IMMIGRATION ENFORCEMENT IN THE UNITED STATES
The Rise of a Formidable Machinery

By Doris Meissner, Donald M. Kerwin, Muzaffar Chishti, and Claire Bergeron

Migration Policy Institute

January 2013

© 2013 Migration Policy Institute.
All Rights Reserved.

ISBN: 978-0-9831591-4-8
e-ISBN: 978-0-9831591-5-5

Library of Congress Control Number: 2012955920

No part of this publication may be reproduced or transmitted in any form by any means, electronic or mechanical, including photocopy, or any information storage and retrieval system, without permission from the Migration Policy Institute. A fulltext PDF of this document is available for free download from www.migrationpolicy.org.

Information for reproducing excerpts from this report can be found at www.migrationpolicy.org/about/copy.php. Inquiries can also be directed to: Permissions Department, Migration Policy Institute, 1400 16th Street, NW, Suite 300, Washington, DC 20036, or by contacting communications@migrationpolicy.org.

Cover image: Modified version of "Gears Blueprint Vector Illustration" (#40476499) by adistock via www.shutterstock.com.
Cover Design: April Siruno, MPI
Inside Layout: Erin Perkins, LeafDev

Suggested citation: Meissner, Doris, Donald M. Kerwin, Muzaffar Chishti, and Claire Bergeron. 2013. *Immigration Enforcement in the United States: The Rise of a Formidable Machinery.* Washington, DC: Migration Policy Institute.

Printed in the United States of America.

TABLE OF CONTENTS

EXECUTIVE SUMMARY 1
    I. OVERVIEW: A STORY OF DRAMATIC GROWTH IN ENFORCEMENT RESOURCES 2
        1. Border Enforcement 3
        2. Visa Controls and Travel Screening 4
        3. Information and Interoperability of Data Systems 5
        4. Workplace Enforcement 6
        5. The Intersection of the Criminal Justice System and Immigration Enforcement 7
        6. Detention and Removal of Noncitizens 7
    II. FINDINGS 9
    III. CONCLUSIONS 11

CHAPTER ONE – INTRODUCTION 15

CHAPTER TWO – OVERVIEW: A STORY OF DRAMATIC GROWTH IN ENFORCEMENT RESOURCES 17
    OVERALL GROWTH 17
        A. Growth of Key Agencies and Programs 19
            1. US Customs and Border Protection (CBP) 19
            2. US Immigration and Customs Enforcement (ICE) 20
            3. United States Visitor Immigrant Status and Information Technology (US-VISIT) 20
        B. Immigration Enforcement Relative to DHS and to Other Federal Enforcement Spending 20
    FINDINGS 23

CHAPTER THREE – BORDER ENFORCEMENT 25
    I. PROGRAMS AND RESULTS 25
        A. Mobilizing People, Infrastructure, and Technology 25
            1. First National Border Control Strategy 26
            2. 2012-16 Strategic Plan 26
            3. National Guard Support 27
        B. Determining Border Control 28
        C. Technology and Border Infrastructure 30
            1. Secure Border Initiative (SBI) 30
            2. Fencing 32
        D. Consequence Delivery System (CDS) 33
        E. Deaths at the Border 35
        F. Ports of Entry (POE) 37
            1. Secure Border Crossing Documents 38
            2. Trusted-Traveler Programs 39
            3. POE Infrastructure 40
        G. US-Canada Border 40
        H. Border Enforcement beyond Immigration Control 41
    II. PROGRAM CRITIQUES AND FINDINGS 42
        A. Measurement 43
        B. Evaluating Consequence Enforcement 44
            1. Painting the Full Border Enforcement Picture 44
            2. Data Anomalies in POE Reporting 45
            3. Visa Overstays 45
            4. Humanitarian Issues in Border Control 46
    FINDINGS 48

CHAPTER FOUR – VISA CONTROLS AND TRAVEL SCREENING 51
I. PROGRAMS AND RESULTS 52
A. Visa Issuance Screening and Controls 52
1. Personal Interviews 52
2. Decline and Rebound in Visa Issuances and Demand 53
3. Visa Waiver Program 57
B. Travel Screening — US-VISIT 60
1. Ports of Entry Screening 61
2. Exit Controls 61
C. International Cooperation 62
D. Migrant Interdiction 63
II. PROGRAM CRITIQUES AND FINDINGS 64
A. Travel and Tourism 64
B. Limitations and Risk Management 65
FINDINGS 66

CHAPTER FIVE – INFORMATION AND INTEROPERABILITY OF DATA SYSTEMS 69
I. PROGRAMS AND RESULTS 70
Key Databases and Information Systems 70
1. US-VISIT: The IDENT and ADIS Databases 70
2. FBI Terrorist Screening Database 72
3. Visa Screening Systems 73
4. SEVIS 73
5. Border Enforcement Screening Systems 74
6. Enforcement Integrated Database (EID) and ENFORCE 75
7. The Central Index System (CIS) of US Citizenship and Immigration Services 75
II. PROGRAM CRITIQUES AND FINDINGS 76
FINDINGS 79

CHAPTER SIX – WORKPLACE ENFORCEMENT 81
I. PROGRAMS AND RESULTS 81
A. The E-Verify Program 82
1. State E-Verify Laws 85
2. Improvements and Unresolved Issues in E-Verify 86
B. Shift in Worksite Enforcement Policy 87
C. Labor Standards Enforcement 89
WHD and ICE Cooperation 90
II. PROGRAM CRITIQUES AND FINDINGS 92
A. Electronic Verification 91
B. State Law Experiences 93
C. Labor Standards Enforcement 94
FINDINGS 96

CHAPTER SEVEN – THE INTERSECTION OF THE CRIMINAL JUSTICE SYSTEM AND IMMIGRATION ENFORCEMENT 97
I. PROGRAMS AND RESULTS 97
A. Increase in Immigration Crimes and Prosecutions 98
1. Unprecedented Growth in Numbers of Prosecutions 98
2. Operation Streamline 101
B. Increase in Crimes with Automatic Consequence of Removal 103
C. Expansion of Programs Targeting Criminals 104
1. The Criminal Alien Program (CAP) 105
2. The National Fugitive Operations Program (NFOP) 107
3. The 287(g) Program 108
4. The Secure Communities Program 112

- D. Targeting Transnational Criminal Enterprises 117
  - 1. Operation Predator 117
  - 2. Border Enforcement Security Task Forces (BEST) 117
  - 3. Operation Community Shield 117
- II. PROGRAM CRITIQUE AND FINDINGS 118
  - A. Concerns Related to Immigration Prosecutions 119
  - B. Criticism of Programs Targeted at Criminal Aliens 119
  - **FINDINGS** 121

CHAPTER EIGHT – DETENTION AND REMOVAL OF NONCITIZENS 123
- I. PROGRAMS AND RESULTS 123
  - A. Removal of Criminal Aliens 123
    - 1. Issuing Removal Orders 124
    - 2. Expedited Removal 127
    - 3. Criminal Aliens 128
    - 4. Stipulated Orders 129
    - 5. Reinstated Orders 129
    - 6. More Removals, Fewer Returns 129
  - B. The Immigration Detention System 130
    - 1. Mandatory Detention 132
    - 2. Detention Reform 133
    - 3. Alternatives to Detention (ATD) 135
  - C. The Immigration Court System 136
    - Prosecutorial Discretion 137
- II. PROGRAM CRITIQUE AND FINDINGS 139
  - A. Scale of Detention 141
  - B. Pressures on Immigration Courts 142
  - C. Removals Outside the Court System 142
  - **FINDINGS** 144

CHAPTER NINE – CONCLUSIONS 147
- A. Immigration and National Security 148
- B. The 1996 Laws 148
- C. The Great Recession 148
- D. Immigration Enforcement 149
- E. New Fiscal Realities 149
- F. The Future 150

APPENDICES 151
WORKS CITED 159
ACKNOWLEDGMENTS 179
ABOUT THE AUTHORS 181

EXECUTIVE SUMMARY

From the early 1970s until the Great Recession that began in 2008, the United States experienced high levels of illegal immigration. Congress first attempted to address the problem in 1986, when it passed the *Immigration Reform and Control Act* (IRCA), which marked the beginning of the current immigration enforcement era. IRCA incorporated the key recommendations of a congressionally mandated commission, although it took more than six years of debate and repeated legislative attempts to enact.

Characterized by its sponsors as a "three-legged stool," IRCA made the hiring of unauthorized workers illegal for the first time in US history. In addition, it called for strengthened border enforcement and provided for legalization for a large share of the unauthorized immigrant population, which then numbered about 3 million to 5 million. The legal status provision, combined with new enforcement measures, was intended to "wipe the slate clean" of the problem of illegal immigration.

Implementation of IRCA's key provisions proved to be disappointing. Employer sanctions — the law's centerpiece — have been ineffective in the absence of a reliable method for verification of work eligibility. It took until the mid-1990s to mobilize stepped-up border enforcement. IRCA's legalization programs were seen as largely successful, having granted legal status to about 3 million individuals, the number estimated to have been eligible.

The defects in IRCA, combined with unprecedented growth and job creation by the US economy in the 1990s and early 2000s, as well as deeply ingrained migration push factors in Mexico and, more recently, Central America, enabled illegal immigration to continue to grow. By the mid-2000s, the unauthorized population was estimated to number 11 million to 12 million and affected nearly every part of the country to varying degrees. Thus, illegal immigration and enforcement have been the dominant focus and concern driving immigration policymaking for more than 25 years.

During this time, there has been strong and sustained bipartisan support for strengthened immigration enforcement, along with deep skepticism over the federal government's will or ability to effectively enforce the nation's immigration laws. Support for enforcement has been heightened by the inability of lawmakers to bridge political and ideological divides over other reforms to the nation's immigration policy. As a result, a philosophy known as "enforcement first" has become *de facto* the nation's singular response to illegal immigration, and changes to the immigration system have focused almost entirely on building enforcement programs and improving their performance.

Enforcement-first proponents argue that effective immigration enforcement should be a precondition for addressing broader reform and policy needs. In fact, the nation's strong, pro-enforcement consensus has resulted in the creation of a well-resourced, operationally robust, modernized enforcement system administered primarily by the Department of Homeland Security (DHS), but with multiple Cabinet departments responsible for aspects of immigration mandates.

The combined actions of these federal agencies and their immigration enforcement programs constitute a complex, cross-agency system that is interconnected in an unprecedented fashion. This modern-day immigration enforcement system, which evolved both by deliberate design and by unanticipated developments, is organized around what this report identifies as six distinct pillars.

They are:

- Border enforcement
- Visa controls and travel screening
- Information and interoperability of data systems
- Workplace enforcement
- The intersection of the criminal justice system and immigration enforcement
- Detention and removal[1] of noncitizens

This report lays out the programs and results and the critiques of each of these six pillars. It describes for the first time the totality and evolution since the mid-1980s of this current-day immigration enforcement machinery. The report's key findings demonstrate that the nation has reached an historical turning point in meeting long-standing immigration enforcement challenges. While the facts on the ground have steadily and dramatically changed, public perceptions have not caught up with new realities. More than ten years after the September 11, 2001 terrorist attacks and 26 years after IRCA, the question is no longer *whether* the government is willing and able to enforce the nation's immigration laws, but *how* enforcement resources and mandates can best be mobilized to control illegal immigration and ensure the integrity of the nation's immigration laws and traditions.

I. Overview: A Story of Dramatic Growth in Enforcement Resources

Funding, technology, and personnel growth are the backbone of the transformations in immigration enforcement. They are the products of nearly 20 years of sizeable, sustained budget requests and appropriations made by the executive branch and by Congress, respectively, under the leadership of both parties. They represent a convergence of rising public unease over illegal immigration that sharply intensified after 9/11.

Spending for the federal government's two main immigration enforcement agencies — US Customs and Border Protection (CBP) and US Immigration and Customs Enforcement (ICE) — and its primary enforcement technology initiative, the US Visitor and Immigrant Status Indicator Technology (US-VISIT) program, surpassed $17.9 billion in fiscal year (FY) 2012.[2] This amount is nearly 15 times the spending level of the US Immigration and Naturalization Service (INS) when IRCA was enacted.[3]

---

1. The terms *removal and deportation* are used interchangeably in this report. Though *deportation* is more commonly used in public discourse, *removal* is the formal term used by the federal government for the expulsion of a noncitizen, most typically one who is in the country illegally. Prior to the *Illegal Immigration Reform and Immigrant Responsibility Act of 1996*, removal encompassed two separate procedures: deportation (for noncitizens present in the United States) and exclusion (for those seeking entry to the United States). IIRIRA consolidated these procedures. Noncitizens in and admitted to the United States, in other words both unauthorized immigrants and legally admitted noncitizens who have run afoul of US laws, may now be subject to removal on grounds of deportability or inadmissibility.
2. US Department of Homeland Security (DHS), *FY 2013 Budget in Brief* (Washington, DC: DHS, 2012): 85, 99, 134, www.dhs.gov/xlibrary/assets/mgmt/dhs-budget-in-brief-fy2013.pdf.
3. US Department of Justice (DOJ), "Budget Trend Data for the Immigration and Naturalization Service (INS), 1975 Through the President's 2003 Request to Congress," Budget Staff, Justice Management Division, Spring 2002, www.justice.gov/archive/jmd/1975_2002/btd02tocpg.htm.

In the ensuing 26 years, the nation has spent an estimated $186.8 billion[4] ($219.1 billion if adjusted to 2012 dollars) on immigration enforcement by INS and its successor agencies, CBP and ICE, and the US-VISIT program.

This investment, which has funded the use of modern technologies and the creation and expansion of new programs, coupled with aggressive use of administrative and statutory authorities, has built an unparalleled immigration enforcement system that rests upon six pillars:

1. Border Enforcement

Effective border control encompasses a broad sweep of responsibilities, geographies, and activities that involve the nation's air, land, and sea entry and admissions processes. Enforcement at US territorial borders — especially the Southwest border with Mexico — represents the most heavily funded and publicized element of border enforcement, and is thus the most prominent pillar of the immigration enforcement system. Historic resource increases have been allocated to CBP for border enforcement. The growth has included dramatic increases in CBP staffing, particularly for the Border Patrol, which has doubled in size over seven years to 21,370 agents as of FY 2012.[5] Large sums have also flowed to infrastructure, technology, and port-of-entry staffing.

The Border Patrol's strategy of "deterrence through prevention," first introduced in 1994, served as the basis for a multi-year build-up of border resources and enforcement infrastructure. In spring 2012, the Border Patrol announced a new phase in its work, which it calls a "Risk-Based Strategic Plan." The plan states that for the period ahead, the resource base that has been built and the operations that have been conducted over the past two decades enable it to focus on "high-risk areas and flows" and target "responses to meet those threats."[6] The plan depicts an organization that envisions steady-state resources and operational challenges, and seeks to refine its programs and capabilities.

In assessing its successes and effectiveness, the Border Patrol has traditionally measured fluctuations in border apprehensions, which reached a peak for the post-IRCA period of almost 1.7 million in FY 2000,[7] and have fallen significantly since. The decreases have been across all nine Southwest Border Patrol sectors and reflect a combination of the weakening of the US economy, strengthened enforcement, and changes in push factors in Mexico. Apprehensions in FY 2011 numbered 340,252, one-fifth of the 2000 level and the lowest level since 1970.[8]

In adopting a risk-management approach to border security, DHS has defined its task as managing, not sealing, borders. Thus, it has rejected the idea of preventing all illegal

---

[4] The $186.8 billion estimate includes the fiscal year (FY) 1986-2002 budgets for the US Immigration and Naturalization Service (INS) and the FY 2003-12 budgets of US Customs and Border Protection (CBP), US Immigration and Customs Enforcement (ICE), and the US Visitor and Immigrant Status Indicator Technology (US-VISIT) program. The INS was abolished and its functions absorbed by the new Department of Homeland Security (DHS) that came into operation in March 2003. CBP, ICE, and US-VISIT are the DHS components that assumed most INS functions. DOJ, "Budget Trend Data for the Immigration and Naturalization Service (INS), 1975 Through the President's 2003 Request to Congress;" DHS, *Budgets in Brief, FY 2004-FY 2013* (Washington, DC: DHS, 2003-13), www.dhs.gov/dhs-budget.
[5] DHS, *FY 2012 Budget in Brief* (Washington, DC: DHS, 2011): 9, www.dhs.gov/xlibrary/assets/budget-bib-fy2012.pdf.
[6] US Border Patrol, *2012-2016 Border Patrol Strategic Plan* (Washington, DC: CBP, 2012), http://nemo.cbp.gov/obp/bp_strategic_plan.pdf.
[7] The number of apprehensions in 2000 was 1,676,438, slightly lower than the historic peak of 1,692,544 in 1986; Border Patrol, "Nationwide Illegal Alien Apprehensions Fiscal Years 1925-2011," www.cbp.gov/linkhandler/cgov/border_security/border_patrol/usbp_statistics/25_10_app_stats.ctt/25_11_app_stats.pdf.
[8] Ibid.

entries as a goal because it is not an attainable outcome of border enforcement.[9]

A prominent feature of today's border enforcement is significant change in the tactics of enforcement being used along the Southwest border. The Border Patrol has steadily introduced new measures and programs to impose what it terms "consequence enforcement" on those arrested. As a result, voluntary return as the prevailing enforcement response to illegal crossing for many years is now being supplanted by a variety of actions (e.g. criminal prosecution or repatriation into the Mexican interior or at a location elsewhere along the US-Mexico border) that are more consequential, both for the migrant and for the immigration system more broadly. The objective is to increase deterrence by raising the cost — monetary, legal, and psychological — of illegal migration to migrants and smugglers alike.

Enforcement at ports of entry (POE) complements CBP's between-ports enforcement. POEs are responsible for both facilitation of legitimate trade and travel and for preventing the entry of a small but potentially deadly number of dangerous people as well as lethal goods, illicit drugs, and contraband. As border security improves and border enforcement makes illegal crossing between ports ever more difficult, the potential for misuse of legal crossing procedures increases.

POE inspections functions have been substantially strengthened, both through increased staffing and new tools, especially the US-VISIT program that provides for biometrically-based travel screening and post-9/11 secure identity document requirements for land border crossers from Mexico and Canada. However, physical infrastructure resource needs at ports of entry have not kept pace with advances in screening and documentation technologies.

At present, evidence of significant improvements in border control relies primarily on metrics regarding resource increases and reduced apprehension levels, rather than on actual deterrence measures, such as size of illegal flows, share of the flow being apprehended, or changing recidivism rates of unauthorized crossers. The ability of immigration agencies and DHS to reliably assess and persuasively communicate border enforcement effectiveness will require more sophisticated measures and analyses of enforcement outcomes.

2. Visa Controls and Travel Screening

Visa controls and travel screening serve as the first line of defense in many aspects of border control and a critical pillar of the immigration system. Dramatic improvements in the nation's screening systems and capabilities have been fielded since the September 11, 2001 terrorist attacks as part of strengthened border control. Visa and immigration port-of-entry officers have access to and check against cross-government data repositories for every individual they clear for entry into the United States. The result has been to increasingly "push the border out" from US territory, a long-held goal of immigration enforcement strategies.

The inherent tension between tighter screening requirements and facilitation of travel led to a dramatic drop in the numbers of nonimmigrant visas issued after 9/11. FY 2011 figures show that the overall number of nonimmigrant visas issued returned to its FY 2001 peak for the first time since 9/11.[10] There has been growth in some categories of visitor and foreign student visa issuances. However, it has been uneven across coun-

---

9 Statement of Janet Napolitano, Secretary of Homeland Security, "Press Conference with Secretary of Homeland Security Janet Napolitano; Immigration and Customs Enforcement Director John Morton; Los Angeles County, California, Sheriff Lee Baca; Harris County, Texas, Sheriff Adrian Garcia; Fairfax County, Virginia, Sheriff Stan Barry on New Immigration Enforcement Results" (briefing, Washington, DC, October 6, 2010).

10 US Department of State, "Nonimmigrant Visa Issuances by Visa Class and by Nationality FY1997-2011 NIV Detail Table," http://travel.state.gov/visa/statistics/nivstats/nivstats_4582.html.

tries and regions. In general, predominantly Muslim country visa issuances have not rebounded as quickly as the worldwide levels.

The 9/11 aftermath also brought into view long-standing concerns about the Visa Waiver Program (VWP) as a potential source of vulnerability.[11] Post-9/11 imperatives led to broad changes that have significantly tightened the program, including requirements for VWP travelers to submit biographic information for screening in advance of boarding an airplane to the United States.[12]

A further layer of travel screening occurs through US-VISIT, the electronic screening system used to clear foreign-born individuals and visitors as they physically enter the United States at ports of entry. As with visa processing, the system is based on biometric information that enables DHS officials to screen noncitizens, including lawful permanent residents, against immigration, criminal, and terrorist databases. The broad-based use of biometric screening in visa and immigration processes represents among the most significant technology improvements of the post-9/11 period in immigration enforcement.

3. Information and Interoperability of Data Systems

Executive-branch agencies have significantly expanded, upgraded, and integrated immigration, criminal, and national security screening information systems and information exchange as part of government-wide efforts to "connect the dots" in the aftermath of 9/11. New, linked data systems capabilities equip consular and immigration enforcement officials with essential information to carry out their immigration enforcement responsibilities.

In addition, with the breakup of INS and creation of DHS in 2003, the organizational machinery for administering the nation's immigration laws has become decentralized. Information and interoperability of data systems serve as the connective tissue tying today's immigration agencies together, and as a critical pillar of the US immigration enforcement system.

Frontline immigration officials have access to all information that the government possesses on dangerous and suspect individuals. This information is, in turn, available at each step of the immigration process (e.g. visa issuance, port-of-entry admission, and border enforcement), as well as removal, political asylum, and myriad other immigration-related procedures applicable to foreign-born persons already in the United States.

US-VISIT, with its IDENT database, stores more than 148 million fingerprint files that grow by about 10 million annually.[13] IDENT is the largest law enforcement biometric database in the world. It makes vast numbers of records accessible to immigration and other authorized law enforcement officials, for use in programs such as Secure Communities.

Immigration fingerprint records are also compatible with Federal Bureau of Investigation (FBI) criminal background records.[14] This interoperability has enabled criminal information to be readily and systematically cross-checked across government law

---

11 Statement of Michael Bromwich, Inspector General, US Department of Justice, on May 5, 1999, before the House Judiciary Committee, Subcommittee on Immigration and Claims, *Nonimmigrant Visa Fraud*, 106th Cong., 1st sess., www.justice.gov/oig/testimony/9905.htm; Jess T. Ford, US General Accounting Office (GAO), *Border Security: Implications of Eliminating the Visa Waiver Program* (Washington, DC: GAO, 2002): 17, www.gao.gov/assets/240/236408.pdf.
12 DHS, "Changes to the Visa Waiver Program to Implement the Electronic System for Travel Authorization (ESTA) Program," *Federal Register* 73, no. 111 (June 9, 2008): 32440 (codified at 8 C.F.R. 217).
13 Email from Robert Mocny, Director, US-VISIT, to Doris Meissner, Senior Fellow and Director, US Immigration Program, Migration Policy Institute, November 29, 2012 (email on file with authors).
14 DHS, *IDENT, IAFIS Interoperability* (Washington, DC: DHS, 2005), www.dhs.gov/xlibrary/assets/foia/US-VISIT_IDENT-IAFISReport.pdf.

enforcement agency databases as a routine matter. Further integration is underway with Department of Defense (DOD) biometric information, which will make the federal government's three biometric identification systems — DHS, FBI, and DOD — interoperable for immigration enforcement purposes.[15]

Although significant investments have been made in automating information and linking databases, the investments have been uneven, tilting heavily toward border security, less toward interior enforcement, and considerably less toward legal immigration processes. In addition, DHS agencies have been slow to use new information capabilities for travel facilitation and trusted traveler initiatives.

4. Workplace Enforcement

Since 1986, employers have the obligation to verify the work eligibility of those they hire. Because of inadequate statutory mandates, however, employer compliance and enforcement have been weak and largely ineffective as tools for frustrating illegal immigration. Some employers do not comply because they see little risk in noncompliance and anticipate the likelihood of competitive advantages in hiring cheaper labor. However, for many others the primary reason has been the array of documents — many of them easy to counterfeit — permitted for meeting employer verification requirements, in the absence of a secure identifier or automated employment verification system. This requirement, popularly called "employer sanctions," is an essential pillar of immigration enforcement because of the job magnet that draws workers into the country illegally.

As a partial solution, the federal government has developed a steadily improving voluntary electronic employment verification system known as E-Verify. By FY 2011, E-Verify had processed more than 17 million queries.[16] Currently less than 10 percent of the nation's 7 million or more employers are enrolled in E-Verify.[17] But the program has been deployed at a fast pace and is becoming more widely accepted. In addition, E-Verify is now required in varying degrees by 19 states.[18]

Government program evaluations report that DHS has made substantial progress in addressing error rates, a serious deficiency in the program's early years. DHS reduced the percentage of E-Verify cases receiving tentative nonconfirmation notices from 8 percent between 2004 and 2007, to 2.6 percent in 2009.[19]

DHS has also changed worksite enforcement strategies dramatically. It has shifted to targeting employers for their hiring practices, which was the goal of the sanctions provisions of IRCA, rather than mounting large-scale raids and arrests of unauthorized workers. Since January 2009, ICE has audited more than 8,079 employers, debarred 726 companies and individuals, and imposed more than $87.9 million in monetary fines for violating employer sanctions laws.[20]

---

15 US-VISIT, 8th Anniversary Briefing, January 5, 2012. Notes on file with authors; DHS, *IDENT, IAFIS Interoperability*.
16 USCIS, "E-Verify History and Milestones," www.uscis.gov/portal/site/uscis/menuitem.eb1d4c2a3e5b9ac-89243c6a7543f6d1a/?vgnextoid=84979589cdb76210VgnVCM100000b92ca60aRCRD&vgnextchannel=84979589cdb76210VgnVCM100000b92ca60aRCRD.
17 For a full description of MPI's methodology in estimating the percentage of employers enrolled in E-Verify, see Chapter Six.
18 ImmigrationWorksUSA, "At a Glance: State E-Verify Laws," July 2012, http://www.immigrationworksusa.org/index.php?p=110.
19 Richard M. Stana, *Employment Verification: Federal Agencies Have Taken Steps to Improve E-Verify, But Significant Challenges Remain* (Washington, DC: Government Accountability Office, 2010): 16, www.gao.gov/new.items/d11146.pdf.
20 Testimony of Janet Napolitano, Homeland Security Secretary, before the House Committee on the Judiciary, *Oversight of the Department of Homeland Security*, 112th Cong., 2nd sess., July 17, 2012, www.dhs.gov/news/2012/07/17/written-testimony-dhs-secretary-janet-napolitano-house-committee-judiciary-hearing.

5. The Intersection of the Criminal Justice System and Immigration Enforcement

One of the most important and potent developments of the last two decades has been the interplay between immigration enforcement and the criminal justice system. The growing interconnectedness, combined with increased resources, congressionally mandated priorities, and broad programs for federal-state-local cooperation are responsible for placing ever larger numbers of removable noncitizens — both unauthorized and authorized — in the pipeline for removal.

Over the last decade, the number of criminal prosecutions for immigration-related violations has grown at an unprecedented rate. Today more than half of *all* federal criminal prosecutions are brought for immigration-related crimes.[21] The two most heavily prosecuted immigration crimes by US attorneys have been illegal entry (a misdemeanor) and illegal re-entry following removal (a felony).[22] The spike in immigration-related prosecutions can be partly credited to Operation Streamline, a Border Patrol initiative that seeks to deter illegal migration by prosecuting unauthorized border crossers instead of engaging in the traditional practice of granting voluntary return.

Equally important has been a series of enforcement programs targeting the removal of noncitizens arrested or convicted of a criminal offense. These programs include the Criminal Alien Program (CAP), the 287(g) program, the National Fugitive Operations Program (NFOP), and the Secure Communities program. The 287(g) and Secure Communities programs reflect the growing involvement of state and local law enforcement as an extension of federal immigration enforcement. Authorization for such involvement dates back to 1996 statutory changes, but grew rapidly in the post-9/11 environment.

Between FY 2004-11, funding for these programs increased from $23 million to $690 million.[23] They have led to substantial increases in both the overall number of removals, and in the proportion of removals of unauthorized immigrants with criminal convictions. In FY 2011, almost 50 percent of those removed by DHS had criminal convictions.[24]

The expanded use of criminal prosecution and state and local law enforcement programs have drawn heavy criticism from immigrant- and civil-rights advocates and from many law enforcement professionals. ICE has updated and elaborated its enforcement priorities in an effort to ensure that these programs meet their stated goals of identifying and removing dangerous criminal aliens and threats to national security, as opposed to ordinary status violators.

6. Detention and Removal of Noncitizens

Substantial expansion of detention capabilities to support removal outcomes and the adjudication of cases subject to removal make up the sixth pillar of the immigration enforcement system. As removal of noncitizens has accelerated, two trends have become evident: an increase in the removal of criminal aliens and extensive use of administrative (versus judicial) orders to effect removals.

Beginning in the 1990s and continuing today, the removal of criminal aliens — a broad group that includes both authorized and unauthorized noncitizens who have committed

---

21 Transactional Records Access Clearinghouse (TRAC), "Going Deeper" tool, "Federal Criminal Enforcement, FY 2011," http://tracfed.syr.edu/; (noting that out of 162,997 total federal prosecutions filed in FY 2011, 82,250 were for immigration-related offenses).
22 TRAC, "Going Deeper" tool, "Immigration Prosecutions for 2011," http://tracfed.syr.edu/.
23 Marc R. Rosenblum and William A. Kandel, *Interior Immigration Enforcement: Programs Targeting Criminal Aliens* (Washington, DC: Congressional Research Service, 2011): 1, http://digital.library.unt.edu/ark:/67531/metadc83991/m1/1/high_res_d/R42057_2011Oct21.pdf.
24 DHS, *Immigration Enforcement Actions 2011* (Washington, DC: DHS, 2012), www.dhs.gov/sites/default/files/publications/immigration-statistics/enforcement_ar_2011.pdf.

crimes that make them removable — has been a high priority.[25] The result has been an increase in the relative proportion of noncitizens in removal proceedings with criminal records. In FY 2011, DHS removed 391,953 noncitizens, 48 percent of whom (188,382) had criminal convictions.[26] This continues an upward trend, rising from 27 percent in FY 2008[27] to 33 percent in FY 2009,[28] and 44 percent in FY 2010.[29]

ICE manages a large, complex and sprawling detention system that holds a highly diverse population in a number of types of facilities.[30] A significantly larger number of individuals are detained each year in the immigration detention system than are serving sentences in federal Bureau of Prisons facilities for all other federal crimes.[31]

ICE's considerable detention management challenges have been complicated by rapid growth in the numbers of those removable, and by laws that mandate the detention of some categories of noncitizens, even when they do not represent a danger or flight risk. In addition, ICE treats even its most restrictive alternative-to-detention (ATD) programs as "alternatives to" rather than "alternative forms of" detention.

Detention reform — particularly designing and implementing a civil detention system — has been a goal of the current administration. Accordingly, ICE has made a series of policy changes in the detention system. They include opening the first "civil" detention center, a facility designed for 600 low-security male detainees with a less restrictive environment than penal detention.

Like the detention system, the demands on the immigration court system have grown enormously. The ratio of immigration proceedings completed to the number of full-time immigration judges rose from fewer than 400 per judge during the years 2000-03 to more than 600 per judge in 2008 and 2009.[32] Even with the increased workload for immigration judges, court backlogs have risen and delays increased, sometimes to more than two years.

To reduce the immigration court backlog and ensure that immigration enforcement resources are being used primarily to remove noncitizens who pose a public safety or national security threat, DHS began implementing a new prosecutorial discretion policy

---

25 Testimony of David Venturella, Executive Director of Secure Communities, before the House Appropriations Committee, Subcommittee on Homeland Security, *Priorities Enforcing Immigration Law,* 111th Cong., 1st sess., April 2, 2009, www.aila.org/content/fileviewer.aspx?docid=28622&linkid=200232. ("Secretary Napolitano has made the identification and removal of criminal aliens a top priority for ICE.")
26 DHS, *Immigration Enforcement Actions: 2011,* 6.
27 DHS, *Immigration Enforcement Actions: 2008* (Washington, DC: DHS, 2010): 4, http://www.dhs.gov/xlibrary/assets/statistics/publications/enforcement_ar_08.pdf.
28 DHS, *Immigration Enforcement Actions: 2009* (Washington, DC: DHS, 2010): 4, www.dhs.gov/xlibrary/assets/statistics/publications/enforcement_ar_2009.pdf.
29 DHS, *Immigration Enforcement Actions: 2010* (Washington, DC: DHS, 2011): 4, www.dhs.gov/immigration-enforcement-actions-2010.
30 Donald Kerwin and Serena Yi-Ying Lin, *Immigrant Detention: Can ICE Meet Its Legal Imperatives and Case Management Responsibilities?* (Washington, DC: Migration Policy Institute, 2009), www.migrationpolicy.org/pubs/detentionreportSept1009.pdf.
31 The federal prison system is fundamentally different than immigration detention in that it incarcerates individuals serving sentences for committing federal crimes. Nonetheless, the relative size of each system illustrates the challenges of scale embedded in ICE's mission. There were 209,771 prisoners under the jurisdiction of federal correctional authorities as of December 31, 2010. In contrast, ICE detained 363,064 individuals that year, and 429,247 in 2011; Paul Guerino, Paige M. Harrison, and William J. Sabol, *Prisoners in 2010* (Washington, DC: DOJ, Bureau of Justice Statistics, 2012), http://bjs.ojp.usdoj.gov/content/pub/pdf/p10.pdf; ICE, "ERO Facts and Statistics," December 12, 2011, www.ice.gov/doclib/foia/reports/ero-facts-and-statistics.pdf.
32 National Research Council of the National Academies, *Budgeting for Immigration Enforcement: A Path to Better Performance* (Washington, DC: National Research Council of the National Academies, 2011): 51.

in 2011.[33] ICE officers have been advised not to place an unauthorized immigrant in removal proceedings or pursue a final order of removal if that person has been deemed "low priority."

A preliminary analysis of this prosecutorial discretion policy has found that immigration courts have issued fewer removal orders, and roughly 1,801 cases have been administratively closed pursuant to the policy.[34] Nonetheless, the backlog in cases pending before the immigration courts has increased, and as of March 2012 stood at a record 305,556 cases.[35]

II. Findings

In all, the report makes 52 findings. The report paints a picture of a wide-reaching, multi-layered network of discrete programs that reside within an interrelated system that has not before been described in its totality. It is a system that is unique in both scope and character as a federal law enforcement endeavor. However, to place that totality into context, some of the findings make comparisons with federal criminal law enforcement system metrics. That is because immigration enforcement increasingly embodies enforcement authorities, methods, and penalties that are akin to criminal enforcement, even though immigration is statutorily rooted in civil law.

Perhaps the most important of the report's findings: *the US government spends more on its immigration enforcement agencies than on* all *its other principal criminal federal law enforcement agencies combined. In FY 2012, spending for CBP, ICE, and US-VISIT reached nearly $18 billion. This amount exceeds by approximately 24 percent total spending for the FBI, Drug Enforcement Administration (DEA), Secret Service, US Marshals Service, and Bureau of Alcohol, Tobacco, Firearms, and Explosives (ATF), which stood at $14.4 billion in FY 2012.*[36]

Judging by resource levels, case volumes, and enforcement actions, which represent the only publicly available comprehensive measures of the performance of the system, immigration enforcement can thus be seen to rank as the federal government's highest criminal law enforcement priority.

Among the report's other key findings:

» *Border Patrol staffing, technology, and infrastructure have reached historic highs, while levels of apprehensions have fallen to historic lows.* Today, there is no net new illegal immigration from Mexico for the first time in 40 years. Between FY 2000-11, Border Patrol apprehensions fell from a peak of more than 1.6 million to 340,252, or one-fifth of the 2000 high point. The drop has been 53 percent since just FY 2008.[37]

» *While enforcement between border ports has improved dramatically, enforcement at land ports of entry is a growing border control challenge.* The gap in the numbers apprehended between ports and those denied

---

33 ICE, Memorandum Re: Exercising Prosecutorial Discretion Consistent with the Civil Immigration Enforcement Priorities of the Agency for the Apprehension, Detention, and Removal of Aliens (June 17, 2011), www.ice.gov/doclib/secure-communities/pdf/prosecutorial-discretion-memo.pdf.
34 TRAC, *Historic Drop in Deportation Orders Continues as Immigration Court Backlog Increases* (Syracuse, NY: TRAC, April 24, 2012), http://trac.syr.edu/immigration/reports/279/.
35 TRAC, *ICE Prosecutorial Discretion Initiative: Latest Figures* (Syracuse, NY: TRAC, April 19, 2012), http://trac.syr.edu/immigration/reports/278/.
36 DOJ, "Summary of Budget Authority by Appropriation," accessed November 11, 2012, www.justice.gov/jmd/2013summary/pdf/budget-authority-appropriation.pdf; DHS, *FY 2013 Budget in Brief*, 25.
37 US Border Patrol, "Nationwide Illegal Alien Apprehensions Fiscal Years 1925-2011."

admission at ports of entry is narrowing. At the FY 2000 peak, between-port apprehensions were nearly three times the 559,000 found to be inadmissible at ports of entry.[38] By FY 2011, between-port apprehensions were only 1.5 times the number denied admission at ports of entry.[39] The gap is likely to narrow further as illegal crossing between ports becomes more difficult and fewer unauthorized entries occur. Despite significant advances, land ports have not experienced improvements on par with between-ports enforcement. The lag is especially evident when it comes to the physical infrastructure needs that are necessary to fully utilize important new technologies such as secure, biometric border-crossing documents and US-VISIT screening.

» *DHS border enforcement data under-report total immigration border enforcement activity.* DHS figures — which are widely used to gauge border enforcement and deterrence — tally the numbers apprehended between ports by the Border Patrol, and those who are found inadmissible by inspections officers at ports of entry. The DHS figures do not include the significant numbers of individuals who arrive at ports of entry but ultimately withdraw their applications for admission because they have been found inadmissible, sometimes for technical reasons. Nevertheless, such actions represent enforcement decisions that add to the scope of border enforcement that is actually taking place.

» *As border enforcement between ports of entry becomes ever more effective, an increasing share of the unauthorized population is likely to be comprised of those who have been admitted properly through ports of entry and overstay their visas.* As a result, the relative share of the unauthorized population from countries other than Mexico and Central America will likely increase beyond the current estimates that 40 to 50 percent of unauthorized immigrants overstayed their visas.[40]

» *Protocols that rely on comprehensive information and interoperability of data systems are now embedded in virtually all critical immigration processes and agency practices.* Today, noncitizens are screened at more intervals, against more databases, which contain more detailed data, than ever before. Thus, when immigration officials do routine name checks, they are able to learn whether an individual re-entering the country or under arrest was, for example, previously deported, has an outstanding arrest warrant, or was convicted of a crime that would make him or her subject to immigration enforcement actions.

» *CBP and ICE together refer more cases for prosecution than all Department of Justice (DOJ) law enforcement agencies combined, including the FBI, DEA, and ATF.* CBP alone refers more cases for prosecution than the FBI.[41]

» *Over 50 crimes categorized as aggravated felonies carry the automatic consequence of removal.* State-level prosecutions of these crimes have placed an unprecedented number of noncitizens into immigration removal proceedings. In addition, programs involving federal, state, and local law enforcement agency cooperation have become major new forces in identifying such cases and apprehending immigration violators. Between FY 2006-11, the number of Notices to Appear (NTAs) issued through the Criminal Alien Program (CAP)

---

38 INS, *Yearbook of Immigration Statistics, FY 2000* (Washington, DC: INS, 2002): 234, 242, www.dhs.gov/xlibrary/assets/statistics/yearbook/2000/Yearbook2000.pdf.
39 DHS, *Immigration Enforcement Actions: 2011*, 1.
40 Pew Hispanic Center, *Modes of Entry for the Unauthorized Migrant Population* (Washington, DC: Pew Hispanic Center, 2006), www.pewhispanic.org/2006/05/22/modes-of-entry-for-the-unauthorized-migrant-population/.
41 TRAC, "Going Deeper" tool, "Prosecutions for 2011," http://tracfed.syr.edu/.

rose from 67,850 to 212,744.[42] In FY 2010, the 287(g) program screened 46,467 noncitizens identified for removal.[43] The same year, ICE reported issuing 111,093 detainers through Secure Communities,[44] a rapid increase from the 20,074 detainers it reported in FY 2009.[45]

» *Since 1990, more than 4 million noncitizens, primarily unauthorized immigrants, have been deported from the United States.* Removals have increased dramatically in recent years — from 30,039 in FY 1990, to 188,467 in FY 2000, and a record 391,953 in FY 2011.[46] The groundwork for this level of removals was laid over many years of congressional mandates, increased detention funding, administrative actions, and improved data systems.

» *Fewer than half of the noncitizens who are removed from the United States are removed following hearings and pursuant to formal removal orders from immigration judges.* DHS has made aggressive use of its administrative authority, when removals without judicial involvement are permitted. In FY 2011, immigration judges issued 161,354 orders of removal, whereas DHS carried out 391,953 removals.[47]

» *The average daily population of noncitizens detained by ICE increased nearly five-fold between FY 1995-11 — from 7,475 to 33,330.* Over the same period, the annual total number of ICE detainees increased from 85,730 to 429,247.[48] Although immigration detention is unique, in that its purpose is to ensure appearances in administrative law proceedings, not to serve criminal law sentences, a significantly larger number of individuals are detained each year in the immigration detention system than are serving sentences in federal Bureau of Prisons facilities for all other federal crimes.

III. Conclusions

This report depicts an historic transformation of immigration enforcement and the emergence of a complex, modernized, cross-governmental immigration enforcement system that projects beyond the nation's borders and at the same time reaches into local jails and courtrooms across the United States to generate an unparalleled degree of enforcement activity. The system's six pillars have been resourced at unprecedented levels and a panoply of enforcement mandates and programs have been implemented that demonstrate the federal government's ability and will to enforce the nation's immigration laws.

Beginning in the 1990s and intensified since 9/11, Congress, successive administrations, and the public have supported building a muscular immigration enforcement infrastructure within which immigration agencies now define their goals and missions principally in terms of national security and public safety. Immigration enforcement

---

42 ICE, "ERO Facts and Statistics." ICE, *Second Congressional Status Report Covering the Fourth Quarter Fiscal Year 2008 for Secure Communities: A Comprehensive Plan to Identify and Remove Criminal Aliens* (Washington, DC: DHS, 2008): 2, www.ice.gov/doclib/foia/secure_communities/congressionalstatusreportfy084thquarter.pdf; (noting that 67,850 detainers were issued as a result of CAP in FY 2006).
43 Rosenblum and Kandel, *Interior Immigration Enforcement: Programs Targeting Criminal Aliens*, 24.
44 ICE, *IDENT/IAFIS Interoperability Statistics* (Washington, DC: ICE, 2011): 2, www.ice.gov/doclib/foia/sc-stats/nationwide_interoperability_stats-fy2011-feb28.pdf.
45 ICE, "Secure Communities Presentation," January 13, 2010, www.ice.gov/doclib/foia/secure_communities/secu-recommunitiespresentations.pdf.
46 DHS, *Immigration Enforcement Actions: 2011*, 5
47 Ibid; DOJ, Executive Office for Immigration Review, *FY 2011 Statistical Yearbook* (Falls Church, VA: EOIR, 2012): D2, www.justice.gov/eoir/statspub/fy11syb.pdf.
48 ICE, "ERO Facts and Statistics."

has been granted new standing as a key tool in the nation's counterterrorism strategies, irrevocably altering immigration policies and practices in the process.

From the standpoint of resource allocations, case volumes, and enforcement actions, which represent the only publicly available measures of the system's performance, immigration patrol enforcement can be seen to rank as the federal government's highest criminal law enforcement priority.

The effects of these new enforcement developments have been magnified by their convergence with statutory changes enacted in 1996 that made retroactive and substantially broadened the list of crimes — including some relatively minor crimes — for which noncitizens (not just unauthorized immigrants) are subject to deportation. These laws placed powerful tools — including authority to engage state and local law enforcement officials in immigration enforcement — in the hands of enforcement officials. Such tools have further extended the impact of dramatic growth in resources.

The worst US recession since the Depression has played an important role in altering decades-long patterns of illegal immigration. Historic changes in Mexico, including significantly lower fertility rates, fewer younger workers entering the labor force, steady economic growth, and the rise of a middle class are changing migration push factors. The numbers leaving Mexico fell by more than two-thirds since the mid-2000s.[49] However, strengthened border and interior enforcement and deterrence have also become important elements in the combination of factors that explain dramatic changes in illegal immigration patterns.

The nation has built a formidable immigration enforcement machinery. The "enforcement-first" policy that has been advocated by many in Congress and the public as a precondition for considering broader immigration reform has *de facto* become the nation's singular immigration policy.

Looking ahead, deep reductions in federal spending are likely, and immigration agencies could be facing straight-line funding or cuts for the first time in nearly 20 years. In the face of these new fiscal realities, DHS and Congress will be forced to look at immigration enforcement return on investment through a more strategic lens. A sharp focus on impact and deterrence — not simply growth in resources — is all but inevitable. Yet few meaningful measures have been developed to assess results and impact from the very significant immigration enforcement expenditures — nearly $187 billion — the country has made since 1986.

How much is needed and where? What is the relative cost-effectiveness among various enforcement strategies? And at what point does the infusion of additional resources lead to dwindling returns or unnecessarily impact other national interests and values?

Today, the facts on the ground no longer support assertions of mounting illegal immigration and demands for building an ever-larger law enforcement bulwark to combat it. Border Patrol apprehensions fell to a 40-year low in FY 2011,[50] bringing the net growth of the resident unauthorized population, which had been increasing at a rate of about 525,000 annually, to a standstill. Economic and demographic forecasts suggest that the changed conditions will persist, with continuing high unemployment in the United

---

49 Mark Stevenson, "Mexico Census: Fewer Migrating, Many Returning," *The Washington Post*, March 3, 2011, www.washingtonpost.com/wp-dyn/content/article/2011/03/03/AR2011030303965.html; Institutuo Nacional de Estadística y Geografía (INEGI), "Tasas Brutas de Migración Internacional al Cuarto Trimestre de 2010," (press release, March 17, 2011), www.inegi.org.mx/inegi/contenidos/espanol/prensa/Boletines/Boletin/Comunicados/Especiales/2011/Marzo/comunica32.pdf.

50 Jeffrey Passel, D'Vera Cohn, and Ana Gonzalez-Barrera, *Net Migration from Mexico Falls to Zero—and Perhaps Less* (Washington, DC: Pew Hispanic Center, 2012), www.pewhispanic.org/2012/04/23/net-migration-from-mexico-falls-to-zero-and-perhaps-less/.

States and sluggish economic growth that is unlikely to generate millions of low-wage jobs in the near term that attracted large numbers of young, foreign-born, unauthorized workers in prior years.

The bulwark is fundamentally in place. Its six pillars represent a durable, institutionalized, machinery that is responding to rule-of-law and enforcement-first concerns. While the system is imperfect, it now represents the federal government's most extensive and costly law enforcement endeavor.

Even with record-setting expenditures and the full use of a wide array of statutory and administrative tools, enforcement alone is not sufficient to answer the broad challenges that immigration — illegal and legal — pose for society and for America's future. Meeting those needs cannot be accomplished through more enforcement, regardless of how well it is carried out. Other changes are needed: enforceable laws that both address continuing weaknesses in the enforcement system, such as employer enforcement, and that better align immigration policy with the nation's economic and labor market needs and future growth and well-being.

Successive administrations and Congresses have accomplished what proponents of "enforcement first" sought as a precondition for reform of the nation's immigration policies. The formidable enforcement machinery that has been built can serve the national interest well if it now also provides a platform from which to address broader immigration policy changes suited to the larger needs and challenges that immigration represents for the United States in the 21st century.

CHAPTER I

INTRODUCTION

There has been strong and sustained bipartisan support over successive administrations and Congresses for strengthened immigration enforcement, even as there has been deep ideological and partisan division over broader immigration reform. A decade-long debate over comprehensive immigration reform (CIR) legislation has repeatedly foundered, in part over the question of whether the federal government has the will and ability to effectively enforce the nation's immigration laws.

CIR would increase enforcement but would also provide new avenues for future worker flows and allow for legalization of the existing unauthorized population. Opponents of CIR point to the presence of an estimated 11 million unauthorized residents[51] as proof of the government's failure to enforce the law and as the reason not to enact broader reform measures, especially a legalization program, such as that included in the *Immigration Reform and Control Act of 1986* (IRCA).[52]

This opposition has been instrumental in preventing passage of CIR and more modest measures, such as the *DREAM Act*, which would provide a pathway to legal status for certain unauthorized immigrants who were brought to the United States as children and who meet certain educational or military service criteria. Some opponents of CIR argue for an "enforcement-first" policy, i.e. that the United States must first establish that it can and will enforce its laws before broader immigration policy measures can be considered. Proponents of CIR contend that effective enforcement is only possible with laws that are enforceable. Thus, the statutory framework that guides the immigration system must, according to this point of view, be reworked to achieve effective enforcement.

This political stalemate has persisted for at least a decade. Meanwhile, the facts on the ground have steadily and dramatically changed. Now, more than ten years after the September 11, 2001 terrorist attacks and 26 years after IRCA — which ushered in the current era of immigration control policies — enforcement first has *de facto* become the nation's singular policy response to illegal immigration.

---

51 Michael Hoefer, Nancy Rytina, and Bryan Baker, *Estimates of the Unauthorized Immigrant Population Residing in the United States* (Washington, DC: Department of Homeland Security, 2012), www.dhs.gov/xlibrary/assets/statistics/publications/ois_ill_pe_2011.pdf.
52 *Immigration Reform and Control Act* (IRCA), Pub. L. No. 99-603, 100 Stat. 3359 (November 6, 1986).

Enforcement-first demands have been an important driver in building a well-resourced, operationally robust, multidimensional enforcement system. Immigration enforcement has evolved into a complex, interconnected system administered by multiple Cabinet departments, most importantly the Department of Homeland Security (DHS), the Department of Justice (DOJ), and the Department of State (DOS). The federal government's lead immigration enforcement and policy agency has become DHS, which houses three separate immigration agencies whose core missions are closely aligned with DHS' national security mandate. Today, the combined actions of these agencies and their programs make up an extensive cross-agency system that is organized around what this report identifies as the six pillars that constitute the nation's immigration enforcement system. They are:

- Border enforcement
- Visa controls and travel screening
- Information and interoperability of data systems
- Workplace enforcement
- The intersection of the criminal justice system and immigration enforcement
- Detention and removal[53] of noncitizens

This report, which characterizes and examines each of these pillars, for the first time describes the totality of the immigration enforcement machinery that began with IRCA's enactment and has evolved — by design and by unanticipated developments — into a complex, interlocking system. The report provides program results and summarizes key critiques of agencies' performance. Its findings and conclusions lay out where immigration enforcement stands and future challenges for policymakers and for the nation.

The report demonstrates that the United States has reached an historical turning point in meeting long-standing immigration enforcement imperatives. Despite continued calls from some for greater border control and attrition through enforcement, the evidence shows that the question is no longer *whether* the government is willing and able to enforce the nation's immigration laws. Instead, the question now should be *how* enforcement resources and mandates can best be mobilized to curb illegal immigration and to mitigate the severest human costs of immigration enforcement, thereby ensuring the integrity of the nation's immigration laws and traditions. ⤳

---

53 The terms *removal* and *deportation* are used interchangeably in this report. Though *deportation* is more commonly used in public discourse, *removal* is the formal term used by the federal government for the expulsion of a noncitizen, most typically one who is in the country illegally. Prior to the *Illegal Immigration Reform and Immigrant Responsibility Act of 1996*, removal encompassed two separate procedures; deportation (for noncitizens present in the United States) and exclusion (for those seeking entry to the United States). IIRIRA consolidated these procedures. Noncitizens in and admitted to the United States (in other words both unauthorized immigrants and legally admitted noncitizens who have run afoul of US laws) may now be subject to removal on grounds of deportability or inadmissibility.

CHAPTER 2

OVERVIEW: A STORY OF DRAMATIC GROWTH IN ENFORCEMENT RESOURCES

Funding, personnel growth, and technology are the backbone of the post-IRCA transformations in immigration enforcement. Between 1986, when IRCA was enacted, and 2012, the funding allocated to the federal government's core immigration enforcement agencies and functions has grown exponentially. The construction of hundreds of miles of fencing and vehicle barriers along the Southwest border, expansion of criminal alien apprehension programs, historic highs in the numbers of removals, and unprecedented caseloads pending before the nation's immigration and federal courts are all manifestations of dramatic growth in immigration enforcement spending and programs.

Overall Growth

At the time of IRCA's passage, the Immigration and Naturalization Service (INS), was responsible for almost all of the country's immigration enforcement efforts. Its budget was $574.7 million in 1986.[54] Accounting for inflation, this amount represents roughly $1.2 billion in 2012 dollars.[55]

Twenty-six years later, funding for the federal government's two main immigration enforcement agencies — US Customs and Border Protection (CBP) and US Immigration and Customs Enforcement (ICE) — and its primary enforcement technology initiative, the US Visitor and Immigrant Status Indicator Technology (US-VISIT) program surpassed $17.9 billion in fiscal year (FY) 2012.[56] With inflation, this is nearly 15 times the 1986 spending level of $1.2 billion. Overall, INS funding during FY 1986-2002, and that for CBP, ICE, and US-VISIT from FY 2003-12, adds up to an estimated $186.8 billion, or $219.1 billion when converted to FY 2012 dollars (see Figure 1).

Funding for immigration enforcement did not remain static even prior to the formation of DHS in 2003. Between 1990 and 2002, INS's budget rose more than fivefold.[57] By FY 2002, it stood at $6.2 billion ($7.9 billion in 2012 dollars).[58] However, following the creation of DHS, funding for immigration enforcement increased even more rapidly. Between FY 2002-06, funding for CBP, ICE, and US-VISIT more than doubled, rising from

---

54 US Department of Justice (DOJ), "Budget Trend Data for the Immigration and Naturalization Service (INS), 1975 Through the President's 2003 Request to Congress," Budget Staff, Justice Management Division, Spring 2002, www.justice.gov/archive/jmd/1975_2002/btd02tocpg.htm.
55 All adjusted figures were converted to 2012 dollars using the Bureau of Labor Statistics' Consumer Price Index (CPI) calculator, available at www.bls.gov/data/inflation_calculator.htm.
56 US Department of Homeland Security (DHS), *FY 2013 Budget in Brief* (Washington, DC: DHS, 2012): 85, 99, 134, www.dhs.gov/xlibrary/assets/mgmt/dhs-budget-in-brief-fy2013.pdf.
57 Doris Meissner and Donald Kerwin, *DHS and Immigration: Taking Stock and Correcting Course* (Washington, DC: Migration Policy Institute, 2009): 100, www.migrationpolicy.org/pubs/DHS_Feb09.pdf.
58 Ibid.

$6.2 billion to $12.5 billion ($14.2 billion in 2012 dollars).[59] By FY 2012, the funding had increased by an additional 43 percent.[60]

Figure 1. Immigration Enforcement Spending Adjusted to 2012 Dollars, 1986-2012

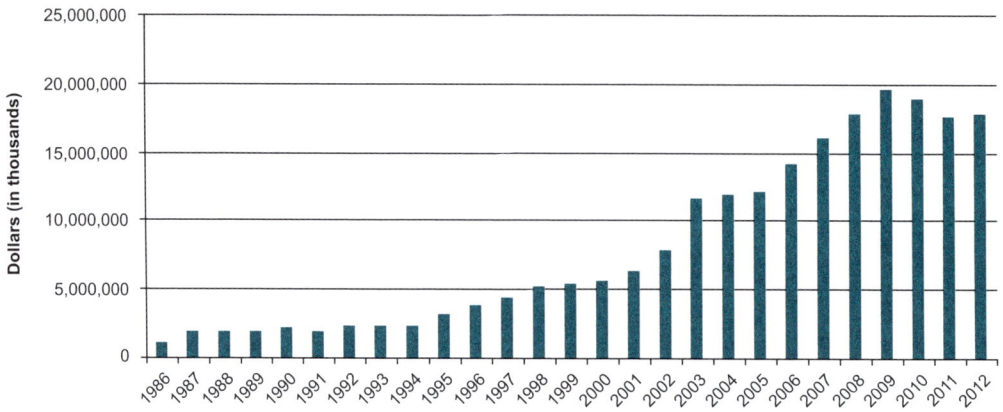

Immigration Enforcement Spending Adjusted to 2012 Dollars ($000)

Notes: The funding encompasses the budgets of the US Immigration and Naturalization Service (INS) for fiscal years (FY) 1986-2003, and the budgets of its successor agencies — US Customs and Border Protection (CBP), US Immigration and Customs Enforcement (ICE), and the US Visitor and Immigrant Status Indicator Technology (US-VISIT) program — for FY 2003-12. All figures were adjusted to 2012 dollars to account for inflation, using the Consumer Price Index (CPI) calculator offered through the Bureau of Labor Statistics. Numbers were rounded to the nearest $100,000. To obtain the most accurate statistics, spending figures were taken from the Department of Homeland Security (DHS) *Budgets in Brief* two years after the applicable year. The FY 2012 statistics are from the *FY 2013 Budget in Brief*.

Sources: US Department of Justice (DOJ), "Immigration and Naturalization Service Budget, FY 1986-2002," www.justice.gov/archive/jmd/1975_2002/2002/html/page104-108.htm; DHS, *DHS Budgets in Brief,* FY 2003-13 (Washington, DC: DHS, various years), www.dhs.gov/dhs-budget.

Agencies beyond CBP and ICE and the US-VISIT program also carry out enforcement responsibilities as part of their core mandates. For example, US Citizenship and Immigration Services (USCIS), the third immigration agency in DHS, administers E-Verify, the federal government's online employment verification program. During FY 2012, that program received over $102 million.[61] The US Coast Guard mission includes migrant interdiction at sea. The lion's share of consular work performed by the US Department of State involves visa screening and issuance. Their budgets do not separately identify funding for these immigration enforcement functions, so it is not possible to paint a full picture of federal agency resources devoted to immigration enforcement. Thus, the calculation of a 15-fold increase in funding is almost certainly an underestimate of the growth in resources expended for today's immigration enforcement system.[62]

---

59 DHS, *Budget-in-Brief FY 2008* (Washington, DC: DHS, 2007): 28, 37, 81, www.dhs.gov/xlibrary/assets/budget_bib-fy2008.pdf.
60 DHS, *Budget in Brief FY 2013.*
61 *Consolidated Appropriations Act of 2012,* Pub. L. 112-74, 125 Stat. 966 (December 23, 2011), www.gpo.gov/fdsys/pkg/BILLS-112hr2055enr/pdf/BILLS-112hr2055enr.pdf.
62 Notably, this estimate does not include the substantial funding expended by the Department of State (DOS) to carry out the visa screening and issuance functions that are a key frontline defense against improper entry to the country, or funding for the Coast Guard for its migrant interdiction operations. At the same time, both ICE and CBP missions encompass broader programs and activities than immigration enforcement. They include enforcement of customs laws and other border security operations, as well as investigation and enforcement of drug smuggling and other criminal activity. Because the annual *Budgets in Brief* do not indicate the shares of ICE, CBP, and US-VISIT funding that is allocated to these activities, we did not subtract from the ICE, CBP, and US-VISIT budget totals the amounts devoted to these non-immigration enforcement activities.

A. Growth of Key Agencies and Programs

Border enforcement suffered from chronic resource deficiencies for much of the period between the early 1970s and the formation of DHS in 2003. That has now radically changed. Border enforcement has won strong, sustained public and bipartisan support over many years, which has heightened in the decade since 9/11. Today, the United States allocates more funding for border enforcement than for all of its other immigration enforcement and benefits programs combined.

1. US Customs and Border Protection (CBP)

CBP carries out border enforcement at and between legal ports of entry. Funding for CBP has increased significantly since its creation in DHS. By sometimes significant margins, Congress through annual and supplemental appropriations has allocated funding for CBP beyond the amounts requested by both the Bush and Obama administrations.

Between FY 2005-12, CBP's budget rose from $6.3 billion to $11.7 billion,[63] an increase of approximately $5.4 billion, or 85 percent. CBP staffing grew approximately 50 percent, from 41,001 personnel to 61,354.[64] The largest share went to the Border Patrol, which basically doubled between FY 2005-12.[65] CBP's FY 2012 budget funded 21,370 Border Patrol agents and 21,186 immigration inspectors and support staff at ports of entry.[66]

CBP funding continues a trend of significant staffing increases for the Border Patrol, which has grown from 2,268 agents in 1980 to 3,715 in 1990, 9,212 in 2000, 11,264 in 2005, and 20,558 in FY 2010.[67] The growth has occurred not only along the Southwest border, but also on the northern border with Canada, which has seen the number of agents deployed there rise from 340 agents in 2001 to over 2,237 in 2011[68] — an increase of almost 560 percent since 9/11.[69]

Another recent trend has been substantial staffing growth in CBP's Office of Field Operations (OFO), which is responsible for inspecting people entering the country through air, land, and sea ports of entry (POEs). POE inspector staffing traditionally received less attention and fewer resources than the Border Patrol. Staffing of inspector positions is now virtually on par with Border Patrol agent-staffing between the ports, as indicated above. However, Border Patrol resources have doubled since 2005, while port-of-entry increases have grown about 45 percent.[70]

---

63 DHS, *Budget-in-Brief FY 2007* (Washington, DC: DHS, 2006): 17, www.dhs.gov/xlibrary/assets/Budget_BIB-FY2007.pdf; DHS, *Budget-in-Brief FY 2013*, 6, 25.
64 DHS, *FY 2012 Budget in Brief* (Washington, DC: DHS, 2011): 65, www.dhs.gov/xlibrary/assets/budget-bib-fy2012.pdf; DHS, *Budget in Brief FY 2005* (Washington, DC: DHS, 2004): 19, www.dhs.gov/dhs-budget-brief-fiscal-year-2005.
65 US Border Patrol, "Border Patrol Agent Staffing by Fiscal Year," www.cbp.gov/linkhandler/cgov/border_security/border_patrol/usbp_statistics/staffing_92_10.ctt/staffing_92_11.pdf.
66 DHS, *FY 2012 Budget in Brief*, 9.
67 Transactional Records Access Clearinghouse (TRAC), *Border Patrol Agents, 1975-2005* (Syracuse, NY: TRAC, 2006), http://trac.syr.edu/immigration/reports/143/; Border Patrol, "Border Patrol Agent Staffing by Fiscal Year," www.cbp.gov/linkhandler/cgov/border_security/border_patrol/usbp_statistics/staffing_92_10.ctt/staffing_92_11.pdf.
68 Ibid.
69 Ibid.
70 DHS, *Budget-in-Brief FY 2007*, 26; (noting that there were 15,893 employees at ports of entry and 11,955 between ports of entry in 2005); DHS, *FY 2012 Budget in Brief*, 85; (noting that there were 23,053 employees at ports of entry and 23,675 between ports of entry in 2012).

2. US Immigration and Customs Enforcement (ICE)

ICE is responsible for interior enforcement functions, including investigations and the detention and removal of unauthorized immigrants. Like CBP, funding for ICE has risen significantly in recent years. Between FY 2005-12, ICE funding increased from $3.1 billion to $5.9 billion, an increase of nearly 87 percent.[71]

ICE growth has been particularly rapid for its detention and removal functions. Between FY 2006-07, Congress increased funding for ICE detention from 20,800 to 27,500 detainee beds.[72] By 2009, Congress provided funding to maintain 33,400 beds;[73] the number rose to 34,000 beds in FY 2012.[74]

3. United States Visitor Immigrant Status and Information Technology (US-VISIT)

Congress' mandate for an entry-exit system to track arrivals and departures of noncitizens, which was first enacted in 1996, became a reality only after the September 11, 2001 terrorist attacks. US-VISIT, which provides biometric identification information for immigration agencies to confirm the identity of noncitizens entering the country, was launched in 2004[75] with $330 million in funding.[76] Its FY 2012 budget was $307 million.[77] During the intervening nine years, the initiative has received $3.16 billion in support.[78] Funding levels for US-VISIT were most substantial during the program's start-up period in the aftermath of 9/11.

B. *Immigration Enforcement Relative to DHS and to Other Federal Enforcement Spending*

Since 2009, funding allocated to immigration enforcement agencies has leveled off somewhat, a trend that reflects the federal fiscal constraints that emerged after the onset of the recession in 2008 (see Figure 2). Still, the percentage of overall DHS funding allocated to CBP has increased from roughly 16-17 percent in 2005 and 2006, to close

---

71 DHS, *FY 2013 Budget in Brief*, 25; (noting that ICE received $5,862,453,000 in FY 2012); DHS, *Budget-in-Brief FY 2007*, 17; (noting that the agency received $3,127,078,000 in FY 2005).
72 Chad C. Haddal and Alison Siskin, *Immigration Related Detention: Current Legislative Issues* (Washington, DC: Congressional Research Service, 2010): 11, http://digitalcommons.ilr.cornell.edu/key_workplace/707/.
73 Ibid; Testimony of John Morton, Assistant Secretary of Immigration and Customs Enforcement (ICE), before the House Appropriations Committee, Subcommittee on Homeland Security, *U.S. Immigration and Customs Enforcement FY 2012 Budget Request*, 112th Cong., 1st sess., March 11, 2011, www.ice.gov/doclib/news/library/speeches/031111morton.pdf. ("Beginning in 2010, Congress included statutory language in the *Homeland Security Appropriations Act* requiring ICE to maintain an average daily detention capacity of at least 33,400 beds."); Testimony of Janet Napolitano, Secretary of Homeland Security, before the Senate Homeland Security and Governmental Affairs Committee, *DHS Fiscal Year 2012 Budget Request*, 112th Cong., 1st sess., February 17, 2011, www.dhs.gov/news/2011/02/17/testimony-secretary-janet-napolitano-united-states-senate-committee-homeland.
74 *Consolidated Appropriations Act 2012*, 125 Stat. 950.
75 Remarks by Under Secretary Asa Hutchinson on the Launch of US-VISIT during speech to the Center for Strategic and International Studies, May 19, 2003), http://csis.org/files/media/csis/events/030519_hutchinson.pdf.
76 *Department of Homeland Security Appropriations Act 2004*, Pub. L. 108-90, 117 Stat. 1137 (October 1, 2003).
77 DHS, *FY 2013 Budget in Brief*, 134.
78 *Department of Homeland Security Appropriations Act 2005*, Pub. L. 108-334, 118 Stat. 1298 (October 18, 2004); *Department of Homeland Security Appropriations Act 2006*, Pub. L. 109-90, 119 Stat. 2064 (October 18, 2005); *Department of Homeland Security Appropriations Act of 2007*, Pub. L. 109-295, 120 Stat. 1355 (October 4, 2006); *Consolidated Appropriations Act, 2008*, Pub. L. 110-161, 121 Stat. 1844 (December 26, 2007); *Consolidated Security Disaster Assistance and Continuing Appropriations Act of 2009*, Pub. L. 110-329, 122 Stat. 3574 (September 30, 2008); *Department of Homeland Security Appropriations Act of 2010*, Pub. L. 111-83, 123 Stat. 2142 (October 28, 2009); *Department of Defense and Full Year Continuing Appropriations Act of 2011*, Pub. L. 112-10, 125 Stat. 38 (April 15, 2011); *Consolidated Appropriations Act of 2012*, Pub. L. 112-74, 125 Stat. 786 (December 23, 2011).

to 21 percent in recent years.[79] ICE's share of the total DHS budget, which was roughly 8 percent in FY 2005, now stands at close to 11 percent.[80] Taken together, the funding for CBP, ICE, and the US-VISIT program represents about one-third of total DHS funding.[81]

Figure 2. Total CBP, ICE, and US-VISIT Budget Authority, FY 2005-12

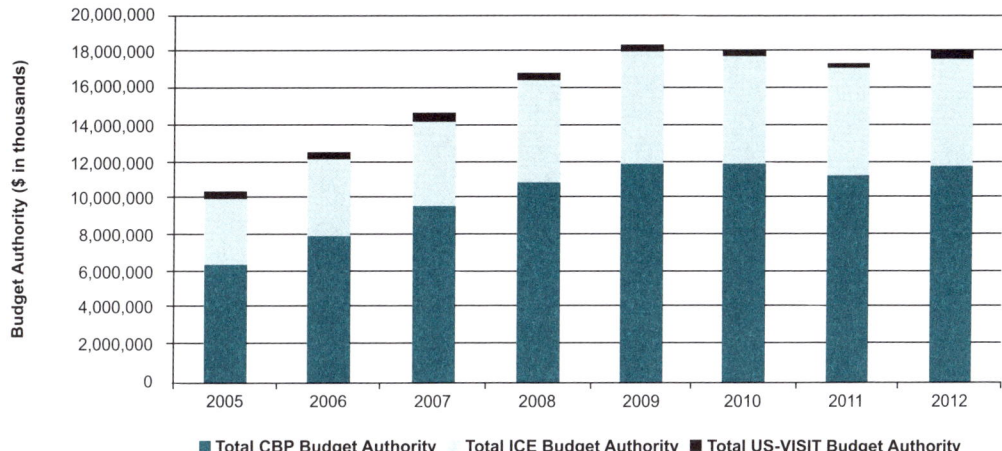

Source: DHS, *Budgets in Brief*, FY 2007-13.

However, the increase in today's levels of immigration enforcement spending is perhaps most telling when viewed in the context of federal spending for other principal federal criminal law enforcement functions. The primary agencies charged with those missions and activities are the Federal Bureau of Investigation (FBI), the Drug Enforcement Administration (DEA), the Secret Service, the US Marshals Service, and the Bureau of Alcohol, Tobacco, Firearms, and Explosives (ATF).[82] In 1986, the total amount allocated to the INS ($574,700,000) represented about half the amount allocated to the FBI ($1,157,000,000).[83] That level of INS funding amounted to approximately one-quarter the total funding allocated to the FBI, DEA, Secret Service, US Marshals Service, and ATF (see Figure 3).[84]

Today, funding for CBP, ICE, and US-VISIT exceeds funding for all the other principal federal criminal law enforcement agencies combined. With a total FY 2012 budget of nearly $18 billion (approximately $11.7 billion for CBP, $5.9 billion for ICE, and $307 million for US-VISIT),[85] the immigration enforcement budgets represent a funding level of about 24 percent greater than that allocated to all other principal federal criminal

---

79 DHS, *Budget-in-Brief FY 2007*, 17; DHS, *Budget-in-Brief FY 2008*, 19; DHS, *Budget in Brief 2009* (Washington, DC: DHS, 2008): 19, www.dhs.gov/xlibrary/assets/budget_bib-fy2009.pdf; DHS, *Budget-in-Brief FY 2010* (Washington, DC: DHS, 2009): 19, www.dhs.gov/xlibrary/assets/budget_bib_fy2010.pdf; DHS, *Budget in Brief FY 2011* (Washington, DC: DHS, 2010): 17, www.dhs.gov/xlibrary/assets/budget_bib_fy2011.pdf; DHS, *FY 2012 Budget in Brief*.
80 DHS, *FY 2013 Budget in Brief*, 25; DHS, *Budget-in-Brief FY 2007*, 12.
81 DHS, *FY 2013 Budget in Brief*, 3, 85, 99, 134. DHS absorbed functions from 22 federal agencies, and has a huge portfolio beyond immigration enforcement – covering everything from the Federal Emergency Management Agency (FEMA) to the Secret Service and Federal Protective Service.
82 DOJ, "Summary of Budget Authority by Appropriation," accessed November 11, 2012, www.justice.gov/jmd/2013summary/pdf/budget-authority-appropriation.pdf.
83 DOJ, "Budget Trend Data for the Immigration and Naturalization Service (INS), 1975 Through the President's 2003 Request to Congress."
84 Ibid.
85 DHS, *FY 2013 Budget in Brief*, 85, 99; DOJ, "Summary of Budget Authority by Appropriation."

law enforcement agencies. This comparison illustrates a paradigm shift in federal law enforcement spending that undergirds the transformation of the immigration enforcement system.

Figure 3. Spending for Immigration Enforcement Compared to All Other Principal Law Enforcement Agencies, FY 1986 and FY 2012

INS & All Other Principal Federal Law Enforcement Agencies, FY 1986

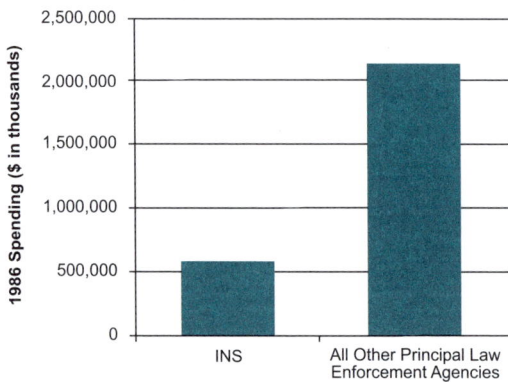

ICE, CBP, US-VISIT & All Other Principal Federal Law Enforcement Agencies, FY 2012

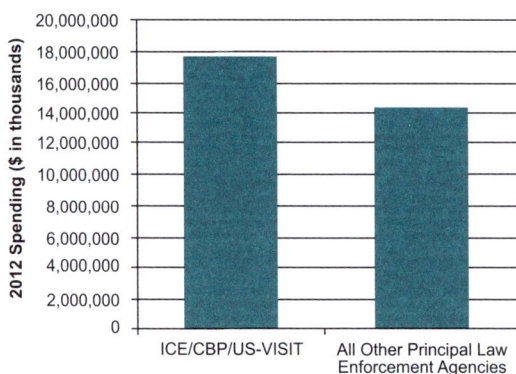

Notes: The principal federal law enforcement agencies listed here outside the immigration arena are the Federal Bureau of Investigation (FBI), Drug Enforcement Administration (DEA), Secret Service, US Marshals Service, and Bureau of Alcohol, Tobacco, Firearms, and Explosives (ATF).

Sources: DOJ, "Budget Trend Data, 1975 Through President's 2003 Request to Congress," www.justice.gov/archive/jmd/1975_2002/btd02tocpg.htm; DHS, *Budget in Brief, FY 2013*, "Total Budget Authority by Organization;" DOJ, "FY 2013, Summary of Budget Authority by Appropriation," www.justice.gov/jmd/2013summary/pdf/budget-authority-appropriation.pdf.

FINDINGS

■ **The US government spends** more on its immigration enforcement agencies than on all all its other principal criminal federal law enforcement agencies *combined*. In FY 2012, spending for the primary immigration enforcement agencies — CBP and ICE — and for US-VISIT, reached nearly $18 billion. This amount exceeds the total spending level of $14.4 billion for the FBI, DEA, Secret Service, US Marshals Service, and ATF combined by approximately 24 percent.

■ **With inflation, the spending level for immigration enforcement** agencies today represents 15 times the spending for the INS in 1986, when the current era of immigration enforcement began.

■ **Border enforcement has seen the largest budget increases.** Between FY 2005-12, CBP's budget rose by approximately 85 percent, from $6.3 billion to $11.7 billion in absolute dollars. CBP funding is greater than that for all the other immigration enforcement and benefits agencies combined.

■ **CBP staffing levels have increased dramatically.** The largest share has gone to the Border Patrol, which has doubled in the past eight years — from 10,819 agents in FY 2004 to 21,370 in FY 2012. Between FY 2004-11, overall CBP staffing grew approximately 50 percent, from 41,001 personnel to 61,354. That staffing includes growth for air, land, and sea ports of entry, which increased from 18,762 in FY 2010 to 23,643 in FY 2012. Among the increases: 2,237 Border Patrol agents were assigned to the US-Canada border in FY 2011, a 560 percent hike in staffing since 9/11.

■ **The ICE budget increased nearly 87 percent,** from $3.1 billion to $5.9 billion between FY 2005-12. ICE growth has been particularly rapid for its detention and removal functions. Between FY 2006-12, Congress funded increases in bed space to hold a daily detainee population rising from 27,500 to 34,000.

CHAPTER 3

BORDER ENFORCEMENT

Border enforcement encompasses a broad sweep of responsibilities, geographies, and activities that involve the nation's air, land, and sea entry and admissions processes. Enforcement at US territorial borders — especially the Southwest land border with Mexico — represents the most heavily funded and publicized element of border enforcement. It is the most prominent pillar of the immigration enforcement system.

CBP is the agency within DHS that is tasked with regulating immigration and trade at the nation's borders, both at and between official ports of entry. CBP is made up of the Office of the Border Patrol (OBP), whose agents secure the border between ports of entry, and the Office of Field Operations (OFO), whose immigration inspectors administer air, land, and sea port-of-entry operations.

The Border Patrol arrests unauthorized immigrants and intercepts illegal shipments of narcotics and other contraband. OFO oversees the authorized entry of large volumes of persons, goods, and conveyances, and seeks to intercept the unauthorized persons and goods concealed among them. Border Patrol and port-of-entry operations are essential complements to achieving effective border control. A major goal and challenge of DHS has been to create seamless enforcement at the borders, a core rationale for the creation of CBP and DHS following the 9/11 attacks.

Although illegal immigration is typically understood as synonymous with illegal land border crossings, estimates are that 40 to 50[86] percent of the unauthorized population may have entered the country legally through authorized ports of entry with properly issued visas and overstayed the period of their admission.[87] Others obtained and then lost legal status once within the United States. Still others violated the terms of their visas by entering as students, for example, but failed to pursue a course of studies, or came as visitors and instead found employment without having work authorization.

Thus, control of the borders is a complex task that must manage both illegal and legal immigration flows. Even if there were no unauthorized crossings at the Southwest border, the United States would still experience illegal immigration and have a sizeable resident unauthorized population.

I. Programs and Results

A. Mobilizing People, Infrastructure, and Technology

Since the mid-1990s, successive administrations and Congresses have been committed to establishing border control by allocating large sums for people, infrastructure, and technology. The strategies for achieving control have evolved over time.

---

86   The range of 40 to 50 percent, published by the Pew Hispanic Center, reflects an estimated 4 million to 5.5 million nonimmigrant visa overstayers in addition to 250,000 to 500,000 border crossing card violators, adding up to a range of 4.5 million to 6 million unauthorized individuals who entered legally with inspection; see Pew Hispanic Center, "Modes of Entry for the Unauthorized Migrant Population" (fact sheet, May 22, 2006), www.pewhispanic.org/2006/05/22/modes-of-entry-for-the-unauthorized-migrant-population/.

87   Ibid.

1. **First National Border Control Strategy**

In 1994, the INS introduced the first formal national border control strategy.[88] The strategy, based on the principle of prevention through deterrence, was updated in 2004 to reflect post-9/11 threats and unprecedented resource infusions.

The national strategy called for targeting resources and gaining control of the border in phases, beginning with the four historically highest crossing corridors from Mexico. Implementation began with Operation Hold the Line in the Juarez-El Paso area and Operation Gatekeeper in the Tijuana-San Ysidro area south of San Diego. The Rio Grande Valley in South Texas and the Nogales corridor south of Tucson followed. The expectation was that as resource infusions were deployed, apprehensions would rise because strengthened enforcement would result in stopping larger numbers and percentages of those attempting to cross. As migrants and smugglers experienced less success in crossing, apprehensions would taper off and longer-term deterrence would set in.[89]

The strategy called for positioning resources as close as possible to the actual border line, so that the Border Patrol's work would increasingly be that of prevention of entry, as compared with apprehending individuals once they had entered the United States, often some distance from the border. Forward placement of new resources — at somewhat reduced levels from the initial infusions — was to be permanent in order to establish and then maintain border control. To that end, entire swaths near the border were bulldozed to build roads enabling Border Patrol vehicle access, install lighting, add fencing and other barriers, position surveillance equipment, and facilitate use of night-vision and tracking technology to locate and apprehend unauthorized entrants and contraband.

Although the strategy anticipated changes in crossing patterns and shifts in the flow, it did not sufficiently contemplate the speed and scale at which migrant crossing patterns would adapt to the enforcement successes experienced in the El Paso and San Diego sectors. Nor could the multi-year resource buildup and dramatic physical changes taking place along the border keep up with the shifts. As a result, success in gaining control of key border areas also led to a funnel effect in others, with migrants crossing in ever-larger numbers across increasingly difficult terrain and dangerous, historically isolated desert areas, especially in Arizona.

2. **2012-16 Strategic Plan**

In spring 2012, the chief of the Border Patrol announced the current iteration of border control, termed a "Risk-Based Strategic Plan."[90] In this 2012-16 plan, the Border Patrol states that the resource base that has been built and the operations that have been conducted over the past two decades enable it to focus on risk going forward. It calls for "identifying high-risk areas and flows and targeting our responses to meet those threats" through information, integration, and rapid response.[91]

To secure flows of goods and people by assessing and managing risk, the strategic plan lays out a vision of intelligence-driven operations that tap and analyze all of the information embedded in its considerable technology and agent experience base. It also underscores the importance of working closely with federal, state, local, tribal, and international partners in managing the "shared border." The plan further highlights a commitment to becoming a more "mature and sophisticated law enforcement organization" by providing ongoing support and investment in the skills and abilities of the agency's people.

---

88   One of the authors of this report, Doris Meissner, was INS Commissioner in 1994 and oversaw the development and implementation of the national border control strategy.
89   Border Patrol, *Border Patrol Strategic Plan: 1994 and Beyond* (Washington, DC: CBP, 1994): 9-10.
90   Border Patrol, *2012-2016 Border Patrol Strategic Plan* (Washington, DC: US Customs and Border Protection, 2012): 4, http://nemo.cbp.gov/obp/bp_strategic_plan.pdf.
91   Ibid., 4, 7.

This commitment may reflect the dramatic growth of the Border Patrol in recent years, which has made the level of officer experience, particularly mid-level supervisors, an ongoing concern. For example, the General Accounting Office (GAO) found that the percentage of agents with less than two years of experience had almost tripled from 14 to 39 percent between 1994 and 1998.[92] In 2007, congressional investigators reported that agent-to-supervisor ratios in Southwest border sectors ranged from 7 to 1 and 11 to 1, although CBP stated that a 5-to-1 ratio was desirable.[93] More recently, the Border Patrol staffing picture has stabilized. By FY 2011, the percentage of agents with less than two years of experience had fallen below 12 percent.[94]

The emphasis on rapid response recognizes the need to be nimble in the face of continual changes, including possible threats of terrorism or other public harm. Among recent steps to institutionalize rapid-response capabilities more fully, CBP has developed mobile response teams involving up to 500 agents to provide surge capabilities when changes in border activity occur.[95] Steep staffing increases have also allowed the Border Patrol to deepen its readiness and training to be able to cope with border safety exigencies that arise regularly in the border's frequently harsh climate and terrain. The Tucson, AZ sector, for example, has trained staff to provide emergency medical assistance and maintains rescue platforms where migrants can radio for help.[96]

Overall, the 2012 plan depicts an organization that envisions steady-state resources and operational challenges, and that seeks primarily to refine its existing programs and capabilities. A notable new theme is the heavy emphasis given to partnerships, especially with neighboring nations, that would have been "unthinkable" until recently.[97]

3. National Guard Support

Beyond the DHS strategies on border control, successive administrations have supported assistance from outside DHS — often due to political pressure from border states — to add manpower on a short-term basis as new agent recruitment and training took place. In May 2010, for example, President Obama announced the deployment of up to 1,200 National Guard personnel to the Southwest border.[98] Through Operation Phalanx, the National Guard provided logistical, surveillance, and other support to the Border

---

92 Chad Haddal, *Border Security: The Role of the US Border Patrol* (Washington, DC: Congressional Research Service, 2010): 33, www.fas.org/sgp/crs/homesec/RL32562.pdf.
93 Letter from Richard M. Stana, Director, Homeland Security and Justice Issues, Government Accountability Office (GAO), to the Honorable Mike Rogers, March 30, 2007, www.gao.gov/new.items/d07540r.pdf.
94 Border Patrol, "Border Patrol Agent Experience: FY 2004/FY 2006/FY 2011 YTD," (prepared for Migration Policy Institute, August 3, 2011). On file with authors.
95 Testimony of Mark Borkowski, Assistant Commissioner, Office of Technology, Innovation, and Acquisition, US Customs and Border Protection (CBP); Michael Fisher, Chief, US Border Patrol; and Michael Kostelnik, Assistant Commissioner, Office of Air and Marine, CBP, before the House Committee on Homeland Security, Subcommittee on Border and Maritime Security, *After SBInet - the Future of Technology on the Border*, 112th Cong., 1st sess., March 15, 2011, www.dhs.gov/ynews/testimony/testimony_1300195655653.shtm; Statement of Janet Napolitano, Secretary of Homeland Security, before the Senate Committee on Homeland Security and Governmental Affairs, *Securing the Border: Progress at the Federal Level What Remains to be Done?* 112th Cong., 1st sess., May 4, 2011, www.dhs.gov/ynews/testimony/testimony_1304459606805.shtm; Border Patrol, Border Patrol Strategic Plan, 12.
96 Briefing by Border Patrol for the Committee on Estimating Costs of Immigration Enforcement in the Department of Justice, National Research Council of the National Academies, during a visit to the Tucson Sector, September 2010. Notes on file with authors.
97 Border Patrol, *2012-2016 Border Patrol Strategic Plan*, 5.
98 Letter from General James L. Jones, National Security Advisor, and John O. Brennan, Assistant to the President for Homeland Security and Counterterrorism, to The Honorable Carl Levin, Chairman, Committee on Armed Services, United States Senate, May 25, 2010, www.whitchouse.gov/sites/default/files/Letter_to_Chairman_Levin.pdf.

Patrol in California, Arizona, New Mexico, and Texas. As of May 2011, Operation Phalanx had assisted in the seizure of 14,000 pounds of illegal drugs and the arrest of more than 7,000 illegal border crossers.[99]

Though the program was scheduled to end on June 30, 2011, the deployment was extended at the request of national, state, and local elected leaders.[100] The operation was slated to continue through December 2012,[101] with approximately 300 National Guard personnel who are limited to providing air surveillance and air mobility support operations to enhance the Border Patrol's ability to detect and deter illegal activity at the border.[102]

B. Determining Border Control

In assessing its successes and effectiveness, the Border Patrol has traditionally relied on border apprehensions data and changes in detected flows.

Border apprehensions reached a peak for the post-IRCA period of almost 1.7 million in 2000[103] and have fallen significantly in the years since. Apprehensions in FY 2011 numbered 340,252, one- fifth of the FY 2000 level — and the lowest level since 1970.[104] The most precipitous drop took place from 2008 to 2011 when apprehensions declined by 53 percent.[105] The post-2008 decline corresponds to the onset of the Great Recession and the sudden loss of jobs, particularly in the construction, hospitality, and tourism sectors, which served as major sources of employment for unauthorized migrants, especially from Mexico and Central America.

Other changes have also been taking place in the interplay between border enforcement tactics and programs and traditional migration patterns across the US-Mexico border. A recent Congressional Research Service (CRS) study, which analyzed the apprehension histories of individuals in the IDENT database, reported that the prevalence of recidivist border crossers (individuals apprehended twice or more in one year) declined from a peak of 28 percent in FY 2007 to 20 percent in FY 2011.[106] The number of unique individuals (as compared with apprehensions) intercepted by the Border Patrol peaked in 2000 at 880,000 and fell to approximately 618,000 in 2003, before rising again to 818,000 in 2005. The number has steadily declined each year since then, falling to 269,000 unique individuals in FY 2011.[107]

---

99 US Army. "Army National Guard Operation Phalanx," (Stand-To! newsletter, May 20, 2011), www.army.mil/standto/archive/2011/05/20/.

100 Letter from Representative Candice Miller to President Obama, April 1, 2011, http://candicemiller.house.gov/2011/04/miller-the-national-guards-mission-on-the-southwest-border-must-continue.shtml.

101 Joint testimony of Ronald D. Vitello, Deputy Chief, US Border Patrol, and Martin E. Vaughn, Executive Director, Southwest Region, Office of Air and Marine, CBP, before the House Committee on Homeland Security, Subcommittee on Border and Maritime Security, *Boots on the Ground or Eyes in the Sky: How Best to Utilize the National Guard to Achieve Operational Control*, 112th Cong., 2nd sess., April 17, 2012, www.dhs.gov/news/2012/04/17/written-testimony-us-customs-and-border-protection-house-homeland-security.

102 DHS, "DHS and DOD Announce Continued Partnership in Strengthening Southwest Border Security," (press release, December 20, 2011), www.dhs.gov/ynews/releases/20111220-dhs-dod-partnership-southwest-border-security.shtm.

103 Apprehensions in 2000 reached 1,676,438 — slightly lower than the historic peak of 1,692,544 in 1986. Border Patrol, "Nationwide Illegal Alien Apprehensions Fiscal Years 1925-2011," accessed November 15, 2012, www.cbp.gov/linkhandler/cgov/border_security/border_patrol/usbp_statistics/25_10_app_stats.ctt/25_11_app_stats.pdf.

104 Ibid.

105 CBP, "CBP's 2011 Fiscal Year in Review," (press release, December 12, 2011), www.cbp.gov/xp/cgov/newsroom/news_releases/national/2011_news_archive/12122011.xml; Border Patrol, "Total Illegal Alien Apprehensions by Fiscal Year," www.cbp.gov/linkhandler/cgov/border_security/border_patrol/usbp_statistics/99_10_fy_stats.ctt/99_11_fy_stats.pdf.

106 Marc R. Rosenblum, *Border Security: Immigration Enforcement Between Ports of Entry* (Washington, DC: CRS, 2012): 25, http://fpc.state.gov/documents/organization/180681.pdf.

107 Ibid.

Beyond significantly fewer apprehensions and individuals arrested, net illegal immigration from Mexico has fallen to zero or become slightly negative (fewer coming than leaving) for the first time in 40 years.[108] These changes can be traced to stronger growth in Mexico's economy than in that of the United States and to fundamental demographic change in Mexico, including lower birth rates, fewer people under the age of 15, and reduced numbers of young workers entering the labor force.[109]

However, border enforcement is also having an effect. Apprehensions along the Southwest border have declined in all nine Border Patrol sectors. The decline has been most dramatic in the Yuma, AZ sector (a 96 percent decrease between 2005 and 2011), the El Paso, TX sector (a 92 percent decrease), and the Del Rio, TX sector (a 76 percent decrease). (See Figure 4).

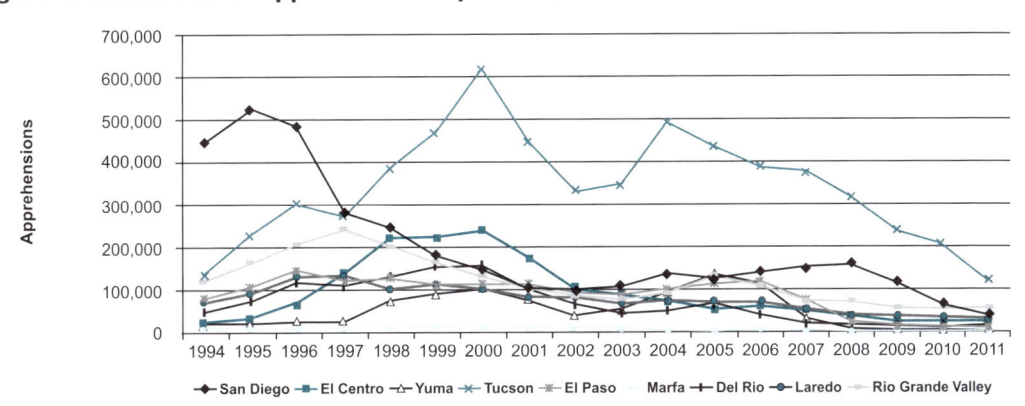

Figure 4. Border Patrol Apprehensions by Sector, 1994-2011

Source: DHS, *Yearbooks of Immigration Statistics*, FY 2003-FY 2011 (Washington, DC: DHS, various years), www.dhs.gov/yearbook-immigration-statistics.

In recent years, CBP has identified the Tucson, AZ sector as its greatest challenge in establishing control across the full Southwest border.[110] The sector, which recorded 123,285 apprehensions in FY 2011, accounted for twice as many arrests as the next highest sector (the Rio Grande Valley, with 59,243).[111] At the same time, the Tucson sector has experienced a 42 percent drop in apprehensions since 2011, and a 72 percent decline since 2005. Thus, although its arrest levels are comparatively high, the declines place it among sectors that have seen the most significant progress in recent years.

---

108 Elliot Spagat, "AP Exclusive: Border Patrol to Toughen Policy," Associated Press, January 17, 2012, www.denverpost.com/immigration/ci_19757370; Douglas S. Massey, "It's Time for Immigration Reform," CNN, July 7, 2011, http://globalpublicsquare.blogs.cnn.com/2011/07/07/its-time-for-immigration-reform/; Jeffrey Passel and D'Vera Cohn, *U.S. Unauthorized Immigration Flows are Down Sharply Since Mid-Decade* (Washington, DC: Pew Hispanic Center, 2010), www.pewhispanic.org/2010/09/01/us-unauthorized-immigration-flows-are-down-sharply-since-mid-decade/; Jeffrey Passel and D'Vera Cohn, *Unauthorized Immigrant Population: National and State Trends, 2010* (Washington, DC: Pew Hispanic Center, 2011), http://pewhispanic.org/files/reports/133.pdf; Rosenblum, *Border Security: Immigration Enforcement Between Ports of Entry*, 1.
109 Aaron Terrazas, Demetrios G. Papademetriou, and Marc R. Rosenblum, *Evolving Demographic and Human Capital Trends in Mexico and Central America and their Implications for Regional Migration* (Washington, DC: MPI and Woodrow Wilson International Center for Scholars, 2011), www.migrationpolicy.org/pubs/RMSG-human-capital.pdf.
110 Remarks by CBP Commissioner Alan Bersin at the Migration Policy Institute (Leadership Visions address, MPI, Washington, DC, October 14, 2010), http://vimeo.com/15887500.
111 DHS Office of Immigration Statistics, *2011 Yearbook of Immigration Statistics* (Washington, DC: DHS, Office of Immigration Statistics, 2012): 95, www.dhs.gov/sites/default/files/publications/immigration-statistics/yearbook/2011/ois_yb_2011.pdf.

Such changes raise the question of how to define and measure border control. The *Secure Fence Act*, enacted in 2006, calls for operational control of the border, defining it as "the prevention of all unlawful entries into the United States, including entries by terrorists, other unlawful aliens, instruments of terrorism, narcotics, and other contraband."[112] DHS argues that preventing *all* unlawful entries is not an attainable outcome. Homeland Security Secretary Janet Napolitano has stated that DHS will never be able to "seal the border" in the sense of preventing all illegal migration.[113]

Instead, the department has adopted a risk-management approach to border security, seeking to "detect and prevent the entry of dangerous people."[114] CBP defines operational control as being able to detect illegal entries, identify and classify them based on the threat they present, respond to them, and "bring each event to a satisfactory law enforcement resolution."[115] In FY 2010, the Border Patrol reported achieving operational control of 44 percent of the US-Mexico border, as defined by being able to "respond to illegal activity after entry."[116]

More recently, the Border Patrol has been re-assessing its definition of border control and the metrics to be used in determining control. Part of its thinking may involve the concept of determining and monitoring baseline flows. As in other areas of law enforcement, where some degree of law-breaking is expected to occur and is met with policing responses, CBP argues that certain baseline flows of people and drugs crossing the border illegally will exist. Thus, the goal is distribution of baseline flows as evenly as possible so that no location is taking the brunt, and effective responses and deterrence keep them to a minimum. Low-level, distributed flows, under this theory, constitute "risk mitigation" consistent with law enforcement practices that see success as reducing risk to a point of low probability of high-risk occurrences, especially terrorism.

For FY 2011, the Tucson sector had 123,285 apprehensions. The Border Patrol states that at that level, given the steep percentage declines of recent years, the Tucson sector could be reaching the level of its baseline flows, as have San Diego, El Paso, and the other sectors that now experience a degree of illegal crossing attempts but are able to respond to them and are, therefore, deemed to be under control.

C. Technology and Border Infrastructure

Technology initiatives for border enforcement have experienced a troubled history over recent decades and the results of highly touted technology solutions have often been disappointing.

1. Secure Border Initiative (SBI)

The most recent example of technology difficulties has been the high-tech component of the Secure Border Initiative (SBI), which DHS launched in late 2005. Described as a "comprehensive multi-year plan to secure America's borders and reduce illegal

---

112 *Secure Fence Act of 2006*, Pub. L. 109-367, 120 Stat. 2638, 2638 (October 26, 2006).
113 Homeland Security Secretary Janet Napolitano, "Press Conference with Secretary of Homeland Security Janet Napolitano; ICE Assistant Secretary John Morton; Los Angeles County, California, Sheriff Lee Baca; Harris County, Texas, Sheriff Adrian Garcia; Fairfax County, Virginia, Sheriff Stan Barry on New Immigration Enforcement Results," Washington, DC, October 6, 2010), www.ice.gov/news/releases/1010/101006washingtondc2.htm.
114 CBP, *Secure Borders, Safe Travel, Legal Trade: US Customs and Border Protection Fiscal Year 2009-2014 Strategic Plan* (Washington, DC: DHS, July 2009): 11, www.cbp.gov/linkhandler/cgov/about/mission/strategic_plan_09_14.ctt/strategic_plan_09_14.pdf.
115 Ibid., 13-4.
116 Statement of Richard M. Stana, Director, Homeland Security and Justice Issues, GAO, before the House Committee on Homeland Security, Subcommittee on Border and Maritime Security, *Border Security: Preliminary Observations on Border Control Measures for the Southwest Border*, 112th Cong., 1st sess., February 15, 2011, www.gao.gov/new.items/d11374t.pdf.

immigration," SBI sought to combine physical fencing with technology advances and increases in law enforcement personnel to gain operational control[117] of the US-Mexico border.[118] The technology component, known as SBInet, was intended to produce a "common operating picture" of the border, i.e. a snapshot of images compiled from cameras, ground sensors, and radar working in concert.[119]

In September 2006, Boeing Company won a three-year contract to construct SBInet,[120] which DHS renewed several times. The government paid Boeing approximately $860 million for the project.[121] SBInet was to be deployed over 387 miles of the Southwest border by the end of 2008.[122]

However, shortly after the project got off the ground it began experiencing significant technical difficulties, as documented by the Government Accountability Office (GAO) in reports to Congress between 2007 and 2010. Despite more than a dozen GAO reports warning of serious SBInet deficiencies, senior administration officials and members of Congress, continued to back the SBInet program through 2009.

In January 2010, GAO highlighted a new series of problems, including that DHS and Boeing had uncovered 1,300 defects in SBInet between March 2008 and July 2009, and that new defects were being found at a faster rate than problems were being fixed.

DHS in 2010 froze the funding that had been allocated for SBInet, with the exception of funds designated for the first two blocks of SBInet technology in the Tucson and Ajo Border Patrol sectors.[123] The department announced plans to conduct a "comprehensive, science-based assessment of alternatives.[124] One year later, in January 2011, Homeland Security Secretary Janet Napolitano announced that DHS was canceling the project.[125]

Secretary Napolitano has since testified that SBInet began as "an attempt to provide a single one-size-fits-all technology solution" for the border that did not provide the return on investment needed to justify it.[126] The current technology plan is to apply SBInet resources to proven technologies for border surveillance that are tailored to different terrains. The goal is to enable technology infusions to be operational more quickly with the funding that SBInet continues to provide, because technology acquisition is less time-consuming and protracted than design and engineering.

---

117 CBP defines operational control as being able to detect illegal entries, to identify and classify them based on the threat they present, to respond to them, and to "bring each event to a satisfactory law enforcement resolution."
118 DHS, "Secure Border Initiative," (press release, November 2, 2005), www.hsdl.org/?view&did=440470.
119 Statement of David Aguilar, Chief of Border Patrol, and Gregory Giddens, Executive Director of Secure Border Initiative, before the House Committee on Homeland Security, Subcommittee on Border, Maritime, and Global Counterterrorism, *Project 28: The Future of SBInet*, 110th Cong., 1st sess., June 7, 2007, http://chsdemocrats.house.gov/SiteDocuments/20070607154822-79256.doc.
120 Griff Witte, "Boeing Wins Deal for Border Security," *The Washington Post*, September 20, 2006, www.washingtonpost.com/wp-dyn/content/article/2006/09/19/AR2006091901715.html.
121 Susan Ragland, *Secure Border Initiative: Controls over Contractor Payments for the Technology Component Need Improvement* (Washington, DC: GAO, 2011): 2, www.gao.gov/new.items/d1168.pdf.
122 Statement of Richard M. Stana, Director, Homeland Security and Justice Issues, GAO, before the House Committee on Homeland Security, Subcommittees on Border, Maritime, and Global Counterterrorism and Management, Investigations, and Oversight, *Secure Border Initiative: Observations on Selected Aspects of SBInet Program Implementation*, 110th Cong., 1st sess., October 24, 2007, www.gao.gov/new.items/d08131t.pdf.
123 Ibid.
124 Testimony of Mark Borkowski, Director, Secure Border Initiative, and Michael Fisher, Acting Chief, US Border Patrol, before the House Homeland Security Committee, Subcommittees on Management, Investigations, and Oversight, and Border, Maritime, and Global Counterterrorism, *SBInet: Does it Pass the Border Security Test?*, 111th Cong., 2nd sess., June 17, 2010, http://chsdemocrats.house.gov/Hearings/index.asp?ID=259.
125 Julia Preston, "Homeland Security Cancels 'Virtual Fence' after $1Billion is Spent," *The New York Times*, January 14, 2011, www.nytimes.com/2011/01/15/us/politics/15fence.html?scp=1&sq=virtual%20fence&st=cse.
126 Testimony of Janet Napolitano, Secretary of Homeland Security, before the US House of Representatives Committee on the Judiciary, *Oversight of the Department of Homeland Security*, 112th Cong., 1st sess., October 26, 2011, www.dhs.gov/ynews/testimony/20111026-napolitano-house-judiciary.shtm.

In addition, the new approach allows for nonintrusive inspection equipment at ports of entry and already tested, commercially available technologies between the ports. They include remote video surveillance systems, mobile surveillance systems, thermal imaging, radiation portal monitors, mobile license plate readers, and unmanned aircraft.[127] Predator drone coverage now spans the entire Southwest border.[128] Fixed and mobile surveillance systems, which function as on-the-ground radar, are steadily replacing long-used ground sensors. Such surveillance technology allows a single agent to monitor seven miles of border area and classify the level of threat of detections for enforcement response.[129]

2. Fencing

The first fencing along the Southwest border was constructed in 1990.[130] Additional fencing was erected during the 1990s and early 2000s along a 14-mile stretch in the San Diego sector[131] and in short segments at other key points, generally in areas that were heavily urbanized, such as El Paso and Nogales. Where communities in Mexico and the United States merged at the border, a clear demarcation and barrier channeled illegal crossings to more open areas outside of the city where enforcement officers could more readily impede illegal entry.

However, fencing is expensive and was considered an enforcement tool to be used sparingly and in combination with other resources only when other measures were insufficient.

Prior to 2005, DHS had constructed approximately 78 miles of pedestrian fencing and 57 miles of vehicle barriers, concentrated in urban areas along the Southwest border where it is now referred to as legacy fencing.[132]

In the mid-2000s, physical and "virtual" (technology-based) fencing proposals, such as SBInet, gained momentum. They began to be championed as the ultimate answer to border control, in response to public impatience with record levels of illegal immigration.

After broader immigration reform legislation failed to win approval, Congress enacted the *Secure Fence Act* in 2006. The law called for constructing 700 miles of physical fencing along the Southwest border and "systematic surveillance" of the border through the use of unmanned aerial vehicles, ground-based sensors, satellites, radar coverage, and cameras.[133]

The *REAL ID Act*, passed in May 2005, ultimately helped to implement the *Secure Fence Act*,[134] by giving the Homeland Security secretary authority to waive any laws deemed to interfere with the expeditious construction of border "barriers and roads." *REAL ID* also provided that federal district courts would have sole jurisdiction to adjudicate

---

[127] Testimony of Janet Napolitano, Secretary of Homeland Security, before the US Senate Committee on Homeland Security and Governmental Affairs, *Securing the Border: Progress at the Federal Level: What Remains to be Done?* 112th Cong., 1st sess., May 3, 2011, www.dhs.gov/news/2011/05/03/secretary-janet-napolitano-senate-committee-homeland-security-and-governmental.

[128] Ibid.

[129] Ibid.

[130] Blas Nuñez-Neto and Stephen R. Vina, *Border Security: Fences Along the U.S. International Border* (Washington, DC: CRS, 2005): CRS-1, http://fpc.state.gov/documents/organization/47819.pdf.

[131] Ibid., CRS-2.

[132] Richard M. Stana, *Secure Border Initiative Fence Construction Costs* (Washington, DC: GAO, 2009): 6, www.gao.gov/assets/100/95951.pdf.

[133] *Secure Fence Act of 2006*, Pub. L. 109-367, 120 Stat. 2638, 2638 (October 26, 2006); *Consolidated Appropriations Act, 2008,* Pub. L. 110-161, 110th Cong, 121 Stat. 1844, 2090 (December 27, 2007).

[134] Omnibus legislation incorporating the *REAL-ID Act of 2005: Emergency Supplemental Appropriations Act for Defense, the Global War on Terror, and Tsunami Relief, 2005*, Pub. L. 109-13, 119 Stat. 231, 306 (May 11, 2005).

constitutional challenges to the waiver authority, with direct review by the US Supreme Court.[135]

By the end of FY 2008, CBP had completed 357 miles of fencing[136] and Homeland Security Secretary Michael Chertoff waived more than 30 laws dealing with environmental protection, Native American autonomy, and historic preservation to facilitate fence construction.[137] Legal challenges brought by environmental groups and local governments were unsuccessful.[138] By February 2012, CBP had completed 651 miles of fencing, a number that has come to be seen as having met the 700-mile mandate.[139]

D. Consequence Delivery System (CDS)

A prominent feature of today's border enforcement is significant change in the enforcement tactics used along the Southwest border. As its resources have grown, the Border Patrol has steadily introduced new measures and programs to impose "enforcement consequences" on those arrested. The stated purpose for these measures is to break the smuggling cycle and networks by separating migrants from smugglers, and to raise the cost — monetary, legal, and psychological — of illegal migration to migrants and smugglers alike.

Some of the tactics, such as interior repatriation to Mexico, have been used in discrete circumstances for many years. Others, such as expedited removal, constitute more recent practice. Used systematically, this Consequence Delivery System (CDS) represents a sharp departure from past enforcement policy and practice.

The modus operandi that had long characterized Southwest border enforcement involved liberal use of voluntary return of removable migrants. With voluntary return, an unauthorized migrant subject to removal may waive the right to a hearing and return voluntarily to his or her country of origin, typically Mexico.[140] The advantage to the government is that voluntary return is fast and relatively inexpensive; the advantage to the migrant is that it does not lead to long-term detention or a formal removal order that bars future immigration. Migrants removed pursuant to a formal order issued by an immigration judge are ineligible for a visa to return for ten years and then for 20 years after any additional removal.[141] Moreover, illegal entry after a formal order of removal is a felony.[142]

Until recently, about 90 percent of deportable migrants located since 1980 have been allowed voluntary return.[143] Voluntary return as the prevailing enforcement response to illegal crossing is now being supplanted by a variety of actions that are more consequential, both for the migrant and for the immigration system more broadly.

---

135 Ibid., 119 Stat. 306.
136 DHS, *Budget-in-Brief FY 2010*, 57.
137 DHS, "Determination Pursuant to Section 102 of the *Illegal Immigration Reform and Immigrant Responsibility Act of 1996*," 73 *Federal Register* 68, 19077-01, April 8, 2008.
138 Linda Greenhouse, "Legacy of a Fence," *The New York Times*, January 23, 2011, http://opinionator.blogs.nytimes.com/2011/01/22/legacy-of-a-fence/.
139 CBP, "Southwest Border Fence Construction Progress," February 10, 2012, www.cbp.gov/xp/cgov/border_security/ti/ti_news/sbi_fence/.
140 *Immigration and Nationality Act* ("INA") §240B(a)
141 INA § 212(a)(9)(A).
142 INA §276; see also National Research Council of the National Academies, *Budgeting for Immigration Enforcement: A Path to Better Performance* (Washington, DC: National Research Council of the National Academies, 2011): 51.
143 Ibid., 48.

Consequence enforcement actions include:

- ***Expedited removal*** — constitutes formal removal without a hearing before an immigration judge for individuals who entered illegally within the two weeks prior to their apprehension or were apprehended within 100 miles of a land or coastal border.[144] Barring a request for political asylum, expedited removal is based on the presumption that those who just entered illegally do not have any grounds for relief from removal. The process was initially used only at ports of entry but was extended in 2002 to include those who arrive by sea and in 2004 for Border Patrol apprehensions.[145]

- ***End of "catch and release"*** — requires detention for all non-Mexicans arrested in certain sectors instead of release, pending immigration hearings. Introduced in 2005-06, the change was intended to stop widespread failure to appear at hearings by mostly Central American migrants who were typically released and then became part of the unauthorized population.[146]

- ***Operation Streamline*** — provides for criminal prosecution of illegal border crossers in federal court. Subsequent illegal re-entry after conviction for illegal border crossing is a felony. Introduced in 2005 in the Del Rio sector and later expanded to parts of five[147] additional sectors, Operation Streamline is intended to focus on recent entrants, many of whom do not have roots in US communities. Through FY 2011, 164,639 people had been referred to the US Attorney's office for prosecution.[148]

- ***The Mexican Interior Repatriation Program (MIRP)*** — returns Mexican migrants to locations inside Mexico far from where they crossed into the United States. The program is designed to make it more difficult and costly for migrants to attempt repeat crossings and to return migrants closer to their homes as a humanitarian matter. MIRP flies migrants back to their hometowns or to nearby locations under an agreement with Mexico. CBP reports that only 11 percent of returnees were later re-apprehended.[149] However the program was suspended in the summer of 2012 because reduced migrant inflow lessened the cost-effectiveness of repatriation flights. A substitute pilot program is underway to determine future uses and forms of interior repatriation.[150]

- ***The Alien Transfer Exit Program (ATEP)*** — transports arrestees to land-border return crossing points for repatriation at points further east or west far from where they entered the United States.[151] Its purpose is to remove people from where they entered so as to disrupt the connection between migrants and smugglers, thereby raising the cost and reducing the likelihood of repeat migration. CBP estimates that less than 24 percent of those removed through

---

144 CBP, "DHS Expands Expedited Removal Authority Along Southwest Border," (press release, September 14, 2005), www.cbp.gov/xp/cgov/newsroom/news_releases/archives/2005_press_releases/092005/09142005.xml.
145 DOJ, "Notice Designating Aliens Subject to Expedited Removal Under Section 235(b)(1)(A)(iii) of the *Immigration and Nationality Act*," 67 *Federal Register* 219, 68924-26, November 13, 2002; DHS, "Notice Designating Aliens for Expedited Removal," 69 *Federal Register* 154, 48877, August 11, 2004.
146 Ibid., 9.
147 Rosenblum, *Border Security: Immigration Enforcement Between Ports of Entry*, 10.
148 Ibid.
149 Testimony of Janet Napolitano, Secretary of Homeland Security, before the US Senate Committee on Homeland Security and Governmental Affairs, *Securing the Border: Progress at the Federal Level*, 111th Cong., 2nd sess., May 3, 2011, www.dhs.gov/news/2011/05/03/secretary-janet-napolitano-senate-committee-homeland-security-and-governmental.
150 Elliot Spagat, "U.S. Stops Immigration Flights to Mexico," Associated Press, September 10, 2012, www.theledger.com/article/20120910/NEWS/120919988?p=1&tc=pg&tc=ar.
151 Rosenblum, *Border Security: Immigration Enforcement Between Ports of Entry*, 10.

ATEP re-enter.[152]

- **Operation Against Smugglers Initiative on Safety and Security (OASISS)** — returns select suspected smugglers to Mexico for prosecution pursuant to a 2005 agreement between the two countries. Through FY 2011, 2,617 people had been transferred.[153] In addition, cases take 12 to 18 months to prosecute in Mexico, as compared with about six months in the United States — putting smugglers out of business for longer periods.[154]

These programs are being used to varying degrees in each Southwest border sector. Consequence enforcement entails using all of these programs in a coordinated way. CDS was spearheaded by the Tucson sector, where a grant of voluntary return requires approval from a second-line supervisor. Ninety percent of the sector's apprehensions are resolved through consequence enforcement, rather than through voluntary return.[155]

CDS requires agents — based on a matrix of actions correlated to severity of offense — to determine which consequence enforcement option is appropriate. For example, those with prior criminal records are likely to be referred to Operation Streamline for criminal prosecution. For first-time crossers, ATEP is the likely consequence. Daily bus-runs transport those apprehended in the Tucson and Yuma, AZ sectors to El Centro and San Ysidro, CA for border repatriation.[156]

The Border Patrol states that its intelligence shows that smugglers along different parts of the border do not cooperate with each other, so at a minimum, ATEP delays return attempts. At best, it discourages migrants from trying again altogether. Border Patrol officials believe that the certainty of strict consequences will deter illegal migration, as compared with voluntary return which they believe resulted in what has been widely characterized as a revolving door.

Consequence enforcement was adopted border-wide during 2012. If implemented as envisioned, voluntary return — historically the prevailing enforcement practice on the US-Mexico border for many decades — will be limited to a relatively small subgroup of illegal crossers, primarily unaccompanied minors and humanitarian cases.

E. Deaths at the Border

Strengthened border enforcement along the Southwest border has made it significantly more difficult to cross the border between ports of entry. As border enforcement has tightened, smugglers have increasingly led migrants through more isolated terrain, particularly remote desert areas of eastern California and Arizona,[157] and migrant deaths have risen. A series of studies have documented this rise, though each presents

---

152 Testimony of Janet Napolitano, Secretary of Homeland Security, before the US Committee on Homeland Security and Governmental Affairs, *Securing the Borders and America's Points of Entry: What Remains to be Done?* 111th Cong., 1st sess., May 20, 2009.
153 Rosenblum, B*order Security: Immigration Enforcement Between Ports of Entry*, 10.
154 Briefing by Border Patrol during a visit to the Tucson Sector by the Committee on Estimating Costs of Immigration Enforcement in the Department of Justice.
155 Ibid; Remarks by Alan Bersin, Commissioner, CBP, at the Center for American Progress, Washington, DC, August 4, 2011; (noting that in Arizona, save for juveniles and special humanitarian cases, nine out of ten people who are apprehended at the border are subject to some sort of "consequence delivery" method).
156 Ibid.
157 Meissner and Kerwin, *DHS and Immigration: Taking Stock and Correcting Course*, 15-7.

slightly different estimates.[158] In 2006, GAO released a report showing that between FY 1999-2005, the number of border-crossing deaths almost doubled from 241 to 472.[159]

The increases were almost entirely due to a dramatic rise in the number of deaths reported in the Tucson sector, which includes much of the Arizona desert.[160] A University of Houston study found more modest increases in numbers, but the causes of death had changed from car accidents, for example, to exposure and dehydration.[161]

Since 2005, the number of migrant deaths reported each year has leveled off.[162] DHS estimates that migrant deaths along the border reached their highest point in 2005 (at 492 deaths). They averaged approximately 431 deaths per year during the period from 2005-09.[163] The death rate then fell to an average of 360 deaths per year during the 2010-11 timeframe.[164]

Despite the recent slight drop, the average number of deaths reported in recent years is significantly greater than the number reported by INS in 1999 (250). In addition, because apprehensions along the border have fallen dramatically, the ratio of deaths to apprehensions has increased. Thus, the risk of dying while attempting to cross the border has risen in recent years.[165]

The Border Patrol has established the following initiatives aimed at reducing the risk of crossing deaths:

- ***Border Safety Initiative (BSI)*** — created in 1998 to reduce the migrant death rate,[166] BSI includes a series of public service announcements issued by the Border Patrol in Mexico to deter would-be crossers. Rescue beacons also have been installed at remote migrant crossing points.[167]

- ***Border Patrol Search, Trauma, and Rescue (BORSTAR)*** — these search and rescue teams are made up of Border Patrol agents specially trained in emergency medical care, first aid, and search-and-rescue techniques.[168]

- ***Arizona Border Control Initiative (ABCI)*** —included a media campaign that warned would-be migrants of the dangers of crossing through the desert.[169]

---

158 Ibid; see also Haddal, *Border Security: The Role of the U.S. Border Patrol*, 1; Maria Jimenez, *Humanitarian Crisis: Migrant Deaths at the U.S.-Mexico Border* (New York: American Civil Liberties Union ACLU of San Diego & Imperial Counties and Mexico's National Commission of Human Rights, 2009), www.aclu.org/immigrants-rights/humanitarian-crisis-migrant-deaths-us-mexico-border.
159 Laurie E. Ekstrand, *Border-Crossing Deaths Have Doubled Since 1995: Border Patrol's Efforts to Prevent Deaths Have Not Been Fully Evaluated* (Washington, DC: GAO, 2006): 4, www.gao.gov/assets/260/251173.pdf.
160 Ibid.
161 Karl Eschbach, Jacqueline Maria Hagan and Néstor Rodriguez, "Causes and Trends in Migrant Deaths along the U.S.-Mexico Border, 1985-1998" (Center for Immigration Research Working Paper Series 01-4, University of Houston, March 2001).
162 Some members of the human-rights community contend that the Border Patrol undercounts fatalities by excluding skeletal remains, victims in car accidents, and corpses discovered by other agencies or local law enforcement officers and does not attempt to estimate the number of migrants who died but were never found.
163 Rosenblum, *Border Security: Immigration Enforcement Between Ports of Entry*, 33.
164 Ibid.
165 Jimenez, *Humanitarian Crisis: Migrant Deaths at the U.S.-Mexico Border*, 8; Testimony of Douglas Massey, Professor of sociology and public affairs, Princeton University, before the US Senate Judiciary Committee, *Securing the Borders and America's Points of Entry, What Remains to be Done?* 111th Cong., 1st sess., May 20, 2009, www.judiciary.senate.gov/hearings/hearing.cfm?id=e655f9e2809e5476862f735da149ad69.
166 Jimenez, *Humanitarian Crisis: Migrant Deaths at the U.S.-Mexico Border*, 32.
167 Ibid; Ekstrand, *Border-Crossing Deaths Have Doubled Since 1995*, 9.
168 CBP, "BORSTAR Fact Sheet," June 3, 2009, www.cbp.gov/linkhandler/cgov/newsroom/fact_sheets/border/border_patrol/borstar.ctt/borstar.pdf.
169 Ibid.

Despite these efforts, the Border Patrol continues to face criticism over its response to migrant deaths. In 2006, GAO concluded that there was insufficient evidence to determine that humanitarian Border Patrol efforts had actually reduced migrant deaths.[170] GAO also found that the Border Patrol lacked a consistent method across sectors for tracking migrant deaths, a failure that made it difficult to evaluate the progress of its humanitarian initiatives.[171] In addition, the Border Patrol does not count migrant deaths that occur in Mexico, and thus has been criticized for undercounting deaths.

F. Ports of Entry (POE)

The POE mission is arguably the most difficult and complex element of border security. CBP's immigration inspectors question, under oath, persons seeking entry in order to determine their admissibility. POEs are responsible for both facilitation of legitimate trade and travel — which are vital for the economies and social well-being of the United States and most countries around the world — and for preventing the entry of a small but potentially deadly number of dangerous people as well as lethal goods, illicit drugs, and contraband. As border security improves and border enforcement makes illegal crossing between ports ever more difficult, the potential for misuse of legal crossing procedures builds and can be expected to steadily increase.

CBP estimates that it processed more than 340 million travelers in FY 2011.[172] With such volumes, inspectors have very little time on average to determine whether a traveler is authorized to enter. Covert testing by GAO at land, sea, and airport entry points from 2003-07 found that inspectors routinely failed to detect counterfeit documents or did not request documents at all.[173] A separate study found that the probability of an unauthorized migrant being apprehended while passing illegally through a POE was about one-half as high as the probability of being apprehended while crossing between ports of entry.[174] Persons seeking to cross illegally have growing incentives to try to enter at a POE, rather than risk their lives crossing illegally between ports.

In recent years, the gap between the number of noncitizens apprehended by the Border Patrol and the number found inadmissible by CBP at ports of entry has narrowed considerably. At the FY 2000 peak, the number of between-ports apprehensions numbered nearly three times the 559,000 actions against noncitizens found to be inadmissible by enforcement at ports of entry.[175] In contrast, the 340,252 apprehensions recorded in FY 2011 were only 1.5 times the number of denials based on inadmissibility at ports of entry.[176]

The inspections function has been substantially strengthened, both through continuing staffing and technology infusions, and through other initiatives that support the inspections screening mission with new tools, especially the US-VISIT program, described in a later section. CBP has implemented numerous additional improvements to strengthen security at POEs.

---

170 Ekstrand, *Border-Crossing Deaths Have Doubled Since 1995*, 5.
171 Ibid., 25.
172 CBP, "CBP's 2011 Fiscal Year in Review," (press release, December 12, 2011), www.cbp.gov/xp/cgov/newsroom/news_releases/national/2011_news_archive/12122011.xml.
173 GAO, *Border Security: Summary of Covert Tests and Security Assessments for the Senate Committee on Finance, 2003 – 2007* (Washington, DC: GAO, 2008): 6-10, www.gao.gov/new.items/d08757.pdf.
174 Rosenblum, *Border Security: Immigration Enforcement Between Ports of Entry*, 34.
175 INS, *Yearbook of Immigration Statistics, FY 2000* (Washington, DC: INS, 2002): 234, 242, www.dhs.gov/xlibrary/assets/statistics/yearbook/2000/Yearbook2000.pdf.
176 DHS, *Immigration Enforcement Actions: 2011*, 3.

1. **Secure Border-Crossing Documents**

Since January 2007, the Western Hemisphere Travel Initiative (WHTI) has required all travelers to present specified documents to prove citizenship and identity to enter the country at POEs,[177] ending inspectors' acceptance of verbal declarations of citizenship. The requirement represented a dramatic change from past practices on the Mexican and Canadian land borders where roughly 621,874 people — most of whom live and work in border areas — cross daily.[178]

The change provoked particular concern and tension in the US-Canadian relationship, because the initial WHTI requirements called for all crossers to present passports, which many Canadian crossers did not possess. The United States subsequently agreed to accept enhanced drivers' licenses that are designed to meet WHTI document requirements, issued both by Canada and a number of northern border states, including Washington, Vermont, and New York. The United States also began to issue a new document, known as a passport card, to meet the statutory requirements.[179] According to CBP, the changes have had a high rate of compliance, without increasing wait times at ports of entry or seriously inconveniencing travelers.[180]

Land border inspections have become significantly more reliable and secure as a result of the change, as well as requirements for new border crossing cards (BCC) on the southern border. Lawful crossers now possess high-quality digital documents that are produced on the same platform as "green" cards and incorporate their same security features. Photo substitution on documents — a major problem for decades on land borders — is virtually impossible with currently available methods.[181]

Despite the document integrity, today's problem is look-a-likes: people crossing with legitimate documents they have obtained from others with similar appearances.[182] Given the high volume of land-border crossings and facility constraints, it has not been possible to scan the fingerprints of Mexican border crossers with BCCs, or of Canadian visitors — thereby "assuring" identity through biometrics — except for individuals referred for more in-depth screening, known as secondary inspection.[183]

---

177 Maura Harty, Assistant Secretary of State for Consular Affairs, and Elaine Dezenski, Acting Assistant Secretary for Border and Transportation Security Policy and Planning, DOS, "DOS Special Briefing on Western Hemisphere Travel Initiative," (DOS briefing, Washington, DC, April 5, 2005), http://2001-2009.state.gov/r/pa/prs/ps/2005/44286.htm.
178 US Customs and Border Protection, "On a Typical Day in Fiscal Year 2011," www.cbp.gov/linkhandler/cgov/about/accomplish/typical_day_fy11.ctt/typical_day_fy11.pdf.
179 DOS, "US Passport Card Frequently Asked Questions," March 2011, http://travel.state.gov/passport/ppt_card/ppt_card_3921.html.
180 Statement of Richard M. Stana, Director, Homeland Security and Justice Issues, GAO, before the Senate Committee on Homeland Security and Governmental Affairs, *DHS Progress and Challenges in Securing the U.S. Southwest and Northern Borders*, 112th Cong., 1st sess., March 30, 2011, www.gao.gov/new.items/d11508t.pdf; Joint Statement of DHS Acting Assistant Secretary for Policy Richard Barth and CBP Office of Field Operations Assistant Commissioner Thomas Winkowski before the House Committee on Homeland Security, Subcommittee on Border, Maritime, and Global Communications, *Implementing the Western Hemisphere Travel Initiative at Land and Sea Ports of Entry: Are we Ready?*, 110th Cong., 1st sess., May 7, 2009, www.cbp.gov/xp/cgov/newsroom/congressional_test/whti_ready_testify.xml.
181 Jess T. Ford, *Border Security: Security of New Passports and Visas Enhanced, but More Needs to be Done to Prevent Their Fraudulent Use* (Washington, DC: GAO, 2007): 3, 13-4, www.gao.gov/products/GAO-07-1006; Dr. Nabajyoti Barkakati, *Improvements in the Department of State's Development Process Could Increase the Security of Passport and Border Crossing Cards* (Washington, DC: GAO, 2010): 7, 13-4, www.gao.gov/assets/310/305134.pdf; CBP, "Securing America's Borders: CBP Fiscal Year 2009 in Review Fact Sheet," November 24, 2009, www.cbp.gov/xp/cgov/about/accomplish/previous_year/fy2009_stats/11242009_5.xml.
182 Ibid.
183 DHS US-VISIT, "US-VISIT Biometric Procedures: Applicability to Canadian Citizens," October 2, 2009, www.dhs.gov/files/programs/editorial_0695.shtm; DHS US-VISIT, "US-VISIT Biometric Procedures: Applicability to Mexican Citizens," October 2, 2009, www.dhs.gov/files/programs/editorial_0696.shtm.

2. Trusted-Traveler Programs

The vast majority of temporary admissions to the country are by Canadians and Mexicans. In FY 2009, Mexicans with BCCs and Canadians traveling with short-term visas for business or tourism comprised 126.8 million, or 78 percent, of the 163 million nonimmigrant admissions to the United States.[184] Given these high volumes, risk-segmentation techniques — such as trusted-traveler programs — are imperative.

The rationale for such programs is to allow low-risk crossers — the vast majority of travelers — who cross frequently to qualify through a one-time in-depth background security screening and personal interview that establishes their eligibility for designation as a trusted traveler. Subject to periodic random fuller screening, pre-approved participants may move quickly through inspections procedures and enter the United States through designated travel lanes.

Such programs also allow CBP inspectors to focus their attention on the small proportion of crossers who may represent a threat.

Currently, CBP manages the following trusted-traveler programs:

- The Secure Electronic Network for Travelers Rapid Inspection (SENTRI) and NEXUS programs, which enable prescreened frequent border crossers to enter through designated lanes at certain land ports of entry along the southern and northern borders

- The Free and Secure Trade (FAST) program, which allows approved Mexican and Canadian commercial drivers to enter the United States through special lanes

- Global Entry, which enables enrolled air travelers to skip regular immigration and customs processing and enter to the United States at designated kiosks.

Travel-facilitation programs that had been developed and evolved separately for the northern and southern borders are being combined. They will have the same application procedure, fee, and technology platform. Among such programs, NEXUS on the US-Canada border and SENTRI on the Southwest border, have approximately 650,000 and 264,000 enrollees, respectively.[185] To grow and further streamline trusted-traveler facilitation, CBP envisions integration with Travel Security Administration (TSA) procedures, so that low-risk, prescreened travelers can navigate both CBP and TSA screening expeditiously.[186]

Still, program participants make up only a fraction of the number of individuals who enter the United States annually.[187] Streamlining travel processes for the 99 percent of

---

[184] Ruth Ellen Wasem, *US Immigration Policy on Temporary Admissions* (Washington, DC: CRS, 2011), www.fas.org/sgp/crs/homesec/RL31381.pdf.

[185] *The Economist*, "Border Accord," December 8, 2011, www.economist.com/blogs/gulliver/2011/12/canada-us; Jacob Goodwin, "CBP Aims to Boost Enrollment in its Trusted Traveler Programs," *Government Security News Magazine*, September 16, 2011, www.gsnmagazine.com/node/24541; DHS, "NEXUS Fact Sheet," March 2012, www.cbp.gov/linkhandler/cgov/travel/trusted_traveler/nexus_prog/nexus_facts.ctt/nexus_facts.pdf.

[186] US Transportation Security Administration (TSA), "TSA Pre-Check," accessed November 16, 2012, www.tsa.gov/what_we_do/escreening.shtm.

[187] According to CBP statistics, nearly 650,000 people are registered participants in NEXUS; see DHS, "NEXUS Fact Sheet." And 87,000 commercial drivers participate in the Free and Secure Trade (FAST) program; CBP, "FAST Fact Sheet," www.cbp.gov/linkhandler/cgov/newsroom/fact_sheets/travel/fast/fast_fact.ctt/fast_fact.pdf. *The New York Times* has reported that just 3-4 percent of air passengers currently use automated kiosks, such as those provided through the Global Entry program, in order to clear customs and immigration processing; see Susan Stellin, "A Long Wait Gets Longer," *The New York Times*, August 22, 2011, www.nytimes.com/2011/08/23/business/long-customs-lines-a-growing-concern.html?_r=1&scp=30&sq=fy%202011%20decrease%20in%20border%20patrol%20officers&st=cse.

travelers who represent economic, social, and cultural benefits to the nation remains a work in progress.

3. POE Infrastructure

Meeting the physical infrastructure needs at POEs has not kept pace with advances in documentation and screening developments. Communities such as Nogales, AZ, for example, have two ports that typically handle 15,000 pedestrian and 20,000 vehicle crossings daily (3.5 million pedestrians and 4.7 million vehicles annually). The POEs are equipped with technology that permits 100 percent license plate reading and document scanning. However, when traffic wait times exceed 60 minutes, inspectors typically "flush" traffic through, pulling aside only obvious high-risk crossers, in an effort to reconcile their facilitation and enforcement missions under trying conditions.

Despite significant advances, land ports have not experienced improvements on par with those realized between ports. As a result, the potential for land POE inspections to be a weak link remains a critical enforcement challenge.

G. US-Canada Border

The northern border is more than 4,000 miles long (excluding the Alaska-Canada border) and over twice the length of the US border with Mexico. The fact that several terrorists (not affiliated with the 9/11 plot) entered the United States from Canada prior to 9/11 led to criticism from Congress over northern border security following the 2001 attacks.[188] Because apprehension levels along the northern border are dramatically lower than along the southern border, CBP's northern border strategy differs significantly from its southern one. In particular, a key part of northern border security efforts continues to be enhanced partnerships between US and Canadian law enforcement agencies.[189]

In December 2011, the United States and Canada announced a new plan for a unified binational approach to security, customs, and trade.[190] Under the agreement, legitimate travel and trade at the countries' shared border will be streamlined while the focus of border protection will shift to a redefined external border around the two countries.

Guided by the principle that a threat to either country is a threat to both, the new plan calls for the United States and Canada to align their border security understandings, goals, and capabilities in three key ways:

- Adopt a common approach to screening entrants through interoperable identity information databases. Canada will develop an electronic database for visa waiver travelers[191] modeled after the US Electronic System for Travel Authorization (ESTA).[192] Canada will also pilot a system for screening passenger name

---

188 Haddal, *Border Security, the Role of the U.S. Border Patrol*, 21.
189 CBP, *Office of the Border Patrol, National Border Patrol Strategy* (Washington, DC: CBP, 2004): 6, www.au.af.mil/au/awc/awcgate/dhs/national_bp_strategy.pdf; Testimony of Alan Bersin, Commissioner, CBP, before the Senate Judiciary Committee, Subcommittee on Immigration, Refugees, and Border Security, *Improving Border Security and Facilitation of Commerce at America's Northern Border and Ports of Entry*, 112th Cong., 1st sess., May 17, 2011, www.cbp.gov/xp/cgov/newsroom/congressional_test/bersin_testifies.xml.
190 DHS, *United States-Canada Beyond the Border: A Shared Vision for Perimeter Security and Economic Competitiveness, Action Plan* (Washington, DC: DHS, 2011), www.dhs.gov/xlibrary/assets/wh/us-canada-btb-action-plan.pdf.
191 The United States Visa Waiver Program (VWP) allows nationals of 37 countries to travel to the United States for business or tourism purposes for up to 90 days without a visa. Since 2009, VWP participants have been required to obtain clearance through the US Electronic System for Travel Authorization (ESTA), which screens travelers' biographic information against immigration, criminal, and terrorism databases. Canada also allows nationals of certain countries to travel visa-free.
192 DHS, *United States-Canada Beyond the Border: A Shared Vision for Perimeter Security and Economic Competitiveness, Action Plan*, 8.

records for ship and airplane passengers that is modeled after the US Advance Passenger Information System (APIS).[193]

- Develop data systems that share travelers' biographic and biometric information, watch list data, immigration histories, and criminal records in some cases.[194] Such information sharing may ultimately be used to enhance bilateral cooperation on asylum and illegal migration. Both countries also seek to share information about certain high-risk individuals, consistent with existing bilateral agreements.[195]

- Create an exit-entry system which automatically registers an individual's entry into one country as an exit from the other.[196]

The agreement also seeks to facilitate legitimate trade and travel at the US-Canada border by initiating new programs that expedite passage at POEs, and expand the use of existing trusted-traveler programs such as NEXUS.[197] The two countries have agreed to make investments in infrastructure and technology at large and small POEs to deepen officials' capacity to quickly move and monitor imports, exports, and travel.

The action plan further calls for enhanced binational law enforcement coordination to respond to incidents on the border involving criminals, fugitives, and unauthorized migrants. Currently, a pilot program called Shiprider deploys US and Canadian border officers to maritime areas and Integrated Border Enforcement Teams (IBETs) and Border Enforcement Security Task Forces (BEST) already operate across the land border. Under the plan, these programs will be continued, broadened, and supplemented with new cross-border law enforcement initiatives designed to improve intelligence, criminal investigations, and enforcement between POEs.[198]

H. Border Enforcement beyond Immigration Control

Today's border enforcement is a multi-faceted, sophisticated enterprise that encompasses not only immigration enforcement but wide-ranging national security, anti-narcotics, criminal enforcement, intelligence, regulatory, trade, federal, state, local, tribal, binational, and multinational missions, programs, and partnerships.

Examples of these broader functions and capabilities include:

- A new Border Intelligence Fusion program at DEA's El Paso Intelligence Center (EPIC) established by DHS with the DEA and the Department of Defense to provide border-wide common intelligence assessments in addition to customary operational intelligence of suspect activities in specific locations.[199]

- Interoperable, cross-border communications with Mexico to support law enforcement coordination and public-safety responses, in combating smuggling and other cross-border and international criminal enterprises. US-Mexico cooperation is more wide-ranging and effective than it has ever been, according to officials in both countries, with trust and joint efforts steadily improving

---

193 Ibid.
194 Ibid., 9.
195 Ibid., 8.
196 Ibid., 10.
197 Ibid., 11-2.
198 Ibid., 21.
199 See testimony of Michael J. Fisher, Chief, US Border Patrol, before the House Committee on Homeland Security, Subcommittee on Border and Maritime Security, *Securing our Borders—Operational Control and the Path Forward*, 112th Cong., 1st sess., February 15, 2011, www.cbp.gov/xp/cgov/newsroom/congressional_test/fisher_testifies/chief_fisher.xml.

- One-quarter of ICE personnel are assigned to the border region to investigate transnational crimes.[200]

- Screening of southbound rail traffic and random vehicle screening for weapons and cash bound for drug cartels in Mexico.[201]

- The Alliance to Combat Transnational Threats (ACTT) is a law enforcement collaboration among DHS, Arizona, and Mexican law enforcement agencies to disrupt and interdict criminal enterprises and individuals. In two years, ACTT operations have seized substantial amounts of narcotics, undeclared currency, weapons, and criminal aliens.[202]

In 2009, DHS reaffirmed and updated the prior administration's Southwest Border Initiative (SBI), coupling Southwest border security with "reinvigorated, smart" enforcement of immigration laws in the country's interior.[203] DHS goals for 2009-14 continue to stress its mission as a "homeland security" agency, thus maintaining bipartisan support for the broad responses to the 9/11 attacks that have been implanted during the past decade.

> *In the aggregate, the picture is one of a complex, professional, heavily resourced border-control-and-security regime where law enforcement agencies define border control as a core role and responsibility.*

II. Program Critiques and Findings

The need for effective border enforcement and control is among the few points of agreement in the national immigration debate. However, what constitutes effective or acceptable levels of border enforcement is often in sharp dispute.

CBP continues to rely almost entirely on apprehensions as its measure of effectiveness. DHS argues that the border is safer than it has ever been and that depicting the border as out of control "is just plain wrong" and ignores "all of the statistical evidence."[204] It has acknowledged the need for new ways to measure results and has committed to providing a border conditions index to measure border enforcement "comprehensively and systematically."[205] The index is being developed but has not yet been made public.

Reduced flows are the result of a combination of factors, beginning with the US economic recession. Still, most experts agree that increased border enforcement and unprecedented investment in border personnel, infrastructure, technology, and binational and international enforcement partnerships have been a contributing factor in historic decreases in apprehensions.[206]

Nonetheless, establishing that border control has significantly improved relies primar-

---

200 DHS, "DHS' Progress in 2011: Southwest Border," accessed November 16, 2012, www.dhs.gov/xabout/2011-dhs-accomplishments-southwest-border.shtm.
201 Ibid; See also Bersin, Leadership Visions speech at MPI.
202 Ibid.
203 Ibid.
204 Homeland Security Secretary Janet Napolitano, "Remarks on Border Security at the University of Texas at El Paso," January 31, 2011, www.dhs.gov/ynews/speeches/sp_1296491064429.shtm.
205 Statement of Janet Napolitano, Secretary of Homeland Security, before the Senate Committee on Homeland Security and Governmental Affairs, *Securing the Border: Progress at the Federal Level What Remains to be Done?* 112th Cong., 1st sess., May 4, 2011, www.dhs.gov/ynews/testimony/testimony_1304459606805.shtm.
206 Meissner and Kerwin, *DHS and Immigration: Taking Stock and Correcting Course*, 15-7.

ily on inputs (e.g., resource increases) — not on outcomes and impact (e.g. deterrence measures, such as size of illegal flows, share of the flow apprehended, or changing crosser recidivism rates). Ultimately, the ability of immigration agencies and DHS to communicate change, overcome misperceptions, and combat distorted charges about inadequate border control will require evidence and analysis of such outcomes.

A. Measurement

Apprehensions are insufficient as sole measures of effectiveness because they count activity or workload, not persons. In the past, the Border Patrol has cited both surges and reductions of apprehensions as evidence of deterrence.[207] Apprehensions are a valid proxy for reduced flows and deterrence, particularly when they demonstrate a trend, as has occurred with the steep apprehension declines in recent years. However, more sophisticated, valid measures for estimating flows across the border are long overdue.

CBP and DHS are working on developing additional measures in the effort to develop a border conditions index. CBP collects many other kinds of data that are amenable to assessing effectiveness:

- *IDENT* — These data can be mined for information about repeat entries, smuggling, and changes in crossing patterns to determine the success of enforcement initiatives and to indicate how many people enter illegally, the likelihood of apprehension per crossing attempt, the percentage of migrants who ultimately succeed in entering, and the reasons that illegal entries increase or decrease.[208] IDENT data are particularly valuable for a methodology known as the "repeated trials model" that is used to estimate sizes of populations where actual counting is not possible, such as wildlife. Such research would capture the overall flow across the Southwest border, changes in the flow, and apprehension rates.[209] DHS analysts are using the model, but the research requires further support and operational information.

- *Border surveillance* — Improved camera and other technology increasingly allows for "seeing" a full and accurate picture of border crossings. Used operationally for dispatching agents and tracing crossing patterns and adaptations by smugglers to avoid detection, these data can also help inform analyses such as the repeated trials model, as well as allow for statistical sampling of actual flows. Ascertaining actual flows — as compared with apprehensions — is the key information that has never been known and is essential for determining enforcement effectiveness and deterrence.

- *Crime rates* — Assessing effective border control would look systematically at crime rates, particularly those associated with illegal immigration, such as breaking and entering, trespassing, and car theft. The rates are down substantially in all US border communities and well below national averages.[210] With these indices, the experience from El Paso, San Diego, and elsewhere is that public perceptions change as migrants are no longer crossing private property

---

207 Donald Kerwin, *Chaos on the U.S.-Mexican Border* (Washington, DC: Catholic Legal Immigration Network, Inc., 2001): 8-10, www.lexisnexis.com/practiceareas/immigration/pdfs/web305.pdf.
208 Edward Alden and Bryan Roberts, "Are US Borders Secure? Why We Don't Know, and How to Find Out," *Foreign Affairs* 90, no. 4 (2011), www.foreignaffairs.com/articles/67901/edward-alden-and-bryan-roberts/are-us-borders-secure; Blas Nuñez-Neto, *Border Security: The Role of the US Border Patrol* (Washington, DC: CRS, updated November 20, 2008): 11-2, http://digitalcommons.ilr.cornell.edu/cgi/viewcontent.cgi?article=1577&context=key_workplace&sei-redir=1#search=%22Nunez%20neto%20role%20US%20border%20patrol%22.
209 Randy Capps, Doris Meissner, and Michael Fix, "Measuring Effective Border Control: What Can We Know?" (unpublished working paper, MPI, July 2012).
210 Dennis Wagner, "Violence Is Not Up on Arizona Border Despite Mexican Drug War," *Arizona Republic*, May 2, 2010, www.azcentral.com/news/articles/2010/05/02/20100502arizona-border-violence-mexico.html.

and dangerous highways, neighborhoods feel safe, and webs of foot trails littered with trash disappear from rural landscapes. CBP is replicating that experience across the Southwest border as the mark of a sustainable borderland.

Systematic measurement of critical elements of border control such as these would allow for a more informed, realistic public debate if DHS could fully mobilize, communicate, and institutionalize them as indispensable ingredients in carrying out its border control mission.

B. *Evaluating Consequence Enforcement*

The cost effectiveness and deterrence of different enforcement strategies — in particular, consequence enforcement — should also be subject to measurement. The degree to which increased consequences for illegal entry and re-entry are effective deterrents is unknown. CBP data on illegal re-entries offer a means to assess the deterrent effects of these policies. Comparisons of IDENT recidivism data would help determine whether formal deportations and criminal prosecutions deter repeat attempts as compared with lateral and interior repatriation or voluntary return, for example. Such information will be increasingly important in the budget climate ahead, as some elements of consequence enforcement are substantially more expensive than others and have significantly different downstream effects on other parts of the immigration and federal criminal justice systems, as well as for the individuals who are removed.

1. Painting the Full Border Enforcement Picture

A primary rationale for the creation of DHS was to ensure greater cooperation and coordination among border officials and agencies. An integrated or seamless approach to border control responds to the need to counteract the flexibility and resourcefulness of terrorists, human-smuggling networks, and determined border crossers.

If deterrence succeeds in a particular Border Patrol sector, illegal crossers will pursue other more amenable crossing methods and routes. For example, a recent surge in the smuggling by boat of Mexican nationals into California has been attributed to increased land border security.[211] Increased Border Patrol activity has been associated with higher rates of unauthorized people entering through POEs.[212] Yet the Border Patrol's strategic plans do not speak to enforcement issues facing land border POEs that are co-located in their areas of jurisdiction, even though both Border Patrol and POE inspections functions are organizationally housed in the same DHS agency, CBP.

In 2003, Homeland Security Secretary Tom Ridge launched the "One Face at the Border" initiative, which was designed to merge the work of legacy immigration, customs, and agricultural inspectors at POEs, but evolved into a broader initiative "to increase efficiencies, eliminate redundancies, and harmonize conflicting policies."[213] Nearly ten years after DHS's creation, the question remains whether integration of border enforce-

---

[211] Jason Kandel, "Maritime Smuggling to California on the Rise," Reuters, July 30, 2011, www.reuters.com/article/2011/07/30/us-usa-mexico-boats-idUSTRE76T1J920110730; United Nations Office on Drugs and Crimes, *Issue Paper—Smuggling of Migrants by Sea* (Vienna, Austria: United Nations Office on Drugs and Crime, 2011): 17, www.unodc.org/documents/human-trafficking/Migrant-Smuggling/Issue-Papers/Issue_Paper_-_Smuggling_of_Migrants_by_Sea.pdf; Carrie Kahn, "Small Fishing Boats Smuggle People to California," NPR, November 16, 2011, www.npr.org/2011/11/16/142133395/small-fishing-boats-smuggle-people-to-california.

[212] Wayne Cornelius, *Reforming the Management of Migration Flows from Latin America to the United States* (San Diego, CA: Center for Comparative Immigration Studies, 2008): 5-7, http://ccis.ucsd.edu/wp-content/uploads/2009/07/WP-170.pdf; Richard M. Stana, *Illegal Immigration: Status for Southwest Border Strategy Implementation* (Washington, DC: GAO, 1999): 2, www.gao.gov/archive/1999/gg99044.pdf; Rosenblum, *Border Security: Immigration Enforcement Between Ports of Entry*, 34.

[213] Deborah Waller Meyers, *One Face at the Border: Behind the Slogan* (Washington, DC: MPI, 2005): 9, www.migrationpolicy.org/pubs/Meyers_Report.pdf.

ment agencies and responsibilities is occurring and how overall coordination among immigration agencies within DHS can be improved.

2. Data Anomalies in POE Reporting

An example of broad, unmet coordination needs involves Border Patrol and Office of Field Operations (OFO) reporting of their enforcement actions. OFO does not regularly report on arrests at POEs, even though POEs are increasingly the locus of illegal entries. In FY 2011, CBP reported that it denied entry to 215,600 people seeking admission to the United States at air, land, or sea POEs[214] because they were found to be inadmissible.[215] Similarly, more than 3,100 individuals were turned back from boarding flights abroad to the United States by inspectors stationed at one of 15 pre-clearance sites in other countries,[216] e.g. Canada, Ireland, and the Bahamas.[217]

At the same time, DHS reported that all of its other (non-OFO) entities totaled 613,003 arrests in FY 2009.[218] It likewise reported that the agency as a whole "located" the same number (613,003) of "deportable aliens" during the year.[219] If the "arrest" and "located" figure refers to the same group, it raises problems of definition, since not all of those "arrested" would ultimately be found "deportable." The figures also raise questions about what other data DHS may not count in its statistical reporting.

Such anomalies go to core unresolved issues within CBP and DHS. The two parts of CBP work together at the operational level in Southwest border locations, but they continue to treat their enforcement roles and actions differently. OFO relies heavily on permitting withdrawal of applications to enter and on voluntary return — even as the Border Patrol has turned to consequence enforcement — and does not categorize all of them as enforcement actions for statistical reporting purposes. In addition, it is not clear how OFO handles the inadmissible persons it encounters. When does it admit them? Under what circumstances are individuals allowed to withdraw their applications for admission? What are the definitions of "withdrawals," "turnbacks," "encounters," and "adverse actions"?

The absence of consistent definitions and systems for reporting OFO case dispositions and enforcement actions impede DHS' ability to provide an accurate, complete picture of border enforcement efforts. Policymakers and the public would get a more accurate picture of effectiveness and the overall scope of immigration enforcement if it was possible to learn and compare total numbers of arrests/withdrawals/returns at POEs with established reporting of border apprehension and removal statistics.

3. Visa Overstays

Another fundamental element of assessing immigration enforcement and border control is the rate of visa overstays. There have been two authoritative studies on overstays. One was done by the INS in 1997 and the other by the Pew Hispanic Center in 2006. The more recent study estimated that visa overstays comprised up to 40-50 percent of the unauthorized population, or about 4 million to 5.5 million, with an additional 250,000 to 500,000 persons who would have entered the United States lawfully (mostly Mexicans and Canadians), but without a visa.[220]

---

214 CBP, "CBP's 2011 Fiscal Year in Review," (press release, December 12, 2011), www.cbp.gov/xp/cgov/newsroom/news_releases/national/2011_news_archive/12122011.xml.
215 Ibid.
216 Ibid.
217 CBP, "Preclearance Locations," March 30, 2011, www.cbp.gov/xp/cgov/toolbox/contacts/preclear_locations.xml.
218 DHS, *Immigration Enforcement Actions: 2009* (Washington, DC: DHS, 2010): 3, www.dhs.gov/xlibrary/assets/statistics/publications/enforcement_ar_2009.pdf; (noting that the Border Patrol, in addition to ICE's Office of Investigations and ICE's Office of Detention and Removal Operations made 613,003 arrests).
219 DHS, *2009 Yearbook of Immigration Statistics* (Washington, DC: DHS, 2010): 91, www.dhs.gov/xlibrary/assets/statistics/yearbook/2009/ois_yb_2009.pdf.
220 Pew Hispanic Center, "Modes of Entry for the Unauthorized Migrant Population."

Estimates of visa overstays have not been updated since the recession and the recent historic drop in apprehensions. As border control has become more effective, it is likely that an increasing share of the resident unauthorized population is or will be comprised of those who have overstayed, rather than crossed the land border illegally.

US-VISIT has begun to identify visa overstayers by comparing arrival records with airline departure records and with I-94 arrival-departure forms. In May 2011, DHS officials announced that by cross-checking US-VISIT data against the agency's I-94 database and other passenger information databases, it had been able to identify and begin vetting 757,000 potential overstay leads.[221] By the end of July 2011, DHS began an overstay initiative by examining these biographic information-identified overstay leads and prioritizing them for review and targeted enforcement based on national security and public-safety concerns.[222] According to DHS, ICE is now pursuing cases from within that population that are deemed high enforcement priorities.[223] Thus, despite the lack of comprehensive exit information about temporary visitors, overstay estimates are being developed for enforcement follow-up.

By analyzing its operational data and working with outside demographers and experts conversant with unauthorized population data and estimation methods, DHS should be able to develop a benchmark estimate of overstays — in total and as a percentage of the unauthorized population. Such estimates could then be regularly updated to round out a full picture that informs public and policymakers' understanding of the scope and profile of illegal immigration and of the effectiveness of border control efforts overall.

4. Humanitarian Issues in Border Control

Critics argue that the border has been inappropriately militarized for friendly, neighboring countries. Indeed, border control and deterrence of future illegal immigration have had corollary impacts that create serious concerns and challenges. The most familiar and acute have been increased numbers of deaths while attempting to cross the border illegally.

Immigrant advocates have criticized the agency for failing to work more collaboratively with humanitarian organizations that provide water and first-aid kits for migrants.[224] They have also called for the creation of a centralized database tracking migrant death information that would reconcile data discrepancies between government and NGO reports by establishing a uniform methodology for counting deaths, and assist family members of deceased migrants in identifying the dead and recovering remains.[225]

Consequence enforcement, with its goal of separating migrants from smugglers, has introduced additional new humanitarian issues and enforcement challenges. Mexico's border cities — especially Tijuana, which receives the largest number of migrants returned through lateral repatriation — now see migrants with no ties or contacts in the area and no money, either to pay another smuggler the $3,000 to $3,500 required to attempt another crossing or to return to home communities distant from the border. Many join growing ranks of the homeless, where they are vulnerable to violence and

---

[221] Statement of John Cohen, Principal Deputy Coordinator for Counterterrorism, DHS, before the House Homeland Security Committee, Subcommittee on Border and Maritime Security, *Ten Years After 9/11: Can Terrorists Still Exploit Our Visa System?* 112th Cong., 1st sess., September 13, 2011, http://homeland.house.gov/hearing/ten-years-after-911-can-terrorists-still-exploit-our-visa-system.

[222] Joint written testimony of John Cohen, DHS Deputy Counterterrorism Coordinator, and Peter Edge, ICE Homeland Security Investigations Deputy Executive Associate Director, before the House Committee on Homeland Security, Subcommittee on Border and Maritime Security, *From the 9/11 Hijackers to Amine el-Khalifi: Terrorists and the Visa Overstay Problem*, 112th Cong., 2nd sess., March 6, 2012, www.dhs.gov/ynews/testimony/20120306-ctwg-ice-visa-overstays.shtm.

[223] Cohen, *Ten Years After 9/11: Can Terrorists Still Exploit Our Visa System?*

[224] Jimenez, *Humanitarian Crisis: Migrant Deaths at the U.S.-Mexico Border*, 37, 43-6, 55.

[225] Ibid., 43.

easy prey for drug traffickers looking for recruits to cross the border carrying narcotics, or to engage in other illegal activity to earn enough for return passage.

In addition, the profile of the typical border crosser is changing as enforcement, reduced push-pull factors, and the fear of violence along traditional migrant routes slow the flow. In general, those who now try to come are no longer young, first-time crossers propelled by the tradition of El Norte to seek a better life. Instead, they are largely experienced men and women who have crossed before — sometimes many years ago. Data show that 56 percent of those now apprehended fit such a profile, compared with 44 percent just five or six years ago.[226]

Such crossers are less likely to be deterred, even with consequence enforcement, because of their determination to resume their lives with families in the United States and slight, if any, remaining ties in their countries of birth. With fewer new arrivals, this pattern is likely to deepen, given the rate of removals and the length of time the large resident unauthorized population has lived in the United States. Nearly two-thirds of the roughly 11 million unauthorized immigrants have been in the United States for a decade or longer.[227]

The intractability of issues such as these demonstrates that regardless of how well resourced and effective enforcement policies and programs are, there always will be limits to the degree enforcement measures alone can resolve the problem of illegal immigration.

---

[226] Damien Cave, "Crossing Over, and Over," *The New York Times*, October 2, 2011, www.nytimes.com/2011/10/03/world/americas/mexican-immigrants-repeatedly-brave-risks-to-resume-lives-in-united-states.html?pagewanted=all.

[227] Paul Taylor, Mark Hugo Lopez, Jeffrey Passel, and Seth Motel, U*nauthorized Immigrants: Length of Residency, Patterns of Parenthood* (Washington, DC: Pew Hispanic Center, 2011), www.pewhispanic.org/2011/12/01/unauthorized-immigrants-length-of-residency-patterns-of-parenthood/.

FINDINGS

■ **Border Patrol staffing, technology, and infrastructure** have reached historic highs, while levels of apprehensions have fallen to historic lows. Today, there is no net new illegal immigration from Mexico for the first time in 40 years. Between FY 2000-11, Border Patrol apprehensions fell from a peak of more than 1.6 million to 340,252, or one-fifth of the 2000 high point. The drop has been 53 percent since just FY 2008.

■ **While Border Patrol apprehensions since 2000 have dropped significantly,** the drop has been uneven across Border Patrol sectors. The decline has been most dramatic in three sectors: Yuma, AZ (96 percent decrease between 2005-11), El Paso, TX (92 percent decrease), and Del Rio, TX (76 percent decrease). However, even the Tucson sector, which has had disproportionately high numbers of apprehensions, has experienced a 72 percent drop since 2005, thus becoming increasingly closely aligned with border-wide decreases.

■ **The share of repeat border crossers among those apprehended** has declined from a peak of 28 percent in FY 2007 to 20 percent in FY 2011. Furthermore, the 340,252 apprehensions made by the Border Patrol in 2011 involved just 269,000 unique individuals. The narrowing of the numerical gap between unique individuals arrested and overall apprehensions points to a decline in repeat border crossings since 2007.

■ **Border Patrol enforcement practices** that historically relied heavily on voluntary returns have been supplanted by a policy of enforcement actions that have more severe consequences for those arrested. Termed "consequence enforcement," the new policy aims to break smuggling cycles and networks by separating migrants from smugglers. The objective is to increase deterrence by raising the cost — monetary, legal, and psychological — of illegal migration to both migrants and smugglers. The Border Patrol began implementing the policy border-wide during 2012.

■ **The fullest use of consequence enforcement** has been in the Tucson sector. Historically, 90 percent of those apprehended there received voluntary return. Today, 90 percent are subject to consequence enforcement. The only exceptions are humanitarian cases.

■ **The Southwest border enforcement build-up** has led to increasing numbers of deaths among border crossers. Although the death rate fell to an average of 360 deaths per year during 2010-11, from the peak average of approximately 431 during 2005-09, the ratio of deaths to apprehensions is at its highest level since formal counting began in the 1990s.

■ **The security features of land border-crossing documents,** including the border crossing card (BCC) used on the Southwest border, and Western Hemisphere Travel Initiative (WHTI)-compliant enhanced driver's licenses and passport cards, are comparable to the sophistication of "green" cards. They are required of all land border crossers, as are visas and passports at air and sea ports.

■ **While enforcement between border ports has improved dramatically,** enforcement at land ports of entry is a growing challenge. The gap in the numbers apprehended between ports and those denied admission at ports of entry is narrowing. At the FY 2000 peak, between-port apprehensions were nearly three times the 550,000 found to be inadmissible at ports of entry. By FY 2011, between-port apprehensions were only 1.5 times the number denied admission at ports of entry. The gap is likely to narrow further as illegal crossing between ports is increasingly difficult and fewer crossings occur. Despite significant advances, land ports have not experienced improvements on par with between-ports enforcement. The lag is especially evident in meeting physical infrastructure needs required to fully utilize important new technologies, such as secure, biometric border-crossing documents and US-VISIT screening.

- **DHS border enforcement data under-report** total immigration border enforcement activity. DHS figures — which are widely used to gauge border enforcement and deterrence — tally the numbers apprehended between ports by the Border Patrol, and those that are found "inadmissible" by inspections officers at ports of entry. The DHS figures do not include the significant numbers of individuals who arrive at ports of entry but ultimately withdraw their applications for admission, often for technical reasons. Nevertheless, such actions represent enforcement decisions that add to the scope of border enforcement that is actually taking place.

- **As border enforcement between ports of entry has become more effective,** an increasing share of the unauthorized population is likely to be comprised of those who have been admitted properly through ports of entry and overstay their visas. Thus, the relative share of the unauthorized population from countries other than Mexico and Central America will likely increase.

CHAPTER 4

VISA CONTROLS AND TRAVEL SCREENING

Visa controls and travel screening serve as the first line of defense in many aspects of border enforcement, thus constituting a core pillar of a robust immigration enforcement system. Dramatic improvements in the nation's screening systems and capabilities have been fielded since the September 11, 2001 terrorist attacks, as part of strengthened border control.

Because the 9/11 hijackers traveled to the United States with valid visas (albeit fraudulently obtained),[228] visa processing and screening systems came under special scrutiny after the 2001 terrorist attacks and raised issues of the most immediate concern. Similarly, the revelation that many of the hijackers were known to some US intelligence and law enforcement agencies highlighted the pressing need for improved information sharing.[229]

The vast majority of people who must apply for visas to enter the United States are coming for legitimate business, educational, cultural, tourism, family, or other reasons that are in the national interest. Reliable screening mechanisms to identify the relatively few who seek to harm the United States became — and remain — an urgent priority.

Effective screening, the linchpin of the visa system as well as every other immigration process, depends on the ability to verify an applicant's identity to ensure he or she does not raise public safety, national security, or other concerns. Sophisticated screening systems contribute to another policy goal that has emerged since 9/11: to "push the border out" by preventing those who pose a public safety or national security threat or who do not have permission to enter from ever reaching a US airport or a land or coastal port-of-entry. This goal is expressed in different ways:

- Creating a "layered defense," for example, emphasizes the importance of redundancy in trying to stop dangerous people from reaching and entering the United States.

- Establishing a North American security zone or perimeter highlights the importance of working with Mexico and Canada to prevent and deter unwanted migration.[230]

- Building "extraterritorial controls" describes US operations in international waters, such as migrant interdiction by the US Coast Guard, or beyond US borders. It also refers to an array of agreements and working relationships with other countries to intercept migrants, pursue transnational criminals, repatriate deportees, develop secure identification documents, and share information.

---

228 National Commission on Terrorist Attacks Upon the United States, "Entry of the 9/11 Hijackers into the United States" (Staff Statement No. 1, National Commission on Terrorist Attacks Upon the United States, Washington, DC, January 2004), http://govinfo.library.unt.edu/911/staff_statements/staff_statement_1.pdf.
229 National Commission on Terrorist Attacks Upon the United States, *The 9/11 Commission Report* (Washington, DC: National Commission on Terrorist Attacks Upon the United States, 2004): 383-90, 416-9, www.9-11commission.gov/report/index.htm.
230 Ibid., 392-3; DHS, FY 2012 *Budget in Brief*, 76.

New intelligence and information-sharing initiatives have been implemented during the past decade, leading to dramatic improvements in the nation's screening systems and capabilities.

I. Programs and Results

The following are the principal programs and initiatives that have been introduced or strengthened.

A. Visa Issuance Screening and Controls

Since 9/11, the United States has substantially strengthened its system of screening noncitizens seeking to enter the country for temporary stays — which can last for just a few days to multiple entries and long-term periods — as well as for permanent immigration. As described in the next chapter, executive-branch agencies have significantly expanded, upgraded, and integrated immigration, criminal, and national security screening information systems and information-exchange capabilities and procedures.

In addition, DHS plays an active role in vetting potentially suspect applications. The ICE Office of Investigations' Visa Security Program now operates in 19 high-risk locations in 15 nations.[231] In FY 2010, it screened 950,000 visa applicants, vetted 260,000 applications, recommended refusal of more than 1,000 applicants based on derogatory information, and added 50 persons to the terrorist watch list.[232]

1. Personal Interviews

In 2003, the Department of State (DOS) amended its regulations to require in-person interviews for most applicants for nonimmigrant (temporary) visas.[233] Consular officers were permitted to waive the interview requirement only for diplomats/foreign government representatives and those under ages 16 or over 60, as well as certain individuals applying for visa renewals. In 2004, Congress enacted the *Intelligence Reform and Terrorism Prevention Act* (IRTPA), which required consular interviews of all nonimmigrant visa applicants ages 14-79.[234] IRTPA allowed only limited categories of exceptions in which a consular officer could waive this requirement.[235]

Since 2004, there have been efforts to broaden use of these exceptions. For example, in 2008, the US Consulate in Moscow announced that it would no longer require interviews

---

231 DHS, *Implementing the 9/11 Commission Recommendations Progress Report* (Washington, DC: DHS, 2011): 24, www.dhs.gov/xlibrary/assets/implementing-9-11-commission-report-progress-2011.pdf.
232 DHS, *FY 2012 Budget in Brief*, 79.
233 DOS, "Waiver of Personal Appearance Revision," (Cable to All Diplomatic and Consular Posts, May 3, 2003), http://travel.state.gov/visa/laws/telegrams/telegrams_1421.html.
234 *Intelligence Reform and Terrorism Prevention Act of 2004* (IRTPA), Pub. L. 108-458, 118 Stat. 3638, (December 17, 2004).
235 Ibid. The law provided that consular officers would only be allowed to waive the interview requirement if: 1) the person applying for a visa was a diplomat/foreign government official, or 2) the applicant had previously applied for and been granted a visa: a) not more than 12 months after the date on which his or her prior visa expired, b) in the same visa class as before, c) at the post in the country where he was a citizen or resident, and d) DOS had no reason to believe that the applicant previously violated US immigration law. The 2004 law further stated that DOS was required to interview all applicants who: 1) were not nationals or residents of the country in which they were applying, 2) were previously refused a visa and had not overcome the ground of inadmissibility or been granted a waiver, 3) were listed in CLASS, or 4) were a national or resident of country designated as a state sponsor of terrorism. See also www.state.gov/documents/organization/87421.pdf for the *Foreign Affairs Manual* (FAM) provision laying out these requirements.

for certain individuals reapplying for visas in the same visa category.[236] More recently, Senators Mike Lee (R-UT) and Charles Schumer (D-NY) introduced legislation that calls for videoconferencing for visa interviews.[237] Such reactions result from the increased wait times that mandatory interviews have caused. However, IRTPA requirements limit DOS's ability to waive nonimmigrant visa interviews outside narrow waiver delegations in the statute.

2. Decline and Rebound in Visa Issuances and Demand

Tightened screening requirements led to a dramatic drop in the number of nonimmigrant visas issued in the aftermath of 9/11. Between 2001 and 2002, the total number of nonimmigrant visas issued by DOS fell by 24 percent, from 7,588,778 visas in 2001 to 5,769,437 in 2002 (see Figure 5). During the same timeframe, the number of B1/B2 (tourist/business) visas fell by 28 percent (see Figure 6), and the number of student (F) visas issued fell by 20 percent (see Figure 7).

Since 2003, the total number of nonimmigrant visas issued, as well as the number of tourist/business and student visas, has essentially rebounded. The overall number of nonimmigrant visas granted in FY 2011 stands at 7,507,939, just slightly shy of the pre-9/11 peak of 7,588,778 in FY 2001. Within that total, for the first time since 9/11, visa issuance for B-1/B-2 tourist/business visas exceeded the 2001 level, by 23 percent. In the case of student (F) visas, the rebound began in 2004. In 2011, the United States issued 447,410 student visas, a figure that is 53 percent greater than the number granted in 2001.

---

236 US Embassy, Moscow, "Waiver of Interview Requirement for Certain Visa Applicants," http://moscow.usembassy.gov/intwaiver.html, accessed November 21, 2012. Under IRTPA, DOS has the authority to waive the visa interview requirement for certain individuals who: 1) are applying not more than 12 months after the date on which such alien's prior visa expires; 2) are applying for the visa classification for which such prior visa was issued; 3) are seeking a visa from the consular post located in the country of such alien's usual residence; and 4) a consular officer has certified have not violated US immigration law.

237 US Senator Mike Lee (R-UT), "Lee, Schumer Introduce Immigration Reform Bill," (press release, October 20, 2011), http://lee.senate.gov/public/index.cfm/press-releases?ID=7d71bb4f-3752-4e86-af5f-85ecc9c0c142.

Figure 5. Total Number of Nonimmigrant Visas Issued, FY 1997-2011

Source: US Department of State, "Nonimmigrant Visa Issuances by Visa Class and by Nationality, FY 1997-2011 NIV Detail Table," www.travel.state.gov/xls/FYs97-11_NIVDetailTable.xls.

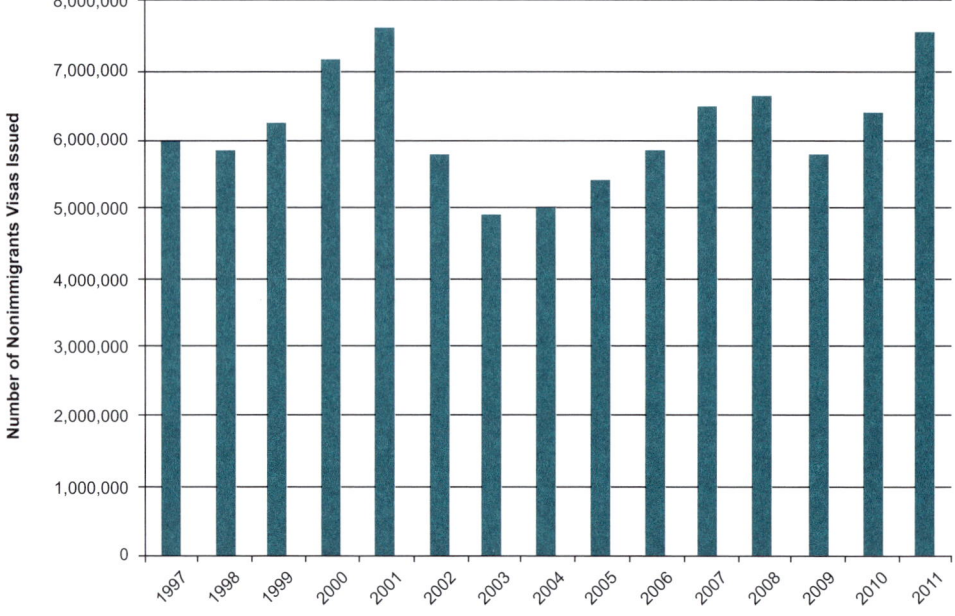

Figure 6. Total Number of Tourist/Business (B1/B2) Visas Issued, FY 1997-2011

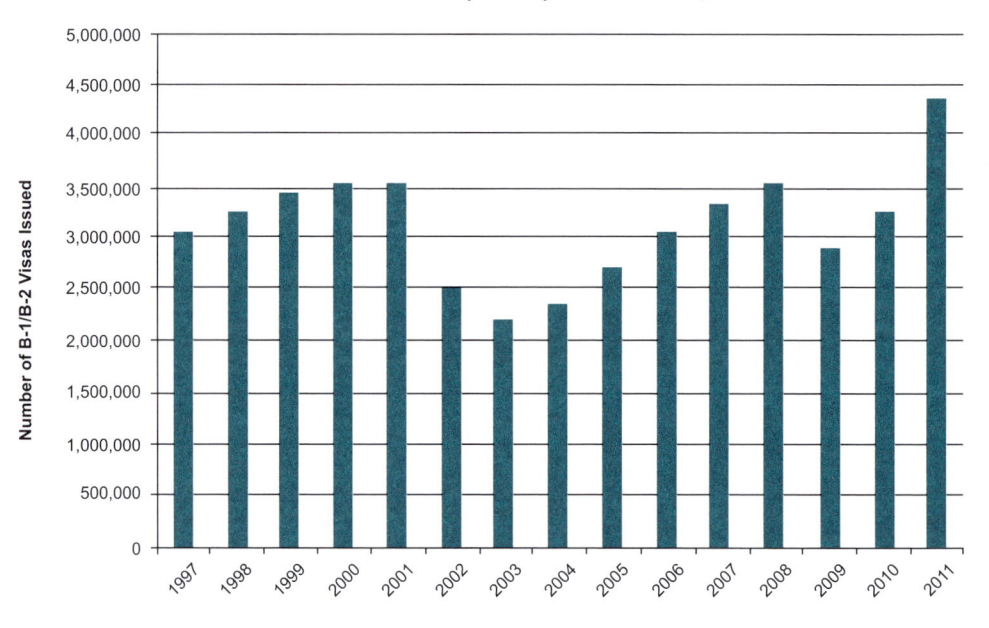

Source: US Department of State, "Nonimmigrant Visa Issuances by Visa Class and by Nationality FY 1997-2011 NIV Detail Table."

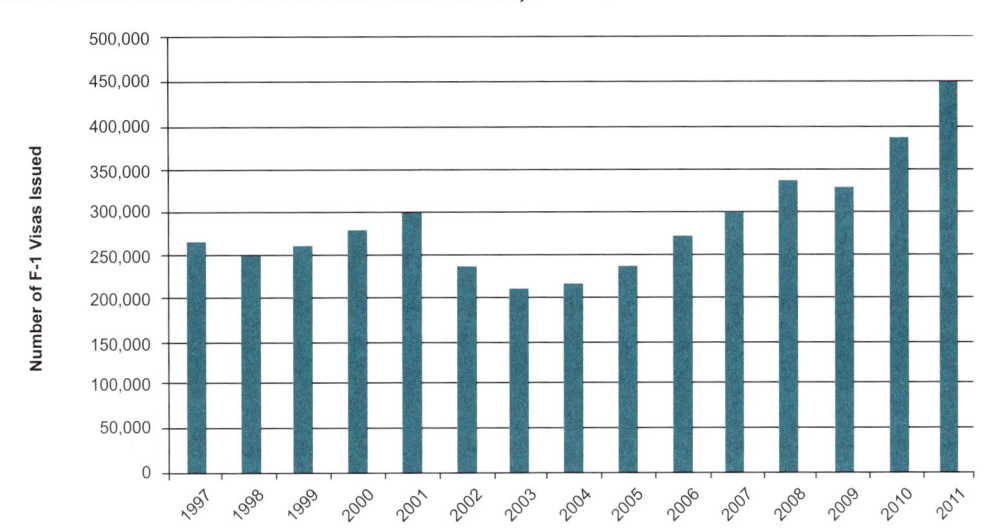

Figure 7. Total Number of Student Visas Issued, FY 1997-2011

Source: US Department of State, "Nonimmigrant Visa Issuances by Visa Class and by Nationality FY 1997-2011 NIV Detail Table."

The rebound in student visa issuance has been largely driven by a rapid increase in students from China. During the late 1990s and early 2000s, between 5 and 10 percent of total student visas were issued to Chinese nationals annually. However, between 2005 and 2011, the number of visas for Chinese students rose more than sevenfold, from 21,642 to 153,206. By 2011, Chinese accounted for almost 35 percent of all student visas issued (447,410). South Korea, Saudi Arabia, and India also send significant numbers of students to the United States, but even the combined number of F-1 visas issued to nationals of those countries is lower than the number of visas issued to students from China.

Post-9/11 policies had a dramatic impact on the number of visas issued to individuals from predominantly Muslim countries, whose nationals became subject to a new registration program — the National Security Entry-Exit Registration System (NSEERS) — that focused on 24 countries that the United States associated with an al Qaeda presence.[238] For those countries, the decline across nonimmigrant visa categories has rebounded, but still falls short of the 2001 levels.

---

[238] In June 2002, Attorney General John Ashcroft announced the start of the National Security Entry-Exit Registration System (NSEERS). The program required certain individuals seeking admission to the United States from designated countries to comply with specialized entry requirements, including having their fingerprints and digital photographs taken, and participating in follow-up interviews. In addition, male noncitizens ages 16 and older from designated countries who were already residing in United States were required to participate in "special registration" interviews with immigration officials. Between September 2002 and January 2003, 25 countries were designated for special registration. With the exception of North Korea, all of the designated NSEERS countries were predominantly Muslim: Afghanistan, Algeria, Bahrain, Bangladesh, Egypt, Eritrea, Indonesia, Iran, Iraq, Jordan, Kuwait, Lebanon, Libya, Morocco, North Korea, Oman, Pakistan, Qatar, Saudi Arabia, Somalia, Sudan, Syria, Tunisia, United Arab Emirates, and Yemen. Other countries with large or majority Muslim populations were not designated for the NSEERS program seemingly because they were not associated with an al Qaeda presence. See Stephen Yale-Loehr, Demetrios G. Papademetriou, and Betsy Cooper, *Secure Borders, Open Doors: Visa Procedures in the Post-September 11 Era* (Washington, DC: MPI, 2005): 19, www.migrationpolicy.org/pubs/visa_report.pdf; Muzaffar Chishti, Doris Meissner, Demetrios G. Papademetriou, Jay Peterzell, Michael J. Wishnie, and Stephen W. Yale-Loehr, *America's Challenge: Domestic Security, Civil Liberties, and National Unity After September 11* (Washington, DC: MPI, 2003), www.migrationpolicy.org/pubs/Americas_Challenges.pdf.

Between 2001 and 2002, the overall number of nonimmigrant visas issued to individuals from NSEERS countries fell by 55 percent, with a drop of 63 percent in B1/B2 visa issuances and 61 percent for F student visas. (See Figure 8.) For four NSEERS countries in the Arabian Peninsula — Yemen, Qatar, United Arab Emirates, and Saudi Arabia — the B1/B2 drop was even greater, at 82 percent.

More recent data show that while overall visa issuances have increased, the number of B1/B2 visas for NSEERS countries was still 11 percent lower in 2011 than in 2001 (see Figure 9).

Moreover, the disparity between overall B1/B2 visa issuance and the number granted to travelers from predominantly Muslim nations is greater than the figures indicate because ten countries have been added to the US Visa Waiver Program since 2001 — a change that would be expected to lower B1/B2 visa issuance levels, as potential visa applicants become eligible to travel visa-free.

Figure 8. F Visas Issued to Individuals from Predominantly Muslim NSEERS Countries, FY 1997-2011

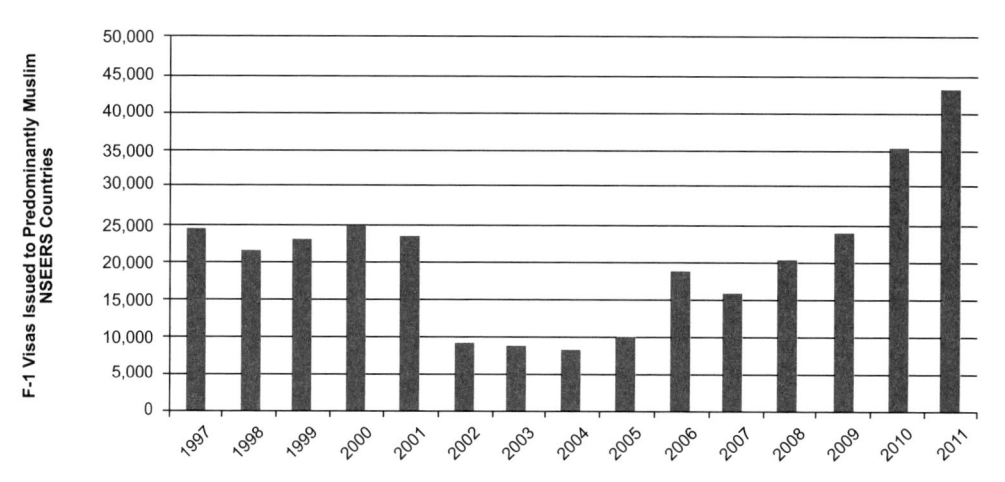

Source: US Department of State, "Nonimmigrant Visa Issuances by Visa Class and by Nationality FY 1997-2011 NIV Detail Table."

Figure 9. B1/B2 Visas Issued to Individuals from Predominantly Muslim NSEERS Countries, FY 1997-2011

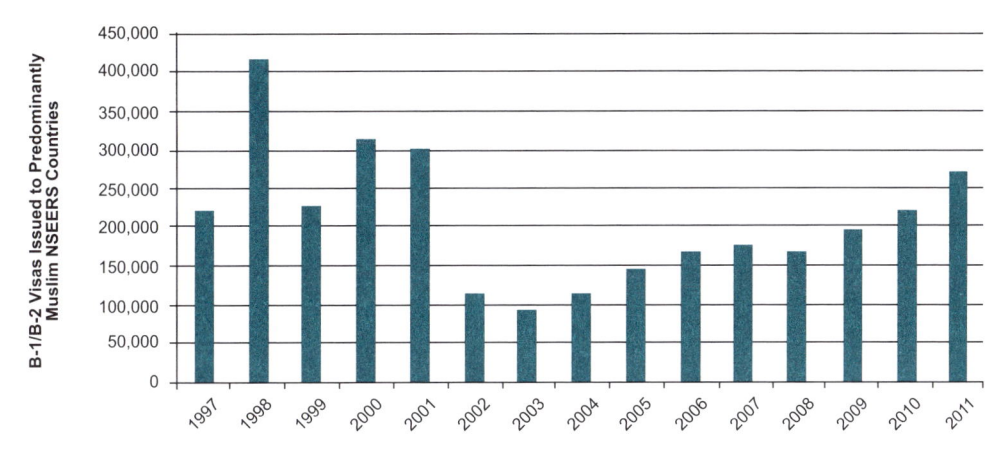

Source: US Department of State, "Nonimmigrant Visa Issuances by Visa Class and by Nationality FY 1997-2011 NIV Detail Table"

For F student visas, the numbers reached 43,236 by 2011, an increase of almost 82 percent over the 2001 level of 23,793. This increase appears to be driven largely by a spike in the number of student visas issued to nationals of Saudi Arabia, which now make up 64 percent of F visas issued to these predominantly Muslim countries. Saudi Arabia is the third-largest source country of foreign students who come to the United States, next to China and South Korea.

3. Visa Waiver Program

The US Visa Waiver Program (VWP) allows citizens from specified countries to enter for brief periods without a visa for business or tourism reasons.

The original purpose of the program was to facilitate low-risk travel between participating nations, so that enforcement resources could be focused on nationals from higher-risk countries.[239] However, VWP has also taken on an important foreign policy dimension. It is viewed by participating nations, and especially by those who desire visa-waiver designation, as an affirmation of their status as mature, advanced nations whose nationals can be permitted to travel with minimal restrictions.

At the same time, the 9/11 attacks brought into the open long-standing concerns about the program as a potential source of vulnerability.[240] Several terrorists — including Zacarias Moussaoui, the French national convicted of conspiring to kill Americans as part of the 9/11 plot, and Richard Reid, the British "shoe bomber"— exploited the program.[241] In September 2007, the Director of National Intelligence testified that al Qaeda was recruiting Europeans as terrorists because those individuals could enter the United

---

[239] DOS, "Visa Waiver Program," accessed November 11, 2012, www.travel.state.gov/visa/temp/without/without_1990.html.

[240] In March 1999, for example, the DOJ Office of the Inspector General (OIG) reported that terrorists, criminals, and smugglers were attempting to enter the United States using counterfeited, stolen, and altered passports from Visa Waiver Program countries. Statement of Michael Bromwich, Inspector General, DOJ, before the House Judiciary Committee, Subcommittee on Immigration and Claims, *Nonimmigrant Visa Fraud*, 106th Cong., 1st sess., May 5, 1999, www.justice.gov/oig/testimony/9905.htm. ("Our review found that terrorists, criminals, smugglers, and others have attempted to enter the United States using stolen blank passports from a Visa Waiver country or by altering or counterfeiting these passports.")

[241] Jess T. Ford, GAO, *Border Security: Implications of Eliminating the Visa Waiver Program* (Washington, DC: GAO, 2002): 17, www.gao.gov/assets/240/236408.pdf.

States without a visa.[242]

Post-9/11 imperatives led to broad changes that have significantly tightened the program:

- Participating nations must now issue tamper-proof, electronic, and biometric passports with digital photographs, enter into an agreement with the United States to share information on lost or stolen passports as well as other law enforcement information, and accept repatriation of nationals ordered removed from the United States.[243]

- A new system, the Electronic System for Travel Authorization (ESTA), requires VWP travelers to submit their biographic information for screening in advance of boarding an airplane to the United States.[244]

ESTA screening became a requirement for all VWP participants on January 12, 2009,[245] thereby allowing for passenger information to be checked against terrorist watch lists and all visa-processing databases to determine whether an applicant is eligible to travel to the United States.[246] According to DHS, the vast majority of ESTA applicants are automatically confirmed. In 2011, the denial rate for ESTA applicants was 0.3 percent.[247] ESTA clearance is normally valid for two years.[248]

Certification through ESTA does not establish admissibility. Persons cleared through ESTA must present themselves for admission at a US port of entry upon arrival on US territory, where they are again subject to inspection by CBP officials and screening through US-VISIT.[249] DHS anticipated that ESTA would reduce the number of travelers found to be inadmissible to the United States after arrival at a port of entry, since many would instead be flagged through ESTA and stopped before embarking upon their travel.[250] DHS does not publish statistics on the number of VWP applicants who are deemed inadmissible at ports of entry, so it is not possible to know if a decrease has occurred.

After reaching a peak in 2000, admissions through the VWP declined substantially in the immediate aftermath of 9/11. By FY 2002, the number of visa waiver admissions stood at just 13,320,001, a drop of nearly 25 percent from the FY 2000 level (17,697,919).[251] However, VWP participation has grown since, and by FY 2008, the number of VWP admissions exceeded pre-9/11 levels.

Some of the growth, especially within the last three years, is due to the designation of new visa-waiver countries. DHS designated eight new VWP countries in 2008: the

---

242 Jess T. Ford, GAO, *Visa Waiver Program: Actions Are Needed to Improve Management of the Expansion Process, and to Assess and Mitigate Program Risks* (Washington, DC: GAO, 2008): 2, www.gao.gov/new.items/d08967.pdf.
243 DHS, "Changes to the Visa Waiver Program to Implement the Electronic System for Travel Authorization (ESTA) Program," 73 *Federal Register* 111, 32440 (June 9, 2008) (codified at 8 C.F.R. 217).
244 Ibid.
245 Alison Siskin, *Visa Waiver Program* (Washington, DC: CRS, 2011): 5, www.fas.org/sgp/crs/homesec/RL32221.pdf.
246 Ibid.
247 DHS, *Congressional Budget Request for FY 2013*, US Customs and Border Protection, Budget Request and Supporting Information (Washington, DC: DHS, 2012): 40, www.dhs.gov/xlibrary/assets/mgmt/dhs-congressional-budget-justification-fy2013.pdf.
248 Siskin, *Visa Waiver Program*, 6.
249 DHS, "US-VISIT Enrollment Requirements," accessed November 18, 2012, www.dhs.gov/files/programs/editorial_0527.shtm.
250 DHS, "Changes to the Visa Waiver Program to Implement the Electronic System for Travel Authorization (ESTA) Program."
251 INS, *Yearbook of Immigration Statistics, FY 2000*, Table C (Washington, DC: INS, 2002); *INS, Yearbook of Immigration Statistics, FY 2002*, Table F (Washington, DC: INS, 2003).

Czech Republic, Estonia, Hungary, Latvia, Lithuania, South Korea, Malta, and Slovakia.[252] Greece was added to the list in 2010 and Taiwan in 2012.[253] They were the first additional countries to be admitted to the program since 1999.[254]

Thirty-seven countries now participate in VWP. They include the majority of members of the European Union, as well as Australia, New Zealand, Japan, Singapore, South Korea, Taiwan, and Brunei.[255] Since the beginning, the bulk of admissions under VWP have come from a relatively small share of participating nations. This trend has continued in recent years.

As Figure 10 demonstrates, in FY 2011, travelers from the top ten participating VWP countries accounted for 87 percent of total admissions. Nationals from the United Kingdom, the top sending VWP country, made up 22 percent of the total VWP admissions. Nationals from Japan constituted an additional 18 percent.

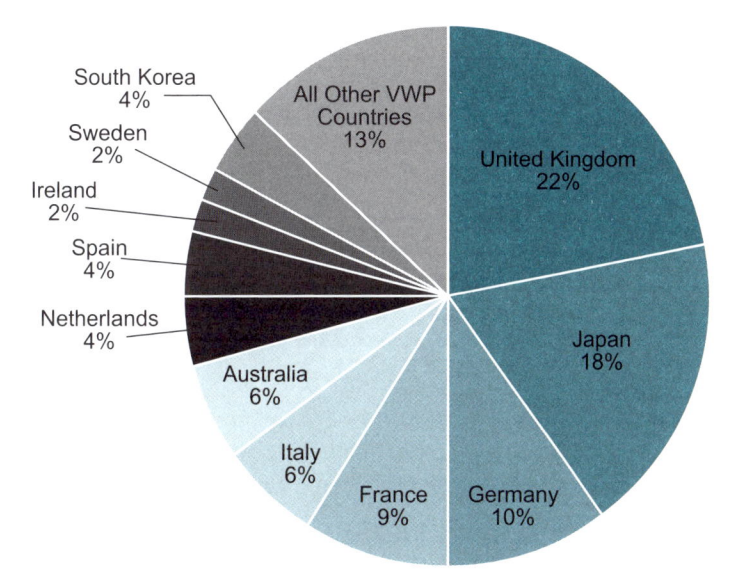

Figure 10. Share of VWP Admissions, Select Countries, FY 2011

Source: DHS, *Yearbook of Immigration Statistics, FY 2011* (Washington, DC: DHS, 2012), www.dhs.gov/sites/default/files/publications/immigration-statistics/yearbook/2011/ois_yb_2011.pdf.

The number of admissions from the traditional large VWP participating countries has declined or remained fairly constant over the last five years, even as program participation has grown. As a result, the US Travel Association and others have called for expanding the program to countries such as Brazil, China, and India, which are likely

---

252 DHS added the Czech Republic, Estonia, Hungary, Latvia, Lithuania, South Korea, and Slovakia on November 17, 2008. DHS, "Additional Countries Designated for Visa Waiver Program," 73 *Federal Register* 222, 67711 (November 17, 2008) (codified at 8 C.F.R. 217). Malta was added on December 30, 2008; DHS, "Designation of Malta for the Visa Waiver Program," 73 *Federal Register* 250, 79595, (December 30, 2008) (codified at 8 C.F.R. 217).
253 DHS, "Designation of Greece for the Visa Waiver Program," 75 *Federal Register* 61, 15991 (March 31, 2010) (codified at 8 C.F.R. 217); DHS, "DHS Announces Taiwan's Designation into the Visa Waiver Program," (press release, October 2, 2012), www.dhs.gov/news/2012/10/02/dhs-announces-taiwan%E2%80%99s-designation-visa-waiver-program.
254 Ford, *Visa Waiver Program: Actions Are Needed to Improve Management of the Expansion Process, and to Assess and Mitigate Program Risks*, 6.
255 DOS, "Visa Waiver Program Frequently Asked Questions," accessed November 18, 2012, http://travel.state.gov/visa/temp/without/without_1990.html.

to represent a growing share of international travelers.[256] However, DHS is not likely to approve VWP designation of such countries, as they may not fit its program criteria.

B. Travel Screening — US-VISIT

Beyond visa-issuance screening, a further layer of travel screening occurs through US-VISIT, the electronic screening system used to clear foreign-born individuals and visitors as they physically enter the United States by air and sea, as well as certain visitors entering by land.[257] US-VISIT serves as the companion system at ports of entry to visa-screening systems at consulates abroad. As in consular processing, the system is based on biometric information — digital photos and electronic fingerprints — that enables DHS officials to screen foreign nationals, including lawful permanent residents, against immigration, criminal, and terrorist databases.

The origins of US-VISIT trace back to the *Illegal Immigration Reform and Immigrant Responsibility Act of 1996* (IIRIRA), which required the attorney general to develop an automated entry-exit system to screen foreign visitors.[258] In addition, both IRCA and the *Visa Waiver Permanent Program Act of 2000* mandated the creation of similar systems for persons entering the United States under VWP.[259]

However, it took the 9/11 attacks to make such a system an urgent priority. Among other provisions, the *Enhanced Border Security and Visa Entry Reform Act* (EBSVERA), enacted in 2002, required:

- Machine-readable, biometric passports for international travelers from countries permitted visa-free travel to the United States

- A database for arrival and departure data from machine-readable travel documents

- Biometric standards for visas and other travel documents issued to noncitizens.[260] The State Department's Bio Visa Program, established as a partner program to US-VISIT in 2003, required the fingerprinting of visa applicants.[261]

EBSVERA set a timetable, mandating that DHS implement an entry-exit system at all ports of entry by October 26, 2004.[262] Congress backed up its mandate with substantial appropriations. EBSVERA allocated INS $150 million to upgrade entry-screening technology and authorized the Department of State to raise fees for visas to cover the cost of making them machine-readable.[263]

---

256 US Travel Association (USTA), *Ready for Takeoff: A Plan to Create 1.3 Million U.S. Jobs by Welcoming Millions of International Travelers* (Washington, DC: USTA, 2011): 19, www.smartervisapolicy.org/site/documents/VisaReport.pdf.
257 DHS, "US-VISIT Resources and Materials," accessed November 18, 2012, www.dhs.gov/files/programs/gc_1213298547634.shtm. Canadian citizens are generally exempt from US-VISIT entry screening. Mexican citizens crossing by land with a border crossing card are also exempt from US-VISIT entry screening, unless planning to travel outside the border zone or stay for longer than 30 days.
258 Ford, *Border Security: Implications of Eliminating the Visa Waiver Program*, 15.
259 Ibid.
260 *Enhanced Border Security and Visa Entry Reform Act of 2002*, Pub. L. 107-173, 116 Stat. 543 (May 14, 2002).
261 National Science and Technology Council, Biometrics in Government Post-9/11 (Washington, DC: National Science and Technology Council, 2008): 44-6, www.biometrics.gov/Documents/Biometrics%20in%20Government%20Post%209/11.pdf. Notably, the *USA PATRIOT Act*, Pub. L. 107-56, required the attorney general to develop an entry/exit system that incorporated biometrics "with all deliberate speed and as expeditiously as practicable." *The USA Patriot Act*, Pub. L. 107-56, 84 Stat. 1116 (October 26, 2001), Sec. 414.
262 *The Enhanced Border Security and Visa Entry Reform Act of 2002*, 116 Stat. 543, § 303.
263 Ibid., §§ 102-103.

The creation of US-VISIT was announced in 2003 and the program was launched in 2004.[264] US-VISIT uses biometrics to provide "real-time identification" of foreign visitors.[265] Border inspectors can now ensure that an individual admitted to the country is the same person who had been granted a visa by the Department of State and is not on a terrorist watch list.[266]

1. Ports of Entry Screening

US-VISIT screening has grown rapidly. By December 2006, US-VISIT was operational at 115 airports, 14 seaports, and 154 of 170 land ports of entry.[267] By FY 2009, the program was in place at almost all land, sea, and air ports of entry.[268]

In addition, passenger information for all US-bound international flights is electronically transmitted by airline carriers to ports of entry where passenger manifests are checked against watch lists prior to departure in most cases. Thus, dangerous persons can either be prevented from boarding flights or immigration inspectors know in advance which individuals may be suspect and can readily refer them for secondary inspection and in-depth questioning.

US-VISIT fingerprint files[269] make vast numbers of records accessible to immigration and other authorized law enforcement officials and are now also compatible with FBI criminal records.[270] Thus, criminal information can be readily and systematically cross-checked across government databases in both visa issuance and port-of-entry screening, along with terrorist watch lists and other government-wide law enforcement and national security information systems.

2. Exit Controls

Congress mandated exit requirements to verify that people with temporary visas leave the country as specified by the terms of their visas. However, unlike entry screening, implementation of the exit procedures for an entry-exit system has proven difficult and has not been accomplished.

In April 2008, DHS announced its intention to implement a biometric exit-verification program at all of the country's air and sea ports of entry.[271] It proposed that commercial air and sea carriers take primary responsibility for collecting biometrics from all departing travelers and submitting them to DHS.[272] Carriers vigorously protested this requirement and DHS did not publish a final rule.

---

264 Remarks by Homeland Security Undersecretary Asa Hutchinson on the Launch of US-VISIT (speech, Center for Strategic and International Studies, May 19, 2003), http://csis.org/files/media/csis/events/030519_hutchinson.pdf.

265 Eric Lichtblau and John Markoff, "U.S. Nearing Deal on Way to Track Foreign Visitors," *The New York Times*, May 24, 2004, www.nytimes.com/2004/05/24/us/us-nearing-deal-on-way-to-track-foreign-visitors.html?pagewanted=all&src=pm; Edward Alden, *The Closing of the American Border: Terrorism, Immigration, and Security Since 9/11* (New York: Harper Perennial, 2009): 22.

266 Ibid; DHS, "Fact Sheet: US-VISIT," April 2, 2004.

267 Testimony of Randolph Hite, Director, Information Technology Architecture and Systems Issues, GAO, and Richard M. Stana, Director, Homeland Security and Justice Issues, GAO, before the House Committee on Appropriations, Subcommittee on Homeland Security, *US-VISIT Has Not Fully Met Expectations and Longstanding Program Management Challenges Need to be Addressed*, 110th Cong., 1st sess., February 16, 2007, www.gao.gov/new.items/d07499t.pdf; GAO, *Homeland Security: Key US-VISIT Components at Varying Stages of Completion, But Integrated and Reliable Schedule Needed* (Washington, DC: GAO, 2009): 7-8, www.gao.gov/new.items/d1013.pdf.

268 GAO, *Homeland Security: Key US-VISIT Components at Varying Stages of Completion, But Integrated and Reliable Schedule Needed*, 7-8.

269 US-VISIT, 8th Anniversary Briefing, January 5, 2012. Notes on file with authors.

270 DHS, *IDENT/IAFIS Interoperability Statistics* (Washington, DC: DHS, 2005), www.dhs.gov/xlibrary/assets/foia/US-VISIT_IDENT-IAFISReport.pdf.

271 GAO, *Homeland Security: US-VISIT Pilot Options Offer Limited Understanding of Air Exit Options* (Washington, DC: GAO, 2010): 1, www.gao.gov/new.items/d10860.pdf.

272 Ibid.

The *Consolidated Security, Disaster Assistance, and Continuing Appropriations Act of 2009* directed DHS to test two different scenarios for an air exit solution before using additional US-VISIT funding to deploy an exit screening program.[273] Under one scenario, DHS officials would have collected biometrics from departing foreign nationals. Under the other, commercial carriers would have borne this responsibility.[274] DHS launched pilot programs that vest responsibility with carriers between May 2009 and June 2009.[275]

However, according to GAO, these programs were of "limited value" and did not meet the originally stated purpose of operationally evaluating air exit requirements.[276] Among other problems, GAO reported that about 30 percent of the requirements for the exit screening system had not been operationally tested, that evaluation plans did not define standards for gauging the pilot programs' performance, and that biometric screening was frequently suspended to avoid departure delays.[277]

DHS's FY 2011 and FY 2012 budgets did not seek additional funding for a biometric exit verification system. According to Secretary Napolitano's testimony before a House congressional committee in July 2012, DHS had submitted an exit control plan to Congress two months earlier.[278] The plan, however, has not been made public, and exit controls remain an unmet and elusive mandate.[279]

C. International Cooperation

Preventing criminals and potential terrorists from entering the United States requires securing travel routes around the globe, a shared interest among many like-minded nations. Thus, international cooperation is a logical extension of effective visa screening and admissions controls. It has increased substantially in the past decade.

In 2004, the United States and the European Union (EU) signed the first EU-US Passenger Name Record (PNR) Agreement, governing the use of data given to commercial airlines by passengers on transatlantic flights and shared with governments to screen travelers and determine which ones might pose a security risk.[280] PNR data can be cross-referenced with data from other sources, such as law enforcement. Because such data go significantly beyond the basic biographic data gleaned from passports and travel documents, the collection of PNR data has been highly controversial.[281] In April 2012, the European Union renewed a PNR agreement with DHS for seven years[282] with strengthened privacy and civil-rights protections.[283]

---

273 Ibid., 2.
274 Ibid.
275 Ibid.
276 Ibid., 4-5.
277 Ibid.
278 Testimony of Janet Napolitano, Homeland Security Secretary, before the House Judiciary Committee, *Oversight of the Homeland Security Department,* 112th Cong., 2nd sess., July 19, 2012, www.micevhill.com/attachments/immigration_documents/hosted_documents/112th_congress/TranscriptOfHouseJudiciaryCommitteeHearingOnOversightOfTheHomelandSecurityDepartment.pdf.
279 DHS, *Budget in Brief FY 2011*, 102, DHS, *FY 2012 Budget in Brief*, 117.
280 Susan Ginsburg and Kristen McCabe, "Re-envisioning Security and the Movement of People," *Migration Information Source*, February 2011, www.migrationinformation.org/Feature/display.cfm?ID=829.
281 Eric Lipton, "Officials Seek Broader Access to Airline Data," *The New York Times*, August 22, 2006, www.nytimes.com/2006/08/22/washington/22data.html; Nicola Clark and Matthew L. Wald, "Hurdle for U.S. in Getting Data on Passengers," *The New York Times*, May 31, 2006, www.nytimes.com/2006/05/31/world/europe/31air.html?_r=1&th&emc=th&oref=slogin.
282 Council of the European Union, *Agreement Between the United States of America and the European Union on the Use and Transfer of Passenger Name Records to the United States Department of Homeland Security* (Brussels: Council of the European Union, 2011), http://register.consilium.europa.eu/pdf/en/11/st17/st17434.en11.pdf.
283 Ibid; "MEPs back deal to give air passenger data to US," BBC News, April 19, 2012, www.bbc.co.uk/news/world-europe-17764365.

As part of continuing efforts to "push out" the border, US-VISIT has strengthened its international partnerships in order to identify individuals involved in terrorism or immigration and asylum fraud. The United States established data sharing in 2007 with the Five Country Conference (FCC), a forum for cooperation on migration and border security among the United States, Australia, Canada, New Zealand, and the United Kingdom, and signed the High Value Data-Sharing Protocol in 2009. During the agreement's first years, each country shared approximately 3,000 biometric records annually to be matched with entries in the other countries' fingerprint and identity databases. According to Australia's immigration agency, the number of records shared this year has grown and negotiations are underway to increase fingerprint matching to 30,000 records per year.[284] Under the FCC protocol, once a match is found, countries share further information on the subject bilaterally.[285]

Finally, DHS also screens passengers in other countries prior to boarding flights to the United States through long-established preclearance programs; has improved the security of US passports; and promoted machine-readable, biometrically enhanced passports internationally; and has negotiated multiple agreements to share law enforcement and intelligence information with individual nations and groups of nations.

D. Migrant Interdiction

In its role as the primary immigration law enforcement agency at sea, the US Coast Guard interdicts several thousand migrants per year.[286] Since 1982, it has interdicted more than 237,000 persons, nearly 117,000 of them Haitians, as well as large numbers of Dominicans and Cubans. According to the DHS Office of the Inspector General, the Coast Guard reported interdicting 51 percent of migrants attempting to enter the United States illegally by sea in FY 2011.[287] Although US interdiction policies have been criticized for not incorporating sufficient refugee and humanitarian protections, they play an important role in combating human-smuggling enterprises and keeping noncitizens who are not authorized to enter from reaching the United States under highly dangerous conditions.

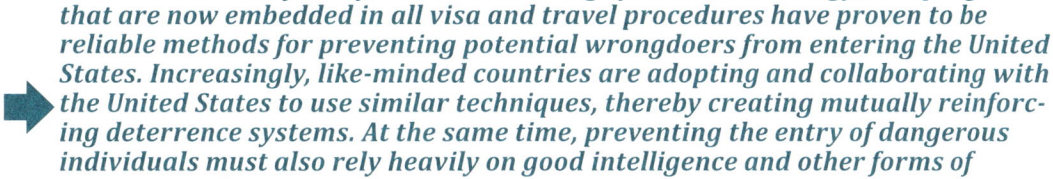

> *The broad reach of today's travel screening systems, technology, and programs that are now embedded in all visa and travel procedures have proven to be reliable methods for preventing potential wrongdoers from entering the United States. Increasingly, like-minded countries are adopting and collaborating with the United States to use similar techniques, thereby creating mutually reinforcing deterrence systems. At the same time, preventing the entry of dangerous individuals must also rely heavily on good intelligence and other forms of international cooperation beyond the scope of immigration enforcement tools and processes.*

---

284 Australian Government Department of Citizenship and Immigration, *Annual Report 2010-11* (Canberra: Department of Citizenship and Immigration, 2011), www.immi.gov.au/about/reports/annual/2010-11/html/outcome-3/identity.htm.
285 Home Office, UK Border Agency, *High value data sharing protocol - Five Country Conference, Privacy Impact Assessment* (London: UK Border Agency, 2010), www.ukba.homeoffice.gov.uk/sitecontent/documents/aboutus/workingwithus/high-value-data-sharing-protocol/.
286 US Coast Guard, "Alien Migrant Interdiction," last updated May 23, 2012, www.uscg.mil/hq/cg5/cg531/AMIO/amio.asp.
287 DHS Office of the Inspector General (OIG), *Annual Review of the United States Coast Guard's Mission Performance* (Washington, DC: DHS, OIG, 2012): 27, www.oig.dhs.gov/assets/Mgmt/2012/OIG_12-119_Sep12.pdf.

II. Program Critiques and Findings

From a broad foreign policy and international relations standpoint, visa policies communicate messages about the United States as a country that values openness to others around the globe. The United States has historically benefitted from its openness to tourists, students, entrepreneurs, business people, scholars, and other visitors. US visa policies and systems have taken on even greater importance in an era characterized by economic interdependence and increasing competition between nations. US competitiveness and even security depend on facilitating legitimate travel and trade.

Openness and its benefits always pose trade-offs, with the risk of vulnerability to those meaning harm. The 9/11 attacks heightened the tension between openness and risk, leading the United States to introduce stringent new visa, document, travel, and entry requirements.

Complaints from those accustomed to traveling regularly to the United States for myriad legitimate reasons were widespread, and many distinguished scholars and dignitaries were among those who publicly denounced requirements they found offensive — particularly fingerprinting — and lengthy processing delays that sometimes included discourteous treatment. Moreover, critics charged government officials with profiling and treating Muslim applicants or those from Middle East and South Asian countries with undue suspicion and especially burdensome requirements and delays.

Indeed, until 2011, young males from certain predominantly Muslim countries had to complete special questionnaires, in addition to undergoing interview and fingerprint requirements, which asked for more specific personal information (e.g. names of relatives, bank accounts) than travelers from other nations.[288] Foreign students and faculty often were unable to return from home visits in time for new school terms, cultural performance dates had to be cancelled because of delays in visa issuances, and laborious background checks left many visa applicants in limbo for months, and even years, with unresolved clearance issues.

Much of the furor has abated, and most of the new systems and procedures have been implemented successfully. Still, the rebound has been unevenly experienced, particularly in predominantly Muslim countries where people-to-people contact with Americans and vice versa are arguably more important in advancing US national interests than ever before. The 9/11 attacks resulted in more than strengthened screening systems. They also led to a fundamental shift in emphasis in visa screening — from concerns and judgments primarily about whether applicants intend to overstay their visas and become part of the large unauthorized population, to whether they pose a danger to national security or public safety.

A. Travel and Tourism

The visa screening system has impacted international travel and the US tourism industry. In May 2011, the US Travel Association released a report noting that while worldwide intercontinental travel increased by roughly 40 percent between 2000 and 2010, it increased by less than 2 percent in the United States during the same decade.[289] USTA attributes this disparity to the country's "burdensome" visa protocols, particularly the requirement for in-person visa interviews, and the long wait times for nationals of

---

288 DHS, "Removing Designated Countries From the National Security Entry-Exit Registration System (NSEERS)," 76 *Federal Register* 82, 23830 (April 28, 2011).
289 USTA, *Ready for Takeoff: A Plan to Create 1.3 Million U.S. Jobs by Welcoming Millions of International Travelers*, 13.

certain countries.[290] For the United States to remain competitive in the growing international tourism market, it must promote and facilitate travel. [291]

B. Limitations and Risk Management

While substantial progress has been made in screening for security vulnerabilities, there are instances where people who pose a national security threat are admitted. The 2011 and 2012 terrorism convictions of two men living in Kentucky who entered as refugees illustrate the need for continuous improvements in screening information and practices.[292] Still, there are limits to what screening tools can do, regardless of their effectiveness. No screening system can identify "clean" operatives, i.e. individuals about whom intelligence and law enforcement agencies do not have information of dangerous activity or reasons for suspicion prior to entering the United States.

Thus, risk-management principles must guide visa screening and travel program decisions. US-VISIT is an example of such principles at work. The cost, inconvenience, and political obstacles represented by exit controls have outweighed their advantages to date. Yet the features of US-VISIT that are now in place, along with new visa issuance procedures and screening systems, have significantly improved the security of the nation's immigration system since 9/11, and have strengthened immigration enforcement and information capabilities overall.

---

290 Ibid. In particular, USTA highlighted the fact that the visa application process can take as long as 145 days in Brazil and 120 days in China, two countries that are among the fastest-growing markets for overseas travel. USTA also noted that the in-person interview requirement for visa applicants is particularly burdensome on individuals who do not live near US consulates. It calculated that there are 27 cities in China and eight in India that have more than 2 million inhabitants, but do not have a US visa processing center.
291 USTA has estimated that worldwide, international arrivals will increase from 930 million to 1.3 billion between 2010 and 2020.
292 Warren Richey, "Iraqi Refugees in Kentucky Charged with Planning to Help Arm Al Qaeda," *Christian Science Monitor*, May 31, 2011, www.csmonitor.com/USA/Justice/2011/0531/Iraqi-refugees-in-Kentucky-charged-with-planning-to-help-arm-Al-Qaeda.

FINDINGS

■ **Visa controls and travel screening have been dramatically strengthened** in the past decade. Visa issuance is now informed by government-wide watch lists, traveler databases, and national security intelligence information. In addition to consular screening, DHS plays an active role in vetting visa applications abroad. The ICE Office of Investigations' Visa Security Program (VSP) operates in 19 "high-risk" locations in 15 countries. Strengthened visa procedures and further screening at ports of entry through the US-VISIT program are key elements of a layered defense against terrorists, transnational criminals, and other persons who pose a risk to the United States.

■ **The Visa Waiver Program** (VWP) has been fortified with security screening procedures to check against its being a weak link in the process of admission to the United States. VWP travelers are cleared through the Electronic System for Travel Authorization (ESTA), a new requirement for VWP that screens against terrorist watch lists and other standard visa-processing databases.

■ **US-VISIT, the post-9/11 biometric fingerprint system,** has proven to be an effective tool in strengthening travel screening and border controls once noncitizens arrive at US ports of entry. US-VISIT screens all foreign-born travelers at air and sea ports of entry, which are the most likely points of access for international terrorists. Since 2009, the program has also become operational in secondary inspection procedures at most land ports of entry.

■ **International data-sharing agreements** between the United States and foreign countries are increasingly being used as a tool for screening and identifying travelers. Under the Five Country Conference High Value Data-Sharing Protocol, the United States, Australia, Canada, New Zealand, and the United Kingdom each exchange and annually compare a specified number of biometric records on travelers deemed to be high-value subjects. Such measures exemplify a key policy goal, which is to "push the border out" by preventing those who pose threats from ever reaching US territory.

■ **Travel to the United States** for business, study, tourism, and other reasons plummeted after 9/11 due to new security and screening requirements. Overall, nonimmigrant visa issuances, which reached a peak in FY 2001, have returned to those levels for the first time since 9/11. The number of nonimmigrant visas issued in FY 2011 (7,507,939) is essentially on par with the 7,588,778 issued in FY 2001. The numbers suggest that balance between security and openness to legitimate travel and trade is being regained. Yet there is considerable variation in the issuances of nonimmigrant visas among different countries and visa categories, especially for predominantly Muslim countries.

■ **By 2008, both the number of B1/B2 tourist and F1 student visas** issued had returned to their pre-9/11 levels. In 2011, the number of B1/B2 visas issued overall was roughly 23 percent higher than in 2001. However, the number of B1/B2 tourist visas granted to individuals from the 24 predominantly Muslim countries designated for the post-9/11 NSEERS registration program was 11 percent lower in 2011 than in 2001.

■ **From FY 2001 to FY 2011**, the number of student visas issued for nationals of all countries grew by 53 percent. Almost 35 percent of these visa issuances are to students from China. During the same period, the number of student visas granted to nationals of predominantly Muslim/NSEERS countries increased by a surprising 82 percent. The increase has been driven by student visas issued to nationals of Saudi Arabia, who account for 64 percent of F visas for predominantly Muslim countries. Saudi Arabia is the third largest source country of foreign students who come to the United States, after China and South Korea.

■ **While the overall number of visas issued** to foreign nationals has rebounded, the United States has lost ground in the share of global travel, which has greatly increased in the past decade. Stringent visa and travel screening requirements may play a role in this shift. However, broad market and competitive forces are also powerful drivers of the change.

CHAPTER 5

INFORMATION AND INTEROPERABILITY OF DATA SYSTEMS

Congressional mandates about government information sharing and interoperability of data systems changed fundamentally after 9/11.[293] Concerns about privacy and "big-brother" dangers that represented the prevailing attitude about federal government information practices before the attacks quickly gave way to demands that government gather and analyze all relevant information for securing travel and immigration procedures.[294] These imperatives have led to significant new data capabilities that constitute a critical pillar of today's immigration enforcement system and reach well beyond their original counterterrorism and national security purposes.

This pillar has not received the attention given to more visible changes, such as the growth of the Border Patrol, for example. However, the investments and progress that have been made in accurate and regularly updated databases, information sharing across law enforcement and intelligence agencies, and interoperability of data systems that make it possible to search immigration, criminal, and terrorist databases at every step in the admissions and immigration process have been transformational in creating a modernized immigration system.

Interoperability of data systems also serves as the connective tissue that ties the various immigration agencies together. With the breakup of INS and the creation of DHS, the organizational machinery for administering the nation's immigration laws has become decentralized. Interoperability of information systems is an indispensable tool for achieving coherence among agencies' programs and activities.

Among the critical failings identified by the 9/11 Commission was the inability of government agencies to "connect the dots" with information gathered and held by the numerous agencies tasked with national security and law enforcement missions.[295] In particular, the 9/11 plot underscored the imperative of making national security information available to frontline actors most likely to come into contact with those meaning to do harm.

---

293 Jerome P. Bjelopera, *Terrorism Information Sharing and the Nationwide Suspicious Activity Report Initiative: Background and Issues for Congress* (Washington, DC: CRS, 2011): 1-3, http://fpc.state.gov/documents/organization/166837.pdf.

294 Bill Zalud, "Less Privacy Concern after Sept. 11," Gale Group, Inc., April 1, 2002: 14, ("After years of use and growth, there are still privacy concerns related to electronic security systems, but many corporate and government security executives now feel that the concern has lessened, primarily because of the 9/11 terrorist attacks."); Adam Liptak, "In the Name of Security: Privacy for Me, Not Thee," *The New York Times*, November 24, 2002, www.nytimes.com/2002/11/24/weekinreview/the-nation-citizen-watch-in-the-name-of-security-privacy-for-me-not-thee.html?pagewanted=all&src=pm; Editors, *New York Times*, "Backward at the FBI: Overreaching New Rules for Surveillance Threaten Americans' Basic Rights," *The New York Times*, June 19, 2011, www.nytimes.com/2011/06/19/opinion/19sun1.html.

295 National Commission on Terrorist Attacks Upon the United States, *The 9/11 Commission Report*, 418; Thomas R. Eldridge, Susan Ginsburg, Walter T. Hempel II, Janice L. Kephart, and Kelly Moore, *9/11 and Terrorist Travel: Staff Report of the National Commission on Terrorist Attacks Upon the United States* (Washington, DC: National Commission on Terrorist Attacks Upon the United States, 2004): 1, 31, 88-9, http://govinfo.library.unt.edu/911/staff_statements/911_TerrTrav_Monograph.pdf.

Such frontline actors include consular and immigration officials, with whom the FBI and intelligence agencies did not share information in a systematic way prior to 9/11.[296] The *Enhanced Border Control and Visa Entry Reform Act* mandated development of an interoperable data system to transmit national security information to immigration control officers.[297] The law explicitly grants access to such data to federal officers responsible for issuing visas, making determinations on admission or removal, and investigating and identifying noncitizens.[298]

Significant resources and high priority have been directed at building sophisticated, new interoperable data systems, aimed at containing all information that the government possesses on dangerous and suspect individuals. Most of the new systems had been envisioned or developed by immigration agencies prior to 9/11, but they had been neither sufficiently funded nor designed and tapped for robust interagency information sharing.

I. Programs and Results

Database screening now accompanies virtually all key interactions between noncitizens and the federal government. Immigration databases capture biographical information (e.g. name, date of birth, and country of origin) and provide information on past entries to the country, immigration status records, criminal history, and possible terrorist connections. Increasingly, the data systems also collect and screen against fingerprints and digital photographs for purposes of identity assurance. Such biometric databases may soon also include iris scans, voice matching, and facial recognition.[299]

Key Databases and Information Systems[300]

The sections below discuss the databases and information systems that are key features of most immigration processes operating today. They support the screening protocols for the five core immigration processes — visa issuance, ports of entry admissions, border apprehensions, arrests and removal of noncitizens, and immigration benefit applications.

1. US-VISIT: The IDENT and ADIS Databases

The scope and use of US-VISIT extends well beyond entry screening, as described in the previous chapter. Data from US-VISIT, which is an identity-assurance program, are tapped in all five of the core immigration processes.

US-VISIT collects biometric data — ten-fingerprint scans and digital photographs — for all noncitizens ages 14-79 except Canadians, Mexican nationals who cross by land borders using border crossing cards, and certain visitors admitted on diplomatic visas.[301]

---

296 Alden, *The Closing of the American Border*, 16, 150.
297 *Enhanced Border Security and Visa Entry Reform Act of 2002*.
298 Ibid.
299 US Federal Bureau of Investigation (FBI), "Next Generation Identification," accessed November 18, 2012, www.fbi.gov/about-us/cjis/fingerprints_biometrics/ngi; US-VISIT, "2011 Year in Review" (Washington, DC: US-VISIT, 2011).
300 See Appendices for a series of diagrams depicting the screening protocols for five core immigration processes: visa applications, authorized entries, border apprehensions, immigration benefit applications, and arrests of unauthorized immigrants in many local jurisdictions.
301 DHS, "US-VISIT at the US-Mexico Land Border," www.dhs.gov/xlibrary/assets/usvisit/usvisit_edu_us_mexico_land_border_info_card_english.pdf. Also exempted from the program are holders of diplomatic visas and Taiwanese visa holders traveling to the United States on E-1 visas; DHS, "US-VISIT Enrollment Requirements," accessed November 18, 2012, www.dhs.gov/files/programs/editorial_0527.shtm. All lawful permanent residents (LPRs) are fingerprinted at air ports but at land ports only if put into secondary inspection.

IDENT — DHS stores these biometric records in a database known as IDENT (Automated Biometric Identification System), which today contains more than 148 million individual fingerprint records,[302] grows by about 10 million new entries per year, and reflects more than 2 billion individual entry events.[303] The system has reciprocal access with the FBI's Integrated Automated Fingerprint Identification System (IAFIS).[304] As a result, law enforcement officials at all levels of government who screen fingerprints have access both to IDENT information regarding past entries and to the FBI's criminal history records.[305] The FBI "criminal master file," which is screened through IAFIS, contains the fingerprints and criminal histories of 70 million persons and 73,000 known or suspected terrorists.[306]

US-VISIT screens foreign nationals against the IAFIS database during secondary inspection. DHS anticipates that by 2013 border inspectors will be able to query both the IDENT (immigration) biometric database and the IAFIS (criminal) biometric database simultaneously during primary inspection.[307]

ADIS — In addition to entry screening that relies on IDENT, US-VISIT administers a comprehensive database of biographic information known as the Arrival and Departure Information System (ADIS).[308] Those data include names, dates of birth, citizenship status, gender, travel document information, nationality, air and sea arrival and departure vessels, ports of arrival and departure, US destination addresses, classes of admission, countries of residence, types of visas issued, countries of birth, social security or alien registration numbers, and terrorist watch list information.[309]

Like IDENT, this database is checked by immigration officers at ports of entry when an individual enters the country.[310] ADIS contains consolidated information from a wide variety of sources. For individuals who are subject to US-VISIT requirements, ADIS stores biographic information collected by CBP from air and sea passenger manifests.[311]

In addition, ADIS contains data from the ICE-administered Student and Exchange Visitor Information System (SEVIS and the Computer Linked Applications Information Management System (CLAIMS 3),[312] managed by USCIS. It also contains data obtained by DHS and DOS officials when an individual attempts entry to the country or applies for a visa.[313] Finally, ADIS may contain data collected by "foreign government border management agencies, or other organizations that collaborate with DHS in pursuing DHS national security, law enforcement, immigration, intelligence, and other DHS mission-related functions."[314]

---

302 E-mail from Robert Mocny, Director, US-VISIT, to Doris Meissner, Senior Fellow and Director, US Immigration Policy Program, Migration Policy Institute, November 29, 2012 (email on file with authors).

303 Ibid; MPI meeting with US-VISIT Chief of Staff Penelope Smith; Section Chief, Systems Operation Services, Diane Stephens; and staff, February 16, 2012. Notes on file with authors.

304 DHS defines interoperability as the sharing of alien immigration history, criminal history, and terrorist information based on positive identification and the interoperable capabilities of IDENT and IAFIS; DHS, *IDENT, IAFIS Interoperability* (Washington, DC: DHS, 2005), www.dhs.gov/xlibrary/assets/foia/US-VISIT_IDENT-IAFISReport.pdf.

305 Ibid.

306 FBI, "The Integrated Automated Fingerprint Identification System," accessed November 18, 2012, www.fbi.gov/about-us/cjis/fingerprints_biometrics/iafis/iafis.

307 US-VISIT, *2011 Year in Review*, 28.

308 Ibid., 17.

309 DHS, *Privacy Impact Assessment for the Arrival and Departure Information System (ADIS)* (Washington, DC: DHS, 2007): 3, www.dhs.gov/xlibrary/assets/privacy/privacy_pia_usvisit_adis_2007.pdf.

310 US-VISIT, *2011 Year in Review*, 17.

311 DHS, *Privacy Impact Assessment for the Advance Passenger Information System (APIS)* (Washington, DC: DHS, 2008): 3, http://foia.cbp.gov/streamingWord.asp?i=38. (Noting that for travelers who are required to enroll in US-VISIT, CBP shares passenger manifest data collected through its own Advance Passenger Information System (APIS) with US-VISIT's ADIS).

312 Ibid., 4.

313 DHS, *Privacy Impact Assessment for the Arrival and Departure Information System (ADIS)* (Washington, DC: DHS, 2007): 3, www.dhs.gov/xlibrary/assets/privacy/privacy_pia_usvisit_adis_2007.pdf.

314 Ibid., 4.

Both IDENT and ADIS are used in a wide variety of other immigration and terrorism screening programs, making them fundamental tools for all parts of the country's immigration enforcement system. For example:

- The Secure Communities program administered by ICE relies on IDENT to verify the identity of arrested noncitizens and provide their immigration information.[315]

- The US Coast Guard uses IDENT to verify the identities of migrants who are apprehended at sea, a process which allows the Department of Justice to prosecute repeat offenders.[316]

- DOS uses both IDENT and ADIS to verify the identities and past immigration histories of visa applicants.[317]

- The US-VISIT program has signed agreements with foreign countries that allow for international collaboration and the sharing of biometric data for "high-value" cases.[318]

Perhaps most significantly, US-VISIT is currently working with the Department of Defense (DOD) to establish interoperability with DOD's biometric database, which contains the fingerprints of foreign nationals encountered by US military personnel abroad in anti-terrorism, combat, and other operations.[319] With this integration, the three core biometric databases of the US government — those administered by the FBI, DOD, and DHS — will be interoperable.[320]

2. FBI Terrorist Screening Database

Another response to the 9/11 attacks has been creation of a comprehensive terrorist watch list database: the FBI's Terrorist Screening Database (TSDB).[321] TSDB maintains lists that number in the hundreds of thousands of individuals believed to be linked with terrorism. It provides "one-stop shopping" to all government screeners, including consular officers issuing visas, airport screeners processing passengers, immigration officers admitting noncitizens, and state and local law enforcement officials.[322] TSDB contains biographic records, biometric data (fingerprint and photograph), and information on terrorist connections.[323] The database is tapped by DOS for every individual it clears during the visa issuance process, through the agency's Consular Lookout and Support System (CLASS) screening system; by CBP through that agency's Advance Passenger Information System (APIS) and TECS (not an acronym) screening systems; and by US-VISIT.[324]

---

315 Ibid., 9.
316 Ibid., 24.
317 Ibid., 19.
318 Ibid., 26. DHS, *Privacy Impact Assessment for the US-VISIT Five Country Joint Enrollment and Information Sharing Project (FCC)* (Washington, DC: DHS, 2009): 2, www.dhs.gov/xlibrary/assets/privacy/privacy_pia_usvisit_fcc.pdf.
319 US-VISIT, *2011 Year in Review:* 21; US-VISIT, 8th Anniversary Briefing.
320 Ibid.
321 Prior to 9/11, the US government maintained nearly a dozen terrorist watch lists controlled by various government agencies; see Edward Alden, *The Closing of the American Border,* 23. The databases had limited interconnectivity, and they varied in the criteria required for an individual to be listed as a suspected terrorist; Eldridge et al., *9/11 and Terrorist Travel: Staff Report of the National Commission on Terrorist Attacks Upon the United States,* 89, 100.
322 FBI, "Terrorist Screening Database, Frequently Asked Questions," accessed November 18, 2012, www.fbi.gov/about-us/nsb/tsc/tsc_faqs.
323 DHS, *Privacy Impact Assessment for the Watchlist Service* (Washington, DC: DHS, 2010): 4, www.dhs.gov/xlibrary/assets/privacy/privacy_pia_dhs_wls.pdf.
324 William J. Krouse and Bart Elias, *Terrorist Watchlist Checks and Air Passenger Prescreening* (Washington, DC: CRS, 2009): 5, 7, 8, www.fas.org/sgp/crs/homesec/RL33645.pdf.

3. Visa Screening Systems

DOS maintains its own databases for use at various stages of immigration and criminal history processing.

The Consular Consolidated Database (CCD) — CCD is the agency's main repository for information collected from applicants for US visas, passports, and US citizen services at US consular offices. It includes biographic information, fingerprints, photographs, and identification numbers. As of December 2009, CCD contained more than 75 million photographs.[325] In February 2010, a State Department official testified that it contained more than 136 million records.[326]

The CCD database is interoperable with a number of other government immigration and security databases, including IDENT and IAFIS, and CBP's TECS.[327] Screening also includes Interpol's Stolen and Lost Travel Documents database. In addition, some, though not all, consular posts have access to the ADIS database[328] of US-VISIT.[329]

The Consular Lookout and Support System (CLASS) — CLASS is a name-check system that uses linguistic algorithms to screen the names of individuals applying for visas against information on persons who may be ineligible to receive a visa or passport. The system contained 26 million records in 2009.[330] CLASS screens against the CCD to determine if an applicant for a visa has a previous visa denial or revocation, as well as against information forwarded from other government agencies, such as DHS and the FBI.

4. SEVIS

Though tracking information on foreign students and exchange visitors dates back many years, it became mandatory after enactment of IIRIRA. The law called upon the attorney general, in consultation with the Secretaries of State and Education, to collect data on foreign students from at least five countries initially and all countries by 2003.[331]

The *USA PATRIOT Act* and the *Enhanced Border Security and Visa Entry Reform Act of 2002* directed that SEVIS be deployed more rapidly,[332] incorporate data from DOS, and individually track pertinent student status data.[333] SEVIS collects biographic information on foreign students (both M and F visa holders) and exchange visitors (J visa holders), as well as their dependents.

Academic institutions seeking to admit foreign students must register with SEVIS. Foreign nationals seeking to study in the United States first apply and are admitted to a SEVIS-certified school. Once the school extends an offer of admission, it enters the admitted student's name and identifying information into SEVIS and issues a ver-

---

325 DOS, *Consular Consolidated Database Privacy Impact Assessment* (Washington, DC: DOS, 2010): 1, www.state.gov/documents/organization/93772.pdf.
326 Statement of Patrick F. Kennedy, Undersecretary of State for Management, before the House Committee on the Judiciary, *Sharing and Analyzing Information to Prevent Terrorism*, 111th Cong., 2nd sess., February 10, 2010, http://travel.state.gov/law/legal/testimony/testimony_4830.html.
327 Ruth Ellen Wasem, *Visa Security Policy: Roles of the Departments of State and Homeland Security* (Washington, DC: CRS, 2011): 7, www.fas.org/sgp/crs/homesec/R41093.pdf.
328 Ibid.
329 Ibid.
330 Ibid.
331 Alison Siskin, *Monitoring Foreign Students in the United States: The Student and Exchange Visitor Information System* (Washington, DC: CRS, 2005): 1, www.ilw.com/immigrationdaily/news/2005,0421-crs.pdf.
332 *The Uniting and Strengthening America by Providing Appropriate Tools Required to Intercept and Obstruct Terrorism Act of 2001* (USA-PATRIOT Act), Public Law 107-56, 115 Stat. 272, 354 (October 26, 2001); *Enhanced Border Security and Visa Entry Reform Act of 2002*, 116 Stat. 543, 560-62.
333 *Enhanced Border Security and Visa Entry Reform Act of 2002*, 116 Stat. 543, 560-62.

ification form, known as an I-20, to the student.[334] Each student must then apply for a student visa at a US embassy or consulate in their home country, where DOS officials use SEVIS to verify the student's biographic and I-20 information, and then screen the applicant against immigration, terrorist, and criminal databases.[335]

When an individual presents the student visa at a US port of entry, his or her information is again screened through SEVIS, as well as through US-VISIT. SEVIS requires subsequent notifications of reporting for classes, changes in majors or courses of study,[336] start dates of terms, failure to enroll, dropping below a full course load, disciplinary action by the school, and early graduation.[337]

By the end of 2010, 10,293 schools and 1,456 exchange visitor programs were participating in SEVIS, and the system contained more than 8.1 million records.[338]

5. Border Enforcement Screening Systems

CBP operates three key database screening systems to review information on individuals (citizens and noncitizens) planning to enter the United States by air or sea.

The Advanced Passenger Information System (APIS) runs citizen and noncitizen "passenger manifest" data against the TSDB terrorist watch list.[339] Such data primarily consist of biographic information collected from machine-readable passports, as well as flight data.[340] Several domestic and international airlines voluntarily submitted passenger manifest data to the US customs and immigration agencies prior to 9/11 when the data were mainly screened in connection with drug-smuggling investigations.[341] Following 9/11, Congress required all airlines to submit such information.[342] Since 2008, international air carriers and vessel operators have been required to submit passenger manifest data prior to their departure.[343]

TECS (not an acronym) is both a database and a screening system.[344] As a database, TECS is CBP's central repository for data on travelers who seek admission to the United States through a port of entry.[345] Whenever a CBP officer admits an individual to the country at an air or sea port, the officer enters that person's basic biographic information into TECS.[346] At land ports, individuals seeking admission are entered into the TECS system only if they are referred to secondary inspection.[347] As a screening system, TECS — like APIS — runs passenger manifest data (or basic biographic data, if the person seeking admission is at a land port of entry) against a series of immigration, terrorism,

---

334 DOS, "Student Visas," accessed November 18, 2012, http://travel.state.gov/visa/temp/types/types_1268.html.
335 Siskin, *Monitoring Foreign Students in the United States*, 4-5.
336 Ibid., 5.
337 Ibid.
338 ICE, *Student and Exchange Visitor Information System: General Summary Quarterly Review for Quarter Ending December 31, 2010* (Washington, DC: DHS, 2011): 3, www.ice.gov/doclib/sevis/pdf/quarterly_report_ending_dec2010.pdf.
339 Krouse and Elias, *Terrorist Watchlist Checks and Air Passenger Prescreening*, 5-6.
340 Ibid., 6.
341 Alden, *The Closing of the American Border*, 28.
342 Krouse and Elias, *Terrorist Watchlist Checks and Air Passenger Prescreening*, 7.
343 DHS, "Advance Electronic Transmission of Passenger and Crew Manifests for Commercial Aircraft and Vessels," 72 *Federal Register*, 163, 48320 (August 23, 2007) (codified at 19 CFR pts. 4 and 122).
344 DHS, *Privacy Impact Assessment for the TECS System: CBP Primary and Secondary Processing* (Washington, DC: DHS, 2010): 2, www.dhs.gov/xlibrary/assets/privacy/privacy_pia_cbp_tecs.pdf.
345 Ibid., 2-3.
346 Ibid.
347 Ibid., 5.

and criminal databases.[348] These include TSDB, as well as databases on previous border crossers, lists of individuals with outstanding warrants, and lists of individuals whose assets were previously seized by CBP.[349]

Automated Targeting System (ATS) is a "decision-support tool," which, like APIS, screens information about individuals who are about to arrive in the United States via air or sea.[350] Unlike APIS, however, ATS screens not just passenger manifest information, but also passenger name records (PNR) data.[351] PNR data include biographic information that appear on passenger manifests and airline data on travelers' booking information, such as travel plans, frequent flyer numbers, and credit card data.[352]

6. Enforcement Integrated Database (EID) and ENFORCE

The Enforcement Integrated Database (EID) is a shared database managed by ICE that contains information about the arrest, detention, and removal of noncitizens. EID, which also connects with CBP and USCIS databases, provides biometric and biographic information gathered and stored by each DHS immigration agency.[353]

DHS personnel, typically ICE agents in the Offices of Homeland Security Investigations (HSI) and Enforcement and Removal Operations (ERO), are able to access EID through software called ENFORCE. Both ENFORCE and EID provide information pertinent to the investigation, arrest, apprehension, booking, detention, and removal of noncitizens encountered by any DHS immigration agency — ICE, CBP, and USCIS.[354] Criminal history information from the FBI's National Crime Information Center (NCIC) database is also available through EID.[355]

To meet ICE needs, EID stores information about subjects' ties to the community, special vulnerabilities, work authorization status, crime victim status, and the number of family members living with the noncitizen.[356] ICE has begun to use the system to establish uniformity in detention decisions and in classifying the priority levels of apprehended noncitizens based on their criminal and immigration histories and community ties.[357]

7. The Central Index System (CIS) of US Citizenship and Immigration Services

The USCIS Central Index System (CIS) tracks immigration benefit applications. The system provides the capability to monitor the status of immigrant, refugee, asylum-seeker, and other applications for immigration benefits filed with USCIS.[358] The database contains biographic records and identification numbers (e.g. social security number, alien registration number).

---

348 Ibid., 8-9.
349 Ibid.
350 Krouse and Elias, *Terrorist Watchlist Checks and Air Passenger Prescreening*, 8-9.
351 Ibid.
352 Ibid.
353 ICE, *Privacy Impact Assessment Update for the Enforcement Integrated Database (EID)Risk Classification Assessment (RCA 1.0), ENFORCE Alien Removal Module (EARM 5.0), and Crime Entry Screen (CES 2.0) DHS/ICE/PIA-015(d)*, (Washington, DC: DHS, 2012), www.dhs.gov/xlibrary/assets/privacy/privacy_piaupdate_EID_april2012.pdf; Alicia Carriquiry and Malay Majmundar, eds., *Options for Estimating Illegal Entries at the U.S.–Mexico Border* (Washington, DC: The National Academies Press, 2013). Prepublication version available at www.nap.edu/openbook.php?record_id=13498&page=R1.
354 ICE, *Privacy Impact Assessment Update*, 2.
355 Ibid., 14.
356 Ibid., 3.
357 Ibid., 3.
358 DHS, *Privacy Impact Assessment for the Central Index System* (Washington, DC: DHS, 2007): 3-4, www.dhs.gov/xlibrary/assets/privacy/privacy_pia_uscis_cis.pdf.

The system receives information from the various USCIS databases used to store information on noncitizens seeking various types of benefits, including CLAIMS 4, the agency's case-tracking database for naturalization cases; CLAIMS 3, the case-tracking database for applications for permanent residence; RAPS, the refugee, asylum, and parole system; and EADS, the employment authorization documentation database.[359]

One of the system's main functions is providing information for E-Verify, the automated employer information verification system described in more detail in the workplace enforcement chapter. In addition, CIS can now be readily tapped by qualified officials in other immigration and law enforcement agencies to obtain information on individuals who have come into contact with the immigration benefit system in one way or another.

> *Taken together, the above-described systems serve to screen noncitizens at more times, against more databases, which possess more data, than ever before. Although the databases and procedures for their use vary by immigration process, they all enable screening for possible terrorist links, criminal background, or immigration history. In addition, their interoperability allows for continually importing and updating data from other databases. Particular databases, such as IDENT, support a broad range of programs and law enforcement purposes well beyond the port-of-entry screening for which it was developed.*

II. Program Critiques and Findings

New and strengthened information systems and interoperability have made it possible for federal immigration agencies to implement their missions far more effectively and broadly. Still, the uses of broad-based information systems and data interoperability remain a work in progress.

Systems such as US-VISIT, while highly adept at storing large quantities of biometric and biographic data, have proven less effective at detecting suspected identity fraud. In August 2012, the DHS Office of the Inspector General (OIG) reported that it had found 825,000 instances in IDENT where one set of fingerprints was linked with more than one set of biographic data.[360] While these inconsistencies constitute less than 1 percent of total IDENT data,[361] and many are likely due to name changes, inconsistent name spellings, typographical errors, or other such "innocent" causes,[362] the OIG concluded that US-VISIT's current data-screening mechanisms do not adequately target individuals who are using multiple identities to enter the United States or entering the country by committing identity fraud.[363] For example, in one instance, the OIG found that the same set of fingerprints was linked to seven different individuals who entered the United States within a few hours of each other.[364] Since 2005, US-VISIT has referred just two instances of suspected biographic fraud to ICE.[365]

Federal security agencies have stressed the need to collect more biometric data as a way of "assuring" identity.[366] Though DHS, DOS, and the FBI already store a vast amount of fingerprint and photographic data, the FBI has been developing Next Generation

---

359 Ibid., 4.
360 DHS Office of the Inspector General, *US-VISIT Faces Challenges in Identifying and Reporting Multiple Biographic Identities* (Washington, DC: DHS, OIG, 2012): 3, www.oig.dhs.gov/assets/Mgmt/2012/OIG_12-111_Aug12.pdf.
361 Ibid; according to the report, the 825,000 records constitute roughly 0.2 percent of the IDENT data.
362 Ibid., 7-8.
363 Ibid.
364 Ibid., 7.
365 Ibid., 5.
366 DHS, "US-VISIT Biometric Identification Services," accessed November 18, 2012, www.dhs.gov/files/programs/gc_1208531081211.shtm.

Identification (NGI), a system to replace IAFIS. NGI will incorporate biometric markers such as facial and voice recognition, palm print, and iris scan capabilities.[367]

The FBI announced in March 2011 that NGI had reached its initial operating capability, but it has not announced a planned implementation date.[368] Because IDENT and IAFIS are interoperable based on fingerprint records, the development of NGI suggests that IDENT could also potentially maintain biometric records beyond fingerprints and photographs. Already, CBP has plans to test the feasibility of iris- and facial-recognition technology in a pilot program at the Border Patrol station in McAllen, TX.[369]

Civil libertarians and other observers have raised concerns over the expansion and consolidation of biometric data, because of possible erosion of privacy, breaches of data security, and projected difficulties in correcting data-entry errors.[370]

Apart from issues of privacy, other concerns stem from the fact that investments in automating information and linking databases have been uneven, tilting heavily toward border security, less toward interior enforcement, and considerably less toward travel facilitation or legal immigration processes. All immigration agencies and activities have benefited from the improvements that have resulted from significant investments in database modernization. For example, CBP's recent announcement that the I-94 arrival departure paper record will become automated signifies a major modernization effort made to streamline legitimate travel. However, the transformation that new data systems and interoperability have generated is far more apparent and dramatic in immigration enforcement than in other realms of immigration activity.

Finally, there has been a frustrating and indefensible lack of transparency and accessible procedures for correcting information mistakenly entered into watch list databases. Even high-profile figures such as the late Senator Edward Kennedy and singer Cat Stevens found themselves on terrorist screening lists. Travelers are inconvenienced repeatedly, and are able to correct their records only after multiple, confounding attempts, if at all.[371]

At a broader level, US-VISIT, in its ability to verify identity using noninvasive, highly reliable techniques, has made the United States the world's leader in identity assurance, an essential requirement facing law enforcement everywhere in carrying out counterterrorism and other public safety responsibilities. When US-VISIT was first introduced, some countries, e.g. Brazil, strenuously objected to fingerprinting requirements and threatened reciprocal procedures. However, the general trend has been one of countries following suit for their own reasons. The United States has been active internationally through the work of the Biometric Partnership Council[372] and agreements it has negotiated with European and other nations. The European Union and India are among those establishing similar biometric identity assurance systems.

The United States can exercise even stronger international leadership by developing identity management and tracking as an analogous capability to financial tracking ("follow the money") requirements that have proved to be potent methods for depriving

---

367 FBI, "Next Generation Identification," accessed November 18, 2012, www.fbi.gov/about-us/cjis/fingerprints_biometrics/ngi.
368 FBI, "FBI Announces Initial Operating Capability for Next Generation Identification System," (press release, March 8, 2011), www.fbi.gov/news/pressrel/press-releases/fbi-announces-initial-operating-capability-for-next-generation-identification-system.
369 NextGov, "Feds Significantly Expand the Use of Iris-Recognition Technology," July 13, 2012, www.nextgov.com/big-data/2012/07/feds-significantly-expand-use-iris-recognition-technology/56776/?oref=ng-HPriver.
370 Ellen Nakashima, "FBI Prepares Vast Database of Biometrics," *Washington Post*, December 22, 2007, www.washingtonpost.com/wp-dyn/content/article/2007/12/21/AR2007122102544.html.
371 Alden, *The Closing of the American Border*, 21-2.
372 Ibid.

terrorists and other criminal enterprises of a key tool they need. Just as access to large amounts of money is essential for terrorists and other criminal elements to succeed, access to international travel is a vital commodity for international criminal networks.

Securing travel mobility through coordinated systems of identity management and information sharing must be consistent with privacy protections, especially among international partners. At the same time, greater ease of movement for frequent and reliable travelers and streamlined travel processes for the more than 99 percent who travel legitimately should be a next-order policy imperative.

In these ways, identity assurance and management can be better leveraged to benefit the nation, partner nations, travelers, and others.

FINDINGS

■ **US-VISIT and its IDENT electronic fingerprint database** rank as the largest law enforcement biometric identity-verification system in the world. The system stores 148 million records that grow by about 10 million per year. More than 2 billion records have been entered since US-VISIT was launched.

■ **Protocols that rely on comprehensive information** and interoperability of data systems are now embedded in virtually all critical immigration processes and agency practices. Today, noncitizens are screened at more times, against more databases, which contain more detailed data, than ever before. Thus, when immigration officials do routine name checks, they are able to learn whether an individual re-entering the country or under arrest was, for example, previously removed, has an outstanding warrant of arrest, or was convicted of a crime that would make him/her subject to immigration enforcement actions.

■ **The integration of IDENT** and the FBI's Integrated Automated Fingerprint Identification System (IAFIS) data systems has been a critical development in harnessing the full scope of the federal government's sources of information for immigration enforcement uses. Today, frontline immigration officers at different levels of government, performing the full range of immigration functions, have access to IDENT, which then provides access to the IAFIS criminal histories of 70 million persons and 73,000 known or suspected terrorists. These new data capabilities reach well beyond their original counterterrorism and national security imperatives. They have enabled immigration agencies to advance conventional immigration enforcement goals through significantly expanded cooperative arrangements with states and localities in programs such as the Criminal Alien Program (CAP), Secure Communities, and 287(g).

■ **US-VISIT is working with the Department of Defense** (DOD) to establish interoperability with DOD's biometric database, which contains the fingerprints of foreign nationals encountered in antiterrorism, combat, and other operations. With this integration, the three core biometric databases of the US government — those administered by the FBI, DOD, and DHS — would be interoperable and accessible for immigration enforcement purposes.

CHAPTER 6

WORKPLACE ENFORCEMENT

Employment in the United States is generally considered to be the driving force for illegal immigration. Noncitizens who enter the United States unlawfully or overstay their visas do so primarily to work. Because of the magnet that employment provides for unauthorized immigrants, and the potential competition illegal immigration represents for authorized US workers, workplace enforcement is an essential pillar of a well-managed immigration enforcement system.

I. Programs and Results

The linchpin of the *Immigration Reform and Control Act of 1986* (IRCA) was to make it unlawful to hire unauthorized workers. The requirement was to be enforced through a system of employer sanctions.[373] However, the law was and remains difficult to enforce and employers can be in technical compliance with the law while still employing unauthorized workers. In 2010, an estimated 8 million unauthorized workers were employed in the United States, constituting 5.2 percent of the US labor force.[374]

Figure 11. Unauthorized Immigrants in the United States, Overall and in Workforce, FY 2000-10

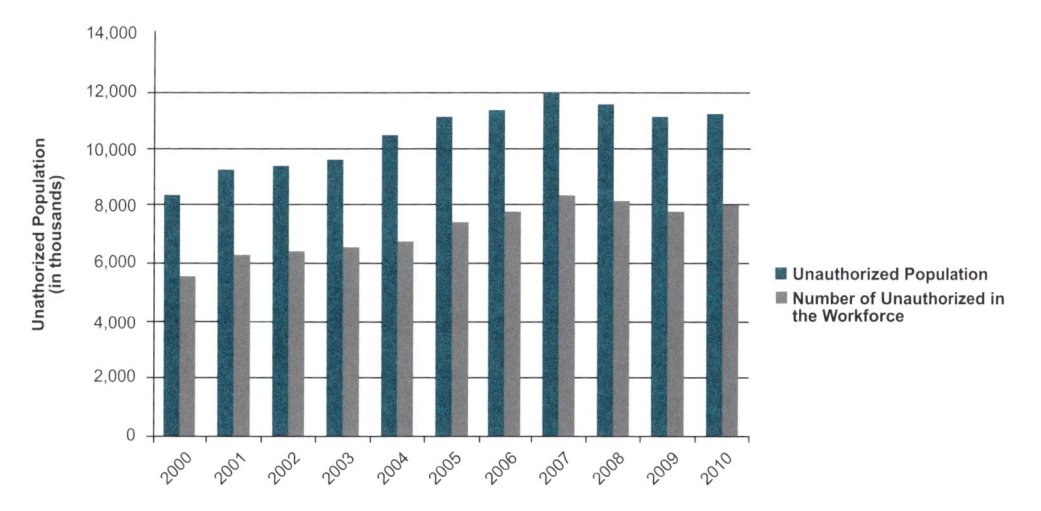

Source: Jeffrey Passel and D'Vera Cohn, *Unauthorized Immigrant Population: National and State Trends 2010* (Washington, DC: Pew Hispanic Center, 2011), www.pewhispanic.org/2011/02/01/unauthorized-immigrant-population-brnational-and-state-trends-2010/.

IRCA provided that employers may not knowingly hire, recruit, or refer for a fee an unauthorized worker. They must establish an employee's identity and work eligibility from a designated list of documents. Employers must attest that they have examined

---

373 INA § 274A(e)-(f).
374 Passel and Cohn, *Unauthorized Immigrant Population: National and State Trends, 2010*.

the appropriate documents and that they appear, on their face, to be genuine.[375] Key features of employer sanctions include:

- Employers are deemed to have complied with the law if they make a good-faith attempt to verify the identity and work eligibility of a worker by completing a form known as the I-9 verification form.[376]

- Employers who request more or different documents than those required, or who refuse to accept documents that appear to be genuine, risk penalties for discrimination based on national origin or citizenship status.[377]

- Employers who violate I-9 hiring requirements can be fined up to $3,200 per unauthorized worker for a first violation, up to $6,500 for a subsequent violation, and up to $16,000 for a third or additional offense.[378]

Employer sanctions are based on the proposition that the large majority of employers will voluntarily comply with the law. A strong tradition of employer compliance exists, for example, with employer tax obligations paid to the Internal Revenue Service and minimum-wage and child labor mandates. Employer adherence to legal status requirements was envisioned as building on that tradition and thereby allowing for scarce enforcement resources to be concentrated on the small fraction of noncompliant employers.

Instead, employer sanctions have been largely ineffective as a tool for controlling illegal immigration. Certain employers do not comply because they see little risk in noncompliance and competitive advantages in hiring a cheaper and more compliant labor force. However, the primary weakness in this system has been the array of documents[379] — many of them easy to counterfeit — that are permitted for meeting I-9 requirements. To respond to the proliferation and abuse of such documents, the federal government has sought to develop a reliable electronic employment verification system.

A. The E-Verify Program

E-Verify is the federal government's online work authorization verification system. The program, which is voluntary, originated from a provision in IIRIRA that required INS to create three four-year pilot programs for employers to screen newly hired workers for work eligibility.[380] The successful pilot, initially called Basic Pilot, was renamed E-Verify in 2007,[381] and is administered by USCIS.

E-Verify allows registered employers to enter the biographic information (name, social

---

375 INA § 274A (b)(1).
376 INA § 274A (a)(3).
377 INA § 274B (a).
378 INA §274A; USCIS, "Penalties," last updated November 23, 2011, www.uscis.gov/portal/site/uscis/menuitem.eb1d4c2a3e5b9ac89243c6a7543f6d1a/?vgnextoid=92082d73a2d38210VgnVCM100000082ca60aRCRD&vgnextchannel=92082d73a2d38210VgnVCM100000082ca60aRCRD.
379 There are 25 different types of documents that employers may use to verify employment authorization. Six of the documents ("List A" documents on Form I-9) may be used to verify both an employee's identity and his or her employment authorization. The remaining documents ("List B" and "List C" documents) may be used to verify either employment authorization or identity. See US Citizenship and Immigration Services (USCIS), "Form I-9 Employment Eligibility Verification," OMB No. 1615-0047, expires 08/31/12, www.uscis.gov/files/form/i-9.pdf.
380 *Omnibus Consolidated Appropriations Act, 1997*, Pub. L. 104-208, 110 Stat. 3009-664 (September 30, 1996) (incorporating the *Illegal Immigration Reform and Immigrant Responsibility Act* (IIRIRA)); USCIS, *Report to Congress on the Basic Pilot Program* (Washington, DC: USCIS, 2004), www.aila.org/content/default.aspx?bc=1016%7C6715%7C16871%7C18523%7C11260.
381 USCIS, "E-Verify History and Milestones," last updated April 5, 2012, www.uscis.gov/portal/site/uscis/menuitem.eb1d4c2a3e5b9ac89243c6a7543f6d1a/?vgnextoid=84979589cdb76210VgnVCM100000b92ca60aRCRD&vgnextchannel=84979589cdb76210VgnVCM100000b92ca60aRCRD.

security number, date of birth, citizenship, and alien registration number) of new hires into an online computer system.[382] The system scans the information against databases administered by the Social Security Administration (SSA) and DHS in order to determine whether the worker is authorized to work. If the database checks confirm that a worker is a US citizen or a noncitizen authorized to work, E-Verify notifies the employer. If work eligibility is not confirmed, the employer receives a "tentative nonconfirmation" (TNC). If a worker fails to correct the problem which led to the TNC within eight business days, the employer must terminate the worker.[383]

While E-Verify has existed since 1997, the program expanded rapidly during the mid-2000s, as follows:

- In December 2003, Congress passed the *Basic Pilot Program Extension and Expansion Act of 2003*, which required DHS to offer E-Verify enrollment to employers in all 50 states.[384]

- By 2006, more than 10,000 businesses had joined the program.[385] Also in 2006, several members of Congress began to advocate making E-Verify a mandatory program for all US employers. The Bush administration made mandatory E-Verify one of the five elements of its comprehensive immigration reform proposal.[386]

- In 2007, after Congress failed to pass a comprehensive immigration reform bill, the administration announced plans to pursue a series of enforcement-only immigration measures, including a push for the continued expansion of E-Verify.[387]

- In November 2008, the administration published a final rule requiring all federal contractors to participate in the program.[388]

By FY 2009, 157,000 employers had registered and the program had processed 8,172,000 queries.[389] In July 2009, the Obama administration announced that it would move ahead with plans to require federal contractors to participate in the program.[390]

In FY 2010, E-Verify processed more than 13 million queries,[391] and more than 17 million queries the following year.[392] Currently there are over 353,822 employers enrolled in the program (see Figure 12).[393] They account for less than 10 percent of the

---

382 Westat, *Findings of the E-Verify Program Evaluation* (Rockville, MD: Westat, 2009), www.uscis.gov/USCIS/E-Verify/E-Verify/Final%20E-Verify%20Report%2012-16-09_2.pdf.
383 Ibid.
384 *Basic Pilot Program Extension and Expansion Act*, Public Law 108-156, 117 Stat. 1944, 1944 (December 3, 2003).
385 DHS, *Budget-in-Brief FY 2008*, 74; USCIS, "E-Verify History and Milestones."
386 White House Office of the Press Secretary, "Basic Pilot: A Clear and Reliable Way to Verify Employment Eligibility," (fact sheet, July 5, 2006), www.swiftraid.org/media/articles/12-20-06BasicPilotFactSheet.pdf.
387 Remarks by Homeland Security Secretary Michael Chertoff and Commerce Secretary Carlos Gutierrez at a press conference on border security and administrative immigration reforms, Washington, DC, August 10, 2007, www.hsdl.org/?view&did=478615.
388 Federal Acquisition Regulation, FAR Case 2007-013 Employment Eligibility Verification, 73 *Federal Register* 221, 67651 (November 14, 2008), http://edocket.access.gpo.gov/2008/pdf/E8-26904.pdf.
389 USCIS, "E-Verify History and Milestones."
390 DHS, "Secretary Napolitano Strengthens Employment Verification with Administration's Commitment to E-Verify," (press release, July 8, 2009), www.dhs.gov/ynews/releases/pr_1247063976814.shtm.
391 USCIS, "E-Verify History and Milestones."
392 Ibid.
393 Ibid.

current number of business firms and establishments in the United States.[394]

Figure 12. Employers Participating in E-Verify and Number of Cases Screened, FY 1997-2011

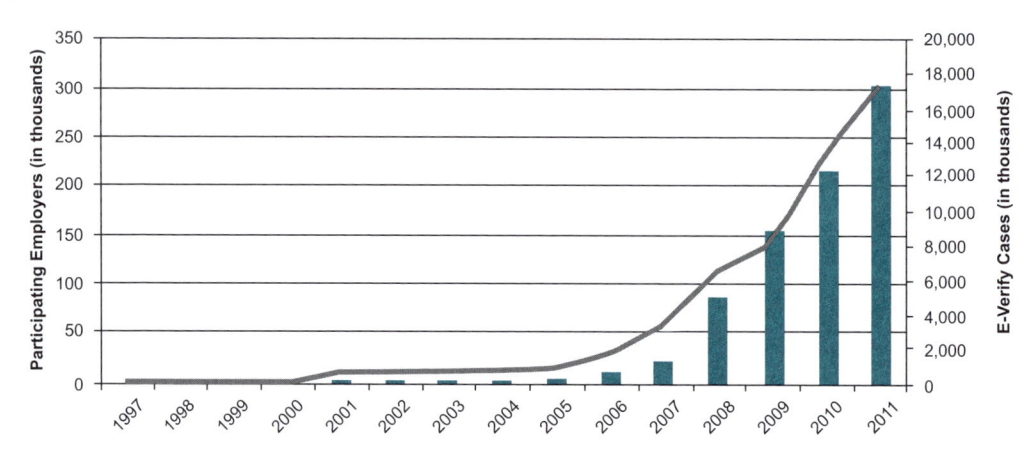

Source: Marc R. Rosenblum, *E-Verify: Strengths, Weaknesses, and Proposals for Reform* (Washington, DC: MPI, 2011), www.migrationpolicy.org/pubs/E-Verify-Insight.pdf.

---

394 The US Census Bureau defines a business establishment as a "single physical location where business is conducted or where services or industrial operations are performed." In contrast, a firm is defined as a "business organization consisting of one or more domestic establishments in the same state and industry that were specified under common ownership and/or control." According to the Census Bureau, there were 7.4 million private nonfarm business establishments in 2009, and 5.8 million business firms. US Census Bureau, "Statistics of U.S. Businesses (SUSB) Main, U.S. & States, Total," www.census.gov/econ/susb/.

> **Box 1. Counting E-Verify Employers**
>
> USCIS reports show that there are currently 353,822 employers enrolled in E-Verify. It is difficult to calculate the exact percentage of all US employers enrolled in E-Verify, both because of the way in which employers enroll in E-Verify and because of the way in which the US Census Bureau calculates the total number of employers in the country.
>
> The Census Bureau issues a count of the number of business "establishments" and "firms" in the country, rather than of "employers." It defines an establishment as a "single physical location where business is conducted or where services or industrial operations are performed." In contrast, a firm is defined as a "business organization consisting of one or more domestic establishments in the same state and industry that were specified under common ownership and/or control."
>
> USCIS defines employer as "any U.S. company, corporation, or business entity that is required to complete an I-9 employment eligibility verification form." All employers enrolling with E-Verify must complete a Memorandum of Understanding (MOU), which details the responsibilities of the employer and USCIS in participating in the program. However, employers with multiple worksites are permitted either to sign one MOU on behalf of their entire company, or to sign multiple MOUs for each worksite. In addition, an employer that signs an MOU enrolling the company in E-Verify may opt not to have all worksite locations participate.
>
> Thus, the total number of employers participating in E-Verify does not precisely correspond with either the total number of participating business firms or establishments.

1. State E-Verify Laws

Although Congress has failed to mandate E-Verify, a handful of states have enacted E-Verify legislation of their own. Colorado passed the first such law in 2006, requiring all public contract recipients to participate in E-Verify. An Idaho law passed in 2006 requires participation by all government contractors.[395] In 2007, Arizona became the first state to require all public and private employers to participate in the program, when it enacted the *Legal Arizona Workers Act* (LAWA). The same year, Illinois passed a measure forbidding participation in E-Verify, prompting the federal government to bring a lawsuit challenging the action. In March 2009, a federal judge struck down the Illinois law as unconstitutional.[396]

In 2011, the US Supreme Court, in *Chamber of Commerce v. Whiting*, upheld the *Legal Arizona Workers Act*, holding that it was not pre-empted by federal law. The court reasoned that although IIRIRA prohibits the federal government from making participation in E-Verify mandatory, it does not forbid states from doing so, and that LAWA's provisions were designed to act in concert with federal law.[397]

There are now 19 states that require all or some employers to participate in E-Verify.[398] Many of these state laws — even those that technically apply to all employers — exempt some discrete categories of workers, and apply to new hires only.

---

395 Marc R. Rosenblum, *E-Verify: Strengths, Weaknesses, and Proposals for Reform* (Washington, DC: MPI, 2011): 3, www.migrationpolicy.org/pubs/E-Verify-Insight.pdf.
396 *United States v. Illinois,* United States District Court for the Central District of Illinois #07-3261 (March 12, 2009), http://op.bna.com/dlrcases.nsf/id/jcwl-7q9mhj/$File/United%20States%20v.%20Illinois%20Op.pdf.
397 *Chamber of Commerce v. Whiting*, 131 S. Ct. 1968, 1985-86 (2011).
398 ImmigrationWorksUSA, "At a Glance: State E-Verify Laws," last updated July 2012, www.immigrationworksusa.org/index.php?p=110.

2. Improvements and Unresolved Issues in E-Verify

A frequent criticism during the program's early years centered on the accuracy and integrity of the databases used by E-Verify. Inaccuracies resulted in both false positive and false negative errors.

False positives — the erroneous confirmation of an unauthorized worker as work authorized — enable someone to work who is not actually authorized to do so. Such errors occur mostly because E-Verify can validate a person's eligibility to work, but does not have the capability to tie an individual's identity to work eligibility.

False negatives — the failure to confirm an authorized worker — can deprive a worker of the opportunity to be hired. False negatives are the result of outdated, missing, inconsistent, or incorrect information stored in federal databases or entered during an E-Verify check, due to employee, employer, or government error. A false negative generates a TNC notice to the employer.

DHS has launched several initiatives aimed at improving the accuracy of E-Verify screening. In 2009, it introduced automatic checks against passport records; in 2010, it established a hotline for employees to register concerns about the program, and in 2011, it developed a "self- check" feature.[399] The self-check feature enables intending job applicants to query the E-Verify system themselves prior to applying for a job to determine whether a TNC would be issued and clear up possible data discrepancies in advance of an employer check.[400]

Recent reports suggest that substantial progress has been made in reducing E-Verify error rates. According to GAO, DHS reduced the percentage of cases receiving TNCs from 8 percent in 2007 to 2.6 percent in 2009.[401] USCIS's own report suggests that in FY 2011, 1.7 percent of cases received a TNC. Of those, 83 percent (1.39 percent of total E-Verify cases) were ultimately not found to be work authorized; a large majority of employees did not contest those nonconfirmations.[402]

Westat, an independent consulting firm hired by DHS to evaluate the program's effectiveness during various stages of implementation, estimated that between April-June 2008, 0.5 percent of workers who were ultimately found to be work eligible were initially flagged for TNCs.[403] The Westat report notes, however, that it is difficult to calculate the number of erroneous TNCs, since errors can be uncovered only if a worker actively takes steps to correct database information or otherwise notifies SSA or DHS of an error. Many do not take this step.[404]

---

399 USCIS, "USCIS Adds Passport Data in E-Verify Process for Foreign-Born Citizens," (press release, March 4, 2009), www.uscis.gov/portal/site/uscis/menuitem.5af9bb95919f35e66f614176543f6d1a/?vgnextoid=b33c436d5f2df110VgnVCM1000004718190aRCRD&vgnextchannel=c94e6d26d17df110VgnVCM1000004718190aRCRD; USCIS, "DHS Unveils Initiatives to Enhance E-Verify," (fact sheet, March 18, 2010), www.uscis.gov/portal/site/uscis/menuitem.5af9bb95919f35e66f614176543f6d1a/?vgnextoid=70beadd907c67210VgnVCM100000082ca60aRCRD&vgnextchannel=de779589cdb76210VgnVCM100000b92ca60aRCRD; USCIS, "Transcript: Press Conference on E-Verify Self-Check," (press conference, Washington, DC, March 22, 2011), www.uscis.gov/USCIS/News/Transcript_SelfCheckSecrtry.pdf.

400 USCIS, "Self-Check Background," last updated February 9, 2012, www.uscis.gov/portal/site/uscis/menuitem.eb1d4c2a3e5b9ac89243c6a7543f6d1a/?vgnextoid=bc417cd67450d210VgnVCM100000082ca60aRCRD&vgnextchannel=bc417cd67450d210VgnVCM100000082ca60aRCRD.

401 Richard M. Stana, *Employment Verification: Federal Agencies Have Taken Steps to Improve E-Verify, But Significant Challenges Remain* (Washington, DC: GAO, 2010): 16, www.gao.gov/new.items/d11146.pdf.

402 USCIS, "E-Verify Statistics and Reports," last updated June 7, 2012, www.uscis.gov/portal/site/uscis/menuitem.eb1d4c2a3e5b9ac89243c6a7543f6d1a/?vgnextoid=7c579589cdb76210VgnVCM100000b92ca60aRCRD&vgnextchannel=7c579589cdb76210VgnVCM100000b92ca60aRCRD.

403 Westat, *Findings of the E-Verify Program Evaluation*, 57.

404 Rosenblum, *E-Verify: Strengths, Weaknesses, and Proposals for Reform*, 7.

Like the I-9 system overall, E-Verify fails to identify unauthorized workers who present the identification documents of authorized workers (false positives). According to Westat, between April-June 2008, 54 percent of the unauthorized workers who submitted biographic information through E-Verify were incorrectly confirmed as work authorized, mostly due to the program's limited ability to detect identity fraud.[405]

While DHS has launched a number of initiatives aimed at stemming identity fraud, including a photo tool that enables employers to compare government-stored digital photographs with the photographs on identity documents presented by workers, these initiatives have thus far had limited success. DHS has the capacity to employ photo-matching for only certain kinds of photos, such as the digital photos used on green cards and employment authorization cards. As a result, of the 14.9 million cases run through the E-Verify system between October 2009 and August 2010, photo matching was able to be used in fewer than 400,000.[406]

In January 2009, Homeland Security Secretary Napolitano issued an action directive calling for a department-wide assessment of a number of key immigration programs, including E-Verify.[407] The directive asked E-Verify program officials to report on strategies to minimize false positives and false negatives.[408] The results have not been made public. However, DHS has continued to build and improve E-Verify and promote employer participation. Though enrollment has increased, partly due to the growing number of state E-Verify laws, it is not mandatory for the vast majority of employers.

B. Shift in Worksite Enforcement Policy

Although claiming a small share of the ICE budget, worksite enforcement became one of the most visible and controversial symbols of the Bush administration's immigration policy actions. A series of large, high-profile raids (or worksite actions, as they were termed) were carried out against some well-known companies, such as Swift & Company and Agriprocessors, Inc. These actions resulted in the arrest and deportation of thousands of unauthorized workers, as well as hundreds of criminal prosecutions for identity fraud and aggravated identity fraud.[409]

The Obama administration changed worksite enforcement strategies dramatically. In a memo issued April 30, 2009, it announced that it would focus efforts on employers who hire unauthorized immigrants, rather than on unauthorized workers themselves. Since then, it has shifted from large-scale actions that netted mostly unauthorized workers to auditing employer compliance with verification requirements and targeting scofflaw employers for civil fines and criminal prosecution.

If ICE determines that an employer has violated the law and should be fined, it issues a Notice of Intent to Fine (NIF). NIFs may result in final orders for monetary penalties, settlements, or case dismissals. Employers who have engaged in a pattern or practice of knowingly hiring unauthorized immigrants can also be criminally prosecuted. However, building a criminal case against an employer — especially proving a knowing violation of the law — can be very difficult.

As a result of the policy shift, between FY 2008-09, the total number of administrative arrests of workers by ICE in its worksite enforcement operations fell from 5,184 to

---

405 Westat, *Findings of the E-Verify Program Evaluation*, 117.
406 Stana, *Employment Verification: Federal Agencies Have Taken Steps to Improve E-Verify, But Significant Challenges Remain*, 22.
407 DHS, "Secretary Napolitano Issues Immigration and Border Security Action Directive," (news release, January 30, 2009), www.dhs.gov/ynews/releases/pr_1233353528835.shtm.
408 Ibid.
409 Meissner and Kerwin, *DHS and Immigration: Taking Stock and Correcting Course*, 32.

1,647.[410] The number of criminal arrests at workplaces also declined, from 1,103 in FY 2008 to 444 in FY 2009, and 448 in FY 2010.[411]

In FY 2008, ICE conducted 503 I-9 audits and debarred one employer from participating in federal contracts. In contrast, since January 2009, ICE has audited more than 8,079 employers and debarred 726 companies and individuals.[412] ICE has announced sanctions against several high-profile targets, including a $1 million settlement with Abercrombie & Fitch and the termination of hundreds of workers from Chipotle restaurants.[413]

Bringing criminal charges against high-level managers of businesses that persistently violate the law is widely believed to operate as an effective deterrent against violating workplace laws. A CRS study of company employees arrested by ICE on criminal charges during worksite enforcement operations in FY 2009 found that of the 403 employees for whom employment information was available, 289 were non-managerial, while 114 were owners, managers, and corporate officials.[414] This represented a decline in the total number of managerial employees arrested on criminal charges during worksite enforcement operations between FY 2008-09.[415] The trend may be attributable to fewer worksite raids overall. However, in FY 2010, ICE reported an increase in arrests (196) of managerial staff. These arrests comprised more than half of all ICE criminal arrests for worksite violations (51 percent) in FY 2010, compared to 28 percent in FY 2009.[416]

According to CRS, the number of final orders assessing civil monetary penalties through worksite enforcement operations increased significantly from 18 in FY 2008 to 237 in FY 2010, as did the total amounts of administrative fines collected and criminal fines imposed.[417] (See Figure 13.) Thus, the policy shift has shown concrete results in targeting employers rather than unauthorized workers, for their hiring practices, which was the goal of the sanctions provisions of IRCA.

---

410 Andorra Bruno, *Immigration-Related Worksite Enforcement: Performance Measures* (Washington, DC: CRS, March 1, 2011): 7, http://assets.opencrs.com/rpts/R40002_20110301.pdf.
411 Ibid.
412 Written testimony of Homeland Security Secretary Janet Napolitano before the House Committee on the Judiciary, *Oversight of the Department of Homeland Security*, 112th Cong., 2nd sess., July 19, 2012, www.dhs.gov/ynews/testimony/20120719-s1-dhs-oversight-hjc.shtm.
413 ICE, "Abercrombie and Fitch Fined after I-9 Audit," (press release, September 28, 2010), www.ice.gov/news/releases/1009/100928detroit.htm; Lisa Baertlein, "Federal Agents Widen Chipotle Immigration Probe," Reuters, May 4, 2011, www.reuters.com/article/2011/05/04/us-chipotle-idUSTRE74307S20110504.
414 Bruno, *Immigration-Related Worksite Enforcement: Performance Measures*, 8.
415 Ibid., 7. ICE estimated that it made 135 arrests of managerial employees through worksite enforcement operations during FY 2008.
416 Bruno, *Worksite Enforcement: Performance Measures*, 8.
417 Ibid., 6, 10.

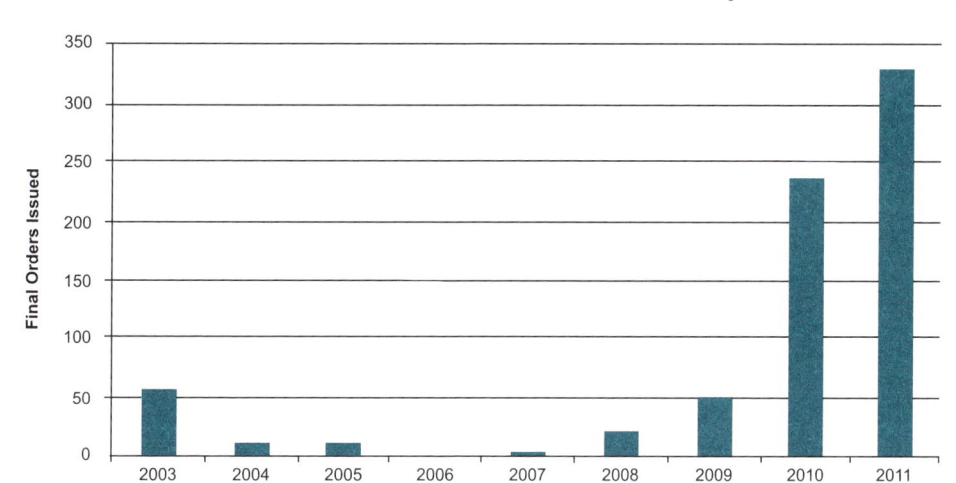

Figure 13. Final Orders for Worksite Enforcement Civil Monetary Penalties, FY 2003-11*

* 2011 data are through September 17, 2011.

Sources: Andorra Bruno, *Immigration-Related Worksite Enforcement Performance Measures* (Washington, DC: CRS, 2012), www.fas.org/sgp/crs/homesec/R40002.pdf; Statement of Kumar Kibble, Deputy Director, US Immigration and Customs Enforcement, before the House Subcommittee on Border and Maritime Security, *Does Administrative Amnesty Harm Our Efforts to Gain and Maintain Operational Control of the Border*, 112th Cong., 1st sess., October 4, 2011, http://homeland.house.gov/sites/homeland.house.gov/files/Testimony%20Kibble_0.pdf.

C. Labor Standards Enforcement

Low-wage immigrants, particularly the unauthorized, are highly concentrated in certain industries that have traditionally experienced substantial labor standards violations. In addition, some employers exploit the fear of deportation to discourage unauthorized immigrants from reporting violations of law and protesting substandard conditions.

Exploitation of unauthorized workers by unscrupulous employers drives down wages and working conditions for all workers, and gives such employers a competitive advantage.[418] Thus, effective labor standards enforcement benefits immigrants, US workers, and law-abiding businesses. However, it has received far fewer resources than other federal enforcement priorities. For example, the FY 2010 combined budgets for three main federal labor standards regulatory agencies was $1.1 billion, making it a modest investment compared to the $17.2 billion budgets for DHS' two immigration enforcement agencies.[419]

The Wage and Hour Division (WHD) of the Department of Labor (DOL) has the lead responsibility for important elements of labor standards enforcement. For FY 2013, the administration has sought a budget increase of $10.7 million for the division, over its FY 2012 total of approximately $227 million.[420] Even with that increase, the division would only have 1,112 investigators to enforce labor laws that cover 135 million workers and

---

[418] White House Office of the Press Secretary, "Remarks by the President on Comprehensive Immigration Reform in El Paso, Texas," (lecture, El Paso, TX, May 10, 2011), www.whitehouse.gov/the-press-office/2011/05/10/remarks-president-comprehensive-immigration-reform-el-paso-texas.

[419] Donald M. Kerwin with Kristen McCabe, *Labor Standards Enforcement and Low-Wage Immigrants: Creating an Effective Enforcement System* (Washington, DC: MPI, 2011): 45, www.migrationpolicy.org/pubs/laborstandards-2011.pdf.

[420] US Department of Labor (DOL), *FY 2013 Congressional Budget Justification: Wage and Hour Division* (Washington, DC: DOL, 2012), www.dol.gov/dol/budget/2013/PDF/CBJ-2013-V2-09.pdf.

7.3 million business establishments.[421] Given the scope of WHD's responsibilities and its modest budget, its priority must, therefore, be to increase voluntary employer compliance, deter violations, and target the most egregious violators of the law.

WHD has become increasingly sophisticated at identifying industries and industry sectors that violate the law at high rates, and at measuring the deterrent effect of its strategies.[422]

WHD has found, for example, that the geographic proximity of enforcement activities, frequency, type of enforcement, and the prominence of the target all influence compliance.[423] It seeks to create a continuous learning-and-enforcement cycle, aimed at deterring violations and promoting widespread compliance.

WHD has particularly targeted fissured industries, which rely extensively on subcontracting, franchising, third-party management, and self-employed contractors. In fissured industries, the dominant employer may be a buyer at the end of a supply chain (e.g. Walmart), a brand-name franchisor (e.g. McDonald's), a central production coordinator (such as national home builder corporations), or a purchaser of services from multiple entities (e.g. building owners).

WHD's research underscores the importance of:

- identifying the lead or dominant entities in fissured industries
- learning which employers "watch" each other and, thus, which employers to target within industries and subsets of industries
- learning how they watch each other, whether through trade journals, membership associations, publicity, or word of mouth in order to publicize enforcement actions
- enlisting the support of lead agencies that can enforce or influence compliance by other entities.

Like CBP and ICE, WHD had traditionally reported on a range of level-of-effort and resource metrics.[424] However, its new direction for targeting scarce resources is a good example of using metrics to heighten deterrence and compliance.

WHD and ICE Cooperation

A pressing labor standards enforcement issue for WHD involves its coordination with ICE. Immigration and labor laws have distinct goals, and enforcement of one set of laws should complement or, at least, not undermine the goals of the other. Like any effective regulatory agency, WHD relies on the cooperation of those most at risk of violations.

---

421 DOL, *FY 2013 Congressional Budget Justification: Wage and Hour Division* (Washington, DC: DOL, February 13, 2012): 13, 17, 19, www.dol.gov/dol/budget/2013/PDF/CBJ-2013-V2-09.pdf.

422 MPI in 2011 released a comprehensive analysis of federal and state labor standards enforcement, with a particular focus on unauthorized immigrants and the enforcement strategies of DOL/Wage and Hour Division (WHD). See Kerwin, *Labor Standards Enforcement and Low-Wage Immigrants*. The report identifies gaps and anomalies in protection in the core federal labor laws: the *Fair Labor Standards Act* (FLSA), which covers minimum wage, overtime, and child labor, and is administered by WHD; the *National Labor Relations Act* (NLRA), which safeguards union organizing and collective bargaining; and the *Occupational Safety and Health Act* (OSHA) which covers safe and healthy workplaces. The report also highlights several DOL goals and strategies that could inform immigration enforcement efforts. Finally, it discusses the need to harmonize ICE and WHD worksite enforcement initiatives.

423 Kerwin, *Labor Standards Enforcement and Low-Wage Immigrants*, 35-6.

424 These include back wages collected, number of employees receiving back wages, complaints registered, concluded cases, WHD-initiated enforcement actions, FLSA registered/concluded cases, civil monetary penalties assessed, and number of WHD investigators.

However, low-wage immigrants, and particularly those who are unauthorized, are reluctant to cooperate with enforcement agencies if to do so may lead to their deportation or the removal of their family members. As a result, DOL and INS/DHS have long operated under formal working arrangements that recognize that their respective missions require distinct and coordinated enforcement tactics.

In 1998, for example, INS and DOL's Employment Standards Administration entered a MOU to coordinate their work and to improve enforcement of both sets of laws.[425] The MOU identified several shared goals:

- reduce unauthorized employment and its adverse impact on the wages and working conditions of US workers by increasing compliance with employment verification requirements

- reduce the incentives to employ unauthorized immigrants and the resulting negative effects on the job opportunities, wages, and working conditions of US workers by increasing compliance with labor standards

- prevent the exploitation of unauthorized workers by employers that threaten to report their employees to immigration officials for exercising their labor rights

- promote employment opportunities for US workers by improving wages, benefits, and working conditions.

On March 31, 2011, DHS and DOL entered a MOU that superseded the earlier agreement, but updated and affirmed its broad goals and principles. The revised MOU seeks to prevent conflicts between DHS and DOL in their civil worksite enforcement activities, to advance their respective missions, and to insulate enforcement from "inappropriate manipulation by other parties."[426]

Under the MOU, ICE must assess whether tips and leads it receives related to immigration violations involve worksites with pending labor disputes or "are motivated by an improper desire to manipulate a pending labor dispute, retaliate against workers for exercising their labor rights, or otherwise frustrate the enforcement of labor laws."

Under the MOU, in cases involving immigration enforcement during a labor dispute, ICE must:

- notify DOL of its activities unless to do so would violate a federal law or would compromise an ICE investigation

- produce detainees for interviews with DOL, provided it does not interfere with or delay removal proceedings

- consider DOL requests to provide temporary immigration status (parole or deferred action) to unauthorized immigrants needed as witnesses in DOL investigations.

The MOU commits the agencies to exchange information on "abusive employment practices against workers regardless of status" and on violations of labor standards, human smuggling and trafficking, child exploitation, and extortion or forced labor. It also creates a joint committee to address implementation issues, and requires DHS and DOL to notify and train their employees on its requirements.

---

425 Kerwin, *Labor Standards Enforcement and Low-Wage Immigrants*, 37.
426 DOL and DHS, "Revised Memorandum of Understanding Between the Departments of Homeland Security and Labor Concerning Enforcement Activities at Worksites (effective March 31, 2011)," www.electronici9.com/wp-content/uploads/2011/04/Revised-MOU-between-DHS-and-DOL.pdf.

In addition to the MOUs, an INS Operation Instruction (OI 287.3a) of December 1996 was issued to ensure that immigration officers do not knowingly get involved in a labor dispute between employers and workers. It directs enforcement officers to take various steps to ascertain that a labor dispute is not in progress before it conducts an enforcement operation pursuant to information regarding presence of unauthorized workers in a workplace.[427]

> *An unauthorized workforce of the current magnitude presents immense challenges to any workplace enforcement strategy. DHS and DOL have ably adjusted and improved their workplace enforcement programs, and E-Verify continues to serve as a rather unique experiment in testing and refining a program in anticipation of possible mandatory use. However, workplace enforcement is fundamentally hobbled by statutory weaknesses that date back to IRCA, and, in the case of labor standards, by resource deficiencies. Until these problems are addressed, employment enforcement will not realize its potential as an important pillar of the immigration enforcement system.*

II. Program Critiques and Findings

Although some have argued that the dramatic growth in the size of the unauthorized population until the recession was due to the failure by INS/DHS to control the border and enforce employer sanctions laws, most experts agree that the principal reason was strong labor market demand in a booming economy, combined with a legal immigration system that is not designed to sufficiently accommodate factors of labor supply and demand.

A. Electronic Verification

For E-Verify to be an effective tool in addressing unauthorized employment, it must be part of a broader policy reform that provides adequate avenues for noncitizens to enter the labor market legally. Only then will it become a broadly practiced and accepted norm upon hiring. This is critical since E-Verify enlists employers as a force multiplier in the effort to reduce illegal immigration. Given the number of US businesses (7.4 million), it is impossible for ICE to enforce the employer verification laws without broad employer buy-in, a straightforward method for compliance, and a significantly reduced unauthorized population.

Legislation would be required for this to happen, as there are substantial limits to what immigration enforcement agencies can accomplish under current law and realities. Nonetheless, the fact that Congress has continuously authorized E-Verify as a voluntary program and supported appropriations to fund it has provided an unusual opportunity for electronic employment verification to develop, grow, and improve, based on feedback from the experience of users — both employers and workers.

Despite significant improvements, E-Verify retains a fundamental vulnerability: an inability to detect unauthorized workers' fraudulent use of the documents of authorized workers. This weakness is because of the absence of a secure means for establishing the identity of those who present work-authorized documents.[428]

---

427 Revised INS Operation Instruction 287.3a (January 27, 1997) reprinted as Appendix IV in 74 *Interpreter Releases*, 199. OI 287.3a has been re-designated as 33.14(h) of the *Special Agent Field Manual* (SAFM) as of April 28, 2000.

428 Written statement of Richard M. Stana, Director, Homeland Security and Justice Issues, GAO, before the House Committee on the Judiciary, Subcommittee on Immigration, Citizenship, Border Security, and International Law, *Employment Verification, Challenges Exist in Implementing a Mandatory Electronic Employment Verification System*, 110th Cong., 2nd sess., June 10, 2008, www.gao.gov/new.items/d08895t.pdf.

There are also legitimate concerns regarding the risk of identity theft in the program and abuse of privacy, mainly because E-Verify allows more public and private administrators access to identification information. Because the program links employment more closely to valid social security numbers and associated biographic data, E-Verify increases the value of such information.[429]

In addition, studies have identified unlawful discriminatory practices by some participating employers. For instance, some employers screen applicants for employment eligibility before making an offer of employment.[430] Such practices not only deny the worker a job, but also the opportunity to contest database inaccuracies. Some employers assume that any worker issued a TNC is not work authorized and therefore restrict work assignments or hours, or alternatively, increase hours and provide substandard working conditions for employees contesting TNCs.[431] There are also concerns about employers using work authorization verification to retaliate against or threaten employees who lodge complaints about labor conditions.

Finally, E-Verify continues to generate a disproportionate number of erroneous TNCs for noncitizens, likely due to discrepancies in name spellings and name hyphenation in some cultural and ethnic groups that the databases have not been able to accommodate.[432]

For the system to work effectively, it must successfully address these vulnerabilities. USCIS has identified various techniques used in the credit-card industry and other sectors that grapple with similar challenges. A series of pilot projects to test some of these techniques could make important contributions to strengthening the system.

B. State Law Experiences

E-Verify laws enacted by states are proving to be a source of important lessons. Even in states that mandate the use of E-Verify by all employers, not all employers participate in the program. In part, this is due to the fact that state E-Verify laws typically require employers to confirm the work eligibility only for new hires; employers are not required to enroll in the program until they have made a new hire.

Nevertheless, research estimating the rate of participating E-Verify employers — both as a share of the state's total number of business establishments and firms[433] — reveals that there is substantial variance among the states in employer E-Verify participation.[434] In states where E-Verify is mandatory for all public and private employers (e.g. Alabama, Arizona, South Carolina, and Mississippi), an estimated 30 to 70 percent of employers with five or more employees currently participate in the program.[435] In the vast

---

429 Marc R. Rosenblum and Lang Hoyt, "The Basics of E-Verify, the US Employer Verification System," *Migration Information Source*, July 2011, www.migrationinformation.org/Feature/display.cfm?ID=846.
430 Temple University Institute of Survey Research and Westat, *Findings of Basic Program Evaluation* (prepared for USCIS, June 2002). See also, National Immigration Law Center (NILC), *Basic Information Brief: Employment Verification Programs—The Basic Pilot and SSNVS* (Washington, DC: NILC, 2005): 2, http://v2011.nilc.org/immsemplymnt/IWR_Material/Attorney/Employment_Verification_Systems_4-05.pdf.
431 Westat, *Findings of the Web Basic Pilot Evaluation* (Rockville, MD: Westat, 2007), www.uscis.gov/files/article/WebBasicPilotRprtSept2007.pdf.
432 Stana, *Employment Verification: Federal Agencies Have Taken Steps to Improve E-Verify, But Significant Challenges Remain*, 19.
433 See Appendix Table A-2.
434 The terms "firm" and "establishment" are used by the Census Bureau to track the number of employers within each state. Appendix Table A-2 explains the definitions of these terms and the methodology MPI employed to calculate the percentage of employers participating in E-Verify.
435 See Appendix Table A-2. Because employers with multiple worksites are permitted to enroll in E-Verify once on behalf of their entire business, or multiple times for each worksite, MPI calculated the percentage of employers participating in E-Verify in each state as a share of each state's business firms and establishments.

majority of states, the percentage of employers participating in E-Verify is far smaller. In eight states, less than 5 percent of employers with five or more employees currently participate in E-Verify.[436] These low levels of participation point to the need for employer education and aggressive monitoring of the program's use should E-Verify become a national mandate.

E-Verify state mandates may also lead to increased informal employment. A March 2011 study by the Public Policy Institute of California concluded that between 2007 and 2009, Arizona's mandatory E-Verify law (LAWA) led to a substantial increase in self-employment (the E-Verify requirement does not apply to the self-employed) by "likely" unauthorized immigrants.[437]

In the two years following LAWA's passage, employment rates of likely unauthorized wage and salaried workers in Arizona were 11 to 12 percent lower than in comparison states without such laws.[438] In addition, Arizona experienced an 8 percent increase in self-employment for likely unauthorized workers over the same period. This is far higher than in comparable states.[439] These findings suggest that employers continue to find ways to hire unauthorized workers, even in states where electronic verification has been mandated.

C. Labor Standards Enforcement

Notwithstanding increased resources, innovative enforcement strategies, and better interagency coordination, the enforcement of labor standards for unauthorized workers remains a challenge. Many unauthorized workers, fearing immigration consequences, are reluctant to bring complaints against their employers.

Even in cases where they do and employers are found violating their labor rights, unauthorized workers are ineligible for the two most significant remedies that can be granted by the National Labor Relations Administration (NLRA). Wrongfully terminated unauthorized workers cannot be reinstated to their jobs. And, following the 2002 decision by the Supreme Court in the Hoffman Plastics case, they do not qualify for back pay.[440] These compromised remedies give certain employers a perverse incentive to hire unauthorized workers.[441]

Effective labor standards enforcement requires federal and state labor agencies to identify and target the industries and firms that habitually violate the law. While there is widespread agreement that unauthorized immigrants are vulnerable to abuse, there is surprisingly little research that systematically compares employers that violate labor standards with those that violate employer verification (i.e. immigration) requirements. Thus, there is no conclusive evidence — one way or the other — on whether employers who hire unauthorized workers are overall more likely than other employers to violate labor standards.

However, there is strong evidence that low-wage immigrants work at high rates in particular industries and firms that substantially violate labor laws. Research that compares industries and industry sectors that violate both labor standards and employer verification laws would benefit both ICE and WHD strategic planning.

---

436 Ibid.
437 Magnus Lofstrom, Sarah Bohn, and Steven Raphael, *Lessons from the 2007 Legal Arizona Workers Act* (San Francisco: Public Policy Institute of California, 2011): 25, www.ppic.org/main/publication.asp?i=915. For the purposes of assessing employment changes, the report used noncitizen Hispanic men ages 16 to 60, who had a high school diploma or less, as its proxy for unauthorized workers.
438 Ibid., 24.
439 Ibid., 25.
440 *Hoffman Plastic Compounds, Inc. v. Nat'l Labor Relations Board*, 535 U.S. 137 (2002).
441 See 535 U.S. at 155. (Breyer, J., dissenting).

Taken together, immigration enforcement agencies in both DHS and DOL are demonstrating initiative and implementing programs that could result in robust employer accountability if scaled up, were new immigration measures were enacted by Congress. In particular, there is evidence now, at least in the formal sector of the economy, that E-Verify can serve as an effective tool for employer compliance.

But to be fully effective, E-Verify must incorporate better identity-verification methods, cover a far larger, national pool of employers, and be coupled with a legalization program or programs that would reduce the size of the unauthorized workforce. These conditions would significantly decrease the likelihood that unauthorized workers whose employment was terminated would be able to obtain employment with other employers that did not use E-Verify or that preferred to hire unauthorized workers to gain an advantage over competitors.[442] In any event, E-Verify will not solve the problems of unauthorized workers in the informal or underground sector of the economy.

---

442 Westat, *Findings of the E-Verify Program Evaluation.*

■ FINDINGS

■ **Though voluntary, E-Verify is being deployed** at a fast pace in US workplaces and is becoming more widely accepted. As of April 2012, more than 353,000 employers were enrolled in the program. In FY 2011, E-Verify processed more than 17.4 million queries. Even with this increase in enrollment, the program still covers less than 10 percent of all US employers. Were it to become a universal requirement, the program would have to reach more than 7 million employers, 154.6 million workers, and process more than 44 million hiring decisions each year.

■ **Seventeen states have enacted separate E-Verify laws** that require all or some categories of employers to participate in the program. Implementation of the *Legal Arizona Workers Act*, the first state statute that mandated participation by all employers, has led to a growth in the underground economy and decreased wages for unauthorized workers. Despite the mandate, just 71.9 percent of firms in Arizona are enrolled in E-Verify.

■ **ICE has shifted its employer enforcement strategy** from worksite raids that focus on persons working illegally to audits of unlawful hiring violations by employers. Between FY 2008-09, the number of administrative arrests by ICE during worksite enforcement operations fell from 5,184 to 1,647. The number of criminal arrests also declined, from 1,103 to 444. In 2008, ICE conducted 503 I-9 audits and debarred one employer from federal contracts. In comparison, since January 2009, ICE has audited more than 8,079 employers, debarred 726 companies, and imposed more than $87.9 million in monetary fines for violating employer sanctions laws.

CHAPTER 7

THE INTERSECTION OF THE CRIMINAL JUSTICE SYSTEM AND IMMIGRATION ENFORCEMENT

One of the most important developments of the last two decades has been the interplay between immigration enforcement and the criminal justice system. Noncitizens today — lawful permanent residents (LPRs), temporary visitors, and unauthorized immigrants — encounter the criminal justice system in unprecedented numbers and situations. This phenomenon represents a profound change that constitutes a potent new pillar of the immigration enforcement system. The increasing interconnectedness between these two formerly distinct law enforcement systems, combined with increased resources, congressionally mandated priorities, and enforcement programs are responsible for placing ever larger numbers of noncitizens into pipelines for emoval.

Five developments have contributed to this trend:

- More immigration violations have been redefined as federal crimes

- New initiatives and funding target these immigration crimes for prosecution

- An increased number of state and federal crimes carry the automatic consequence of removal

- Immigration judges have lost discretion to weigh equitable considerations in recommending relief from removal in cases of noncitizens with criminal records

- New programs, information systems, and resources funnel criminal suspects into the immigration enforcement system, increasingly with state and local law enforcement participation.

I. Programs and Results

US immigration law has historically provided for the exclusion and deportation of noncitizens who have engaged in criminal activity. But until recently, removal of noncitizens for criminal activity was limited to those who had been convicted of serious or violent criminal offenses.

The picture changed radically beginning with the *Anti-Drug Abuse Act of 1988*, the *Antiterrorism and Effective Death Penalty Act of 1996* (AEDPA)[443] and the *Illegal Immigration Reform and Immigrant Responsibility Act of 1996* (IIRIRA).[444] As a result of these laws, the

---

[443] *Anti-Terrorism and Effective Death Penalty Act (AEDPA)* Pub. L. No. 104-32, 110 Stat. 1214, 104th Cong, 2nd sess. (April 24, 1996).
[444] *Omnibus Consolidated Appropriations Act, 1997*, Pub. L. 104-208, 110 Stat. 3009-664 (September 30, 1996) (incorporating the *Illegal Immigration Reform and Immigrant Responsibility Act*).

prosecution of immigration crimes and the number of state and federal crimes leading to removal has vastly expanded, the discretion of immigration judges to suspend the removal of noncitizens based on their equitable ties in the United States has diminished, and the categories of noncitizens subject to mandatory detention have grown.

A. Increase in Immigration Crimes and Prosecutions

Immigration offenses have historically been treated as violations of civil law, leading (at worst) to removal/deportation from the country. That is why many constitutionally guaranteed protections accorded in criminal proceedings do not apply in most immigration proceedings. However, in recent years, Congress has transformed more formerly civil immigration violations into crimes and has increased the penalties for long-standing immigration crimes.[445]

In addition, in the past, INS/DHS and, in particular the Border Patrol, mostly referred only egregious immigration violators for prosecution, e.g. noncitizens who re-entered the country following removal for a criminal offense[446] or those charged with felony immigration or drug offenses.[447] Although less serious offenses such as illegal entry have long been criminal offenses,[448] they were overwhelmingly treated as civil violations.[449]

I. Unprecedented Growth in Numbers of Prosecutions

Over the last decade, the number of criminal prosecutions for immigration-related violations has grown at an unprecedented rate. The two most heavily prosecuted immigration crimes by US attorneys have been illegal entry (a misdemeanor) and illegal re-entry following removal (a felony).[450] They comprise more than 90 percent of immigration-related prosecutions.[451] Both are charges generally referred by border enforcement officials. Between FY 2000-10, the number of aliens prosecuted for illegal entry rose more than tenfold (from 3,900 to 43,700), while the number prosecuted for illegal re-entry following removal more than tripled (from 7,900 to 35,800).[452] In FY 2011, there were 39,305 prosecutions for illegal entry,[453] representing 48 percent of all immigration charges filed, and 36,040 prosecutions for illegal re-entry, representing 44 percent of all immigration charges filed.[454]

---

445 Kerwin, *Chaos on the US-Mexico Border*, 4, 45-9.
446 Ibid., 45.
447 Ibid., 48.
448 *Immigration and Nationality Act*, Pub. L. 82-414, 66 Stat. 163, 229 (the *"McCarran-Walter Act"*) (June 27, 1952), Sec. 275 ("Any alien who (1) enters the United States at any time or place other than as designated by immigration officers, or (2) eludes examination or inspection by immigration officers, or (3) obtains entry to the United States by a willfully false or misleading representation or the willful concealment of a material fact, shall, for the first commission of any such offenses, be guilty of a misdemeanor...").
449 In 1993, for example, federal prosecutors brought just 801 cases for illegal entry, even though INS apprehended 1,327,259 noncitizens during that fiscal year. See TRAC, "Going Deeper" tool records for federal criminal enforcement, "Prosecutions for 8 USC 1325, Entry of an Alien at Improper Time or Place," http://tracfed.syr.edu/trachelp/tools/help_tools_godeep.shtml; INS, 1993 *Statistical Yearbook of the Immigration and Naturalization Service* (Washington, DC: INS, 1994): 158. In contrast, in FY 2010, prosecutors filed 43,688 charges of illegal entry. See TRAC, "Going Deeper" tool, "Prosecutions for 8 USC 1325, Entry of an Alien at Improper Time and Place."
450 TRAC, *Immigration Prosecutions for 2011* (Syracuse, NY: TRAC, 2011), http://tracfed.syr.edu/results/9x754ec2fef8ab.html.
451 Ibid; Donald Kerwin and Kristen McCabe, "Arrested on Entry: Operation Streamline and the Prosecution of Immigration Crimes," *Migration Information Source*, April 2010, www.migrationinformation.org/Feature/display.cfm?ID=780.
452 TRAC, "Graphical Highlights Immigration: Lead Charges for Criminal Immigration Prosecutions FY 1986 – FY 2011," http://trac.syr.edu/immigration/reports/251/include/imm_charges.html.
453 TRAC, "Going Deeper" tool, "Federal Criminal Enforcement, FY 2011."
454 Ibid.

Such prosecutions have also increased dramatically as a percentage of total federal prosecutions for all crimes. Between FY 2000-03, prosecutions for immigration offenses accounted for between 17 and 21 percent of the total number of federal criminal prosecutions.[455] By FY 2004, immigration prosecutions accounted for 31.7 percent of all federal prosecutions.[456] Immigration prosecutions jumped to more than 50 percent of all federal prosecutions between FY 2008-10[457] and remained there in FY 2011.[458]

An insight into this trend comes from a different set of numbers. Immigration-related crimes now constitute the third-largest category of crimes — following drug and traffic offenses — committed by criminal aliens (see Figure 14).[459] Nearly 20 percent of criminal aliens removed from the United States in 2010 had been convicted of immigration-related crimes only.[460] Between FY 1998-2009, the number of people entering federal prison who had been charged with an immigration offense increased by 131 percent, from 9,762 to 22,563.[461] In FY 2010, that number fell slightly to 21,520.[462]

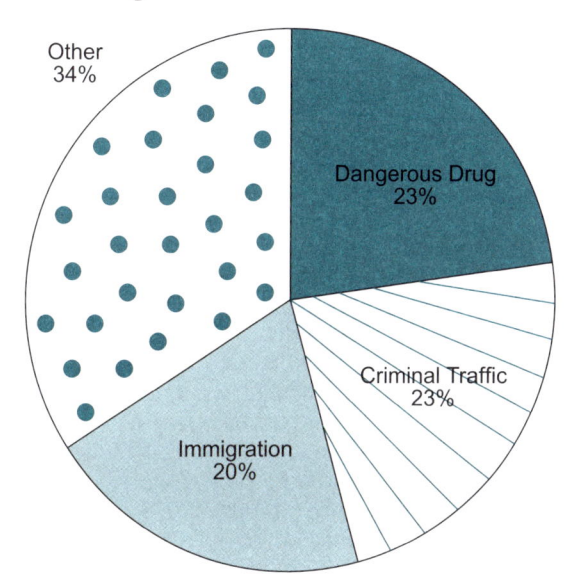

Figure 14. Leading Crime Categories of Convicted Criminal Aliens Removed, FY 2011

- Other 34%
- Dangerous Drug 23%
- Criminal Traffic 23%
- Immigration 20%

Notes: Dangerous drug crimes include the manufacturing, distribution, sale, and possession of illegal drugs; and immigration crimes include entry and re-entry, false claims to citizenship, and alien smuggling.

Source: John Simanski and Lesley M. Sapp, *Immigration Enforcement Actions: 2011* (Washington, DC: DHS, Office of Immigration Statistics, 2012), www.dhs.gov/sites/default/files/publications/immigration-statistics/enforcement_ar_2011.pdf.

To put this trend into context, CBP now refers more cases to US Attorneys for criminal prosecution than does the FBI. Together, CBP and ICE refer more cases for criminal

---

455 TRAC "Going Deeper" tool, "Immigration Prosecutions, FY 2000-2003."
456 Ibid., for FY 2004-07.
457 TRAC "Going Deeper" tool, "Immigration Prosecutions, FY 2008, FY 2009 and FY 2010."
458 TRAC "Going Deeper" tool, "Federal Criminal Enforcement, FY 2011," (noting that out of 162,997 total federal prosecutions filed in FY 2011, 82,250 were for immigration-related offenses).
459 DHS, Office of Immigration Statistics (OIS), *Immigration Enforcement Actions: 2011* (Washington, DC: DHS, OIS, 2012): 6, www.dhs.gov/sites/default/files/publications/immigration-statistics/enforcement_ar_2011.pdf.
460 Ibid.
461 DOJ, Bureau of Justice Statistics, "Federal Criminal Case Processing Statistics, Persons Entering Federal Prison," http://bjs.ojp.usdoj.gov/fjsrc/.
462 Ibid.

prosecution than do all DOJ law enforcement agencies combined.[463] Partly as a result of the new trends in immigration prosecutions, the five federal judicial districts along the US-Mexico border, which are home to less than 10 percent of Americans, now account for nearly half of all federal felony prosecutions in the United States.[464]

Figure 15. Criminal Immigration Prosecutions as Share of Overall Federal Criminal Prosecutions, FY 2000-11

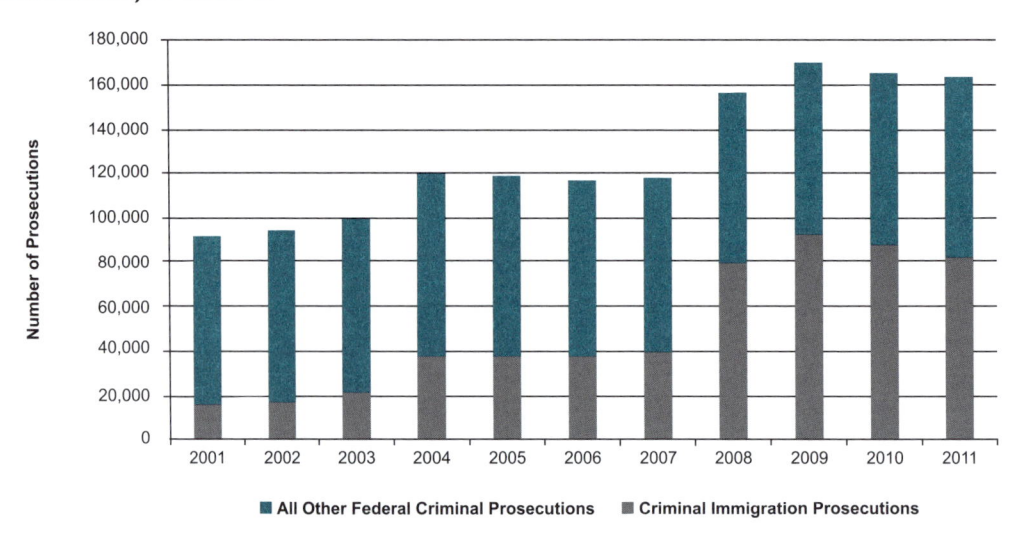

Source: Transactional Access Records Clearinghouse (TRAC), "Going Deeper" tool, http://tracfed.syr.edu/trachelp/tools/help_tools_godeep.shtml.

While ICE is the principal immigration investigative agency within DHS and has responsibility for immigration enforcement within the nation's interior, CBP refers most immigration cases for criminal prosecution, as shown in Figure 16. Between FY 2006-09, the number of CBP-referred cases nearly tripled, from 26,108 to 77,588.[465] Over the same period, ICE-referred cases rose from 7,012 to 12,345.[466] In FY 2011, CBP referred 67,112 immigration cases, while ICE referred 13,007.[467]

In addition to CBP and ICE, USCIS, which handles the adjudication of immigration benefits, also refers cases for criminal prosecution in certain instances. However, between FY 2006-11, the number of USCIS referrals fell from 3,433 to 1,480.[468]

---

463 TRAC "Trac Fed" tool, "Prosecutions for 2011," http://trac.syr.edu/cgi-bin/product/interpreter.pl?p_stat=fil&p_series=annual.
464 TRAC, *Federal Criminal Enforcement and Staffing: How Do the Obama and Bush Administrations Compare?* (Syracuse, NY: TRAC, 2010), http://trac.syr.edu/tracreports/crim/245/.
465 TRAC "Going Deeper" tool, "Immigration Prosecutions, FY 2006-FY 2009."
466 Ibid.
467 Ibid., 2011.
468 Ibid.

Figure 16. Immigration Prosecutions by Originating Agency, FY 2006-11

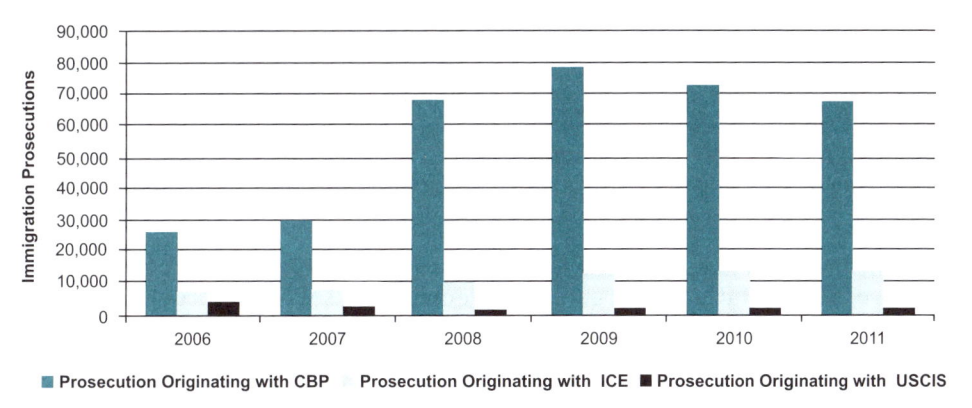

■ Prosecution Originating with CBP   Prosecution Originating with ICE   ■ Prosecution Originating with USCIS

Source: TRAC, "Going Deeper" tool.

Figure 17. Immigration Prosecutions by Originating Lead Charge, FY 2011

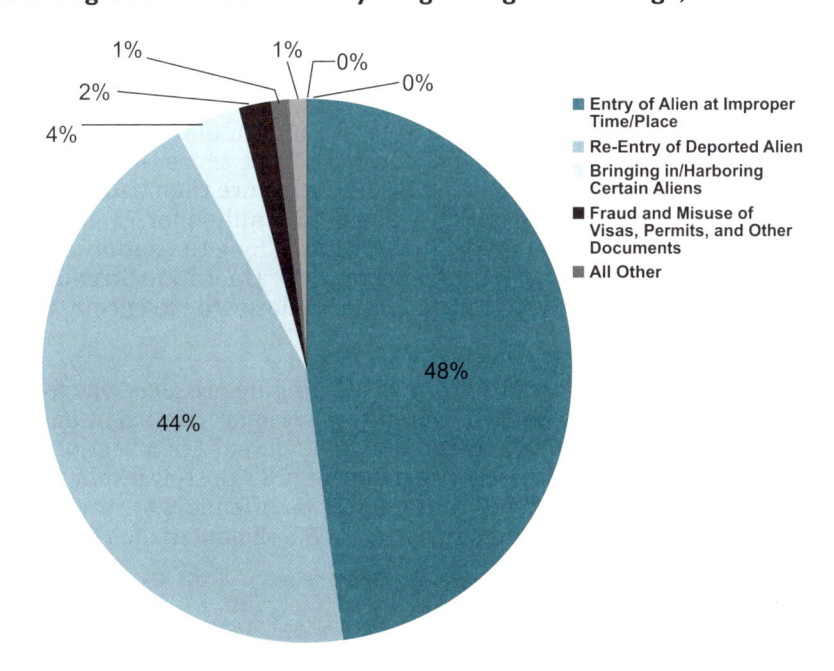

- Entry of Alien at Improper Time/Place: 48%
- Re-Entry of Deported Alien: 44%
- Bringing in/Harboring Certain Aliens: 4%
- Fraud and Misuse of Visas, Permits, and Other Documents: 2%
- All Other: 1%, 1%, 0%, 0%

Source: TRAC, "Going Deeper" tool.

2. Operation Streamline

The spike in immigration-related prosecutions can be partly credited to Operation Streamline, a DHS/CBP initiative that seeks to deter illegal migration by prosecuting border crossers arrested in certain Border Patrol sectors and corridors along the US-Mexico border. DHS launched Operation Streamline in 2005, in response to concerns over record numbers of unauthorized crossings through Del Rio, TX.[469] Since then, the program has expanded to six of the nine[470] Border Patrol sectors along the Southwest

---

[469] Joanna Jacobbi Lydgate, "Assembly-Line Justice: A Review of Operation Streamline" 98 *California Law Review* 481, 483, 491 (2010).

[470] Operation Streamline is being used in the Del Rio, Yuma, Laredo, Tucson, and Rio Grande Valley sectors, and according to several recent research and press reports, in El Paso as well.

border and has also become a cornerstone of consequence enforcement discussed in Chapter Three.[471]

Noncitizens processed through Operation Streamline typically appear before a magistrate judge and generally plead guilty to a criminal immigration violation as a group.[472] DHS characterized Operation Streamline as a "zero-tolerance" program, leading to prosecution of all unauthorized persons arrested in certain border areas, regardless of whether they were charged with felony or misdemeanor offenses (such as illegal entry).[473]

However, the program does not prosecute all arrested noncitizens within an entire Border Patrol sector. Rather, it targets enforcement areas within Border Patrol sectors and caps the number of cases referred each day for prosecution. The Del Rio sector, for example, refers no more than 80 new cases each day and in the Tucson sector, the cap is 70.[474] In addition, CBP rarely refers for prosecution juveniles, parents traveling with minor children, or persons with certain health conditions.[475] As a result, the number of cases referred for prosecution can be far lower than the number of unauthorized immigrants detained by sector.

Nonetheless, the program has led to significant increases in immigration-related prosecutions nationwide. In testimony before the US Sentencing Commission in January 2010, a Tucson magistrate judge estimated that since Operation Streamline's implementation in Tucson in 2008, roughly 30,000 persons had been prosecuted in that sector alone.[476] In May 2011, Homeland Security Secretary Napolitano testified that during the 12-month period between April 1, 2010 and March 31, 2011, more than 30,000 prosecutions were brought under Operation Streamline, with more than half in the Tucson sector.[477] In its FY 2010 budget request, DOJ asked for $8 million for 75 new positions and additional resources to address illegal immigration along the nation's borders.[478] While DOJ has not asked for specific Southwest border or Operation Streamline resources since then, CBP has extended the program to the Yuma sector to encompass the jurisdiction of Ajo, AZ.[479]

DHS has also championed a new initiative aimed at bringing prosecutions for immigration crimes against noncitizens who have committed serious criminal offenses. The program, initiated in 2008 and known as the Violent Criminal Alien Section (VCAS), screens noncitizens who are identified through one of ICE's post-arrest or prison screening programs and refers "recidivist" immigration offenders for prosecution.[480] The program led to the indictment and conviction of 6,842 noncitizens for immigration

---

471 Ibid.
472 Kerwin and McCabe, "Arrested on Entry: Operation Streamline and the Prosecution of Immigration Crimes."
473 DHS, "Fact Sheet: Secure Border Initiative Update," (fact sheet, August 23, 2006), www.hsdl.org/?view&did=476281.
474 Ibid., 496, 500.
475 Ibid.
476 Stephen Lemons, "Operation Streamline Costs Taxpayers Millions, Tramples on the Constitution, Treats Immigrants Like Cattle and Doesn't Work. So Why Are the Feds So Committed To It?" *Dallas Observer*, October 21, 2010, www.dallasobserver.com/2010-10-21/news/operation-streamline-costs-taxpayers-millions-tramples-on-the-constitution-treats-immigrants-like-cattle-and-doesn-t-work-so-why-are-the-feds-so-committed-to-it/.
477 Statement of Janet Napolitano, Secretary of Homeland Security, before the Senate Committee on Homeland Security and Governmental Affairs, *Securing the Border: Progress at the Federal Level What Remains to be Done?* 112th Cong., 1st sess., May 4, 2011, www.dhs.gov/ynews/testimony/testimony_1304459606805.shtm.
478 DOJ, *FY 2010 Budget Request* (Washington, DC: DOJ, 2009): 102, www.justice.gov/jmd/2010summary/pdf/usa-bud-summary.pdf.
479 James Gilbert, "Yuma Sector Expands Operation Streamline," *Yuma Sun*, December 20, 2010, www.yumasun.com/news/sector-66298-operation-yuma.html; *Arizona Republic*, "U.S. Plans Upgraded Security on Border," *Arizona Republic*, July 7, 2011.
480 ICE, "Fact Sheet: Criminal Alien Program," (fact sheet, March 29, 2011), www.ice.gov/news/library/factsheets/cap.htm.

offenses in FY 2009.[481] In FY 2010, convictions increased by an additional 25 percent and indictments by 20 percent.[482]

B. *Increase in Crimes with Automatic Consequence of Removal*

As a result of the passage of the *Anti-Drug Abuse Act of 1988*, IIRIRA, and AEDPA, there are now five distinct categories of crimes for which noncitizens, if convicted, are deportable:

- crimes of moral turpitude[483]
- controlled substance offenses[484]
- firearm or destructive device offenses[485]
- crimes of domestic violence and crimes against children[486]
- aggravated felonies.[487]

Aggravated felonies — a term unique to immigration law — were limited to a list of four felonies in 1988.[488] With the enactment of AEDPA and IIRIRA in 1996, the definition of the term expanded significantly. Today, aggravated felonies encompass some 50 separate crimes that fall into 21 general classes that include serious and relatively minor offenses, including misdemeanors.[489]

Table 1. Classes of Aggravated Felonies

Class	Aggravated Felony
A	Murder, Rape, Sexual abuse of a minor
B	Illicit trafficking of controlled substances; drug trafficking
C	Illicit trafficking in firearms, destructive devices, or explosives
D	Money laundering; or monetary transactions over $10,000 derived from unlawful activity
E	Explosive materials or firearms offenses
F	Crimes of violence (with 1+ year imprisonment term); e.g. Assault, Child Abuse, Criminal Trespass, Burglary, Domestic Violence, DWI/DUI, Evading Arrest, Manslaughter, Robbery, Resisting Arrest.
G	Theft/burglary/receipt of stolen property (with 1+ year imprisonment)
H	Demand for or receipt of ransom
I	Child pornography
J	RICO or gambling offenses
K	Owning, controlling, managing, supervising prostitution business; peonage/slavery/involuntary servitude
L	Gathering/transmitting national defense information; protecting identity of undercover agents

---

481 DHS, *Budget-in-Brief FY 2011*, 63.
482 DHS, *FY 2012 Budget-in Brief*, 79.
483 INA § 237(a)(2)(A)(i)
484 INA § 237(a)(2)(B)
485 INA § 237(a)(2)(C)
486 INA § 237(a)(1)(E)
487 INA § 237(a)(2)(A)(iii); INA § 101(a)(43).
488 *Anti-Drug Abuse Act of 1988*, Pub. L. 100-690, 102 Stat. 4181, 100th Cong., 2nd sess., (November 18, 1988), Sec. 7342.
489 Bertha A. Zuniga, *Aggravated Felony Case Summary* (San Antonio, TX: Executive Office for Immigration Review (EOIR), 2010), www.justice.gov/eoir/vll/benchbook/resources/Aggravated_Felony_Outline.pdf.

Class	Aggravated Felony
M	Fraud or deceit causing loss to victim over $10,000; tax evasion exceeding $10,000
N	Alien smuggling
O	Improper entry/reentry by alien previously deported
P	Falsely making/forging/counterfeiting/mutilating/altering passport; document fraud (with 1+ year imprisonment term)
Q	Failure to appear to serve sentence for an offense punishable by 5+ years
R	Commercial bribery, counterfeiting, forgery, or trafficking in vehicles with altered ID numbers, with term of imprisonment at least 1 year
S	Obstruction of justice, perjury, bribery of a witness, with sentence of at least 1 year
T	Failure to appear after court order to answer felony charge, for which term of 2 years or more may be imposed
U	Attempt or conspiracy to commit any of the above offenses

Source: Bertha A. Zuniga, Aggravated Felony Case Summary (San Antonio, TX: Executive Office for Immigration Review, US Department of Justice, November 15, 2010 update), www.justice.gov/eoir/vll/benchbook/resources/Aggravated_Felony_Outline.pdf.

IIRIRA also made its broadened definition of an aggravated felony effective retroactively.[490] Although the Supreme Court has disallowed the retroactive application of some provisions of IIRIRA,[491] those provisions where Congress expressly contemplated retroactivity have withstood challenge.[492] Thus, since 1996, many long-term residents, including LPRs, notwithstanding their length of residence, family or other equitable ties to the United States, have been removed based on relatively minor crimes that they may have committed years ago.[493]

C. Expansion of Programs Targeting Criminals

Equally important to legislative expansion of criminal deportation grounds has been a series of enforcement programs launched by the executive branch with substantial funding by Congress. Successive administrations and Congress have placed high priority on the removal of noncitizens arrested or convicted of a criminal offense. This priority is reflected in burgeoning post-arrest and post-conviction screening programs and the targeting of noncitizens ordered removed on criminal grounds who have not left

---

490 *Omnibus Consolidated Appropriations Act,* 1997, Pub. L. 104-208, 110 Stat. 3009-664 (September 30, 1996) (incorporating the *Illegal Immigration Reform and Immigrant Responsibility Act [IIRIRA]* Sec. 321(b) [amending INA Section 101(a) (43)]).

491 See *Vartelas v. Holder,* 132 S. Ct. 1479 (2012) (holding that IIRIRA section 301, which allows the government to place in removal proceedings lawful permanent residents who have committed certain crimes and then leave the country and seek readmission, may not be applied retroactively to individuals whose qualifying criminal offenses predate the statute); see also *INS v. St. Cyr,* 533 U.S. 289 (2001) (holding that IIRIRA did not make retroactive the elimination of a discretionary waiver of removal for certain lawful permanent residents).

492 *St. Cyr,* 533 U.S. at 316 (noting that "despite the dangers inherent in retroactive legislation, it is beyond dispute that, within constitutional limits, Congress has the power to enact laws with retrospective effect"); and id. at 318-9 (noting that in the portion of IIRIRA expanding the definition of an "aggravated felony," Congress expressly indicated that it intended the provision to be retroactive); see also *Mohammed v. Ashcroft,* 261 F.3d 1244, 1249 (11th Circuit 2001) (holding that it was proper to apply IIRIRA §321(a)(3) retroactively because Congress made a "clear" and "unambiguous" statement in favor of retroactivity).

493 Catholic Legal Immigration Network, Inc. (CLINIC), *The Impact of Our Laws on American Families* (Washington, DC: CLINIC, 2000), http://cliniclegal.org/sites/default/files/atrisk1.pdf; American Bar Association (ABA), Commission on Immigration, *American Justice Through Immigrants' Eyes* (Chicago: ABA, 2004): 23-44, 59-71, www.protectcivilrights.org/pdf/reports/american-justice/american_justice.pdf.

the country ("absconders"). Between FY 2004-11, funding for these programs increased from $23 million to $690 million, or 2,900 percent.[494]

The four major ICE programs targeting noncitizens who have been arrested for crimes are: the Criminal Alien Program (CAP), the 287(g) program, the National Fugitive Operations Program (NFOP), and the Secure Communities program. In addition, DHS runs a less known, but also high-priority program that targets transnational criminal enterprises.

1. The Criminal Alien Program (CAP)

CAP grew out of two programs launched in the 1980s, the Alien Criminal Apprehension Program (ACAP) and the Institutional Hearing Program (IHP).[495]

Under CAP, ICE assigns deportation officers to federal and state prisons and local jails in order to interview detained noncitizens and determine if they are removable. CAP teams cover all state and federal prisons, as well as more than 300 local jails.[496] The program operates differently from facility to facility. Although ICE screens 100 percent of inmates at a number of "Tier 1" and "Tier 2" prisons, it has 100 percent screening at fewer than 10 percent of local jails.[497] While CAP officers conduct in-person interviews with inmates in some facilities, in others, CAP interviews take place via teleconference.[498]

CAP officers are tasked with identifying removable immigrants — unauthorized immigrants and those who have committed crimes — and issuing them charging documents called Notices to Appear (NTAs).[499] CAP officers also coordinate the issuance of ICE "detainers" (i.e., requests to state or local arresting or correctional agencies to hold a noncitizen until ICE can assume custody).

CAP also encompasses three other programs that target criminal aliens who are not necessarily detained, as follows:

- The Violent Criminal Alien Section (VCAS) targets recidivist immigration offenders, who are referred for criminal prosecution

- The Joint Criminal Alien and Removal Task Force (JCART) targets noncitizens with convictions for drug trafficking, violent crimes, and sex offenses

- Law Enforcement Area Response (LEAR) Teams respond to state and local law enforcement agencies that request ICE assistance.[500]

Another component of CAP, the Rapid Removal of Eligible Parolees Accepted for Transfer

---

494 Rosenblum and Kandel, *Interior Immigration Enforcement: Programs Targeting Criminal Aliens*.
495 Statement of Lowell Dodge, Director, Administration of Justice Issues, General Government Division, GAO, before the US House of Representatives Committee on the Judiciary, Subcommittee on Immigration, Refugees, and International Law, *Criminal Aliens: INS Enforcement*, 101st Cong., 2nd sess., November 1, 1989, 7, 9, http://archive.gao.gov/d48t13/139869.pdf; DOJ, Office of the Inspector General (OIG), *Audit Division, Audit Report: Immigration and Naturalization Service Institutional Removal Program* (Washington, DC: DOJ, OIG, 2002): 1, www.justice.gov/oig/reports/INS/a0241/final.pdf; see also ICE, "Fact Sheet: Secure Communities," (fact sheet, March 28, 2008), www.aila.org/content/default.aspx?docid=25045.
496 Andrea Guttin, *The Criminal Alien Program: Immigration Enforcement in Travis County, TX* (Washington, DC: Immigration Policy Center, 2010): 6, www.immigrationpolicy.org/sites/default/files/docs/Criminal_Alien_Program_021710.pdf.
497 Ibid.
498 Ibid., 5.
499 Once a notice to appear (NTA) is issued, it must still be filed in immigration court.
500 ICE, "Fact Sheet: Criminal Alien Program," (fact sheet, March 29, 2011), www.ice.gov/news/library/factsheets/cap.htm; ICE, "Fact Sheet: ICE Enforcement in Arizona," (fact sheet, November 14, 2011), www.ice.gov/news/library/factsheets/az-enforcement.htm.

(Rapid REPAT program) coordinates the removal of nonviolent criminal offenders who, in exchange for early parole, waive their rights to appeal final orders of removal.[501]

According to DHS, the goal of CAP is to identify and prioritize removals of those determined to pose the greatest risk to the community.[502] In recent years, CAP has led to the detention of more noncitizens than any other ICE program (see Figure 18). In FY 2009, for example, ICE estimated that 48 percent of detained noncitizens in immigration proceedings had come through CAP.[503]

Figure 18. Sources of ICE Apprehensions by Program, FY 2009

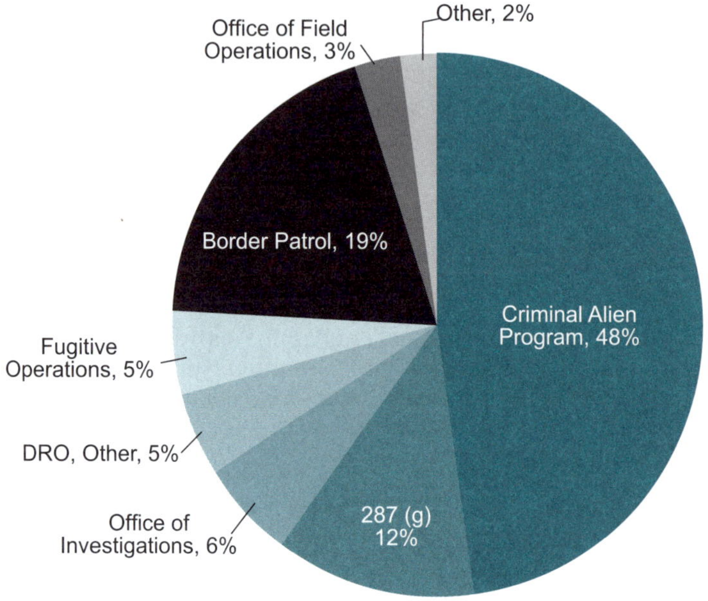

- Criminal Alien Program, 48%
- 287 (g), 12%
- Office of Investigations, 6%
- DRO, Other, 5%
- Fugitive Operations, 5%
- Border Patrol, 19%
- Office of Field Operations, 3%
- Other, 2%

Source: Dora Schriro, *Immigration Detention Overview and Recommendations* (Washington, DC: ICE, 2009), www.ice.gov/doclib/about/offices/odpp/pdf/ice-detention-rpt.pdf.

In recent years, CAP's impact has increased dramatically. Between FY 2006-09, the number of NTAs issued through the program rose from 67,850 to 230,250 (see Figure 19).[504] That number dropped somewhat in FY 2010, when DHS issued an estimated 223,217 NTAs through the program,[505] and dropped again slightly in FY 2011, to 212,744.[506]

---

501 ICE, "Fact Sheet: Criminal Alien Program;" ICE, "Fact Sheet: ICE Enforcement in Arizona;" see also, ICE, "Rapid REPAT," accessed November 18, 2012, www.ice.gov/rapid-repat/.
502 ICE, "Fact Sheet: Criminal Alien Program."
503 Dora Schriro, *Immigration Detention Overview and Recommendations* (Washington, DC: DHS, 2009): 12, www.ice.gov/doclib/about/offices/odpp/pdf/ice-detention-rpt.pdf.
504 ICE, *Secure Communities: Quarterly Report, Fiscal Year 2009 Report to Congress, Fourth Quarter* (Washington, DC: ICE, 2009): 19, www.ice.gov/doclib/foia/secure_communities/congressionalstatusreportfy094thquarter.pdf, (noting that 230,250 detainers were issued as a result of the Criminal Alien Program in FY 2009); ICE, *Second Congressional Status Report Covering the Fourth Quarter Fiscal Year 2008 for Secure Communities: A Comprehensive Plan to Identify and Remove Criminal Aliens* (Washington, DC: ICE, 2008): 2, www.ice.gov/doclib/foia/secure_communities/congressionalstatusreportfy084thquarter.pdf, (noting that 67,850 detainers were issued as a result of the Criminal Alien Program in FY 2006).
505 ICE, "ERO Facts and Statistics," December 12, 2011, www.ice.gov/doclib/foia/reports/ero-facts-and-statistics.pdf.
506 Ibid.

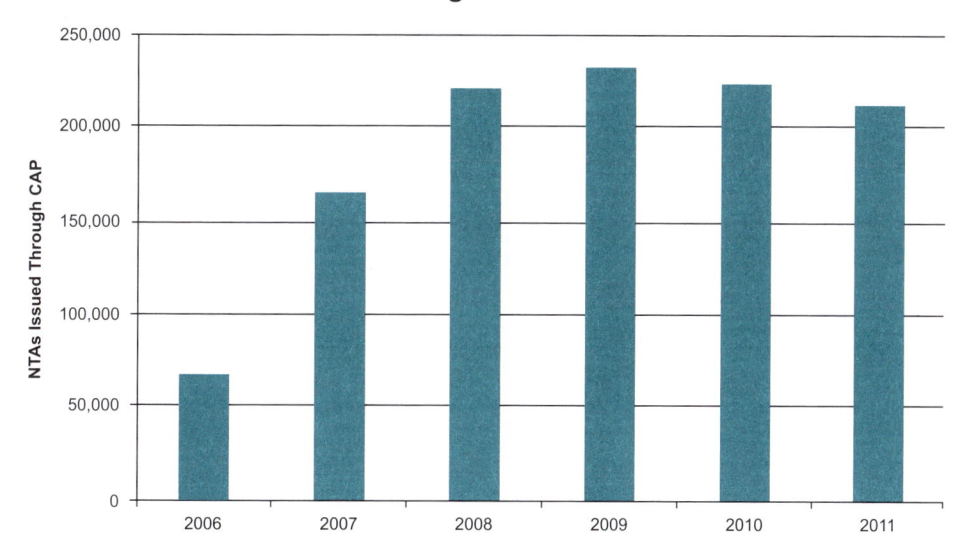

Figure 19. Number of NTAs Issued Through CAP

Sources: Secure Communities Quarterly Reports to Congress FY 2008, 2009 and 2010 (Washington, DC: ICE, various years), www.ice.gov/foia/library/; and ICE, "ERO Facts and Statistics," December 12, 2011, www.ice.gov/doclib/foia/reports/ero-facts-and-statistics.pdf.

2. The National Fugitive Operations Program (NFOP)

NFOP was established in 2002 to identify and arrest absconders, i.e. noncitizens ordered removed, but who had not left the country.[507] In FY 2003, Congress allocated $9 million for the program.[508] By FY 2010, its budget had grown to $230 million.[509] Over the same period, the number of noncitizens apprehended through the program rose from 1,900 to 35,774.[510]

As NFOP grew, its focus shifted from noncitizen criminals to those without criminal convictions. Between 2003 and February 2008, almost three-quarters (73 percent) of the individuals apprehended by NFOP teams had no criminal conviction.[511] In recent years, ICE has placed priority on the arrest of noncitizens with criminal records: 45 percent of those arrested in FY 2009 and 51 percent in FY 2010 were criminal aliens.[512]

Since 2009, ICE has also emphasized that it is prioritizing the arrest of criminal fugi-

---

[507] Margot Mendelson, Shayna Strom, and Michael Wishnie, *Collateral Damage: An Examination of ICE's Fugitive Operations Program* (Washington, DC: MPI, 2009): 4, www.migrationpolicy.org/pubs/NFOP_Feb09.pdf.
[508] Ibid., 3.
[509] DHS, *Congressional Budget Justification FY 2012, US Immigration and Customs Enforcement* (Washington, DC: DHS, 2010): 3, www.dhs.gov/xlibrary/assets/dhs-congressional-budget-justification-fy2012.pdf; see also Mendelson et al., *Collateral Damage*, 9.
[510] DHS, *FY 2012 Budget in Brief*, 80.
[511] Mendelson et al., *Collateral Damage*, 11.
[512] ICE, *Secure Communities: Quarterly Report, Fiscal Year 2009 Report to Congress, Fourth Quarter*: 19; ICE, *Secure Communities Quarterly Report, Fiscal Year 2010 Report to Congress, Fourth Quarter* (Washington, DC: ICE, 2011): 13, www.ice.gov/doclib/foia/secure_communities/congressionalstatusreportfy104thquarter.pdf; ICE, *Secure Communities Quarterly Report, Fiscal Year 2010 Report to Congress, Third Quarter* (Washington, DC: ICE, 2010): 13, www.ice.gov/doclib/foia/secure_communities/r_congressionalfy10rdquarterreport.pdf; ICE, *Secure Communities Quarterly Report, Fiscal Year 2010 Report to Congress, Second Quarter* (Washington, DC: ICE, 2010): 16, www.ice.gov/doclib/foia/secure_communities/congressionalstatusreportfy102ndquarter.pdf; ICE, *Secure Communities Quarterly Report, Fiscal Year 2010 Report to Congress, First Quarter* (Washington, DC: ICE, 2010): 14, www.ice.gov/doclib/foia/secure_communities/congressionalstatusreportfy101stquarter.pdf.

tives through the program.[513] However, as the data from FY 2010 indicate, the number of people arrested through the program classified by ICE as fugitive criminal aliens (those who have a criminal history and are also absconders) remains relatively modest. In that year, DHS reported arresting 35,800 individuals through NFOP,[514] of whom 28 percent (10,150) were classified as fugitive criminal aliens.[515] Thus, more than 70 percent of those arrested through NFOP in 2010 were not fugitive criminal aliens despite the fact that ICE claims that such noncitizens are the program's top priority.

Figure 20. Fugitive Criminal Arrests as Share of Total Arrests Made Through NFOP, By Quarter, 2010

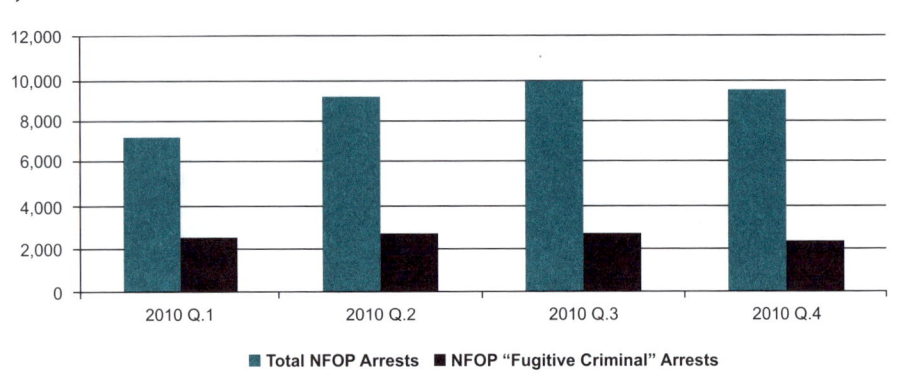

Quarter	Total NFOP Arrests	NFOP "Fugitive Criminal" Arrests
2010 Q.1	~7,200	~2,500
2010 Q.2	~9,300	~2,700
2010 Q.3	~10,100	~2,800
2010 Q.4	~9,600	~2,400

Source: ICE, *Secure Communities Quarterly Reports to Congress, FY 2010* (Washington, DC: ICE, 2011), www.ice.gov/foia/library/index.htm#47.

3. The 287(g) Program

The 287(g) program, named after the relevant section of the *Immigration and Nationality Act* (INA) that established it, was enacted as part of IIRIRA. Under the program, ICE is authorized to enter into agreements with state and local law enforcement agencies to enforce certain aspects of immigration law. Now operating in 57 jurisdictions,[516] the program authorizes state and local law enforcement officers to screen people for immigration status, issue detainers to hold them on immigration violations until ICE takes custody, and begin the process of their removal.

While there are other federal-state partnerships, the 287(g) program is the only one that enables state and local law enforcement officials to enforce federal immigration law directly.

---

513 See ICE, "Memo Re: National Fugitive Operations Program: Priorities, Goals, and Expectations," (memo, December 8, 2009), www.ice.gov/doclib/detention-reform/pdf/nfop_priorities_goals_expectations.pdf.
514 ICE, *Secure Communities: Quarterly Report, Fiscal Year 2010 Report to Congress, First Quarter*, 14; ICE, *Secure Communities: Quarterly Report, Fiscal Year 2010 Report to Congress, Second Quarter*, 16; ICE, *Secure Communities: Quarterly Report, Fiscal Year 2010 Report to Congress: Third Quarter*, 16; ICE, *Secure Communities: Quarterly Report, Fiscal Year 2010 Report to Congress, Fourth Quarter* (Washington, DC: ICE, 2011): 13, www.ice.gov/doclib/foia/secure_communities/congressionalstatusreportfy104thquarter.pdf.
515 Ibid.
516 ICE, "Fact Sheet: Delegation of Immigration Authority Section 287(g) Immigration and Nationality Act," (fact sheet, updated October 16, 2012), www.ice.gov/news/library/factsheets/287g.htm.

Currently, there are three types of 287(g) agreements:[517]

- The *task force model* permits state and local law enforcement officers to question and arrest suspected noncitizens encountered during routine law enforcement operations.

- The *jail enforcement model* enables local officers to question persons who are detained at prisons and jails about their immigration status.

- *"Hybrid" agreements* allow jurisdictions to participate in both the task force and jail models.[518]

While Congress created the program in 1996, the first 287(g) agreement was not signed until 2002, with the state of Florida.[519] Most of the program's growth occurred during 2007 and 2008. During this period, the number of 287(g) agreements jumped from eight to 61.[520] The program's budget also grew significantly, from $5 million (FY 2006) to $42 million (FY 2008).[521] Funding further increased to $68 million by FY 2010,[522] where it remained in FY 2011.[523]

In a January 2009 report, GAO evaluated 29 of the then-existing agreements and found that the program lacked documented program objectives, clear and consistent mechanisms for supervision, and protocols for collection of data. It concluded that in the absence of such controls, it was difficult to determine whether the program advanced the federal government's enforcement objectives.[524]

The Obama administration undertook a number of measures designed to strengthen oversight of 287(g) agreements. In March 2009, DOJ launched an investigation into practices of the Sheriff's Department in Maricopa County, AZ, including complaints of racial profiling during local immigration investigations conducted under its 287(g) agreement.[525] After concluding its investigation in December 2011, DOJ announced that it had found that the sheriff's department was engaged in unlawful racial profiling against Latinos and that its jail policies discriminated against noncitizens who were Limited English Proficient.[526] An expert retained by DOJ to analyze data related to police stops found that Latino drivers in Maricopa County were four to nine times more likely to be stopped by the police than similarly situated non-Latino drivers.[527] Following the DOJ announcement, DHS announced that it was terminating Maricopa County's participation in the 287(g) program.[528]

---

517 Cristina Rodriguez, Muzaffar Chishti, Randy Capps, and Laura St. John, *A Program in Flux: New Priorities and Implementation Challenges for 287(g)* (Washington, DC: MPI, 2010): 5, www.migrationpolicy.org/pubs/287g-March2010.pdf.
518 Ibid., 3.
519 Ibid.
520 ICE, "Fact Sheet: Delegation of Immigration Authority Section 287(g) Immigration and Nationality Act."
521 DHS, OIG, *The Performance of 287(g) Agreements: Report Update* (Washington, DC: DHS, OIG, 2010): 4, www.oig.dhs.gov/assets/mgmt/oig_10-63_mar10.pdf.
522 Ibid.
523 Rosenblum and Kandel, *Interior Immigration Enforcement: Programs Targeting Criminal Aliens*, 22.
524 Richard M. Stana, *Immigration Enforcement: Better Controls Needed Over Program Authorizing State and Local Enforcement of Federal Immigration Laws* (Washington, DC: GAO, 2009): 18-9, www.gao.gov/new.items/d09109.pdf.
525 *United States v. Maricopa County*, complaint, case number 2:10-cv-01878-LOA (filed September 2, 2010), www.justice.gov/opa/documents/maricopa-complaint.pdf.
526 DOJ, "Assistant Attorney General Thomas E. Perez Speaks at the Maricopa County Sheriff's Office Investigative Findings Announcement," (press release, December 15, 2011), www.justice.gov/crt/opa/pr/speeches/2011/crt-speech-111215.html.
527 Ibid.
528 DHS, "Statement by Secretary Napolitano on DOJ's Findings of Discriminatory Policing in Maricopa County," (press release, December 15, 2011), www.dhs.gov/ynews/releases/20111215-napolitano-statement-doj-maricopa-county.shtm.

In February 2012, DOJ presented the sheriff's office with a settlement which the parties failed to negotiate successfully. As a result, in May 2012, DOJ filed a lawsuit against Maricopa County, the Maricopa County Sheriff's Office, and Sheriff Joseph M. Arpaio. The suit alleged:

- discriminatory and otherwise unconstitutional law enforcement actions against Latinos who are frequently stopped, detained, and arrested on the basis of race, color, or national origin;

- discriminatory jail practices against Latino inmates with limited English skills; and

- illegal retaliation against perceived critics, subjecting them to baseless criminal actions, unfounded civil lawsuits, or meritless administrative actions.[529]

In July 2009, ICE announced that it had created a new, standardized 287(g) Memorandum of Agreement (MOA) which all participating agencies would be required to sign.[530] The standardized agreement was designed to provide closer federal oversight and focus the program on the detention and removal of "dangerous" criminals.[531] Among other changes, the new 287(g) agreements directed participating jurisdictions to prioritize 287(g) resources in accordance with three separate ICE-articulated priority levels of criminal aliens.[532] The agreements stipulated that participating jurisdictions should concentrate the most attention on Priority 1 criminal aliens, a category that encompasses noncitizens who have been convicted of or arrested for major drug offenses and violent crimes. Local officials were directed to focus fewer resources on Priority 2 aliens (noncitizens arrested for or convicted of minor drug and property offenses) and Priority 3 aliens (noncitizens convicted of or arrested for other offenses).[533]

Despite these guidelines, the program does not target primarily or even mostly serious or dangerous offenders.[534] Nationally, half of the detainers issued under the program are issued to those who have committed felonies and other crimes that ICE classifies as serious (Priority 1 and 2). The other half are issued to those who have committed misdemeanors or traffic offenses.[535]

More importantly, there is a substantial variation in how the program is implemented across jurisdictions. Many jurisdictions use a "targeted" model for their programs — a model aimed primarily at identifying serious criminal offenders, while others use a "universal" model — that identifies and processes as many unauthorized immigrants as possible, including those who have committed misdemeanors or traffic violations, which may not be consistent with ICE's national enforcement priorities.[536]

---

529 *United States v. Maricopa County*, case number 2:12-cv-00981-LOA (filed May 10, 2012), www.justice.gov/iso/opa/resources/46420125101544060757.pdf.
530 ICE, "Secretary Napolitano Announces New Agreement for State and Local Immigration Enforcement Partnerships and Adds 11 New Agreements," (press release, July 10, 2009), www.ice.gov/news/releases/0907/090710washington.htm.
531 Ibid.
532 Rodriguez et al., *A Program in Flux*, 12.
533 Ibid.
534 Randy Capps, Marc R. Rosenblum, Cristina Rodriguez, and Muzaffar Chishti, *Delegation and Divergence: A Study of 287(g) State and Local Immigration Enforcement* (Washington, DC: MPI, 2011): 2, www.migrationpolicy.org/pubs/287g-divergence.pdf.
535 Ibid.
536 Ibid.

Figure 21. The Growth of 287(g) Agreements, FY 2002-12

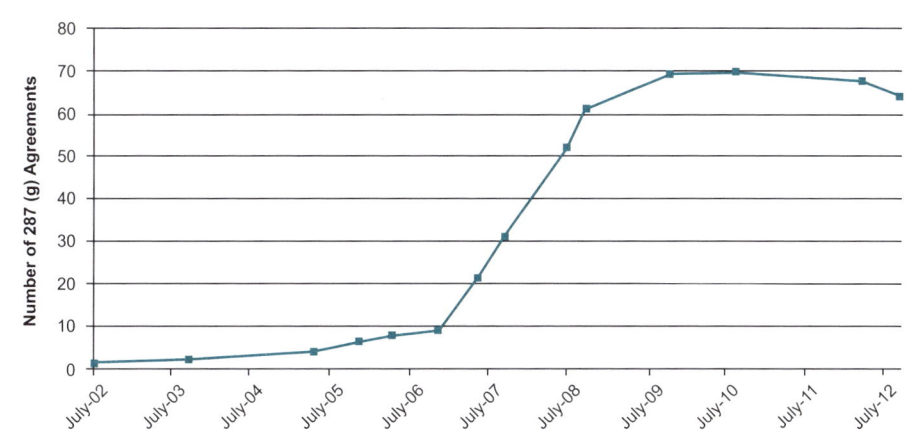

Source: ICE, "Delegation of Immigration Authority Section 287(g) Immigration and Nationality Act," (fact sheet, October 16, 2012), www.ice.gov/news/library/factsheets/287g.htm#signed-moa.

As the 287(g) program grew, so did its output. In FY 2009, state agencies identified 56,116 noncitizens who were "amenable to removal," nearly ten times the number identified in FY 2006 (5,685).[537] In FY 2010, the number fell to 46,467 (see Figure 22).[538] It fell again in FY 2011, when 33,180 noncitizens were identified.[539] Despite the reduced activity in FY 2010, there is no evidence that the revised standardized agreements and new guidelines have had a substantial effect on meeting program priorities or on changing the program's operations or outcomes.[540]

In February 2012, the administration announced that it would seek a decrease in funding for the 287(g) program, requesting $17 million less than the program had received the previous year.[541] In its FY 2013 budget request, DHS attributed the drop in the 287(g) funding request to the recent expansion of the Secure Communities program, and its plans to deploy Secure Communities nationwide by FY 2013.[542]

At a hearing on the FY 2013 budget, ICE Assistant Secretary John Morton stated that the cut in funding would only go toward reducing the number of 287(g) task force agreements and that there would be no reduction in the number of jail enforcement agreements.[543] Morton also said that he had recently approved two additional jail enforcement model agreements,[544] reportedly for Horry County, SC and Knox County, TN.[545]

---

[537] Rosenblum and Kandel, *Interior Immigration Enforcement: Programs Targeting Criminal Aliens*, 24.
[538] Ibid.
[539] Ibid.
[540] Capps et al., *Delegation and Divergence*, 3.
[541] DHS, *FY 2013 Budget in Brief*, 16.
[542] Ibid.
[543] Testimony of ICE Assistant Secretary John Morton before the House Appropriations Committee, Subcommittee on Homeland Security, *FY 2013 Appropriations for the Homeland Security Department's Immigration and Customs Enforcement*, 112th Cong., 2nd sess., March 8, 2012, www.micevhill.com/attachments/immigration_documents/hosted_documents/112th_congress/TranscriptOfHouseAppropriationsSubcommitteeHearingOnFY13ICEAppropriations.pdf.
[544] Ibid.
[545] Keith Rushing, "Rights Groups Say New 287(g) Program in TN and SC to Lead to Bias," Rights Working Group, March 21, 2012, www.rightsworkinggroup.org/content/rights-groups-say-new-287g-program-tn-and-sc-lead-bias.

Figure 22. 287(g) Program Arrests, FY 2006-11

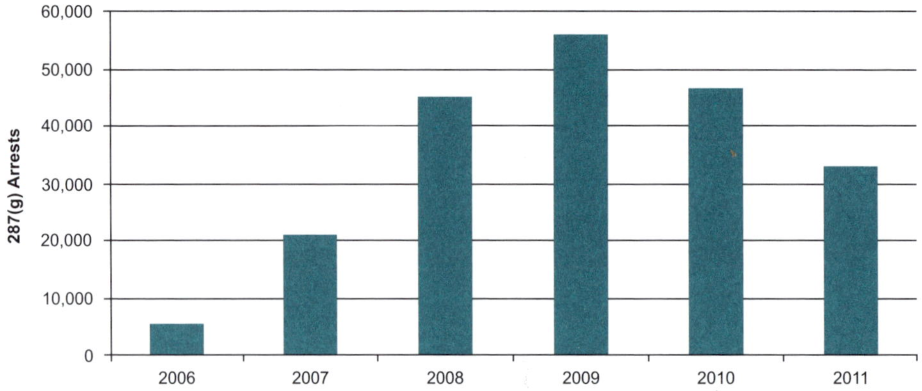

Source: Marc R. Rosenblum and William A. Kandel, *Interior Immigration Enforcement: Programs Targeting Criminal Aliens* (Washington, DC: CRS, 2011): 24, www.fas.org/sgp/crs/homesec/R42057.pdf.

4. The Secure Communities Program

Secure Communities, a program that has been implemented in virtually all of the nation's 3,181 jails and prisons,[546] screens arrested persons whose fingerprints are checked against FBI and DHS databases. Its intent is to enable ICE to prioritize the use of enforcement resources to target noncitizens who have committed serious crimes. The cornerstone for Secure Communities is data systems advances that allow DHS and the FBI to run fingerprints through their respective databases — IDENT (the DHS database that tracks immigration history) and IAFIS (the FBI database for criminal arrests and convictions).[547] In 2008, the two systems became interoperable. Thus, a fingerprint check now provides information about both an individual's immigration and criminal history.

The Secure Communities fingerprint check process begins with a state or local law enforcement or detention officer taking an arrested individual's fingerprints, and ends with the ICE Law Enforcement Support Center (LESC) generating an "Immigration Alien Response" (IAR), which may include a criminal-level classification. Figure 23 illustrates the process.

---

546 ICE, "Activated Jurisdictions," August 22, 2012, www.ice.gov/doclib/secure-communities/pdf/sc-activated.pdf.
547 ICE, *Secure Communities: Quarterly Report, Fiscal Year 2009 Report to Congress, Fourth Quarter*, 3.

Figure 23. The Secure Communities Process

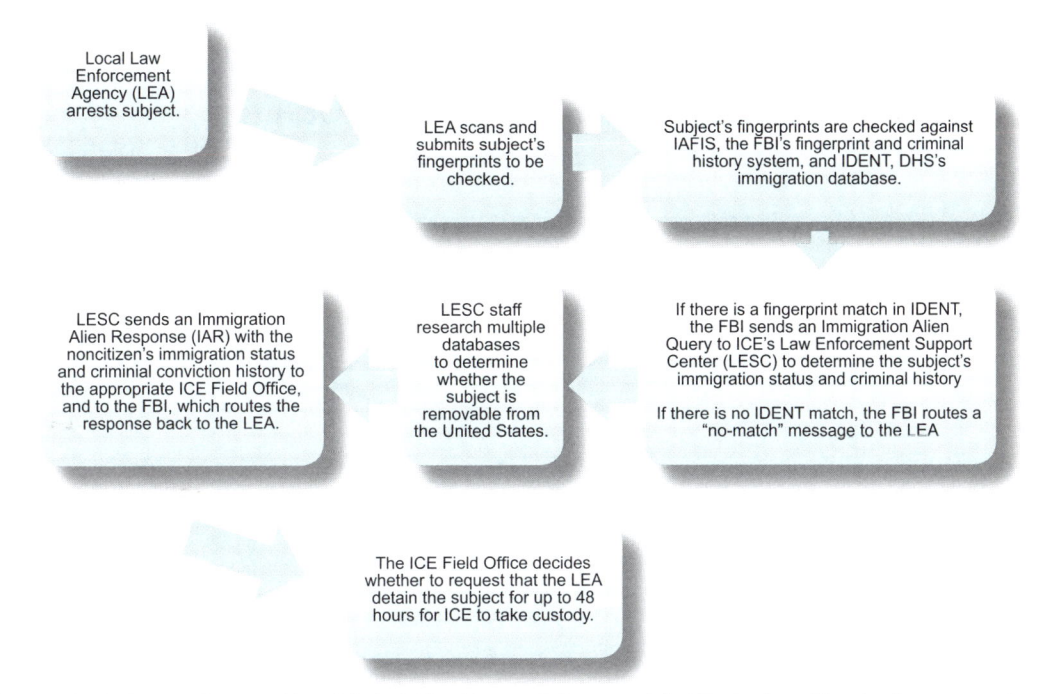

- Local Law Enforcement Agency (LEA) arrests subject.
- LEA scans and submits subject's fingerprints to be checked.
- Subject's fingerprints are checked against IAFIS, the FBI's fingerprint and criminal history system, and IDENT, DHS's immigration database.
- If there is a fingerprint match in IDENT, the FBI sends an Immigration Alien Query to ICE's Law Enforcement Support Center (LESC) to determine the subject's immigration status and criminal history. If there is no IDENT match, the FBI routes a "no-match" message to the LEA.
- LESC staff research multiple databases to determine whether the subject is removable from the United States.
- LESC sends an Immigration Alien Response (IAR) with the noncitizen's immigration status and criminal conviction history to the appropriate ICE Field Office, and to the FBI, which routes the response back to the LEA.
- The ICE Field Office decides whether to request that the LEA detain the subject for up to 48 hours for ICE to take custody.

Source: GAO, *Secure Communities: Criminal Alien Removals Increased, but Technology Planning Improvements Needed* (Washington, DC: GAO, 2012), www.gao.gov/assets/600/592415.pdf.

ICE has emphasized that unlike other criminal alien programs that work in cooperation with state and local law enforcement officials to screen only noncitizens, Secure Communities runs fingerprints of all arrestees through the system, thus eliminating the risk of racial profiling at the screening stage.[548]

The program enables ICE to prioritize the detention and removal of high-interest or dangerous noncitizen criminals. To that end, on June 30, 2010, ICE Assistant Secretary John Morton directed agency staff to target noncitizen criminals who threaten public safety or national security.[549] The Secure Communities memorandum establishes the following classifications:

- Priority 1 — convicted of aggravated felonies, as defined in the INA, as well as those who have been convicted of two or more felonies
- Priority 2 — convicted of at least one felony offense, or three misdemeanors
- Priority 3 — convicted of at least one misdemeanor.[550]

Since its launch in seven jurisdictions in October 2008, Secure Communities has grown dramatically. The percentage of overall removals that have occurred through Secure

---

[548] Testimony of David Venturella, Executive Director of Secure Communities, before the House Appropriations Committee, Subcommittee on Homeland Security, *Priorities Enforcing Immigration Law*, 111th Cong., 1st sess., April 2, 2009, www.aila.org/content/fileviewer.aspx?docid=28622&linkid=200232.
[549] John Morton, Assistant Secretary, ICE, "Memorandum for All ICE Employees: Civil Immigration Enforcement: Priorities for the Apprehension, Detention, and Removal of Aliens (memo, June 2010), www.immilaw.com/FAQ/ICE%20prosecution%20priorities%202010.pdf.
[550] Ibid.

Communities has risen from 4 percent in 2009 to 20 percent in 2011.[551] As of August 22, 2012, the program operated in 3,074 jurisdictions in all 50 states, four territories, and in Washington, DC.[552] ICE plans to have the program operational in all of the nation's 3,181 jurisdictions by March 2013.[553]

Figure 24. Growth of Secure Communities Jurisdictions, FY 2008-12

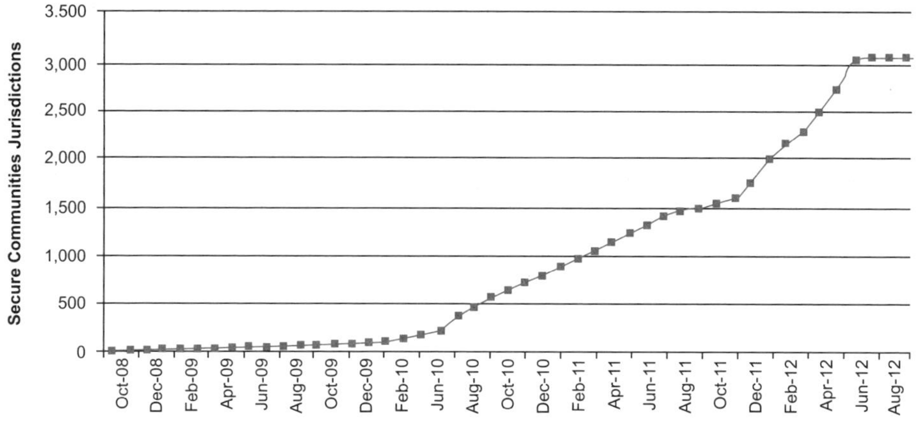

Source: ICE, "Secure Communities Monthly Statistics, July 2012," 52, www.ice.gov/doclib/foia/sc-stats/nationwide_interop_stats-fy2012-to-date.pdf.

Funding for Secure Communities grew significantly between FY 2008-11:

- For 2008, Congress allocated $200 million to be utilized over a two-year period.[554]

- In FY 2009, Congress provided an additional $150 million.[555]

- In FY 2010, ICE received another two-year allocation, providing $200 million.[556]

- For FY 2011, Congress maintained the FY 2010 level through a series of continuing resolutions.

- For FY 2012, Congress allocated $189 million to be utilized over a two-year period.[557]

Secure Communities can operate in tandem with other ICE programs. DHS has used Secure Communities funding to establish automatic fingerprint checks for immigration violations within pre-existing ICE programs, such as CAP and the Joint Criminal Alien Removal Task Force (JCART).[558] ICE has also used Secure Communities funds to support

---

551 GAO, *Secure Communities: Criminal Alien Removals Increased, but Technology Planning Improvements Needed* (Washington, DC: GAO, 2012): 14-5, www.gao.gov/assets/600/592415.pdf.
552 ICE, "Activated Jurisdictions, Nationwide Cumulative Numbers," August 22, 2012, www.ice.gov/doclib/secure-communities/pdf/sc-activated.pdf.
553 Ibid.
554 ICE, "Secure Communities Budget Numbers, FY 2008-FY 2011," www.ice.gov/doclib/foia/secure_communities/budgetnumbers.pdf; ICE, *Secure Communities: Quarterly Report FY 2011, Report to Congress, Second Quarter* (Washington, DC: ICE, 2011): 2, www.ice.gov/doclib/foia/secure_communities/congressionalstatusreportfy112ndquarter.pdf.
555 Ibid.
556 Ibid.
557 *Consolidated Appropriations Act of 2012*, Pub. L. 112-74, 125 Stat. 966 (December 23, 2011).
558 ICE, *Secure Communities: Quarterly Report, Fiscal Year 2010 Report to Congress, Third Quarter*, 12; ICE, *Secure Communities: Quarterly Report, Fiscal Year 2011 Report to Congress, First Quarter*, 11.

IDENT/IAFIS screening systems in national, state, and local jails that we[?] ipating in one of the pre-existing ICE post-arrest screening programs. [?] funds specifically allocated for Secure Communities, ICE uses its gene[?] for salaries and expenses, as well as funding allocated for criminal ali[?] detention and removal generally, to complement Secure Communities effor[?].

The expansion of Secure Communities has spurred a massive increase in the numbers of individuals being screened by ICE. The total number of fingerprints submitted through the program increased from 828,119 in FY 2009 to nearly 3.4 million in FY 2010 to approximately 6.9 million in FY 2011.[560]

It is difficult to assess whether the program is meeting the enforcement priorities established by ICE. This is partly due to the distinction between two sets of priority numbers that ICE tracks and reports. For its reporting purposes, ICE categorizes people at the screening stage and later at the detainer/arrest stage. During the screening/identification stage, ICE categorizes noncitizens as Priority 1, 2, or 3 criminals based on the *charge* for which they were arrested or their prior conviction histories.[561] However, when ICE reports on the number of noncitizens for whom it ultimately issues detainers through Secure Communities, it classifies noncitizens as Priority 1, 2, or 3 criminals based upon actual *convictions*. [562]

This reporting methodology explains the large discrepancy between the number of Priority Category 1 criminals that ICE "identifies" through the program and the number of Priority Category 1 criminals that the agency arrests and detains. Thus, a large number of persons flagged by Secure Communities as Priority 1 criminals may have no criminal conviction, but are classified as such on the basis of their arrest.

Classification aside, the growth in Secure Communities has led to a surge in detainers issued by ICE. In FY 2009, ICE reported issuing 20,074 detainers through Secure Communities.[563] This figure may understate the impact of Secure Communities, because it did not count detainers technically issued through the 287(g) or CAP programs, when they operate in tandem with Secure Communities.

In FY 2010, the number of individuals issued detainers through Secure Communities rose to 111,093.[564] Noncitizens without criminal convictions and Priority Level 3 criminal convictions (misdemeanants) made up 55 percent of those placed in removal proceedings through the program, and 60 percent of those ultimately ordered removed.[565] In FY 2011, such noncitizens made up 55 percent of those removed through Secure Communities, although ICE has indicated that some may fall into other agency priority categories, such as fugitive aliens, individuals who have returned following an order of removal, and recent border crossers (see Figure 25).[566]

---

559 ICE, *Secure Communities: Quarterly Report Fiscal Year 2011 Report to Congress, Third Quarter*, 9.
560 ICE, *Secure Communities: Quarterly Report, Fiscal Year 2011 Report to Congress, First Quarter*, 5; ICE, *IDENT/IAFIS Interoperability Statistics*, 2; ICE, *Secure Communities: Quarterly Report, Fiscal Year 2011 Report to Congress, First Quarter*, 5; ICE, *Secure Communities: Quarterly Report, Fiscal Year 2011 Report to Congress, Second Quarter*, 5; ICE, *Secure Communities: Quarterly Report Fiscal Year 2011 Report to Congress, Third Quarter*, 5; DHS, *Budget in Brief FY 2013*, 96.
561 See ICE, *Secure Communities: Quarterly Report, Fiscal Year 2010 Report to Congress, Third Quarter*, 5, (noting that "IDENT matches for the Level 1, 2, and 3 aliens are based on charge or conviction, which are described in Section 11.1A of this report").
562 Ibid.
563 ICE, "Secure Communities Presentation," January 13, 2010, www.ice.gov/doclib/foia/secure_communities/securecommunitiespresentations.pdf.
564 ICE, *IDENT/IAFIS Interoperability Statistics*, 2.
565 Ibid.
566 ICE, *Secure Communities: Monthly Statistics through January 31, 2012* (Washington, DC: ICE, 2012): 2, www.ice.gov/doclib/foia/sc-stats/nationwide_interoperability_stats-fy2012-to-date.pdf.

Figure 25. Secure Communities Removals by Priority Levels, FY 2011

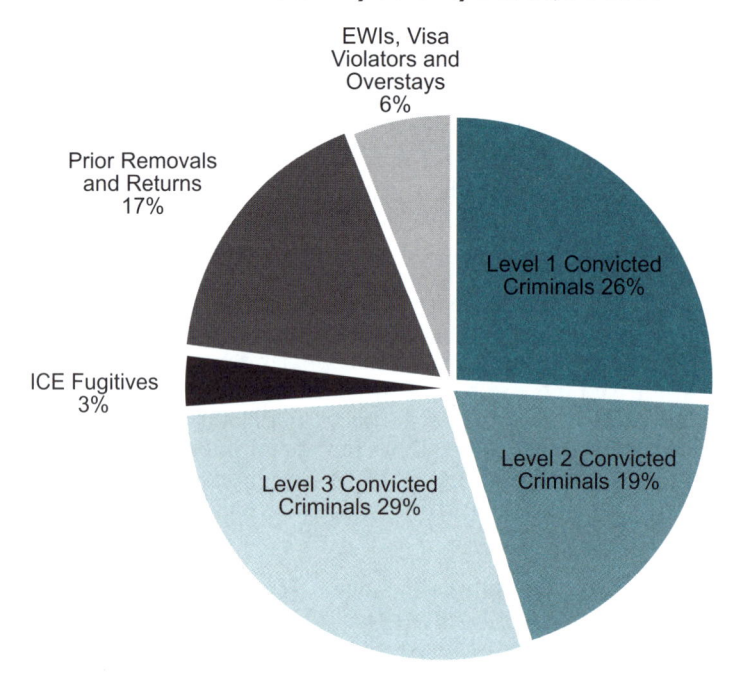

- EWIs, Visa Violators and Overstays 6%
- Prior Removals and Returns 17%
- ICE Fugitives 3%
- Level 1 Convicted Criminals 26%
- Level 2 Convicted Criminals 19%
- Level 3 Convicted Criminals 29%

Source: ICE, "Secure Communities Nationwide Interoperability Statistics, 2011," www.ice.gov/foia/library/index.htm#50.

Initially, ICE indicated that Secure Communities was a voluntary program. Many states expressed unease about their involvement, citing concerns that Secure Communities could undermine cooperation between the police and immigrant communities. In particular, Massachusetts, Illinois, and New York decided against participating in the program,[567] as did a number of localities, such as Arlington, VA; Washington, DC; and Santa Clara and San Francisco, CA.[568] However, what it meant to opt out of the program was unclear.

In October 2010, Homeland Security Secretary Napolitano stated that she did not view Secure Communities as an "opt-in/opt-out" program.[569] On August 5, 2011, ICE terminated all of its Secure Communities Memoranda of Agreement (MOA) with states on the grounds that "[o]nce a state or local law enforcement agency voluntarily submits fingerprint data to the federal government, no agreement with the state is legally necessary for one part of the federal government to share it with another part."[570]

As a result, Secure Communities is now functional in all states, including those that expressed concerns. At the same time, DHS affirmed its intention to "activate" the

---

567 Tara Bahrampour, "ICE Reforms Secure Communities Program," *Washington Post*, June 17, 2011, www.washingtonpost.com/local/ice-reforms-secure-communities-program/2011/06/17/AGMJkaZH_story.html.
568 Elise Foley. "Communities Opt Out of Immigration Enforcement Program," *Washington Independent*, September 29, 2011, http://washingtonindependent.com/99071/communities-opt-out-of-immigration-enforcement-program; Mallie Jane Kim, "Controversial Immigration Program Spurs Federal-State Spat," *US News and World Report*, June 27, 2011, www.usnews.com/news/articles/2011/06/27/controversial-immigration-program-spurs-federal-state-spat.
569 DHS, "Press Conference with Secretary of Homeland Security Janet Napolitano; Immigration and Customs Enforcement Director John Morton; Los Angeles County, California, Sheriff Lee Baca; Harris County, Texas, Sheriff Adrian Garcia; Fairfax County, Virginia, Sheriff Stan Barry on New Immigration Enforcement Results," (briefing, Washington, DC, October 6, 2010).
570 Letter from John Morton, Assistant Secretary, ICE, to the Honorable Jack Markell, Governor of Delaware (August 5, 2011), http://epic.org/privacy/secure_communities/SGN.pdf.

program nationwide by March 2013, which seems to be a reconfirmation of its plans to complete implementation of the program in all local jails by then.

D. Targeting Transnational Criminal Enterprises

DHS does not report extensively on its programs that target transnational criminals. However, this work is a high priority for the agency. In FY 2010, ICE initiated 2,200 human-smuggling investigations, which led to 2,500 arrests, 1,400 indictments, 1,500 convictions, and $15 million in seized assets.[571] In addition, ICE's Office of Investigations (OI) participates in the Extraterritorial Criminal Travel Strike Force (ECT) which targets terrorist travel and human smuggling.[572] Three of DHS's leading programs focused on transnational criminal enterprises are as follows:

1. Operation Predator

ICE launched Operation Predator in 2003 to target citizens and noncitizens who perpetrate child sex abuse crimes.[573] The initiative seeks to identify, investigate, and arrest human traffickers, international sex tourists, Internet pornographers, and "foreign national predators."[574] Operation Predator has resulted in the arrest of over 13,594 individuals, of whom 10,975 were noncitizens, from its launch in 2003 through October 2011.[575]

2. Border Enforcement Security Task Forces (BEST)

The Border Enforcement Security Task Forces (BESTs) target drug trafficking and other criminal organizations along the US southern and northern borders. ICE created the first BEST partnership in Laredo, TX in August 2005.[576] The program has since expanded to 32 task force teams operating in 36 cities in 17 states as well as Puerto Rico and Mexico City; the units are comprised of ICE, CBP, Coast Guard, ATF, and other federal agencies; state and local law enforcement agencies; and, in some jurisdictions, Mexican and Canadian officials.[577] In FY 2010, the task forces made 1,618 criminal and 907 administrative arrests, resulting in 868 indictments and 689 convictions.[578] In FY 2011, BESTs made 2,196 criminal arrests and 1,135 administrative arrests, securing 1,193 indictments and 1,078 convictions.[579]

3. Operation Community Shield

In February 2005, ICE created Operation Community Shield to "disrupt and dismantle violent transnational street gangs."[580] Under the program, ICE partners with federal, state, and local law enforcement agents to share intelligence on gangs and to arrest, prosecute, and remove noncitizen gang members.[581] Two months following its creation,

---

571 DHS, "Enforce and Administer Our Immigration Laws," accessed November 18, 2012, www.dhs.gov/xabout/gc_1240610592951.shtm.
572 Ibid.
573 ICE, "ICE Arrests South Florida Residents for Transferring Obscene Material to a Juvenile," (press release, November 24, 2010), www.ice.gov/news/releases/1011/101124fortpierce.htm.
574 Ibid.
575 Statement of Kumar Kibble, Deputy Director, ICE, before the House Committee on Homeland Security, Subcommittee on Border and Maritime Security, *Does Administrative Amnesty Harm Our Efforts to Gain and Maintain Operational Control of the Border?* 112th Cong., 1st sess., October 4, 2011, www.gpo.gov/fdsys/pkg/CHRG-112hhrg73358/pdf/CHRG-112hhrg73358.pdf.
576 DHS, *Budget-in-Brief FY 2008*, 36, 38.
577 ICE, "Border Enforcement Security Task Force (BEST)," accessed November 18, 2012, www.ice.gov/best/.
578 DHS, *FY 2012 Budget in Brief*, 76.
579 DHS, *FY 2013 Budget in Brief*, 94.
580 DHS, *Budget-in-Brief FY 2007*, 32.
581 ICE, "MS-13 Members Convicted of Federal Racketeering Charges," (press release, December 8, 2010), www.ice.gov/news/releases/1012/101208washington.htm.

Bush administration officials credited the program with the arrest (for immigration violations) of 150 Mara Salvatrucha (MS-13) gang members, including nine leaders and the head of MS-13 in Honduras.[582] The program targets people who are threats to national security, gang leaders, and persons with violent criminal histories.[583] Between its inception and September 1, 2009, Operation Community Shield led to 8,575 criminal and 10,350 administrative arrests, with 226 arrests of reported gang leaders.[584]

In FY 2010, ICE conducted a joint operation with other federal, state, and local law enforcement agencies that targeted transnational street gangs, prison gangs, and motorcycle gangs involved in drug trafficking. The operation led to the arrest of 517 gang members, associates, and others in 83 US cities.[585] In February 2010, ICE launched its first "global" Operation Community Shield Task Force based in Honduras.[586]

> *The new nexus between immigration enforcement and the criminal justice system has been buttressed by substantial resource infusions and new information and data system capabilities. The scope of today's criminal enforcement programs and the numbers of cases they generate for both the federal courts and immigration removal systems have risen steeply over just a few years' time. This pillar depicts a serious new dimension of law enforcement in local jurisdictions all over the country.*

II. Program Critique and Findings

The rapid and increasing interplay between immigration and criminal law has had far-reaching impacts at different levels of law enforcement and the criminal justice system. Perhaps the strongest reaction to the changes came in May 2010, with the landmark Supreme Court decision, *Padilla v. Kentucky*. The high court held that the failure of criminal defense lawyers to advise clients of the immigration consequences of criminal plea agreements constituted ineffective counsel in violation of the Sixth Amendment of the US Constitution.[587] The Supreme Court stated:

The landscape of federal immigration law has changed dramatically over the last 90 years. While there was once a narrow class of deportable offenses and judges wielded broad discretionary authority to prevent deportation, immigration reforms over time have expanded the class of deportable offenses and limited the authority of judges to alleviate the harsh consequences of deportation... These changes to our immigration law have dramatically raised the stakes of a noncitizen's criminal conviction.[588]

The high stakes that criminal convictions present for noncitizens, expanded criminal prosecution of immigration violations, and the rapid growth in programs aimed at criminal aliens have together raised a set of concerns from a variety of perspectives.

---

582 See Statement of John P. Torres, Deputy Assistant Director, Human Smuggling and Public Safety Division, ICE, before the House Committee on International Relations, Subcommittee on the Western Hemisphere, *Gangs and Crime in Latin America, Gangs and Crime in Latin America*, 109th Cong., 1st sess., April 20, 2005, www.ice.gov/doclib/news/library/speeches/042005Gang_testimony_torres.pdf.
583 Ibid.
584 ICE, "MS-13 Members Convicted of Federal Racketeering Charges," (news release, December 8, 2010), www.ice.gov/news/releases/1012/101208washington.htm.
585 DHS, *FY 2012 Budget in Brief*, 78.
586 ICE, "ICE's Operation Community Shield Goes Global with a New Task Force in Honduras: Operation Double Impact from the Videographer's View," (press release, August 11, 2010), www.ice.gov/news/releases/1008/100811washingtondc.htm.
587 *Padilla v. Kentucky,* 130 S. Ct. 1473, 1481-87 (2010).
588 Ibid., 1478.

A. Concerns Related to Immigration Prosecutions

The expanded use of criminal prosecution of immigration violations as an enforcement tool has drawn heavy criticism from immigrant advocates, civil-liberties groups, the media, judges, and public defenders. Operation Streamline has especially drawn scrutiny. Some immigration and civil-liberties advocates argue that it primarily targets low-level immigration violators, a practice at odds with the administration's emphasis on dangerous criminal aliens.[589] Academics have expressed concerns over the program's potential to violate due process since federal public defenders often do not have time to meet with individual clients and to prepare their cases, especially when defendants accept guilty pleas en masse.[590] In addition, federal prosecutors now spend significant time prosecuting immigration cases, which may inhibit their ability to bring cases for more serious offenses, such as illegal drug and arms trafficking.[591]

Even apart from the Supreme Court's decision in *Padilla*, the trend in increased immigration prosecutions has not gone unnoticed by the judicial system. In May 2009, the Supreme Court unanimously held in *Flores-Figueroa v. United States* that the government could not sustain aggravated identity theft charges against a noncitizen who used a false social security card to work, unless it could prove that the person knew that the social security number belonged to another person.[592] Following large-scale worksite enforcement raids during the Bush administration, prosecutors used the threat of prosecution for aggravated identity theft (which carries a mandatory two-year prison sentence) to pressure noncitizens to plead guilty to lesser charges, such as identity fraud.[593]

B. Criticism of Programs Targeted at Criminal Aliens

The four major programs administered by ICE to target criminal aliens have all generated considerable controversy. The criticism has mostly surrounded the extent to which these programs meet their stated goals of identifying and removing criminal aliens, as opposed to ordinary immigration status violators. These programs have also come under scrutiny for their substantial negative family, community, and social impacts.

Commentators have argued that despite its billing as a program that screens for convicted criminals, a large percentage of noncitizens apprehended through CAP do not have criminal convictions. In FY 2010, fewer than 60 percent of CAP arrests had criminal convictions.[594] This is partly due to the fact that CAP teams screen noncitizens who have been arrested but not necessarily convicted of, crimes. In addition, several programs that fall under the CAP umbrella target nonincarcerated persons who may or may not have criminal convictions.[595] The DHS-appointed Task Force on Secure Communities has also raised the concern that the program may undermine the relationship between immigrant communities and local police at the risk of endangering public safety.[596]

---

589 American Civil Liberties Union and National Immigration Forum, "Operation Streamline" (fact sheet, July 21, 2009), www.immigrationforum.org/images/uploads/OperationStreamlineFactsheet.pdf.
590 Lydgate, "Assembly-Line Justice: A Review of Operation Streamline."
591 Ted Robbins, "Border Patrol Program Raises Due Process Concerns," National Public Radio, September 13, 2010, www.npr.org/templates/story/story.php?storyId=129780261.
592 *Flores-Figueroa v. United States*, 556 U.S. 646, 646 (2009).
593 Adam Liptak and Julia Preston, "Justices Limit Use of Identity Theft Law in Immigration Cases," *The New York Times*, May 4, 2009, www.nytimes.com/2009/05/05/us/05immig.html?_r=1&scp=1&sq=aggravated%20identity%20theft&st=cse.
594 DHS, *FY 2012 Budget in Brief*, 79.
595 See Part II, section on the Criminal Alien program, explaining that several of the programs within CAP, including the Violent Criminal Alien Section (VCAS) and the Joint Criminal Alien and Removal Task Forces (JCARTs) target some noncitizens who are not incarcerated or do not have criminal convictions.
596 Task Force on Secure Communities, *Findings and Recommendations* (Washington, DC: Homeland Security Advisory Council, 2011), www.dhs.gov/xlibrary/assets/hsac-task-force-on-secure-communities.pdf.

Recent reports have suggested that NFOP has failed to focus its resources on the priorities Congress intended when it authorized the program. Despite NFOP's mandate to arrest dangerous fugitives, almost three-quarters (73 percent) of the individuals apprehended by Fugitive Operations Teams (FOTs) from 2003 through February 2008 had no criminal convictions.[597] In FY 2010, fugitive criminal aliens constituted less than 30 percent of the total number of people arrested through NFOP.

Likewise, the 287(g) program has been criticized for inconsistent and divergent implementation, often driven by local priorities and political imperatives. Given leeway in interpreting program mandates, some jurisdictions have targeted serious and dangerous criminal offenders, while others have adopted a more universal model that draws in large numbers of unauthorized immigrants with misdemeanors and traffic offenses.[598] Since the universal models have been used heavily in the Southeast, the program's implementation has generated most controversy in that part of the country. The ten sites with the largest share of detainers placed on traffic violators are all in the Southeast.[599]

The universal enforcement models in the 287(g) program have also resulted in substantial community impacts. Many believe that they have created mistrust of authorities in immigrant communities, reduced reporting of crimes, withdrawal of immigrants from public places, and changes in driving behavior.[600]

Secure Communities, the most rapidly expanding of these federal programs, has been similarly criticized from many vantage points, including by state and local officials, academic experts, and immigrant advocates. Like the 287(g) program, it is viewed as undermining public trust in the police, and hampering their ability to conduct their primary job of ensuring public safety.[601] The program has also been discredited for placing in removal proceedings those who may have been wrongfully arrested, or individuals never charged for any crime or possessing no prior criminal record.

---

597 Mendelson et al., *Collateral Damage*, 11.
598 Capps et al., *Delegation and Divergence*, 18-9.
599 Ibid., 23-4.
600 Ibid., 38-41.
601 National Immigration Law Center (NILC), "DHS Proposes Fantasy Remedies to Cure Fundamental Flaws in the Secure Communities Program," July 2011, www.nilc.org/DHS-6-17-11-memos-QA-2011-07.html; Julianne Hing, "Counties Defy Feds, Vow Not to Detain Immigrants on ICE's Behalf," *Colorlines*, October 25, 2011, http://colorlines.com/archives/2011/10/counties_unable_to_opt_out_of_secure_communities_vow_not_to_detain_immigrants_on_ices_behalf.html.

■ FINDINGS

■ **Immigration enforcement is playing** an increasingly dominant role in the federal criminal justice system. Between FY 2001-09, prosecutions for immigration-related crimes rose more than fivefold, from 16,310 to 91,899. Immigration crimes accounted for 17 to 20 percent of total federal prosecutions in FY 2000-03. By FY 2008-11, they represented more than 50 percent of federal prosecutions. Illegal entry (a misdemeanor) and illegal re-entry following removal (a felony) comprise more than 90 percent of such prosecutions.

■ **Among federal law enforcement agencies, CBP** refers more cases for prosecution in federal courts than the FBI. CBP and ICE together refer more cases for prosecution than all of the DOJ law enforcement agencies combined, including FBI, DEA, and ATF.

■ **Among immigration agencies, CBP** refers more cases for criminal prosecution than ICE. In FY 2011, CBP referred 67,112 immigration cases, while ICE referred 13,007.

■ **Since its implementation in 2008, Operation Streamline** has been a key driver of increased immigration prosecutions. The five federal districts along the US-Mexico border, which are home to less than 10 percent of the US population, now account for nearly half of all federal felony prosecutions.

■ **Over 50 crimes categorized as "aggravated felonies"** carry the automatic consequence of removal. State-level prosecutions of these crimes have placed an unprecedented number of noncitizens into immigration removal proceedings. In addition, programs involving federal, state, and local law enforcement agency cooperation have become major new forces in identifying such cases and apprehending immigration violators. Between FY 2006-11, the number of Notices to Appear (NTAs) issued through the Criminal Alien Program (CAP) rose from 67,850 to 212,744. In FY 2010, the 287(g) program identified 26,871 noncitizens for removal. The same year, ICE reported issuing 111,093 detainers through Secure Communities a rapid increase from the 20,074 detainers it reported in FY 2009.

■ **CAP has placed more noncitizens into the ICE detention system** than any other federal-state cooperation program. In FY 2009, ICE estimated that 48 percent of detained noncitizens had come through CAP. CAP teams operate in all state and federal prisons, as well as in more than 300 local jails.

■ **While removal of fugitive criminal aliens** — absconders who are also criminal aliens — is the stated goal of the National Fugitive Operations Program (NFOP), just 28 percent of NFOP arrests in FY 2010 met the fugitive criminal aliens definition. However, the proportion of criminal aliens processed through the program has increased. In FY 2010, 51 percent of those arrested under the program were criminal aliens as compared with FY 2003-February 2008, when 73 percent did not have a criminal history. From FY 2003-10, the number of noncitizens apprehended through NFOP rose from 1,900 to 35,774.

■ **Though authorized by Congress in 1996, the 287(g) program** experienced rapid growth between 2006 and 2008, when the number of agreements signed grew from six to 61. Since 2009, only two new agreements have been signed, and an estimated 14 were not renewed or were terminated. The number of people arrested through the program has fallen, and the administration has requested reductions in funding for the task force model of the program.

■ **Secure Communities is fast replacing the 287(g) program** and has become the predominant federal-state-local enforcement cooperation program. Since its launch in seven jurisdictions in October 2008, Secure Communities has grown dramatically. As of August 1, 2012, the program operated in 3,074 jurisdictions across all 50 states, and is expected to be operational in all of the nation's 3,181 jurisdictions by March 2013.

■ **During FY 2009, Secure Communities programs submitted** 828,119 fingerprints for federal database screening. In FY 2010, the number reached nearly 3.4 million, and rose to 6.9 million in FY 2011. During the same period, Secure Communities-attributed removals rose from 4 percent to 20 percent of all removals.

■ **In FY 2010, noncitizens with no criminal convictions** and Level 3 criminal aliens (misdemeanants) made up 56 percent of those placed in removal proceedings through Secure Communities, and 60 percent of those ultimately were ordered removed.

■ **Targeting transnational criminal enterprises** is a high ICE/DHS priority. Many of these efforts now involve cooperation with state, local, and international partners. Since 2005, ICE has expanded its Border Enforcement Security Task Forces (BESTs), which target drug trafficking and other criminal enterprises along the border, to 32 task force units operating in 36 cities across 17 states, Puerto Rico and Mexico, comprised of ICE, CBP, Coast Guard, ATF, and state and local law enforcement agents. In some jurisdictions, Mexican and Canadian officials participate in BEST teams. ICE has also expanded Operation Community Shield, an initiative that targets gangs and noncitizen gang members. In February 2010, ICE launched its first "global" Operation Community Shield Task Force in Honduras.

CHAPTER 8

DETENTION AND REMOVAL OF NONCITIZENS

Since 1986, more than 4 million deportations of noncitizens from the United States have been carried out. A sharp rise in removals has taken place over the last 15 years — climbing from 30,039 in 1990 to 188,467 in 2000[602] and 391,953 in 2011.[603] The groundwork for these levels of removals was laid over many years of congressional and administrative actions described in the prior chapters. Substantial expansion of detention capabilities to support removal outcomes and the adjudication of cases subject to removal make up the sixth pillar of the immigration enforcement system.

As removal of noncitizens has accelerated, two trends have become evident: an increase in the removal of criminal aliens, and extensive use of administrative (versus judicial) orders to effect removals. The historic rise in removals has brought into sharp focus the system of detaining noncitizens and the administrative court system to adjudicate removal cases.

I. Programs and Results

A. Removal of Criminal Aliens

Beginning in the 1990s and continuing today, the removal of criminal aliens — a broad group that includes both authorized and unauthorized noncitizens who have committed crimes that make them removable — has been a high priority.[604] The result has been an increase in the relative proportion of noncitizens in removal proceedings with criminal records.

As reported by DHS' Office of Immigration Statistics (OIS), in FY 2011, DHS removed 391,953 noncitizens, 48 percent of whom (188,382) had criminal convictions.[605] This continues an upward trend, rising from 27 percent in FY 2008[606] to 33 percent in FY 2009,[607] and 44 percent in FY 2010.[608] ICE, which issues its own statistics on removals and criminal removals (see Box 2 below), reported that in FY 2011, the total number of criminal aliens removed (216,698) exceeded the number of non-criminals removed

---

602 DHS, *Yearbook of Immigration Statistics: 2010*, Table 36 (Washington, DC: DHS, 2011), www.dhs.gov/xlibrary/assets/statistics/yearbook/2010/ois_yb_2010.pdf.

603 DHS, *Immigration Enforcement Actions: 2011*, 5. Notably, ICE publishes its own removals totals that differ somewhat from those listed in DHS's annual *Yearbook of Immigration Statistics*, published by the agency's Office of Immigration Statistics. ICE, "Removal Statistics," www.ice.gov/removal-statistics/. Because the OIS totals account for both ICE- and CBP-effectuated removals, and distinguish formal offers of removal from the various forms of voluntary return, this report cites the OIS numbers wherever possible.

604 Venturella testimony, *Priorities in Enforcing Immigration Law*, ("Secretary Napolitano has made the identification and removal of criminal aliens a top priority for ICE.")

605 DHS, *Immigration Enforcement Actions: 2011*, 6.

606 DHS, *Immigration Enforcement Actions: 2008*, 4.

607 DHS, *Immigration Enforcement Actions: 2009*, 4.

608 DHS, *Immigration Enforcement Actions: 2010* (Washington, DC: DHS, 2011): 4, www.dhs.gov/immigration-enforcement-actions-2010.

(180,208).[609] Regardless of which figures are used, the trend is clear: an increasing number of noncitizens being removed now have criminal convictions.

Figure 26. Criminal Alien Removals vs. Total Number of Removals, FY 2001-11

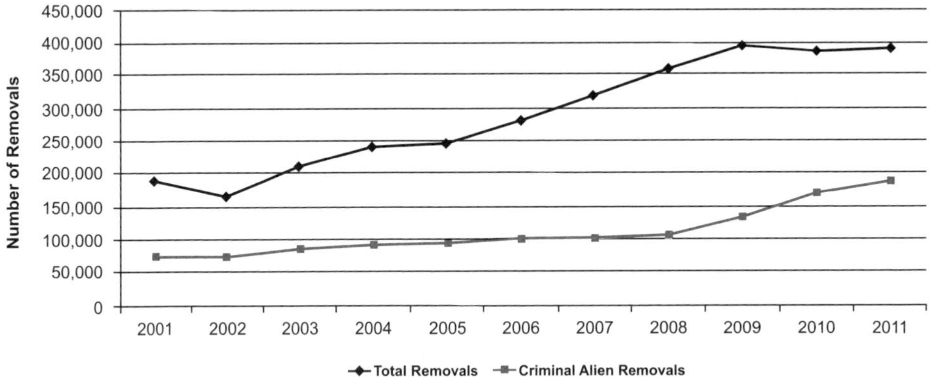

Source: DHS, *Yearbook of Immigration Statistics, FY 2011* (Washington, DC: DHS, 2012), www.dhs.gov/sites/default/files/publications/immigration-statistics/yearbook/2011/ois_yb_2011.pdf.

1. Issuing Removal Orders

Noncitizens can be removed from the United States either through formal proceedings in immigration courts or by an administrative order issued by DHS. In addition, federal judges may issue removal orders under certain circumstances as part of their sentencing of noncitizens convicted of federal crimes.[610] Several studies have examined problems in the immigration court system, including lack of legal counsel, inadequate translation services, and vast disparities in outcomes by different immigration judges.[611] Much less attention has been paid to the growing numbers of removals — roughly half of the total — that occur without a court appearance of any kind.

---

609 ICE, "Removal Statistics."
610 8 USC § 1228(c); Gerald L. Neuman, "Federal Courts Issues in Immigration Law," 78 *Texas Law Review* 1661, 1687 (2000).
611 ABA Commission on Immigration, *Reforming the Immigration System: Proposal to Promote Independence, Fairness, Efficiency, and Professionalism in the Adjudication of Removal Cases* (Washington, DC: ABA, 2010): 5-8, www.americanbar.org/content/dam/aba/administrative/immigration/coi_complete_full_report.authcheckdam.pdf, (noting problems related to the availability of legal counsel for individuals in immigration proceedings); Ibid., 2-26, (citing a 2008 survey of immigration judges which found that 20 percent were dissatisfied with over-the-phone translation services); Jaya Ramji-Nogales, Andrew I. Schoenholtz, and Phillip G. Schrag, *Refugee Roulette: Disparities in Asylum Adjudication and Proposals for Reform* (New York: New York University Press, 2009) (finding gross disparities in the asylum grant rates of various immigration judges); Donald M. Kerwin, *Revisiting the Need for Appointed Counsel* (Washington, DC: MPI, 2005), www.migrationpolicy.org/insight/Insight_Kerwin.pdf, (arguing that recent changes in immigration law have increased the need for competent counsel); ABA Commission on Immigration, *American Justice Through Immigrants' Eyes* (Washington, DC: ABA, 2004): 53-8, (citing concerns with immigrants' lack of access to legal counsel).

> ### Box 2. Reporting Removals
>
> The definitive "count" of the number of noncitizens formally removed from the United States each year has traditionally been the number released by DHS's Office of Immigration Statistics (OIS) in the agency's annual statistical yearbook. OIS defines a removal as the "compulsory and confirmed movement of an inadmissible or deportable alien out of the United States based on an order of removal." A return is defined as "the confirmed movement of an inadmissible or deportable alien out of the United States not based on an order of removal." Returns include individuals who depart pursuant to an order of voluntary departure issued by an immigration judge.
>
> In the most recent statistical yearbook, OIS reported that the United States returned 323,542 noncitizens during FY 2011 and removed 391,953. These figures include removals and returns made by ICE, as well as those made by CBP.
>
> ICE also issues its own statistics detailing the number of noncitizens that it has removed from the country. DHS has generally published the ICE numbers soon after the close of the fiscal year, which is months before OIS publishes the *Yearbook of Immigration Statistics*. The ICE figures differ from the numbers published by OIS, both because ICE includes in its removal statistics some individuals who departed the country without a formal removal order, and because ICE does not count in its number those people removed pursuant to removal orders issued by CBP.
>
> The OIS statistics are also subject to some dispute. While OIS counts departures made pursuant to grants of voluntary departure as returns, only those noncitizens who "check in" with DHS once they have departed may be counted. Although some noncitizens may have strong motivations to check in once they have departed, such as ensuring that their family members in the United States receive back the bond money paid to guarantee the departures, others do not actually check in with DHS once they have departed. This leads to the likelihood that DHS's annual statistical yearbook figures undercount the total number of returns.
>
> In addition, the OIS statistics on returns capture some, but not all, instances in which port of entry officials direct a noncitizen seeking entry to withdraw his or her request for admission. Such withdrawals are frequently employed by CBP's Office of Field Operations (OFO). However, it is unclear when and in what circumstances OFO directs a noncitizen to withdraw his or her application for admission, rather than placing the person in removal proceedings or issuing an expedited order of removal. Thus, an unknown number of port-of-entry enforcement actions are not reported in OIS's statistical yearbook.

Immigration judges acting within DOJ's Executive Office of Immigration Review (EOIR) adjudicate removal cases and can order noncitizens removed. Under the INA, a noncitizen identified by ICE as inadmissible or deportable can be placed in formal removal proceedings after being issued a Notice to Appear (NTA). During the proceedings, he or she can contest removability, and apply for political asylum or seek other discretionary relief from removal.[612]

In recent years, political asylum standards have tightened, new procedural barriers to

---

612 INA §240.

asylum have been erected, and asylum applications have decreased.[613] In addition, as discussed earlier, IIRIRA significantly limited discretionary relief from removal based on family ties and equities in the United States. Finally, only half of persons in removal proceedings — and about 15 percent of detainees — are represented by legal counsel.[614] Lack of representation significantly reduces an applicant's ability to mount an effective defense in complex and adversarial removal proceedings.[615] All these factors have contributed to the rise in removal orders issued by immigration judges.

As illustrated in Figure 27, the number of judicial removal orders fell between FY 2006 and FY 2007, but increased in FY 2008 and FY 2009, then fell again in FY 2010 and FY 2011 (to 161,354 orders).[616] Immigration judges can also order a noncitizen to depart "voluntarily" within a given period of time. Not all removable noncitizens are eligible for voluntary departure. To qualify, a noncitizen must demonstrate that he or she has the financial means to pay for departure, has been a person of "good moral character" for five years preceding the application, and has been physically present in the United States for at least one year.[617] Voluntary departure recipients do not receive formal removal orders, and thus are not subject to many statutory bars to re-enter the United States that apply to those formally removed. However, for statistical purposes, EOIR counts "voluntary departure" orders as removal orders.[618] In FY 2011, immigration judges granted voluntary departure to 30,385 people.[619]

The number of noncitizen removals by DHS each year greatly exceeds the number ordered removed through formal court proceedings. Since 2007, this gap has widened significantly. In FY 2011, DHS processed more than twice as many orders of removal as did immigration judges — with 391,953 and 161,354 respectively.[620] The current trend is the opposite of what it was in 1996, when immigration judges issued far more orders of removal than the number of people formally removed by immigration authorities. During that year, judges issued 147,652 orders of removal, while INS removed just 69,680 people.[621]

---

613 At EOIR, both applications and grants for asylum declined from FY 2007 (58,053 applications and 12,859 grants) to FY 2010 (40,405 applications and 9,906 grants). There was a slight uptick in FY 2011— EOIR received 41,000 applications for asylum and granted 11,504. See EOIR, "Asylum Statistics by Nationality FY 2007," www.justice.gov/eoir/efoia/FY07AsyStats-Current.pdf; EOIR, "Asylum Statistics by Nationality FY 2010," www.justice.gov/eoir/efoia/FY10AsyStats-Current.pdf; EOIR, "Asylum Statistics by Nationality FY 2011," www.justice.gov/eoir/efoia/FY11AsyStats-Current.pdf; Donald M. Kerwin, *The Faltering US Refugee Protection Program: Legal and Policy Responses to Refugees, Asylum Seekers, and Others in Need of Protection* (Washington, DC: MPI, 2011): 13-23, www.migrationpolicy.org/pubs/refugeeprotection-2011.pdf.
614 EOIR, *FY 2010 Statistical Yearbook* (Falls Church, VA: EOIR, 2011): G1, www.justice.gov/eoir/statspub/fy10syb.pdf; EOIR, FY 2011 Statistical Yearbook (Falls Church, VA: EOIR, 2012): G1, www.justice.gov/eoir/statspub/fy11syb.pdf; Human Rights Watch and ACLU, *Deportation by Default: Mental Disability, Unfair Hearings, and Indefinite Detention in the US Immigration System* (New York: Human Rights Watch and ACLU, 2010): 51, www.hrw.org/reports/2010/07/26/deportation-default-0.
615 Donald M. Kerwin, Doris Meissner, and Margie McHugh, *Executive Action on Immigration: Six Ways to Make the System Work Better* (Washington, DC: MPI, 2011): 23-4, www.migrationpolicy.org/pubs/administrativefixes.pdf.
616 EOIR, *FY 2011 Statistical Yearbook* (Falls Church, VA: EOIR, 2012): D2, www.justice.gov/eoir/statspub/fy11syb.pdf.
617 INA §240B (a)(4)(b).
618 EOIR, *FY 2011 Statistical Yearbook*, Q1.
619 EOIR, *FY 2011 Statistical Yearbook*, Q1.
620 DHS, *Immigration Enforcement Actions: 2011*, 6; EOIR, *FY 2011 Statistical Yearbook*, D2.
621 EOIR, *Statistical Yearbook 2000* (Falls Church, VA: EOIR, 2001): 12, www.justice.gov/eoir/statspub/SYB2000Final.pdf.

Figure 27. Overall Noncitizen Removals and Removal Orders, FY 1996-2011

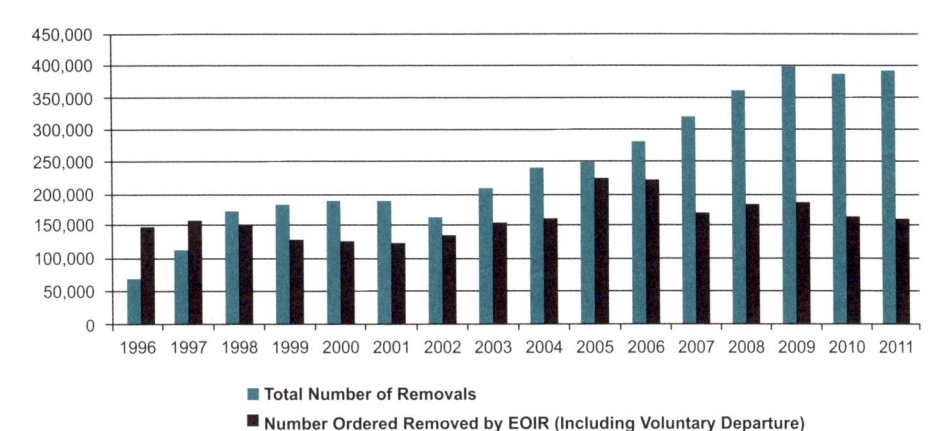

- Total Number of Removals
- Number Ordered Removed by EOIR (Including Voluntary Departure)

Sources: DHS, *Yearbook of Immigration Statistics FY 2011*, 102; EOIR, *Statistical Yearbook, FY 2002-2011* (Falls Church, VA: EOIR, various dates), www.justice.gov/eoir/statspub/syb2000main.htm.

One reason for this wide gap could be simply that DHS is arresting and removing more persons who were issued formal orders of removal in previous years. However, at least part of the increase in actual removals is attributable to increased administrative removals, i.e. people removed by DHS pursuant to administrative orders, rather than ordered removed by an immigration judge.

This increase in the use of administrative orders is rooted in the authority given to DHS officials to issue orders of removal to four categories of noncitizens: those subject to expedited removal, certain criminal aliens who are not lawful permanent residents (LPRs), those covered by stipulated orders of removal, and those subject to reinstatements of orders of removal.

2. Expedited Removal

Today, roughly one-third of total removals are through expedited orders of removal.[622] Persons ordered removed pursuant to the expedited removal process do not receive a hearing before a judge.[623] They are also subject to mandatory detention while awaiting removal.[624]

The authority for the expedited removal process, which Congress created in IIRIRA, comes from two separate provisions.[625] Under the first provision, an immigration officer may issue an expedited order of removal to certain noncitizens who attempt to enter the United States through a port of entry using fraud or false documents,[626] with an exception carved out for individuals who choose to seek asylum.[627]

A separate provision of the IIRIRA statute gives the attorney general the discretion to apply the expedited removal process to designated groups of noncitizens found outside of ports of entry who have been physically present in the United States for less than two years.[628] In the immediate aftermath of IIRIRA's passage, INS applied expedited removal

---

[622] DHS, *Immigration Enforcement Actions: 2011*, 5.
[623] Ibid.
[624] Haddal and Siskin, *Immigration Related Detention: Current Legislative Issues*, 8.
[625] *Omnibus Consolidated Appropriations Act, 1997*, Pub. L. 104-208, 110 Stat. 3009-664 (September 30, 1996), Sec. 302(b)(1)(A)(i) and Sec. 302(b)(1)(A)(iii) (incorporating the *Illegal Immigration Reform and Immigrant Responsibility Act*).
[626] Ibid., sec. 302(b)(1)(A)(i).
[627] Ibid., sec. 302(b)(1)(A)(ii).
[628] Ibid., sec. 302(b)(1)(A)(iii).

procedures only to noncitizens identified at ports of entry.[629]

Beginning in 2002, INS (and later DHS) began designating new groups of noncitizens subject to expedited removal by expanding the reach of the program beyond ports of entry. In a November 13, 2002 *Federal Register* notice, INS announced that it would apply the expedited removal process to noncitizens who had arrived in the United States by sea, had not been admitted or paroled, and could not demonstrate continuous presence in the United States for at least two years.[630] In August 2004, DHS extended the program to noncitizens "encountered" within 100 miles of a US international land border, or who had not been continuously present in the country for more than 14 days.[631]

With these expanded designations, expedited removals increased significantly in FY 2005 (87,888) and FY 2006 (110,663).[632] Since 2006, the number of expedited removals has remained fairly constant. In FY 2010, for example, there were 111,116 removals (29 percent of all removals).[633] In FY 2011, 31 percent of all removals (123,180) were expedited removals.[634] Given significant decreases in illegal border crossings over this period, the ratio of expedited removals to illegal crossings has increased in recent years.

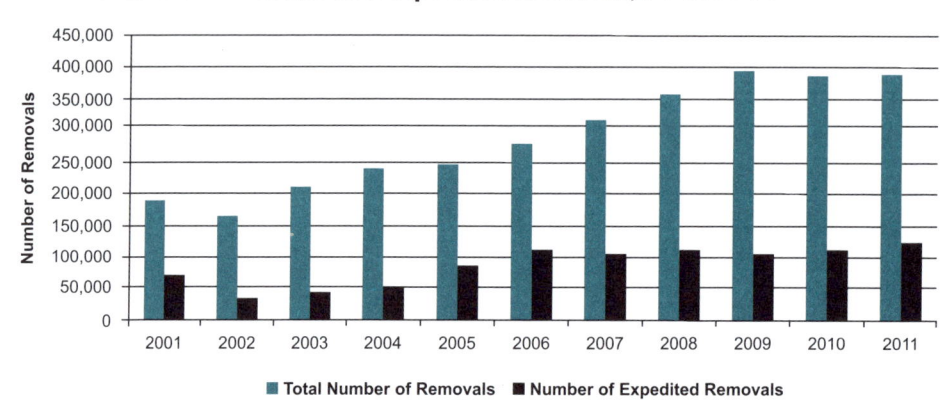

Figure 28. Number of Removals and Expedited Removals, FY 2000-11

Sources: John Simanski and Lesley M. Sapp, *Immigration Enforcement Actions: 2011* (Washington, DC: DHS, Office of Immigration Statistics, 2012), www.dhs.gov/sites/default/files/publications/immigration-statistics/enforcement_ar_2011.pdf; *Immigration Enforcement Actions: 2009* (Washington, DC: DHS, Office of Immigration Statistics, 2010), www.dhs.gov/xlibrary/assets/statistics/publications/enforcement_ar_2009.pdf.

3. Criminal Aliens

In addition to expedited removals, ICE can issue orders of removal to certain criminal aliens who are not LPRs and who have been previously convicted of aggravated felonies.[635] ICE does not release statistics on the number of persons to whom it issues administrative orders of removal. A report by the Transactional Records Access Clearinghouse (TRAC) estimated that 55 percent of the removal orders issued to noncitizens

---

[629] DOJ, "Inspection and Expedited Removal of Aliens; Detention and Removal of Aliens; Conduct of Removal Proceedings; Asylum Procedures; Final Rule," 62 *Federal Register* 44, 10313 (March 6, 1997).
[630] DOJ, "Notice Designating Aliens Subject to Expedited Removal Under Section 235(b)(1)(A)(iii) of the Immigration and Nationality Act," 67 *Federal Register* 219, 68924-26 (November 13, 2002).
[631] DHS, "Notice Designating Aliens for Expedited Removal," 69 *Federal Register* 154, 48877 (August 11, 2004).
[632] DHS, *Immigration Enforcement Actions: 2009*, 4.
[633] DHS, *Immigration Enforcement Actions: 2010*, 4.
[634] DHS, *Immigration Enforcement Actions: 2011*, 5.
[635] INA §238(b).

convicted of aggravated felonies in FY 2006 were issued by ICE, rather than by the immigration court.[636]

4. Stipulated Orders

An unknown number of removal orders are also issued pursuant to stipulated orders of removal. These are signed statements in which a noncitizen agrees to waive his or her rights to a hearing before an immigration judge, acknowledges removability, and accepts a final order of deportation.[637] These orders are typically signed by ICE detainees who seek to avoid prolonged detention.[638] While ICE and EOIR do not release statistics on stipulated orders, an estimated 100,000 noncitizens were removed through this process between FY 2004 and FY 2008.[639] Of those who signed stipulated orders, 94.5 percent were not represented by counsel.[640]

5. Reinstated Orders

Finally, a significant number of removals are reinstatements of orders of removal— old orders of removal that are "called up" and re-counted when an individual who has already been ordered removed comes into contact with DHS officials at a subsequent time. Under the INA, if DHS finds that a noncitizen previously removed from the United States has re-entered the country, the agency may immediately remove the individual by re-effectuating the prior removal order.[641]

Under such circumstances, the prior order is not subject to being reopened or reviewed, and the noncitizen is not eligible for any form of immigration relief.[642] In FY 2011, individuals removed pursuant to the issuance or reinstatements of removal constituted 33 percent (130,006) of the total number of noncitizens removed.[643]

6. More Removals, Fewer Returns

DHS distinguishes between formal orders of removal and confirmed voluntary return of noncitizens to another country, i.e. those physically removed but not pursuant to formal orders of removal.[644]

In recent years, the number of noncitizens removed pursuant to formal orders has increased significantly, while the number of voluntary return actions has steadily declined. In FY 2000, for example, the INS formally removed 184,775 persons, but returned nine times that number (1.7 million).[645] In FY 2010, DHS formally removed 387,242 persons, but returned 476,405, the sixth straight year in which the number of

---

636 TRAC, *New Data on the Processing of Aggravated Felons* (Syracuse, NY: TRAC, 2007), http://trac.syr.edu/immigration/reports/175/.
637 Human Rights Watch and ACLU, *Deportation by Default*, 9.
638 Ibid.
639 Jayashri Srikantiah and Karen Tumlin, "Stipulated Removal" (Backgrounder, National Immigration Law Center and Stanford Immigrants' Rights Clinic, Stanford, CA, 2008): 1, www.law.stanford.edu/program/clinics/immigrantsrights/pressrelease/Stipulated_removal_backgrounder.pdf.
640 Ibid., 3.
641 INA §241(a)(5).
642 Ibid. There is a minor exception for individuals who express fear of torture or persecution in their home countries. Such individuals are referred first to an asylum officer, who determines whether their expressed fear meets the "reasonable fear of persecution" standard. If it does, they are referred to immigration proceedings before an immigration judge, who is authorized only to determine whether they qualify for withholding of removal or relief under the international Convention Against Torture (CAT). See DHS, OIG, *DHS Detainee Removals and Reliance on Assurances* (Washington, DC: DHS, OIG, 2011), www.oig.dhs.gov/assets/Mgmt/OIG_11-100_Nov11.pdf.
643 DHS, *Immigration Enforcement Actions 2011*, 5.
644 DHS, *2009 Yearbook of Immigration Statistics*, 95.
645 INS, *Statistical Yearbook of the Immigration and Naturalization Service, 2000* (Washington, DC: INS, 2002): 245, www.dhs.gov/xlibrary/assets/statistics/yearbook/2009/ois_yb_2009.pdf.

voluntary returns declined.[646] In FY 2011, for the first time, DHS removed more individuals than it returned (the agency removed 391,953 persons pursuant to the issuance of formal orders of removal and returned 323,542).[647]

Most voluntary returns are granted to Mexican and Canadian nationals who are arrested near the border.[648] This trend is likely attributable to the decline in illegal border crossings, the increase in the number of administrative orders issued, and the increase in the number of border crossers referred by CBP for criminal prosecution.

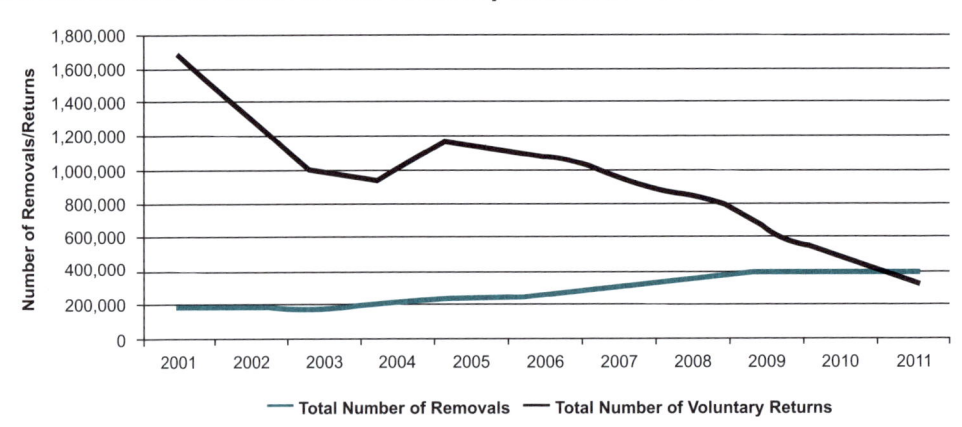

Figure 29. Number of Removals and Voluntary Returns, FY 2000-11

Sources: DHS, *Yearbooks of Immigration Statistics, FY 2010 and 2011* (Washington, DC: DHS, 2011 and 2012), www.dhs.gov/yearbook-immigration-statistics; and INS, *2000 Statistical Yearbook of the Immigration and Naturalization Service* (Washington, DC: INS, 2001), www.dhs.gov/xlibrary/assets/statistics/yearbook/2000/Yearbook2000.pdf.

B. The Immigration Detention System

ICE's detention program is an integral part of the removal system. The purpose or goal of detention authority as part of the INA is to assure that noncitizens appear for their removal proceedings or do not abscond after a final order of removal has been issued. ICE does not detain individuals for punitive reasons or to serve criminal sentences.

Despite this limited mandate, ICE manages a large, complex and sprawling detention system that holds a highly diverse immigrant population in an equally diverse set of facilities: local jails, for-profit prisons, federal prisons, its own Service Processing Centers, special care facilities, and alternative-to-detention (ATD) programs. The detainee population comprises:

- men, women and families
- persons of all ages, backgrounds, religions, and nationalities
- asylum seekers, recent arrivals, and "career" criminals
- persons in removal proceedings and those ordered removed whose countries will not accept their return

---

646 DHS, *Immigration Enforcement Actions: 2010*, 1.
647 DHS, *Immigration Enforcement Actions: 2011*, 1.
648 DHS, *Immigration Enforcement Actions: 2009*, 4 (noting that in FY 2009, 85 percent of returns involved Mexican or Canadian aliens).

- persons with different immigration and criminal histories, subject to different custody and release requirements
- short-term detainees and those who will be in its custody for years.[649]

ICE's considerable detention management challenges have been complicated by rapid growth in the number of those removable, and by laws that mandate the detention of some categories of noncitizens even when they do not represent a danger or flight risk. ICE's daily detainee population more than quadrupled between FY 1995 and FY 2011, rising from 7,475 to 33,330.[650] Over the same period, the total number of individuals ICE detained annually increased from 85,730 to 429,247.[651]

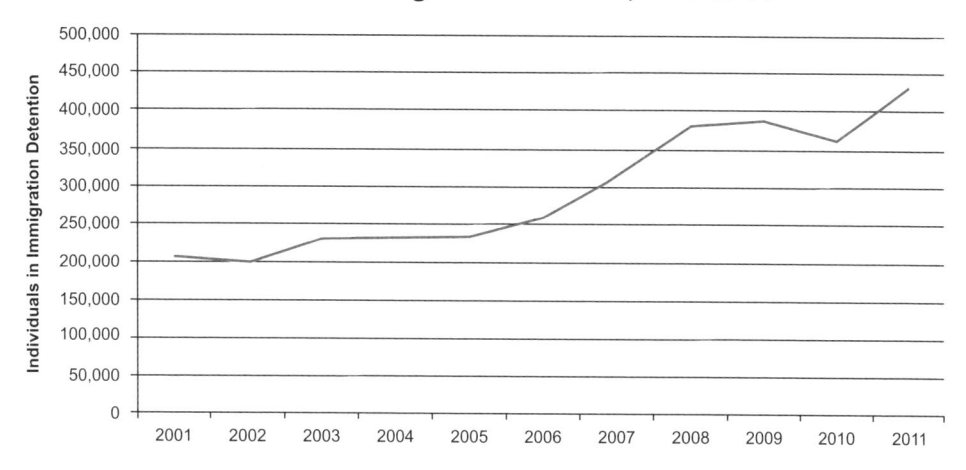

Figure 30. Growth in Number of Immigration Detainees, FY 2001-11

Source: ICE, "Report on ERO Facts and Statistics," December 12, 2011, www.ice.gov/foia/library/.

The size and scope of the immigration detention system can be illustrated by comparing it with Bureau of Prisons (BOP) custody for federal criminal offenders. The federal prison system is fundamentally different than immigration detention in that it incarcerates individuals serving sentences for committing federal crimes. Nonetheless, the relative size of each system illustrates the challenges of scale embedded in ICE's mission. In FY 2001, for example, INS detained 204,459 people, roughly three times the number who entered the federal prison system (66,654).[652] By 2010 the total number of persons detained by ICE had risen to 363,064, more than five times the number of people entering prison for federal criminal offenses.[653] In addition, a significantly larger number of individuals are detained each year in the immigration detention system

---

649 Donald M. Kerwin and Serena Yi-Ying Lin, *Immigrant Detention: Can ICE Meet Its Legal Imperatives and Case Management Responsibilities?* (Washington, DC: MPI, 2009), www.migrationpolicy.org/pubs/detentionreport-Sept1009.pdf.
650 Haddal and Siskin, *Immigration-Related Detention: Current Legislative Issues*, 12; ICE, "ERO Facts and Statistics (2011)."
651 DHS, *Immigration Enforcement Actions: 2010*, 4; DHS, *Immigration Enforcement Actions: 2009*, 3; Donald M. Kerwin, *Detention of Newcomers: Constitutional Standards and New Legislation: Part One* (Washington, DC: Federal Publications, Inc., 1996); ICE, "ERO Facts and Statistics."
652 DOJ, Bureau of Justice Statistics, "Federal Criminal Case Processing Statistics," http://bjs.ojp.usdoj.gov/fjsrc/var.cfm?t=new; ICE, "ERO Facts and Statistics."
653 Comparison is of US Bureau of Prisons "book-ins" to detainees entering ICE detention; Ibid.

than are serving sentences in federal Bureau of Prisons facilities for all other federal crimes.[654]

It is also notable that of the total number of people entering federal prison for criminal offenses, an increasing number are imprisoned for immigration-related offenses. According to DOJ's Bureau of Justice Statistics, among all individuals who entered prison for federal criminal offenses in 2001, 13,167 (approximately 20 percent) had been convicted for immigration-related criminal offenses.[655] By 2009, the number of federal prisoners who had been convicted of immigration-related criminal offenses had risen to 30 percent (22,563) of the total number entering Bureau of Prisons custody.[656]

I. Mandatory Detention

IIRIRA and the *USA PATRIOT Act* expanded the INA's mandatory detention rules to cover broad categories of noncitizens who have committed certain crimes or are deemed security threats. In addition, in the aftermath of 9/11, Congress dramatically increased its funding for ICE detention beds, and required that the agency use the money to detain a minimum number of removable noncitizens.

Congress appropriated funding for 27,500 detainee beds in FY 2007, up from 20,800 beds in FY 2006.[657] By 2009, Congress appropriated sufficient funding for 33,400 beds — a number which remained constant during FY 2010-11,[658] before rising to 34,000 beds in FY 2012.[659]

Congressional budgetary language and testimony have made it clear that Congress views ICE bed allocations as minimum requirements. The *DHS Appropriations Act of 2010*, for example, allocated funding for ICE detention "provided that funding made available ... shall maintain a level of not less than 33,400 detention beds through September 30, 2010."[660] The FY 2012 appropriations bill included similar language, but upped the number of beds to 34,000.[661]

In its FY 2013 budget proposal, DHS requested a slight reduction in the number of bed spaces to 32,800 beds.[662] Homeland Security Secretary Janet Napolitano testified in February 2012 that the reduction in bed spending was requested to offset an increase in spending on alternatives-to-detention (ATD) programs.[663]

---

654 There were 209,771 prisoners under the jurisdiction of federal correctional authorities as of December 31, 2010. In contrast, ICE detained 363,064 individuals that year, and 429,247 in 2011. Paul Guerino, Paige M. Harrison, and William J. Sabol, *Prisoners in 2010* (Washington, DC: DOJ, Bureau of Justice Statistics, 2012),
655 DOJ, Bureau of Justice Statistics, "Federal Criminal Case Processing Statistics."
656 Ibid.
657 Haddal and Siskin, *Immigration Related Detention: Current Legislative Issues*, 11.
658 Ibid; Testimony of John Morton, Assistant Secretary, ICE, before the House Appropriations Committee, Subcommittee on Homeland Security, *The Budget for Immigration and Customs Enforcement*, 112th Cong., 1st sess., March 11, 2011, www.gpo.gov/fdsys/pkg/CHRG-112hhrg67979/pdf/CHRG-112hhrg67979.pdf. ("Beginning in 2010, Congress included statutory language in the *Homeland Security Appropriations Act* requiring ICE to maintain an average daily detention capacity of at least 33,400 beds.); Testimony of Janet Napolitano, Secretary of Homeland Security, before the Senate Homeland Security and Governmental Affairs Committee, *The Homeland Security Department's Budget Submission for Fiscal Year 2012*, 112th Cong., 1st sess., February 17, 2011, www.gpo.gov/fdsys/pkg/CHRG-112shrg66623/pdf/CHRG-112shrg66623.pdf.
659 *Consolidated Appropriations Act of 2012*, Pub. L. 112-74, 125 Stat. 966 (December 23, 2011), www.gpo.gov/fdsys/pkg/BILLS-112hr2055enr/pdf/BILLS-112hr2055enr.pdf.
660 *Department of Homeland Security Appropriations Act, 2010*, Pub. L. 111-83, 123 Stat. 2142, 2149 (October 28, 2009), www.gpo.gov/fdsys/pkg/PLAW-111publ83/pdf/PLAW-111publ83.pdf.
661 *Consolidated Appropriations Act of 2012*.
662 DHS, *U.S. Department of Homeland Security Annual Performance Report Fiscal Years 2011-2013*, 35.
663 Testimony of Homeland Security Secretary Janet Napolitano before the House Appropriations Committee, Homeland Security Subcommittee, *An Examination of the President's FY 2013 Budget Request for the Department of Homeland Security*, 112th Cong., 2nd sess., February 15, 2012.

As of September 1, 2009, 66 percent of the persons in ICE custody were subject to mandatory detention and 51 percent had committed felonies.[664] Eleven percent of the felons had committed violent crimes.[665] However, ICE categorized the vast majority of these offenders as "low custody" or having a "low propensity for violence."[666] According to more recent data released by ICE to Human Rights First, as of May 2, 2011, 41 percent of ICE detainees were classified as Level 1 (lowest-risk) detainees, while only 19 percent were classified as Level 3 (highest-risk) detainees.[667] Nonetheless, the agency informed Human Rights First that "fully 90 percent" of the individuals detained on a daily basis were detained either because their detention was mandatory by law or because their cases fell into one of the agency's immigration enforcement priorities.[668]

Not all mandatory detainees represent a flight or public safety risk, but ICE lacks the discretion to release them. In addition, it treats even its most restrictive ATD programs as *alternatives to*, rather than *alternative forms of* detention.[669] By this interpretation, it cannot place those subject to mandatory detention in these programs, and its flexibility in deciding how to use its resources is further diminished.

ICE statistics also indicate that in recent years, the agency has detained an increasing number of noncitizens with criminal convictions.[670] The agency reports that it detained 79,943 noncitizens with criminal convictions in FY 2001, a figure which rose steadily to the FY 2011 level of 197,472.[671] The percentage of detainees with criminal convictions has risen as well, although at a much slower rate due to large overall increases in the number of detainees. According to ICE, in FY 2011, roughly 46 percent of the detainees entering ICE detention had criminal convictions, compared with 39.1 percent of those entering ICE detention in FY 2001.[672]

2. Detention Reform

Removal proceedings are technically a civil, not a criminal, process. Yet the standards that govern ICE's facilities have been based on American Correctional Association (ACA) standards for local jails and prisons used for pretrial inmates in the criminal justice system.[673]

In August 2009, ICE Assistant Secretary John Morton announced that ICE planned to overhaul its detention system in order to create a "truly civil detention system."[674] ICE created a new Office of Detention Policy and Planning charged with designing and implementing a civil detention system.[675]

---

664 Dora Schriro, *Immigration Detention Overview and Recommendation*, 6.
665 Ibid.
666 Ibid., 2.
667 Human Rights First, *Jails and Jumpsuits: Transforming the U.S. Immigration Detention System—A Two Year Review*, (New York and Washington, DC: Human Rights First, 2011): 2, www.humanrightsfirst.org/wp-content/uploads/pdf/HRF-Jails-and-Jumpsuits-report.pdf.
668 Ibid.
669 DHS, *U.S. Department of Homeland Security Annual Performance Report Fiscal Years 2011-2013*, ICE Budget, 54. ("The ATD program provides alternate detention options for those aliens for whom ICE has determined traditional detention is neither mandated nor appropriate.")
670 ICE, "ERO Facts and Statistics."
671 Ibid.
672 Ibid.
673 See American Correctional Association (ACA), *Performance-Based Standards for Adult Local Detention Facilities, Fourth Edition* (Lanham, MD: ACA, 2004).
674 Nina Bernstein, "US to Reform Policy on Detention for Immigrants," *The New York Times*, August 5, 2009, www.nytimes.com/2009/08/06/us/politics/06detain.html.
675 ICE, "ICE Announces Major Reforms to Immigration Detention System," (news release, August 6, 2009), www.ice.gov/news/releases/0908/090806washington.htm.

Since then, ICE has made a number of policy changes in the detention system. Among them, it:

- Announced a policy to "generally" release asylum seekers who had demonstrated a credible fear of return to their home countries.[676] Under the prior policy, arriving asylum seekers who demonstrated a credible fear had to apply in writing for parole (release), and needed to demonstrate significant community ties[677]

- Created an online detainee locator system to assist family members and attorneys to locate detainees, since many are detained in places far from where they reside or are apprehended[678]

- Reduced the number of its contracts with for-profit prisons, and created statements of work for new "civil" detention facilities

- Launched a 24-hour, toll-free hotline for detainees who believe that they are victims of a crime or are US citizens[679]

- Developed a new risk assessment tool to screen detained individuals and ensure that those eligible are placed in ATD programs[680]

- Deployed new field medical coordinators to all ICE field offices to provide for better coordination with detention facilities and respond more rapidly to medical concerns.[681]

In addition, in February of 2012, ICE released its 2011 "Performance Based National Detention Standards," (PBNDS) the first updated standards governing immigration detention facilities since 2008. While many of the standards mirror the 2008 rules,[682] the new standards expand some medical and privacy protections for particularly vulnerable groups of detainees, such as women, the elderly, and lesbian, gay, bisexual, and transgender (LGBT) individuals. The 2011 standards state that when ICE officers assess new detainees at intake in order to determine whether they will be placed in a high-, medium-, or low-security facility, officers shall give "special consideration" to factors that raise the risk of "vulnerability, victimization, or assault" of the detainee during detention, including whether the person is transgendered, elderly, pregnant, or physically or mentally disabled.[683] The new rules also expand the types of medical care offered to women in ICE detention,[684] and provide that ICE agents shall not, absent "truly extraordinary circumstances," use restraints or shackles on detainees who are pregnant.[685]

---

676 ICE, "ICE Issues New Procedures for Asylum Seekers as Part of Ongoing Detention Reform Initiatives," (press release, December 16, 2009), www.ice.gov/news/releases/0912/091216washington.htm.
677 Ibid.
678 ICE, "ICE Announces Launch of Online Detainee Locator System," (press release, July 23, 2010), www.ice.gov/news/releases/1007/100723washingtondc.htm.
679 ICE, "ICE Establishes Hotline for Detained Individuals, Issues New Detainer Form," (press release, December 29, 2011), www.ice.gov/news/releases/1112/111229washingtondc.htm.
680 Testimony of Kevin Landy, Assistant Director, Office of Detention Policy and Planning, ICE, before the House Committee on the Judiciary, Subcommittee on Immigration Policy and Enforcement, *Holiday on ICE: The U.S. Department of Homeland Security's New Immigration Detention Standards*, 112th Cong., 2nd sess., March 28, 2012, www.judiciary.house.gov/hearings/Hearings%202012/Landy%2003282012.pdf.
681 Ibid.
682 Ibid.
683 ICE, *Performance-Based National Detention Standards 2011* (Washington, DC: DHS, 2012): 64, www.ice.gov/doclib/detention-standards/2011/pbnds2011.pdf.
684 Ibid., 256.
685 Ibid.

The new standards strengthen oversight of the process through which detainees may file grievances. They require facilities to provide two levels of review for detainee grievances,[686] while the 2008 standards required only one.[687] The new rules further provide that formal written grievances regarding medical care should be submitted directly to medical personnel designated to receive them.[688]

Perhaps most notably, in March 2012, ICE announced the opening of its first ICE-designed and -built "civil" detention center, in Karnes, TX.[689] The facility can house roughly 600 low-security male detainees and has incorporated a number of features intended to make it a less restrictive environment, designed for civil rather than penal detention. Detainees are permitted relatively free movement in and out of rooms within the facility; guards — renamed "resident advisors" — do not wear uniforms; and detainees have access to an indoor gym, outdoor playing fields, a barber, and a library with Internet access.[690]

3. Alternatives to Detention (ATD)

Since 2002, ICE has used various ATD programs for detainees who, with proper supervision and monitoring, do not pose a flight risk or a danger to the community.[691] Although there is some dispute over what kinds of programs encompass "alternatives to detention," ICE has used ATD appropriations to fund both physical detention centers, with custody restrictions that are less strict than ordinary jails, as well as electronic monitoring and community-based programs.[692]

At present, ICE offers a full-service (FS) program that includes home and office visits and technological (remote electronic) monitoring, and a less-intensive, technology-assisted (TA) program in which ICE directly supervises participants.[693] Participants in the FS version of the program are assigned to a caseworker who conducts an individual assessment and refers the person to needed services, such as pro bono legal assistance.[694] In TA programs, participants receive the electronic monitoring equipment, but no such case services.[695] As of January 22, 2011, there were 13,583 participants in the FS program and 3,871 participants in the TA program.[696]

Studies have indicated that an overwhelming majority of ATD participants abide by the terms of the program. In FY 2010, for example, about 94 percent of ATD participants appeared at their immigration hearings.[697] In its strategic plan for FY 2010-14, ICE recognized "the value of enforcing removal orders without detaining people" and committed to developing "a cost-effective Alternatives to Detention program that results in

---

686 Ibid., 333-40
687 ICE, *2008 Performance Based National Detention Standards*, Part 6.35, "Grievance System," 6.
688 ICE, *Performance-Based National Detention Standards 2011*, 338.
689 ICE, "ICE Opens its First-Ever Designed and Built Civil Detention Center," (press release, March 13, 2012), www.ice.gov/news/releases/1203/120313karnescity.htm.
690 Ibid; Brian Bennett, "A Kinder, Gentler, Detention System," *Los Angeles Times*, March 17, 2012, http://articles.latimes.com/2012/mar/17/nation/la-na-detention-salad-bar-20120318.
691 ICE, "ICE Fact Sheet: Alternatives to Detention for ICE Detainees," November 6, 2009, www.kolkenandkolken.com/index.php?src=news&srctype=detail&category=Immigration%20Publications&refno=2488.
692 For example, ICE has used ATD funding to pay for the Broward Transitional Center, a custody facility with "less restrictive" detention conditions, such as dormitory-style housing, as well as electronic monitoring and community-based programs. See Lutheran Immigration and Refugee Service (LIRS), *Unlocking Liberty: A Way Forward for U.S. Immigration and Detention Policy* (Baltimore, MD: LIRS, 2012): 29, www.lirs.org/wp-content/uploads/2012/05/RPTUNLOCKINGLIBERTY.pdf.
693 DHS, *U.S. Department of Homeland Security Annual Performance Report Fiscal Years 2011-2013*, 43-4.
694 LIRS, *Unlocking Liberty*, 31.
695 Ibid.
696 Ibid.
697 Ibid., 14.

high rates of compliance."[698] ICE requested $72 million for ATDs in FY 2012, compared to $1.9 billion for detention operations overall.[699] For the FY 2013 budget, ICE increased its request for the ATD program to $111.6 million,[700] compared to nearly $2 billion for overall detention operations.[701]

C. The Immigration Court System

Like the detention system, the immigration court system is an integral part of the removal process. With the spike in removable noncitizens, the demands on the court system have grown enormously.

According to a recent report released by the National Research Council of the National Academies, the ratio of immigration proceedings completed to the number of full-time immigration judges rose from fewer than 400 per judge during the years 2000-03 to more than 600 per judge in 2008 and 2009.[702] A report by the American Bar Association's Commission on Immigration placed the number of proceedings completed per judge in FY 2008 at 1,243 proceedings per judge.[703]

With the increased workload for immigration judges, court backlogs have risen and delays increased. As of March 28, 2012, a record 305,556 cases were pending in immigration courts nationally, compared to 174,935 cases in 2007.[704] As of September 2012, judges took an average of 203 days to complete a removal case and 781 days to complete a case in which relief from removal was ultimately granted.[705] Since immigration judges give priority to removal cases involving those in detention, average delays in the removal cases of nondetainees are far longer.

The high demand on the court system can be attributed to the quantum rise in the number of noncitizens placed in removal proceedings, in large part due to the set of new enforcement initiatives involving cooperative relationships with state and local law enforcement authorities. It can also be attributed to a shortage of judges. Another contributing factor has been minimal levels of discretion exercised by DHS officials in deciding whom to place in removal proceedings.[706]

Forty separate categories of CBP, ICE and USCIS officials — as well as other "delegated" officials — can issue notices to appear (NTAs) that initiate removal proceedings. While ICE issues most of the NTAs, USCIS also issues substantial numbers (nearly as many as CBP in recent years).[707] This is surprising because, with the creation of DHS, immigration enforcement functions were designated as the responsibility of CBP/ICE, and immigrant services and benefits adjudication the responsibility of USCIS. Nonetheless, USCIS may issue NTAs to arriving foreign nationals whom its officers deem to have a "credible fear" of return pursuant to the expedited removal process,[708] to denied asylum

---

698 ICE, *ICE Strategic Plan FY 2010-2014* (Washington, DC: ICE, 2010): 7, www.ice.gov/doclib/news/library/reports/strategic-plan/strategic-plan-2010.pdf.
699 DHS, *U.S. Department of Homeland Security Annual Performance Report Fiscal Years 2011-2013*, 3-4.
700 Ibid., 53.
701 Ibid., 35.
702 National Research Council of the National Academies, *Budgeting for Immigration Enforcement: A Path to Better Performance*, 20.
703 ABA Commission on Immigration, *Reforming the Immigration System*, 2-16.
704 TRAC, *New Judge Hiring Fails to Stem Rising Immigration Case Backlog* (Syracuse, NY: TRAC, 2011), http://trac.syr.edu/immigration/reports/246/; Kerwin et al., Executive Action on Immigration, 21.
705 TRAC, *Immigration Court Processing Time by Outcome* (Syracuse, NY: TRAC, 2012), http://trac.syr.edu/phptools/immigration/court_backlog/court_proctime_outcome.php; TRAC, "Immigration Court Backlog Tool," June 6, 2012), http://trac.syr.edu/phptools/immigration/court_backlog/.
706 Kerwin et al, *Executive Action on Immigration*, 21-2.
707 ABA Commission on Immigration, *Reforming the Immigration System*, 1-13.
708 INA §235(b)(i)(B)(iii).

seekers who applied for asylum "affirmatively" (outside of removal proceedings), and to any noncitizen whose application for legal status is denied and who falls out of status.[709]

In 2006, the CIS Ombudsman recommended that USCIS adopt a policy of placing in removal proceedings all those whose application for legal status is denied and who fell out of status.[710] USCIS did not adopt this recommendation in the belief that that it would undermine the agency's ability to exercise prosecutorial discretion, especially in cases when applications are denied for technical reasons.[711]

Still, the number of NTAs issued by USCIS increased from 32,008 in FY 2006 to 53,185 in FY 2009 (see Figure 31).[712] USCIS does not regularly release data on NTAs issued to those whose asylum applications have been denied, but, according to independent studies, these fell between FY 2004-08.[713] Thus, it appears that the overall increase in NTAs issued by USCIS can mostly be attributed to NTAs issued following the denial of immigration status applications, which has, in turn, contributed significantly to the growth of cases pending in the immigration court system.

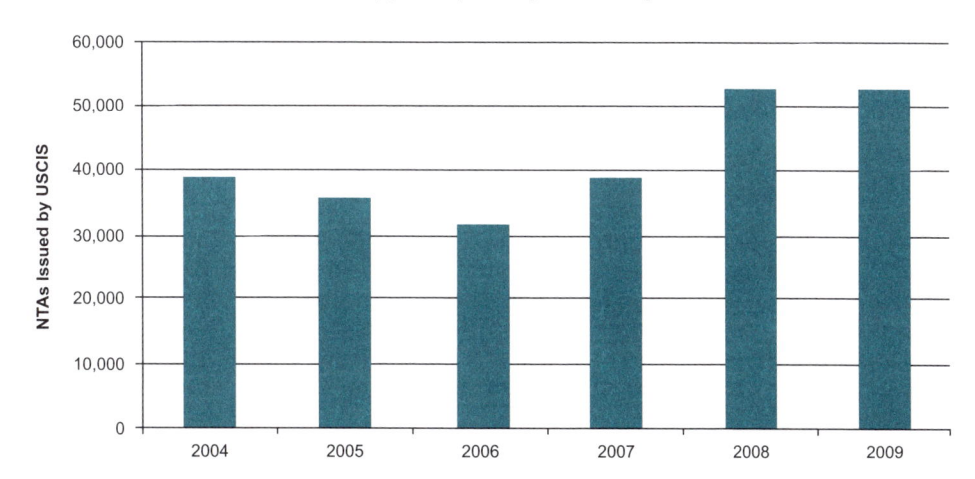

Figure 31. Number of Notices to Appear (NTAs) Issued by USCIS, FY 2004-09

Source: American Bar Association (ABA) Commission on Immigration, *Department of Homeland Security: Reforming the Immigration System -- Proposals to Promote Independence, Fairness, Efficiency and Professionalism in the Adjudication of Removal Cases* (Washington, DC: ABA, 2010), www.americanbar.org/content/dam/aba/migrated/media/nosearch/immigration_reform_executive_summary_012510.authcheckdam.pdf.

Prosecutorial Discretion

In an effort to ensure that immigration enforcement resources are being used primarily to remove noncitizens who pose a public safety or national security threat and to reduce the immigration court backlog, DHS has begun implementing a new prosecutorial discretion policy. In June 2011, ICE Assistant Secretary John Morton issued a memorandum directing ICE officers and attorneys to focus their enforcement efforts to pursue removal cases against noncitizens who had committed serious crimes, posed national security risks, or had recently entered the country illegally.

---

709 ABA Commission on Immigration, *Reforming the Immigration System*, 1-18.
710 Citizenship and Immigration Services (CIS) Ombudsman, *Recommendation from the CIS Ombudsman to the Director, USCIS* (Washington, DC: CIS Ombudsman, 2006), www.dhs.gov/xlibrary/assets/CISOmbudsman_RR_25_EAD_03-20-06.pdf.
711 CIS Ombudsman, *CIS Ombudsman Recommendation* 22, www.dhs.gov/xlibrary/assets/CISOmbudsman_RR_22_Notice_to_Appear_USCIS_Response-04-27-06.pdf.
712 ABA Commission on Immigration, *Reforming the Immigration System*, 1-12.
713 Ibid.

For noncitizens deemed low priority, the memo advised that ICE officers should exercise prosecutorial discretion — for example, deciding not to place an individual in removal proceedings or pursue a final order of removal.[714] The memo outlined a number of factors that could make a person's case low priority, such as long length of residence in the United States, having been brought to the United States as a child, and service in the US military.[715]

Following the ICE memo's release, USCIS issued prosecutorial discretion guidance in November 2011. The guidance stated that while USCIS officers may themselves issue NTAs in certain limited circumstances, they should, in most instances, refer cases to ICE for determinations on whether to issue an NTA to an individual whose application for immigration benefits has been denied.[716] The guidance noted that the new policy is intended to ensure that USCIS's issuance of NTAs "fits within and supports the Government's overall removal priorities."[717]

DHS also launched a case-by-case review process for cases pending in immigration courts. Beginning in November 2011, in two pilot jurisdictions (Denver and Baltimore), ICE attorneys began reviewing all cases pending before the courts to determine whether any of them met the prosecutorial discretion criteria.[718] If ICE determined that a particular case merited prosecutorial discretion, the agency exercised such discretion by allowing the noncitizen the opportunity to administratively close his or her case, so that no order of removal would be issued.

In March 2012, ICE announced that it would expand this review process to other jurisdictions.[719] The agency plans called for a review all of the cases pending before EOIR.

While the full impact of the new prosecutorial discretion policy will not be known for some time, a preliminary analysis of the policy conducted by TRAC in October 2012 found that since DHS has adopted its new prosecutorial discretion policy, ICE has filed fewer removal cases with the immigration courts, and roughly 10,998 cases have been administratively closed pursuant to the new policy.[720] However, TRAC also found that the backlog in cases pending before the immigration courts had increased, and now stands at a record 321,663 cases.[721]

Finally, in a high-visibility decision grounded in the exercise of prosecutorial discretion, the administration announced in June 2012 that unauthorized children and young adults who were brought to the country as minors would be eligible for relief from

---

[714] ICE, "Memorandum Re: Exercising Prosecutorial Discretion Consistent with the Civil Immigration Enforcement Priorities of the Agency for the Apprehension, Detention, and Removal of Aliens," (memo, June 17, 2011), www.ice.gov/doclib/secure-communities/pdf/prosecutorial-discretion-memo.pdf.
[715] Ibid.
[716] USCIS, "Revised Guidance for the Referral of Cases and Issuance of Notices to Appear (NTAs) in Cases Involving Inadmissible and Removable Aliens," (memo, November 7, 2011), www.uscis.gov/USCIS/Laws/Memoranda/Static_Files_Memoranda/NTA%20PM%20(Approved%20as%20final%2011-7-11).pdf.
[717] Ibid.
[718] ICE, "Next Steps in the Implementation of the Prosecutorial Discretion Memorandum and the August 18th Announcement on Immigration Enforcement Priorities," (memo, November 17, 2011), www.aila.org/content/default.aspx?docid=37684.
[719] Alicia Caldwell, "DHS Expanding Deportation Reviews to 4 More Cities," Associated Press, March 29, 2012, www.boston.com/news/nation/washington/articles/2012/03/29/dhs_expanding_deportation_reviews_to_4_more_cities/.
[720] TRAC, *Historic Drop in Deportation Orders Continues as Immigration Court Backlog Increases* (Syracuse, NY: 2012), http://trac.syr.edu/immigration/reports/279/.
[721] TRAC, *ICE Prosecutorial Discretion Initiative: Latest Figures* (Syracuse, NY: TRAC, 2012), http://trac.syr.edu/immigration/reports/278/.

deportation and for work authorization.[722] Titled Deferred Action for Childhood Arrivals (DACA), the program applies to those who arrived in the United States before the age of 16, were under the age of 31 as of June 15, 2012, and have continuously resided in the county in the last five years. They also must either be enrolled in school, or have graduated from high school, obtained a GED, or been honorably discharged from the military or the Coast Guard. In addition, they must not have been convicted of a felony, a significant misdemeanor, or at least three misdemeanors.[723]

The application process for DACA began on August 15, 2012. In December 2012, USCIS reported having received 367,903 applications for processing, scheduled 336,464 biometrics appointments, and approved 102,965 cases.[724] About 1.7 million individuals are estimated to be potentially eligible for the program.[725]

> *Detention and removal can be a serious bottleneck for the immigration system. In order to process the large numbers of removable cases generated by heightened border and interior enforcement, DHS has utilized a wide range of administrative programs and authorities — in addition to immigration court proceedings — to achieve greater numbers of removals each year, particularly of those with criminal convictions. Thus, judging by every available measure, immigration agencies and programs are utilizing every available tool to achieve deterrence, the goal immigration enforcement officials believe to be the primary purpose of immigration enforcement.*

II. Program Critique and Findings

With close to 400,000 people removed from the country each year, the United States is now carrying out historic numbers of removals. Some have argued that this increase has enhanced national security and strengthened the rule of law, especially as DHS reports that a growing share of those removed has criminal convictions. But others argue that these levels of removals have imposed heavy social costs on children, families, and communities of those removed, as well as on the individuals themselves, many of whom may have resided in the United States for decades, have US citizen or permanent resident spouses or family members, and have virtually no avenue to immigrate to the United States lawfully.[726]

Studies estimate that there are now 16.6 million US residents in families with at least

---

722 DHS, "Memorandum: Exercising Prosecutorial Discretion with Respect to Individuals Who Came to the United States as Children," (memo, June 15, 2012), www.dhs.gov/xlibrary/assets/s1-exercising-prosecutorial-discretion-individuals-who-came-to-us-as-children.pdf.

723 Ibid.

724 USCIS, "Deferred Action for Childhood Arrivals Process," December 2012, www.uscis.gov/USCIS/Resources/Reports%20and%20Studies/Immigration%20Forms%20Data/All%20Form%20Types/DACA/DACA%20MonthlyDEC%20Report%20PDF.pdf.pdf.

725 Jeanne Batalova and Michelle Mittelstadt, *Relief from Deportation: Demographic Profile of the DREAMers Potentially Eligible under the Deferred Action Policy* (Washington, DC: MPI, 2012): 1, www.migrationpolicy.org/pubs/FS24_deferredaction.pdf.

726 NYU School of Law Immigrant Rights Clinic, Immigrant Defense Project, and Families for Freedom, *Insecure munities, Devastated Families: New Data on Immigrant Detention and Deportation Practices in New York Cit* York: NYU School of Law Immigrant Rights Clinic, Immigrant Defense Project, and Families for Freed http://familiesforfreedom.org/sites/default/files/resources/NYC%20FOIA%20Report%20201 pdf; ABA, *Reforming the Immigration System: Proposals to Promote Independence, Fairness, Effi alism in the Adjudication of Removal Cases* (Washington, DC: ABA, 2010): 1-48; National Ir *Year One Report Card: Human Rights & the Obama Administration's Immigration Detenti* 2010), www.detentionwatchnetwork.org/sites/detentionwatchnetwork.org/files FULL%20FINAL%202010%2010%2006.pdf; CLINIC, *The Impact of Our Laws on An.* DC: CLINIC, 2000), http://cliniclegal.org/sites/default/files/atrisk1.pdf.

one unauthorized immigrant.[727] Nine million are part of "mixed-status" families that contain at least one unauthorized citizen parent, and one child born in the United States.[728] Of the 10.2 million unauthorized adult immigrants living in the United States in 2010, 63 percent had been in the country for a decade or longer.[729] In 2010, 52 percent of Latinos in the United States reported that they worried that they, a family member, or a close friend could be deported.[730] One-quarter of all Latinos polled reported that they knew someone who had been deported or detained by federal authorities in 2011.[731]

Children who have grown up in the United States and whose parents are ordered removed face the dilemma of either accompanying their parent to a country that is unfamiliar to them, or remaining in the United States separated from a removed parent. The numbers point to the potential scope of this problem. An estimated 4.5 million US-born children have at least one parent who is unauthorized.[732] And, according to DHS, during the six months between January 1, 2011 and June 30, 2011, ICE removed 46,486 noncitizens who claimed to have a US citizen child.[733]

Media reports have documented the struggles that US citizen children face when they accompany a deported parent back to a country with which they have little or no familiarity. The difficulties include language barriers, homesickness, and academic difficulties.[734] Other reports have looked at children whose deported parents opt for them to stay in the United States. In November 2011, the Applied Research Center estimated that there were 5,200 children currently in foster care as a result of a parent being deported.[735] Many more are likely residing in the United States with another family member, an arrangement which often leads to financial and emotional difficulties.[736]

The removals have especially harsh consequences when they involve long-term legal permanent residents. The retroactive application of immigration laws and broad definition of an aggravated felony has resulted in many LPRs being placed in removal proceedings for offenses committed at a time when such offenses were not categorized as deportable offenses. Additionally, unlike many state crimes, the crimes or immigration violations that constitute deportable offenses are not subject to any statute of limitations. Thus, an LPR may be in removal proceedings for a crime or immigration violation that occurred decades ago. And since the passage of IIRIRA and AEDPA, immigration judges no longer have discretion to cancel the removal of long-term permanent residents in especially compelling cases.[737]

---

727 Paul Taylor, Mark Hugo Lopez, Jeffrey Passel, and Seth Motel, *Unauthorized Immigrants: Lengths of Residency, Patterns of Parenthood* (Washington, DC: Pew Hispanic Center, 2011), www.pewhispanic.org/2011/12/01/unauthorized-immigrants-length-of-residency-patterns-of-parenthood/.
728 Ibid.
729 Taylor et al, *Unauthorized Immigrants: Length of Residency, Patterns of Parenthood*, 1.
730 Mark Hugo Lopez, Rich Morin, and Paul Taylor, *Illegal Immigration Backlash Worries, Divides Latinos* (Washington, DC: Pew Hispanic Center, 2010), www.pewhispanic.org/2010/10/28/illegal-immigration-backlash-worries-divides-latinos/.
731 Mark Hugo Lopez, Ana Gonzalez-Barrera, and Seth Motel, *As Deportations Rise to Record Levels, Most Latinos Oppose Obama's Policy* (Washington, DC: Pew Hispanic Center, 2011), www.pewhispanic.org/2011/12/28/as-deportations-rise-to-record-levels-most-latinos-oppose-obamas-policy/.
732 Ibid.
733 ICE, *Deportation of Parents of U.S. Born Citizens: Fiscal Year 2011 Report to Congress* (Washington, DC: ICE, 2012), www.lirs.org/wp-content/uploads/2012/07/ICE-DEPORT-OF-PARENTS-OF-US-CIT-FY-2011.pdf.
734 Damien Cave, "American Children, Now Struggling to Adjust to Life in Mexico," *The New York Times*, June 18, 2012, www.nytimes.com/2012/06/19/world/americas/american-born-children-struggle-to-adjust-in-mexico.html?pagewanted=all.
735 Seth Freed Wessler, *Shattered Families: The Perilous Intersection of Immigration Enforcement and the Child Welfare System* (New York: Applied Research Center, 2011), http://arc.org/shatteredfamilies.
Joanna Dreby, *How Today's Immigration Enforcement Policies Impact Children, Families, and Communities: A View from the Ground* (Washington, DC: Center for American Progress, 2012), www.americanprogress.org/wp-content/uploads/2012/08/DrebyImmigrationFamiliesFINAL.pdf.
Reforming the Immigration System, 1-31-1-34.

The June 2011 ICE prosecutorial discretion memo, which instructs ICE to consider a noncitizen's family ties and length of residence in the United States when deciding whether to remove him or her, begins to address these issues.[738] However, given the size of the affected population, prosecutorial discretion is an inadequate remedy.

A. Scale of Detention

The number of people booked into the immigration detention system each year dwarfs the volume managed by the nation's federal prison system. Yet unlike the Bureau of Prisons, which constitutes a stand-alone, single-mission agency within DOJ, immigration detention is administered by the Detention and Management Division, a subcomponent of ICE's Enforcement and Removal Operations division, which is a subcomponent of ICE, one of the three immigration agencies in DHS.[739] The organizational structure within which ICE detention is administered weakens oversight and engagement by senior DHS officials tasked with setting broad DHS policies and priorities.

Nonetheless, ICE and the Obama administration have placed unusually high priority on detention issues. ICE has recently put in place reforms that address long-standing shortcomings of the detention system. Proponents of detention reform have generally praised ICE's creation of a new "civil" detention center and new detention standards that expand protections for vulnerable populations. However, they have expressed concern over the pace of reform.[740] They point out that the new Performance Based National Detention Standards continue to be based on American Correctional Association Standards for persons awaiting criminal trial, and that the overwhelming majority of detainees continue to be held in jails and jail-like facilities.[741] A particular challenge has been the lack of an analogous "civil" detention system and standards governing such a system.

In addition, DHS information systems do not collect sufficient information to allow ICE to know when it has to consider certain detainees for release.[742] So despite the recent detention reforms, substantial numbers of detainees remain in custody for longer periods of time than warranted.[743]

While ICE has emphasized the importance of developing "a cost-effective Alternatives to Detention program that assures a high rate of compliance,"[744] the resources allocated to ATD programs represent a small share of DHS funding for custody operations overall. Similarly, the number of people participating in ATDs is small compared to the number detained in the traditional detention system. Recent ICE statistics report that just 19 percent of detainees are considered "highest risk,"[745] while 41percent are considered "lowest risk."[746] Allowing more of these lowest-risk detainees to participate in ATDs could ease concerns about the punitive nature of ICE detention facilities without compromising public safety or attendance at court proceedings.

---

738 ICE, "Memorandum Re. Exercising Prosecutorial Discretion Consistent with Civil Immigration Enforcement Priorities of the Agency for the Apprehension, Detention, and Removal of Aliens," (memo, June 17, 2011), www.ice.gov/doclib/secure-communities/pdf/prosecutorial-discretion-memo.pdf.
739 ICE, "Organizational Chart," June 7, 2011, www.dhs.gov/xlibrary/assets/org-chart-ice.pdf.
740 Human Rights First, *Jails and Jumpsuits*; NIJC et al, *Year One Report Card: Human Rights & the Obama Administration's Immigration Detention Reforms*; LIRS, *Unlocking Liberty*.
741 Human Rights First, *Jails and Jumpsuits*, 7-8.
742 Kerwin and Lin, *Immigrant Detention: Can ICE Meet Its Legal Imperatives and Case Management Responsibilities?*, 1.
743 Ibid., 16-20, 25-30.
744 ICE, *ICE Strategic Plan FY 2010-2014*, 7.
745 Human Rights First, *Jails and Jumpsuits*, 2.
746 Ibid.

B. Pressures on Immigration Courts

In immigration proceedings, all foreign nationals, including unauthorized immigrants, are entitled to a fair hearing, with basic procedural protections.[747] Yet, given the ever-increasing volume of cases that immigration courts handle annually, experts have questioned the ability of the courts to offer even these basic protections.[748] Central to this concern is the fact that noncitizens in removal proceedings are not entitled to legal counsel at government expense. A noncitizen's chance of success in his or her removal case goes up significantly if represented by counsel.[749] However, most noncitizens appear in court without representation. Lack of representation is especially problematic for minors, the elderly, or those who are mentally or physically disabled.[750]

Removal proceedings are adversarial and complex and can be lengthy and confusing. Noncitizens who do not speak English are provided with interpreters, but unless the noncitizen has an attorney who speaks his or her language, or the government attorney or immigration judge speaks that language, there is no one to correct interpreter errors. This problem is magnified when hearings are held via televideo, and the interpreter "appears" over the phone.[751] Immigration attorneys further contend that in a televideo hearing, judges cannot properly "read" body language or facial expressions, factors that help establish the credibility of witness testimony.[752]

Cases for detained noncitizens frequently take months to resolve; for non-detained cases, it can take years. As many legal and human-rights groups have pointed out, such delays undermine the integrity of the immigration court system and force qualified asylum seekers and others to wait extended periods of time without the relief to which they may be legally entitled. Some may abandon their claim for relief in order to be released from detention. Detained noncitizens may also be less likely to pursue meritorious appeals of their cases, if they know the end result is that they will spend several more months in detention.[753]

C. Removals Outside the Court System

Because of the expanded use of administrative orders, more than half of those removed depart pursuant to a removal order that is issued outside of the formal immigration court process.[754] In administrative removal, decisions are made not by an independent body but by DHS officials, and noncitizens do not receive the basic due-process protections of being able to present or contest the government's evidence. In addition, because most noncitizens are not represented by counsel,[755] especially in administrative

---

747 *Yamataya v. Fisher*, 189 U.S. 86 (1903).
748 ABA, *Reforming the Immigration System*, 2-15- 2-28.
749 Ramji-Nogales et al., *Refugee Roulette; Kerwin, Revisiting the Need for Appointed Counsel*, 5.
750 Human Rights Watch and ACLU, *Deportation by Default*; Julia Preston, "Young and Alone, Facing Court and Deportation," *The New York Times*, August 25, 2012, www.nytimes.com/2012/08/26/us/more-young-illegal-immigrants-face-deportation.html?pagewanted=all;
751 J. Traci Hong, *Objecting to Video Merits Hearings* (Washington, DC : American Immigration Law Foundation, 2002), www.ailf.org/lac/pa/lac_pa_080902.asp; Aaron Haass, "Videoconferencing in Immigration Proceedings," 5 *Pierce Law Review* 60; ABA, *Reforming the Immigration System*, 2-26, 2-27.
752 ABA, *Reforming the Immigration System*, 2-26, 2-27.
753 Human Rights Watch, *Costly and Unfair: Flaws in US Immigration Detention Policy* (New York: Human Rights Watch, 2010): 2, www.hrw.org/reports/2010/05/06/costly-and-unfair-0.
754 John Simanski and Lesley M. Sapp, *Immigration Enforcement Actions 2011* (Washington, DC: DHS, OIS, 2011): 5, www.dhs.gov/sites/default/files/publications/immigration-statistics/enforcement_ar_2011.pdf, (noting that expedited orders of removal constituted 31 percent of all removals in 2011 and reinstatements of removal constituted another 33 percent).
755 ABA, *Reforming the Immigration System*, 1-31, 1-34; Jennifer Lee Koh, Jayashri Srikantiah, and Karen C. Tumlin, *Deportation Without Due Process* (Palo Alto, CA: Stanford Law School Mills Legal Clinic, Western State University College of Law, National Immigration Law Center): 8, www.nilc.org/document.html?id=6.

removal circumstances, they may not understand that an administrative order carries the same consequences as a removal order issued by an immigration judge.

At the border, the choice between a formal order of removal, which is issued through an administrative mechanism like expedited removal, or voluntary return may appear to be a distinction without a difference. In either case, the noncitizen is returned to his or her country of origin. However, formal orders of removal carry significant future legal consequences. Noncitizens who are formally ordered removed — regardless of whether that order of removal is granted without any judicial involvement — are statutorily barred from returning to the United States for between five and 20 years.[756] If they attempt to re-enter and are apprehended, they face criminal charges and a prison term of two to 20 years.[757] And it is almost impossible for them to re-enter the United States lawfully, even if they have US citizen or LPR family members through whom they would otherwise be eligible for an immigrant visa.

Whether formal removal orders, in place of voluntary return, are a more effective deterrent to re-entering the United States illegally in today's border and interior enforcement environments is not known. The question exemplifies many unknowns that merit more careful analysis about current enforcement policies in order to strike a reasoned balance between deterrence and social costs in the immigration arena.

---

[756] INA § 212(a)(9).
[757] 8 USC § 1326.

FINDINGS

■ **Since 1990, more than 4 million deportations of noncitizens have been carried out.** Removals have increased dramatically in recent years, rising from 30,039 in 1990 to 188,467 in 2000, and reaching a record 391,953 in FY 2011. The groundwork for this level of removals was laid over many years of congressional mandates, detention funding, administrative actions, and improved data systems.

■ **Expedited removals have been a big component of the total removal numbers.** They grew from 87,888 in FY 2005 to 123,180 in FY 2011 and now comprise 31 percent of all removals. Because of significant decreases in illegal border crossings, the ratio of expedited removals to illegal crossings has also increased.

■ **In recent years, ICE has placed high priority on removal of criminal aliens,** which has led to an increase in the proportion of those in removal proceedings with criminal records. In FY 2011, 48 percent, (188,382) had criminal convictions, up from 27 percent in FY 2008.

■ **The number of noncitizens removed pursuant to an administrative order** exceeds the number of removals ordered by immigration judges. This is because DHS has made aggressive use of its administrative authority, when removals without judicial involvement are permitted. In FY 2011, immigration judges issued 161,354 orders of removal, whereas DHS carried out 391,953 removals.

■ **The number of noncitizens removed pursuant to formal orders of removal** has increased significantly, while the number of those returned without such orders has steadily declined. In FY 2000, for example, the INS removed 184,775 persons, but returned nine times that number (1.7 million) without orders. In FY 2011, DHS removed 391,953 persons, and returned 323,542, marking the first time that removals outpaced returns. This trend is likely attributable to the decline in illegal border crossings, the increase in the number of administrative orders issued, and the increase in the number of border crossers referred by CBP for criminal prosecution.

■ **The average daily population of noncitizens detained by ICE** increased nearly fivefold between FY 1995 and FY 2011: from 7,475 to 33,330. Over the same period, the annual total number of ICE detainees increased from 85,730 to 429,247. Although immigration detention is for unique reasons under civil, not criminal law, far more noncitizen detainees are held — by a wide margin — than are incarcerated by the federal Bureau of Prisons for *all federal crimes combined*.

■ **ICE reports that "fully 90 percent" of the individuals it detains** are either subject to mandatory detention or their cases fell into one of the agency's enforcement priorities. During FY 2011, roughly 46 percent of those entering ICE detention had criminal convictions, as compared with 39.1 percent in FY 2001. Forty-one percent were classified as Level 1 (lowest-risk) detainees, while 19 percent were classified as Level 3 (highest-risk) detainees.

■ **Less than 5 percent of the detainee caseload is in Alternative-to-Detention** (ATD) programs. About 94 percent of ATD participants appeared at their immigration hearings in FY 2010.

■ **ICE has recently instituted a number of long-urged reforms in the detention system.** In March 2012, ICE opened its first detention center specifically designed to reflect civil rather than criminal detention standards. In addition, asylum seekers who establish "credible fear" in their first interview are now generally not detained; an online detainee tracking system has been created, making it possible for lawyers and family members to learn where detainees are held; contracts with for-profit prison facilities have been reduced; medical and privacy protections for detainees have been expanded, and grievance procedures have been strengthened. New risk assessment tools have been developed to increase the pool of those who can be placed in ATD programs. These developments have been welcomed, although critics remain concerned about the pace of reforms.

■ **The immigration court system is heavily backlogged,** creating severe pressures on immigration judge workloads and case calendars. As of May 2011, a record 275,316 cases were pending in immigration court, compared to 168,830 cases five years earlier. In September 2012, it took an average of 403 days to complete cases, and 781 days where relief to a noncitizen was ultimately granted. In especially high-volume courts, such as Los Angeles and New York, average decision times in cases where relief was granted reached 1,199 and 819 days, respectively. The ratio of immigration proceedings completed to the number of immigration judges nationwide rose from about 400 per judge during 2000-03 to more than 600 per judge in 2008-09.

CHAPTER 9

CONCLUSIONS

This report depicts an historic transformation of immigration enforcement and the emergence of a complex, modernized, multifunctional, cross-governmental enforcement system. The system has emerged since 1986 by design as well as through unanticipated developments. It is built on what the report identifies as six distinct, but interconnected, pillars — border enforcement, visa screening, information and interoperability of data systems, workplace enforcement, intersections with the criminal justice system, and detention and removal of noncitizens. Above all, the system has become institutionalized through its national security links and unprecedented resource investments in vital capabilities that demonstrate the federal government's ability and will to vigorously enforce the nation's immigration laws.

Judging by resource levels, case volumes, and enforcement actions the only publicly available comprehensive measures of the performance of the system, immigration enforcement can be seen to rank as the federal government's highest criminal law enforcement priority. Those measures tell a dramatic story:

- Current spending for the core immigration enforcement agencies — US Customs and Border Protection (CBP) and US Immigration and Customs Enforcement (ICE) — and the US-VISIT program exceeds that of *all* the other principal federal criminal law enforcement agencies combined.

- In US-VISIT, the United States has built the world's largest law enforcement biometric identity-verification and admissions screening system.

- More than half of all federal court criminal prosecutions are brought for immigration-related crimes.

- CBP alone refers more cases for prosecution than the FBI. CBP and ICE together refer more cases for prosecution than *all* of the Department of Justice (DOJ) law enforcement agencies combined, including the Federal Bureau of Investigation (FBI), Drug Enforcement Administration (DEA), and Bureau of Alcohol, Tobacco, Firearms, and Explosives (ATF).

- A significantly larger number of individuals are detained each year in the immigration detention system than are serving sentences in federal Bureau of Prisons facilities for *all federal crimes combined*.

- Federal enforcement initiatives and federal-state-local enforcement cooperation have generated rates of removals of noncitizens that are at an all-time high.

- More removals are carried out through administrative orders than by orders issued by immigration judges.

These and other findings tell a story of aggressive enforcement of immigration laws at the borders and in the nation's interior, and of immigration agencies that are utilizing wide-ranging statutory and procedural authorities. Moreover, immigration enforcement is increasingly going global through international agreements, unprecedented cross-border cooperation with Mexico and Canada, and special initiatives that combat transnational crime. Dramatic growth, advanced technology, and new programs have cohered to constitute a transformed immigration enforcement system that increasingly implicates foreign relations, national security, counterterrorism, trade, labor standards, states' rights, criminal justice, and civil-rights policy realms.

Beginning in the 1990s and intensified since 9/11, Congress, successive administrations, and the public have supported building a muscular immigration enforcement infrastructure within which immigration agencies now define their goals and missions principally in terms of national security and public safety. Immigration enforcement has been granted new standing as a key tool in the nation's counterterrorism strategies, irrevocably altering immigration policies and practices in the process.

A. *Immigration and National Security*

Of particular significance in the new face of immigration enforcement has been establishment of the Department of Homeland Security (DHS), a new Cabinet agency that is second in size and staffing only to the Department of Defense. Its creation represents the largest reorganization of federal government agencies since World War II. Immigration and border control functions that had been carried out by the former US Immigration and Naturalization Service (INS) in the Department of Justice and the US Customs Service in the Department of the Treasury, were merged, decentralized into three separate agencies within DHS, and designated as national security functions.

The national security responsibilities of these agencies have required access to post-9/11 government-wide data systems. As frontline actors, they participate in information sharing across law enforcement and national security realms and with federal-state-local law enforcement. This shift has made immigration agencies, processes, and systems full partners in the terrorism fight where immigration and national security converge, both domestically and internationally.

At the same time, although immigration laws and programs are essential tools in protecting against terrorism and other threats, the overwhelming majority of day-to-day actions and responsibilities carried out by the new immigration agencies constitute conventional law enforcement and service-providing activities. Thus, their national security missions and capabilities have also implicated large numbers of noncitizens in the country who have nothing to do with terrorism.

B. *The 1996 Laws*

The effects of these new enforcement missions and resources have been magnified by statutory changes enacted in 1996 that significantly toughened traditional immigration enforcement policies and practices. The 1996 laws made retroactive and substantially broadened the list of crimes — including adding some relatively minor crimes — for which noncitizens are subject to removal from the country. The 1996 laws also eliminated most forms of discretion that immigration judges and officials had earlier exercised.

As a result, unprecedented numbers of individuals — including long-time lawful permanent residents ("green card" holders) — became subject to mandatory detention and removal. Armed with tough laws and generous funding, programs to "control the border" and combat illegal immigration by enforcing immigration requirements have become far-reaching.

C. *The Great Recession*

For more than 30 years, the United States has experienced historically high immigration levels, comprised of both legal and illegal flows. Fueled by an economy that generated demand for low-wage workers and by the demographics of aging, illegal immigration from Mexico and Central America, in particular, has been a function of market forces, with laws of supply and demand overriding government policy and law enforcement responses.

The 2008 recession has fundamentally altered this picture. In FY 2011, Border Patrol apprehensions fell to a 40-year low,[758] bringing the net growth of the resident unauthorized population, which had been increasing at rates of about 525,000 annually, to a standstill.

Economic forecasts suggest that the changed conditions will persist. High unemployment in the United States will continue, with sluggish growth that is unlikely to generate millions of low-wage jobs in the near term that attracted large numbers of foreign-born, unauthorized workers in prior years.

Mexico's 2010 census corroborates dramatic changes. The numbers leaving Mexico — the largest source country for illegal immigration to the United States by a wide margin — fell by more than two-thirds since the mid-2000s. The census also shows deeper structural changes in Mexican demographic trends. Mexico has declining numbers of new labor market entrants, significantly reduced fertility rates, a rising middle class, and improved living standards and education levels, including in regions of traditionally high emigration to the United States.

In short, current evidence points to historic shifts in both the United States and Mexico in the dynamics that have driven high levels of illegal immigration.

D. Immigration Enforcement

Strengthened border and interior enforcement and deterrence have become important additional elements in the combination of factors that explain changed illegal immigration patterns. The difficulties and dangers of crossing the border and the greater likelihood of detection and removal once in the United States have become widely experienced by would-be and seasoned migrants alike.

The nation has built a formidable immigration enforcement machinery. A policy idea and political demand known as "enforcement first," which has been advocated by many in Congress and the public as a precondition for considering broader immigration reforms, has *de facto* become the nation's singular immigration policy.

E. New Fiscal Realities

Looking ahead, deep reductions in federal spending and the size of government are likely in the coming decade. Immigration agencies and enforcement programs could be facing straight-line funding or cuts for the first time in nearly 20 years.

In the face of new fiscal realities, immigration enforcement agencies and Congress will be forced to look at return on investment through a more strategic lens. A sharp focus on impact and deterrence — not simply growth in resources to combat mounting levels of illegal immigration — to determine funding and resource allocations is all but inevitable.

Calls for such spending justifications would place new, unfamiliar demands on enforcement agencies. Few meaningful measures have been developed to assess results and impact from the significant expenditures the country has made. How much is needed and where? What is the relative cost effectiveness among various enforcement strate-

---

758 Passel, Cohn, and Gonzalez-Barrera, *Net Migration from Mexico Falls to Zero—and Perhaps Less.*

gies? In which programs are enforcement dollars best invested? What is the relationship between reduced flows and particular enforcement programs? It will be essential for credible, transparent policy development and analysis capabilities to be established in DHS.

F. The Future

The post-9/11 imperative for strengthened enforcement has sidelined concerns over competing core national interests, such as facilitation of trade and travel, or the corollary impacts of stringent enforcement — especially for children, families, and immigrant communities — both in the United States and abroad. To date, appeals to countervailing values and concerns have been overridden because of border security needs, mounting illegal immigration, and demands for building a law enforcement bulwark to combat it. Today, the facts on the ground no longer support such admonitions.

The bulwark is fundamentally in place. Its six pillars represent a durable, institutionalized, machinery that is responding to rule-of-law and enforcement-first concerns. The system is imperfect and would benefit from recalibration in many dimensions of its work — from investment in land port-of-entry infrastructure, to shoring up immigration courts and procedures, to systematic evaluation and impact measurement overall. Nonetheless, a fundamentally new, high-performing immigration enforcement system has been built that ranks as the federal government's most extensive and costly law enforcement endeavor at this time.

Nevertheless, even with record-setting expenditures and the full use of a wide array of statutory and administrative tools, enforcement alone is not sufficient to answer the broad challenges that immigration — illegal and legal — pose for society and for America's future. At this juncture, answering those challenges depends not only on effective enforcement, but also on enforceable laws that both address inherent weaknesses in the enforcement system — such as employer enforcement — and that better rationalize immigration policy to align with the nation's economic and labor market needs and future growth and well-being.

Meeting those needs cannot be accomplished through more enforcement, regardless of how well it is carried out or how much added spending is authorized. Successive administrations and Congresses have accomplished what proponents of "enforcement first" sought as a precondition for reform of the nation's immigration policies. The formidable enforcement machinery that has been built can serve the national interest well if it now also provides a platform from which to address broader immigration policy changes suited to the larger needs and challenges that immigration represents for the United States in the 21st century.

APPENDICES

Appendix A. Visa Screening Process

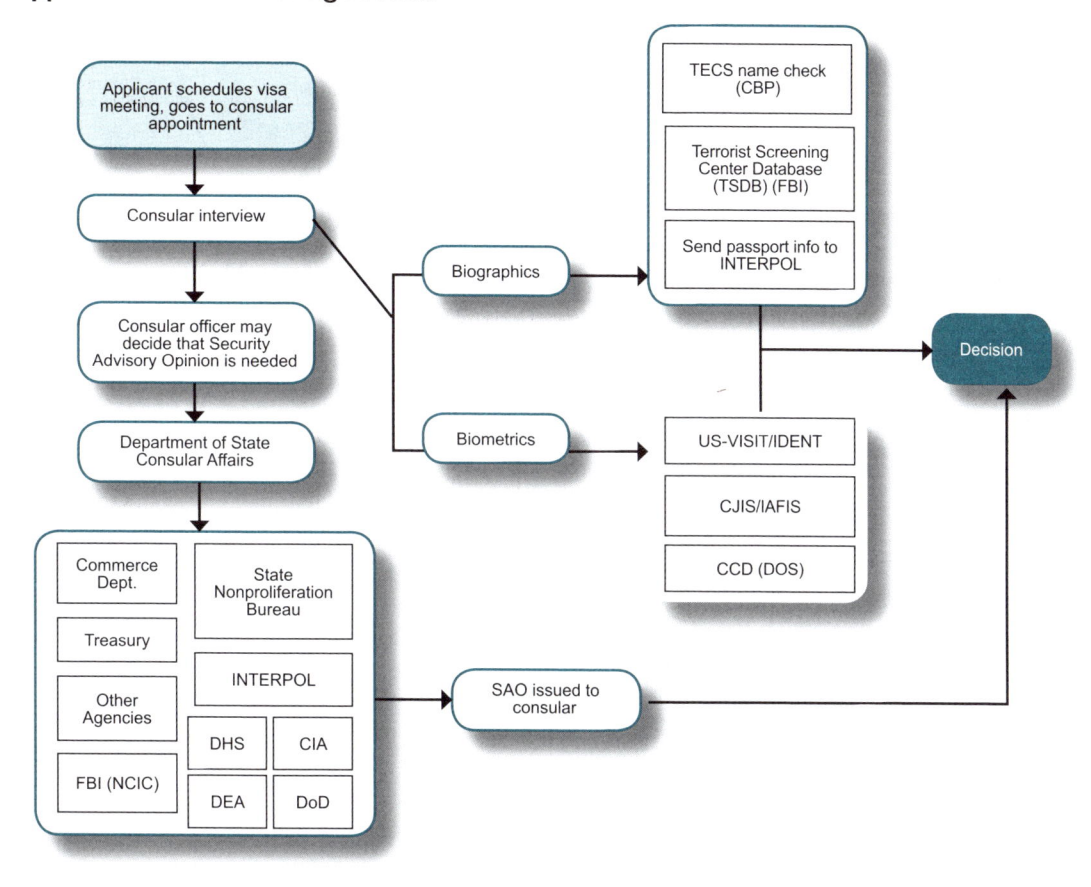

```
Applicant schedules visa meeting, goes to consular appointment
            ↓
Consular interview ─────────────┬──→ Biographics ──→ ┌─────────────────────────┐
            ↓                    │                    │ TECS name check (CBP)    │
Consular officer may decide that │                    │                          │
Security Advisory Opinion is     │                    │ Terrorist Screening      │
needed                           │                    │ Center Database          │
            ↓                    │                    │ (TSDB) (FBI)             │
Department of State              │                    │                          │
Consular Affairs                 │                    │ Send passport info to    │
            ↓                    │                    │ INTERPOL                 │
┌──────────────────────────┐     │                    └─────────────────────────┘
│ Commerce   │ State        │    │                                    ↓
│ Dept.      │ Nonprolif.   │    └──→ Biometrics ──→  US-VISIT/IDENT    → Decision
│            │ Bureau       │                         CJIS/IAFIS
│ Treasury   │              │                         CCD (DOS)
│            │ INTERPOL     │
│ Other      │              │         SAO issued to consular ─────────→ Decision
│ Agencies   │ DHS │ CIA    │
│            │              │
│ FBI (NCIC) │ DEA │ DoD    │
└──────────────────────────┘
```

Appendix B. Entry Screening Process

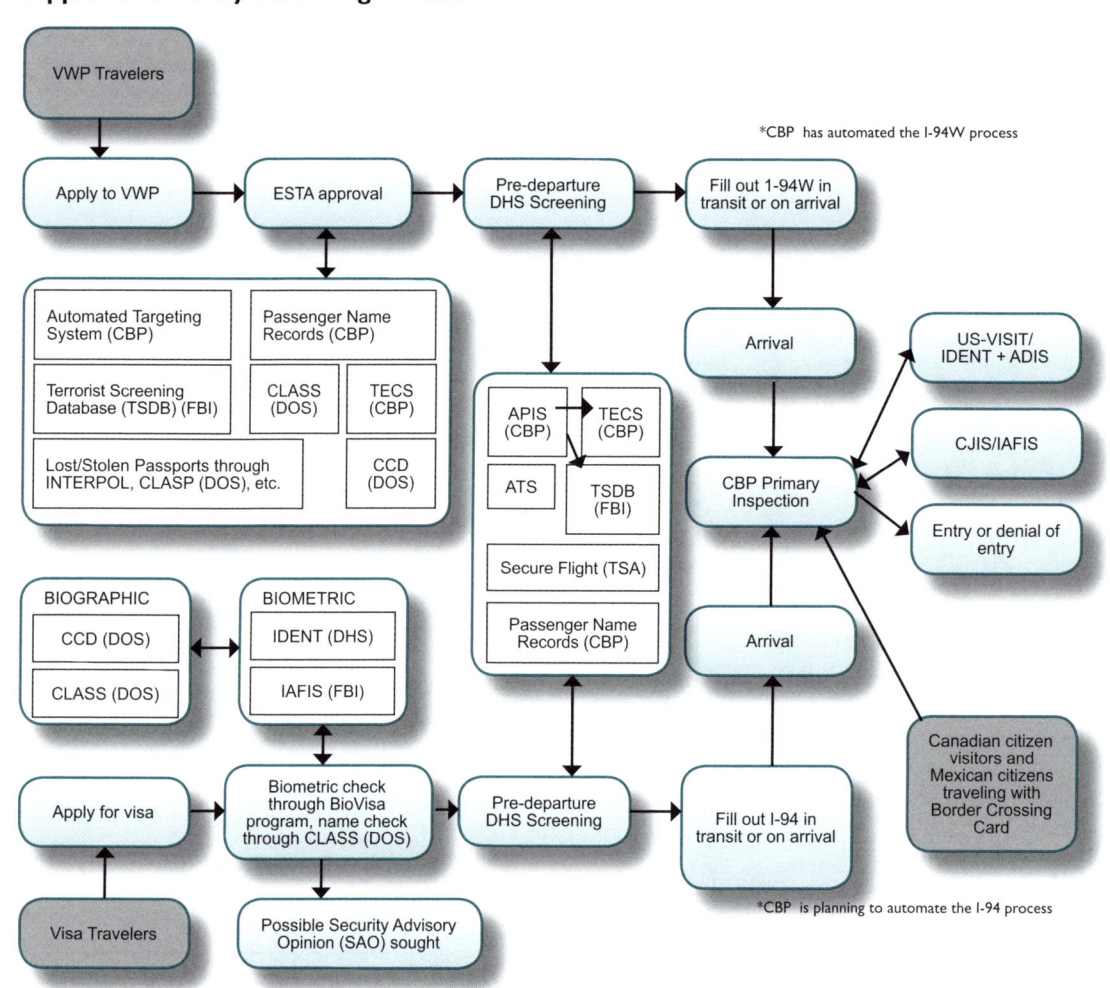

VWP Travelers → Apply to VWP → ESTA approval → Pre-departure DHS Screening → Fill out I-94W in transit or on arrival → Arrival → CBP Primary Inspection

*CBP has automated the I-94W process

ESTA approval draws from:
- Automated Targeting System (CBP)
- Passenger Name Records (CBP)
- Terrorist Screening Database (TSDB) (FBI)
- CLASS (DOS)
- TECS (CBP)
- Lost/Stolen Passports through INTERPOL, CLASP (DOS), etc.
- CCD (DOS)

Pre-departure DHS Screening draws from:
- APIS (CBP) → TECS (CBP)
- ATS
- TSDB (FBI)
- Secure Flight (TSA)
- Passenger Name Records (CBP)

Visa Travelers → Apply for visa → Biometric check through BioVisa program, name check through CLASS (DOS) → Pre-departure DHS Screening → Fill out I-94 in transit or on arrival → Arrival → CBP Primary Inspection

Biometric check draws from:
- BIOGRAPHIC: CCD (DOS), CLASS (DOS)
- BIOMETRIC: IDENT (DHS), IAFIS (FBI)

Possible Security Advisory Opinion (SAO) sought

CBP Primary Inspection →
- US-VISIT/IDENT + ADIS
- CJIS/IAFIS
- Entry or denial of entry

Canadian citizen visitors and Mexican citizens traveling with Border Crossing Card → CBP Primary Inspection

*CBP is planning to automate the I-94 process

152 IMMIGRATION ENFORCEMENT IN THE UNITED STATES: THE RISE OF A FORMIDABLE MACHINERY

Appendix C. Border Patrol and Coast Guard Apprehension Screening

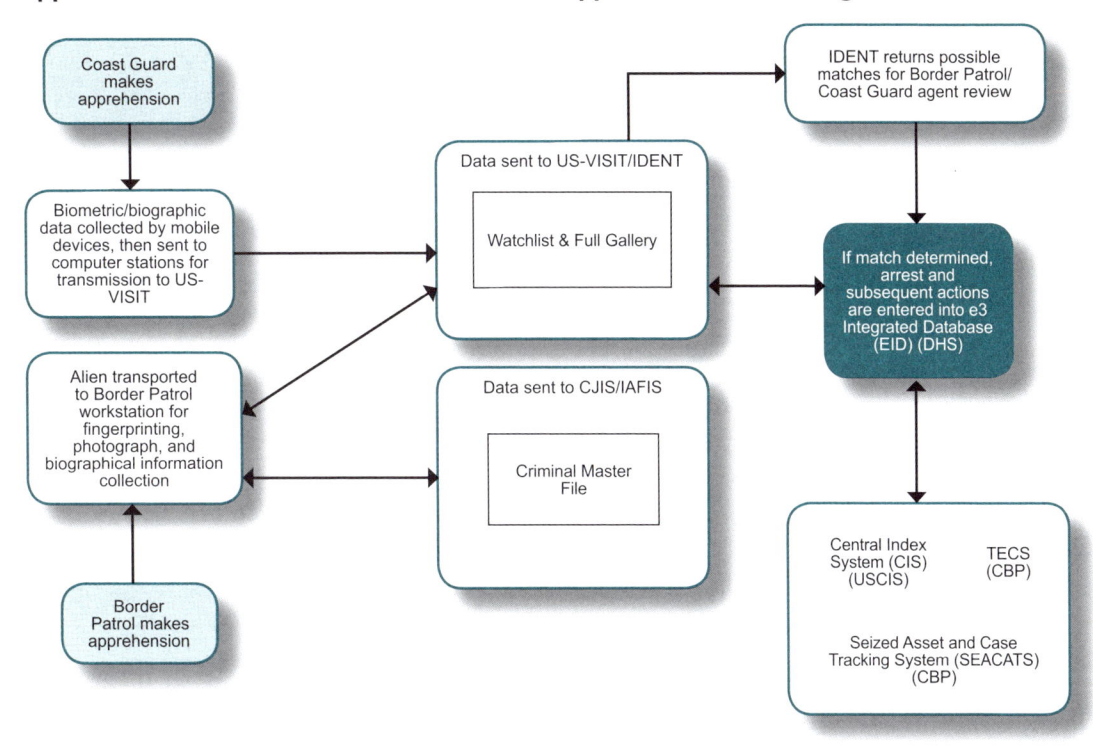

- Coast Guard makes apprehension
- Biometric/biographic data collected by mobile devices, then sent to computer stations for transmission to US-VISIT
- Alien transported to Border Patrol workstation for fingerprinting, photograph, and biographical information collection
- Border Patrol makes apprehension

- Data sent to US-VISIT/IDENT
  - Watchlist & Full Gallery
- Data sent to CJIS/IAFIS
  - Criminal Master File

- IDENT returns possible matches for Border Patrol/Coast Guard agent review
- If match determined, arrest and subsequent actions are entered into e3 Integrated Database (EID) (DHS)
  - Central Index System (CIS) (USCIS)
  - TECS (CBP)
  - Seized Asset and Case Tracking System (SEACATS) (CBP)

Appendix D. Immigration Benefits Application Background Screening

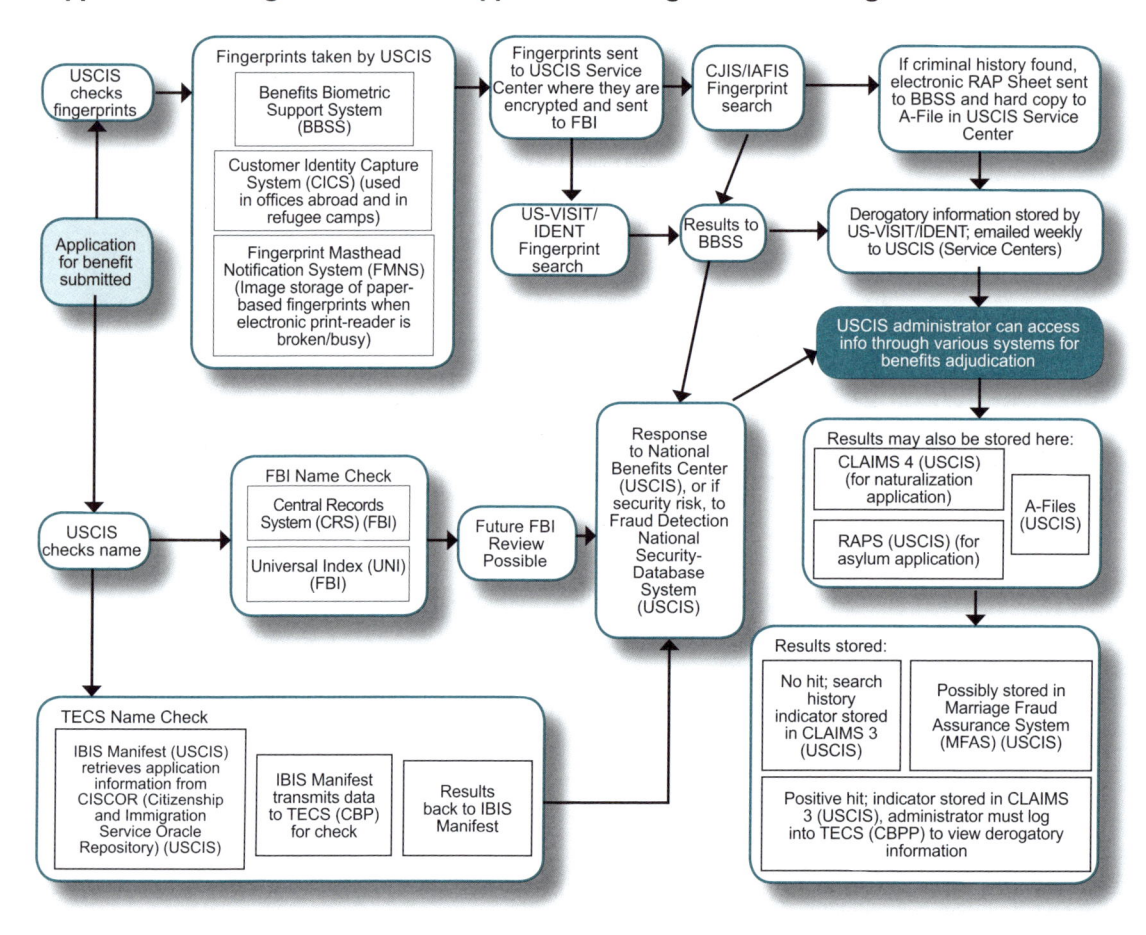

USCIS checks fingerprints

Fingerprints taken by USCIS:
- Benefits Biometric Support System (BBSS)
- Customer Identity Capture System (CICS) (used in offices abroad and in refugee camps)
- Fingerprint Masthead Notification System (FMNS) (Image storage of paper-based fingerprints when electronic print-reader is broken/busy)

Fingerprints sent to USCIS Service Center where they are encrypted and sent to FBI

CJIS/IAFIS Fingerprint search

If criminal history found, electronic RAP Sheet sent to BBSS and hard copy to A-File in USCIS Service Center

US-VISIT/IDENT Fingerprint search

Results to BBSS

Derogatory information stored by US-VISIT/IDENT; emailed weekly to USCIS (Service Centers)

Application for benefit submitted

USCIS administrator can access info through various systems for benefits adjudication

USCIS checks name

FBI Name Check:
- Central Records System (CRS) (FBI)
- Universal Index (UNI) (FBI)

Future FBI Review Possible

Response to National Benefits Center (USCIS), or if security risk, to Fraud Detection National Security-Database System (USCIS)

Results may also be stored here:
- CLAIMS 4 (USCIS) (for naturalization application)
- RAPS (USCIS) (for asylum application)
- A-Files (USCIS)

TECS Name Check:
- IBIS Manifest (USCIS) retrieves application information from CISCOR (Citizenship and Immigration Service Oracle Repository) (USCIS)
- IBIS Manifest transmits data to TECS (CBP) for check
- Results back to IBIS Manifest

Results stored:
- No hit; search history indicator stored in CLAIMS 3 (USCIS)
- Possibly stored in Marriage Fraud Assurance System (MFAS) (USCIS)
- Positive hit; indicator stored in CLAIMS 3 (USCIS), administrator must log into TECS (CBPP) to view derogatory information

Appendix E. Arrests/Secure Communities Screening

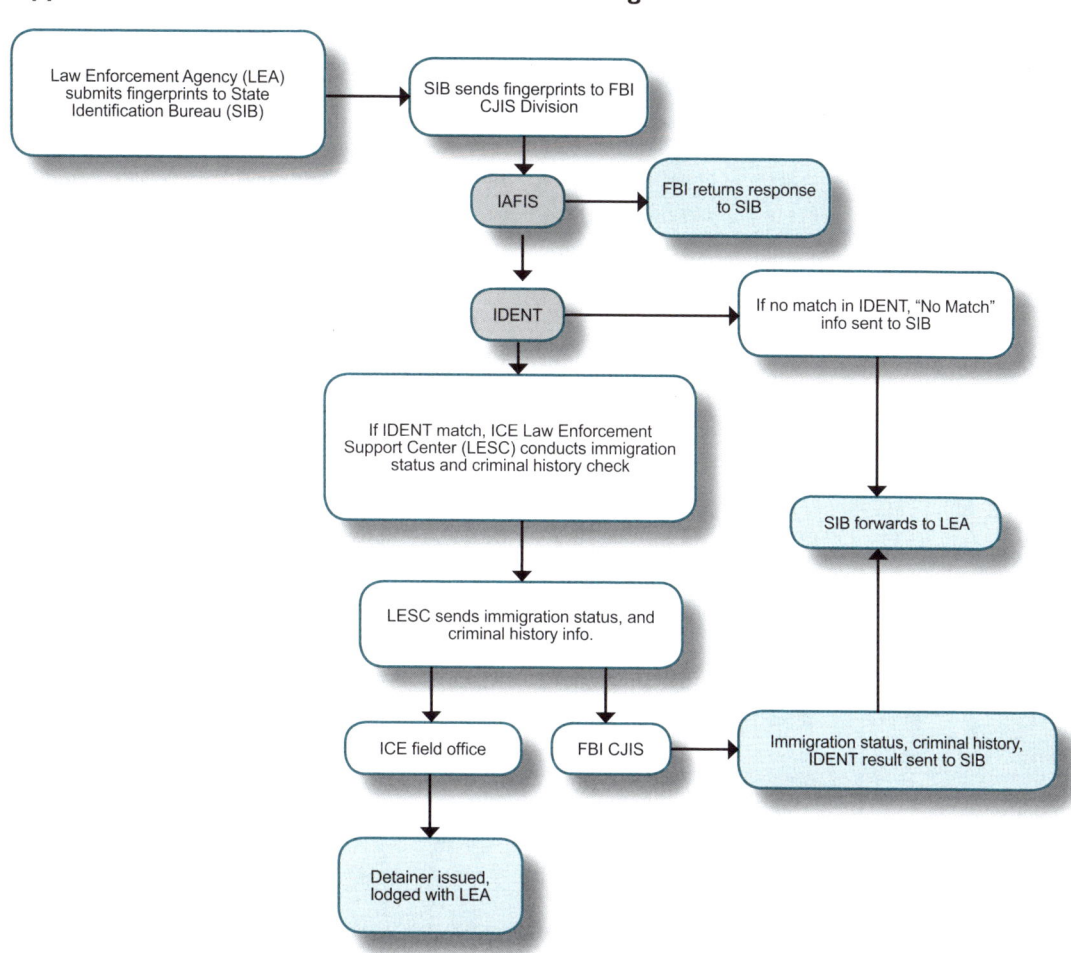

- Law Enforcement Agency (LEA) submits fingerprints to State Identification Bureau (SIB)
- SIB sends fingerprints to FBI CJIS Division
- IAFIS
- FBI returns response to SIB
- IDENT
- If no match in IDENT, "No Match" info sent to SIB
- If IDENT match, ICE Law Enforcement Support Center (LESC) conducts immigration status and criminal history check
- LESC sends immigration status, and criminal history info.
- ICE field office
- FBI CJIS
- Immigration status, criminal history, IDENT result sent to SIB
- SIB forwards to LEA
- Detainer issued, lodged with LEA

APPENDICES 155

Table A-1. Apprehensions between Ports of Entry by Border Patrol Sector, Southwest Border, 1994-2010

	San Diego (CA)	El Centro (CA)	Yuma (AZ)	Tucson (AZ)	El Paso (TX)	Marfa (TX)	Del Rio (TX)	Laredo (TX)	Rio Grande (TX)
1994	450,152	27,654	21,211	139,473	79,688	13,494	50,036	73,142	124,251
1995	524,231	37,317	20,894	227,529	110,971	11,552	76,490	93,305	169,101
1996	483,815	66,873	28,310	305,348	145,929	13,214	121,137	131,841	210,553
1997	283,889	146,210	30,177	272,397	124,376	12,692	113,280	141,893	243,793
1998	248,092	226,695	76,195	387,406	125,035	14,509	131,058	103,433	204,257
1999	182,267	225,279	93,388	470,449	110,857	14,952	156,653	114,004	169,151
2000	151,681	238,126	108,747	616,346	115,696	13,689	157,178	108,973	133,243
2001	110,075	172,852	78,385	449,675	112,857	12,087	104,875	87,068	107,844
2002	100,681	108,273	42,654	333,648	94,154	11,392	66,985	82,095	89,927
2003	111,515	92,099	56,638	347,263	88,816	10,319	50,145	70,521	77,749
2004	138,608	74,467	98,060	491,771	104,399	10,530	53,794	74,706	92,947
2005	126,909	55,726	138,438	439,090	122,689	10,536	68,510	75,342	134,188
2006	142,122	61,469	118,537	392,104	122,261	7,517	42,634	74,843	110,531
2007	152,459	55,881	37,994	378,323	75,464	5,537	22,919	56,715	73,430
2008	162,392	40,962	8,363	317,709	30,310	5,390	20,761	43,659	75,476
2009	118,712	33,520	6,952	241,667	14,998	6,357	17,082	40,571	60,992
2010	68,565	32,562	7,116	212,202	12,251	5,288	14,694	35,287	59,766
2011	42,447	30,191	5,833	123,285	10,345	4,036	16,144	36,053	59,243
Change Since 2000	-72.02%	-87.32%	-94.64%	-80.00%	-91.06%	-70.52%	-89.73%	-66.92%	-55.54%
Change Since 2005	-66.55%	-45.88%	-95.79%	-71.92%	-91.57%	-61.69%	-76.43%	-52.14%	-55.84%

Sources: DHS, *2009 Yearbook of Immigration Statistics* (Washington, DC: DHS, 2010), www.dhs.gov/xlibrary/assets/statistics/yearbook/2009/ois_yb_2009.pdf; *Yearbook of Immigration Statistics, FY 2011* (Washington, DC: DHS, 2012), www.dhs.gov/sites/default/files/publications/immigration-statistics/yearbook/2011/ois_yb_2011.pdf.

Table A-2. Businesses Enrolled in E-Verify, by State and as Share of All Firms and Establishments, FY 2012

State	Businesses Enrolled in E-Verify (5 or More Employees)	Business Firms (5 or More Employees)	Business Establishments (5 or More Employees)	Share of E-Verify Participants as Share of Firms (5 or More Employees)	Share of E-Verify Participants as Share of Establishments (5 or More Employees)
UNITED STATES	298,786	2,208,598	3,868,032	13.53%	7.72%
ARIZONA	30,197	41,998	71,776	71.90%	42.07%
MISSISSIPPI	12,616	20,698	34,133	60.95%	36.96%
ALABAMA	20,535	34,877	58,579	58.88%	35.06%
SOUTH CAROLINA	17,801	34,375	57,407	51.78%	31.01%
GEORGIA	21,906	67,324	114,797	32.54%	19.08%
MISSOURI	13,732	48,125	80,398	28.53%	17.08%
UTAH	5,491	22,322	33,627	24.60%	16.33%
DC	1,658	8,908	13,381	18.61%	12.39%
NEBRASKA	3,152	17,520	27,251	17.99%	11.57%
RHODE ISLAND	1,722	10,398	14,222	16.56%	12.11%
COLORADO	7,262	45,002	71,157	16.14%	10.21%
TENNESSEE	5,542	44,997	78,749	12.32%	7.04%
FLORIDA	15,226	125,172	216,221	12.16%	7.04%
VIRGINIA	7,410	62,360	106,110	11.88%	6.98%
INDIANA	5,921	49,988	83,946	11.84%	7.05%
OKLAHOMA	3,507	30,412	48,451	11.53%	7.24%
NORTH CAROLINA	7,813	69,572	118,585	11.23%	6.59%
LOUISIANA	3,832	37,548	59,338	10.21%	6.46%
MARYLAND	4,655	46,215	72,693	10.07%	6.40%
KANSAS	2,582	25,948	40,942	9.95%	6.31%
NEVADA	2,008	20,393	32,197	9.85%	6.24%
TEXAS	15,765	166,779	293,039	9.45%	5.38%
CALIFORNIA	24,108	268,297	428,275	8.99%	5.63%
MINNESOTA	4,047	47,615	75,233	8.50%	5.38%
WASHINGTON	4,581	56,987	88,533	8.04%	5.17%
NEW MEXICO	1,275	15,961	24,597	7.99%	5.18%
ALASKA	504	6,468	9,927	7.79%	5.08%
HAWAII	855	11,426	18,015	7.48%	4.75%

State	Businesses Enrolled in E-Verify (5 or More Employees)	Business Firms (5 or More Employees)	Business Establishments (5 or More Employees)	Share of E-Verify Participants as Share of Firms (5 or More Employees)	Share of E-Verify Participants as Share of Establishments (5 or More Employees)
OREGON	2,560	35,264	54,478	7.26%	4.70%
MASSACHUSETTS	4,108	57,735	89,661	7.12%	4.58%
ILLINOIS	6,799	100,561	161,302	6.76%	4.22%
NEW JERSEY	4,972	73,779	109,349	6.74%	4.55%
IDAHO	968	14,367	21,158	6.74%	4.58%
ARKANSAS	1,394	22,057	36,030	6.32%	3.87%
DELAWARE	538	8,769	13,528	6.14%	3.98%
CONNECTICUT	1,899	31,778	48,260	5.98%	3.93%
IOWA	1,632	27,457	44,669	5.94%	3.65%
KENTUCKY	1,846	31,536	52,546	5.85%	3.51%
WYOMING	393	7,244	9,875	5.43%	3.98%
NEW HAMPSHIRE	730	13,605	20,080	5.37%	3.64%
PENNSYLVANIA	5,189	100,695	166,153	5.15%	3.12%
OHIO	4,457	87,929	151,491	5.07%	2.94%
MICHIGAN	3,716	74,053	119,246	5.02%	3.12%
WISCONSIN	2,414	49,758	78,742	4.85%	3.07%
NEW YORK	7,176	152,104	226,390	4.72%	3.17%
NORTH DAKOTA	366	7,851	11,442	4.66%	3.20%
SOUTH DAKOTA	419	9,196	13,096	4.56%	3.20%
MONTANA	439	11,483	16,119	3.82%	2.72%
MAINE	434	12,766	19,545	3.40%	2.22%
WEST VIRGINIA	416	14,048	22,963	2.96%	1.81%
VERMONT	218	7,471	10,330	2.92%	2.11%

Notes: The Census Bureau defines a business establishment as a "single physical location where business is conducted or where services or industrial operations are performed." In contrast, a firm is defined as a "business organization consisting of one or more domestic establishments in the same state and industry that were specified under common ownership and/or control." Because a business with multiple locations may enroll in E-Verify for its entire firm but then opt to use the program in only some of its establishments, or, in some cases, enroll each establishment in the program individually, USCIS statistics on the number of employers participating in E-Verify in a given state do not map precisely with either the number of firms or the number of establishments in that state, so as to provide a direct method of comparison. Some businesses may also serve as E-Verify "verification agents" for all other businesses. For that reason, as well as the fact that the numbers above exclude all businesses with fewer than five employees, these estimates should be used with some caution.

Sources: MPI analysis of data from USCIS, "E-Verify Employers and Federal Contractors List," www.uscis.gov/portal/site/uscis/menuitem.eb1d4c2a3e5b9ac89243c6a7543f6d1a/?vgnextoid=0199256ace346310VgnVCM100000082ca60aRCRD&vgnextchannel=0199256ace346310VgnVCM100000082ca60aRCRD; and Census Bureau, "Statistics of U.S. Businesses," 2009, www.census.gov/econ/susb/.

WORKS CITED

Aguilar, David and Gregory Giddens. 2007. Testimony of Chief of Border Patrol and Executive Director of Secure Border Initiative before the House Committee on Homeland Security, Subcommittee on Border, Maritime, and Global Counterterrorism. *Project 28: The Future of SBInet*, 110th Cong., 1st sess., June 7, 2007. http://chsdemocrats.house.gov/SiteDocuments/20070607154822-79256.doc.

Alden, Edward. 2009. *The Closing of the American Border: Terrorism, Immigration, and Security Since 9/11.* New York: Harper Perennial.

Alden, Edward and Bryan Roberts. 2011. Are US Borders Secure? Why We Don't Know, and How to Find Out. *Foreign Affairs* 90 (4). www.foreignaffairs.com/articles/67901/edward-alden-and-bryan-roberts/are-us-borders-secure.

American Bar Association (ABA) Commission on Immigration. 2004. *American Justice Through Immigrants' Eyes*. Chicago: ABA. www.protectcivilrights.org/pdf/reports/american-justice/american_justice.pdf.

_____. 2010. *Reforming the Immigration System: Proposal to Promote Independence, Fairness, Efficiency, and Professionalism in the Adjudication of Removal Cases*. Washington, DC: ABA. www.americanbar.org/content/dam/aba/administrative/immigration/coi_complete_full_report.authcheckdam.pdf.

American Civil Liberties Union and National Immigration Forum. 2009. Operation Streamline. Fact sheet, July 21, 2009. www.immigrationforum.org/images/uploads/OperationStreamlineFactsheet.pdf.

American Correctional Association (ACA). 2004. *Performance-Based Standards for Adult Local Detention Facilities, Fourth Edition.* Lanham, MD: ACA.

Australian Government Department of Citizenship and Immigration. 2011. *Annual Report 2010-11*. Canberra: Department of Citizenship and Immigration. www.immi.gov.au/about/reports/annual/2010-11/html/outcome-3/identity.htm.

Baertlein, Lisa. 2011. Federal Agents Widen Chipotle Immigration Probe. Reuters, May 4, 2011. www.reuters.com/article/2011/05/04/us-chipotle-idUSTRE74307S20110504.

Bahrampour, Tara. 2011. ICE Reforms Secure Communities Program. *Washington Post*, June 17, 2011. www.washingtonpost.com/local/ice-reforms-secure-communities-program/2011/06/17/AGMJka-ZH_story.html.

Barkakati, Nabajyoti. 2010. *Improvements in the Department of State's Development Process Could Increase the Security of Passport and Border Crossing Cards*. Washington, DC: US Government Accountability Office. www.gao.gov/assets/310/305134.pdf.

Barth, Richard and Thomas Winkowski. 2009. Joint Statement of DHS Acting Assistant Secretary for Policy and US Customs and Border Protection Office of Field Operations Assistant Commissioner before the House Committee on Homeland Security, Subcommittee on Border, Maritime, and Global Communications. *Implementing the Western Hemisphere Travel Initiative at Land and Sea Ports of Entry: Are We Ready?* 110th Cong., 1st sess., May 7, 2009. www.cbp.gov/xp/cgov/newsroom/congressional_test/whti_ready_testify.xml.

Batalova, Jeanne and Michelle Mittelstadt. 2012. *Relief from Deportation: Demographic Profile of the DREAMers Potentially Eligible under the Deferred Action Policy.* Washington, DC: Migration Policy Institute. www.migrationpolicy.org/pubs/FS24_deferredaction.pdf.

BBC News. 2012. MEPs back deal to give air passenger data to US. BBC News, April 19, 2012. www.bbc.co.uk/news/world-europe-17764365.

Bennett, Brian. A Kinder, Gentler, Detention System. *Los Angeles Times*, March 17, 2012. http://articles.latimes.com/2012/mar/17/nation/la-na-detention-salad-bar-20120318.

Bernstein, Nina. 2009. US to Reform Policy on Detention for Immigrants. *New York Times*, August 5, 2009. www.nytimes.com/2009/08/06/us/politics/06detain.html.

Bersin, Alan. 2010. Remarks by Commissioner, Customs and Border Protection, at the Migration Policy Institute. Washington, DC: October 14, 2010. http://vimeo.com/15887500.

———. 2011. Remarks by Commissioner, Customs and Border Protection, at the Center for American Progress. Washington, DC: August 4, 2011. www.c-spanvideo.org/program/300899-1.

———. 2011. Testimony of the Commissioner, Customs and Border Protection, before the Senate Judiciary Committee, Subcommittee on Immigration, Refugees, and Border Security. *Improving Border Security and Facilitation of Commerce at America's Northern Border and Ports of Entry*, 112th Cong., 1st sess., May 17, 2011. www.cbp.gov/xp/cgov/newsroom/congressional_test/bersin_testifies.xml.

Bjelopera, Jerome P. 2011. *Terrorism Information Sharing and the Nationwide Suspicious Activity Report Initiative: Background and Issues for Congress.* Washington, DC: Congressional Research Service. http://fpc.state.gov/documents/organization/166837.pdf.

Borkowski, Mark and Michael Fisher. 2010. Testimony of Director, Secure Border Initiative, and Acting Chief, US Border Patrol, before the House Homeland Security Committee, Subcommittees on Management, Investigations, and Oversight, and Border, Maritime, and Global Counterterrorism. *SBInet: Does it Pass the Border Security Test?* 111th Cong., 2nd sess., June 17, 2010. chsdemocrats.house.gov/Hearings/index.asp?ID=259.

Borkowski, Mark, Michael Fisher, and Michael Kostelnik. 2011. Joint Testimony of Assistant Commissioner, Office of Technology, Innovation, and Acquisition, Customs and Border Protection; Chief, US Border Patrol; and Assistant Commissioner, Office of Air and Marine, Customs and Border Protection, before the House Committee on Homeland Security, Subcommittee on Border and Maritime Security. *After SBInet - the Future of Technology on the Border*, 112th Cong., 1st sess., March 15, 2011. www.dhs.gov/ynews/testimony/testimony_1300195655653.shtm.

Bromwich, Michael. 1999. Statement of Inspector General, Department of Justice, before the House Judiciary Committee, Subcommittee on Immigration and Claims. *Nonimmigrant Visa Fraud*, 106th Cong., 1st sess., May 5, 1999. www.justice.gov/oig/testimony/9905.htm.

Bruno, Andorra. 2011. *Immigration-Related Worksite Enforcement: Performance Measures*. Washington, DC: Congressional Research Service. http://assets.opencrs.com/rpts/R40002_20110301.pdf.

Caldwell, Alicia. 2012. DHS Expanding Deportation Reviews to 4 More Cities. Associated Press, March 29, 2012. www.boston.com/news/nation/washington/articles/2012/03/29/dhs_expanding_deportation_reviews_to_4_more_cities/.

Capps, Randy, Marc R. Rosenblum, Cristina Rodriguez, and Muzaffar Chishti. 2011. *Delegation and Divergence: A Study of 287(g) State and Local Immigration Enforcement*. Washington, DC: Migration Policy Institute. www.migrationpolicy.org/pubs/287g-divergence.pdf.

Capps, Randy, Doris Meissner, and Michael Fix. 2012. *Measuring Effective Border Control: What Can We Know?* Unpublished working paper, Migration Policy Institute, July 2012.

Carriquiry, Alicia and Malay Majmundar, eds. 2013. *Options for Estimating Illegal Entries at the U.S.–Mexico Border*. Washington, DC: The National Academies Press. Prepublication version available at www.nap.edu/openbook.php?record_id=13498&page=R1.

Catholic Legal Immigration Network, Inc. (CLINIC). 2000. *The Impact of Our Laws on American Families*. Washington, DC: CLINIC. http://cliniclegal.org/sites/default/files/atrisk1.pdf.

Cave, Damien. 2011. Crossing Over, and Over. *New York Times*, October 2, 2011. www.nytimes.com/2011/10/03/world/americas/mexican-immigrants-repeatedly-brave-risks-to-resume-lives-in-united-states.html?pagewanted=all.

———. 2012. American Children, Now Struggling to Adjust to Life in Mexico. *New York Times*, June 18, 2012. www.nytimes.com/2012/06/19/world/americas/american-born-children-struggle-to-adjust-in-mexico.html?pagewanted=all.

Chertoff, Michael and Carlos Gutierrez. 2007. Remarks by Homeland Security Secretary and Commerce Secretary at a press conference on border security and administrative immigration reforms. Washington, DC: August 10, 2007. www.hsdl.org/?view&did=478615.

Chishti, Muzaffar, Doris Meissner, Demetrios G. Papademetriou, Jay Peterzell, Michael J. Wishnie, and Stephen W. Yale-Loehr. 2003. *America's Challenge: Domestic Security, Civil Liberties, and National Unity After September 11.* Washington, DC: Migration Policy Institute. www.migrationpolicy.org/pubs/Americas_Challenges.pdf.

Citizenship and Immigration Services (CIS) Ombudsman. 2009. *Recommendation from the CIS Ombudsman to the Director, USCIS.* www.dhs.gov/xlibrary/assets/CISOmbudsman_RR_25_EAD_03-20-06.pdf.

Clark, Nicola and Matthew L. Wald. 2006. Hurdle for U.S. in Getting Data on Passengers. *New York Times*, May 31, 2006. www.nytimes.com/2006/05/31/world/europe/31air.html?_r=1&th&emc=th&oref=slogin.

Cohen, John. 2011. Statement of Principal Deputy Coordinator for Counterterrorism, Department of Homeland Security, before the House Homeland Security Committee, Subcommittee on Border and Maritime Security. *Ten Years After 9/11: Can Terrorists Still Exploit Our Visa System?* 112th Cong., 1st sess., September 13, 2011. http://homeland.house.gov/hearing/ten-years-after-911-can-terrorists-still-exploit-our-visa-system.

Cohen, John and Peter Edge. 2012. Joint testimony of Department of Homeland Security Deputy Counterterrorism Coordinator and US Immigration and Customs Enforcement Homeland Security Investigations Deputy Executive Associate Director, before the House Committee on Homeland Security, Subcommittee on Border and Maritime Security. *From the 9/11 Hijackers to Amine el-Khalifi: Terrorists and the Visa Overstay Problem*, 112th Cong., 2nd sess., March 6, 2012. www.dhs.gov/ynews/testimony/20120306-ctwg-ice-visa-overstays.shtm.

Cornelius, Wayne. 2008. *Reforming the Management of Migration Flows from Latin America to the United States.* San Diego, CA: Center for Comparative Immigration Studies. http://ccis.ucsd.edu/wp-content/uploads/2009/07/WP-170.pdf.

Council of the European Union. 2011. *Agreement Between the United States of America and the European Union on the Use and Transfer of Passenger Name Records to the United States Department of Homeland Security.* Brussels: Council of the European Union. http://register.consilium.europa.eu/pdf/en/11/st17/st17434.en11.pdf.

Dodge, Lowell. 1989. Statement of Director, Administration of Justice Issues, General Government Division, Government Accountability Office, before the House Committee on the Judiciary, Subcommittee on Immigration, Refugees, and International Law. *Criminal Aliens: INS Enforcement*, 101st Cong., 2nd sess., November 1, 1989. http://archive.gao.gov/d48t13/139869.pdf.

Dreby, Joanna. 2012. *How Today's Immigration Enforcement Policies Impact Children, Families, and Communities: A View from the Ground.* Washington, DC: Center for American Progress. www.americanprogress.org/wp-content/uploads/2012/08/DrebyImmigrationFamiliesFINAL.pdf.

Economist, The. 2011. Border Accord. *The Economist*, December 8, 2011. www.economist.com/blogs/gulliver/2011/12/canada-us.

Ekstrand, Laurie E. 2006. *Border-Crossing Deaths Have Doubled Since 1995: Border Patrol's Efforts to Prevent Deaths Have Not Been Fully Evaluated.* Washington, DC: Government Accountability Office. www.gao.gov/assets/260/251173.pdf.

Eldridge, Thomas R., Susan Ginsburg, Walter T. Hempel II, Janice L. Kephart, and Kelly Moore. 2004. *9/11 and Terrorist Travel: Staff Report of the National Commission on Terrorist Attacks Upon the United States.* Washington, DC: National Commission on Terrorist Attacks Upon the United States. http://govinfo.library.unt.edu/911/staff_statements/911_TerrTrav_Monograph.pdf.

Eschbach, Karl, Jacqueline Maria Hagan, and Néstor Rodriguez. 2001. Causes and Trends in Migrant Deaths along the U.S.-Mexico Border, 1985-1998. Working Paper Series 01-4. Houston: Center for Immigration Research.

Fisher, Michael J. 2011. Testimony of Chief, US Border Patrol, before the House Committee on Homeland Security, Subcommittee on Border and Maritime Security, *Securing our Borders—Operational Control and the Path Forward*, 112th Cong., 1st sess., February 15, 2011. www.cbp.gov/xp/cgov/newsroom/congressional_test/fisher_testifies/chief_fisher.xml.

Foley, Elise. 2011. Communities Opt Out of Immigration Enforcement Program. *Washington Independent*, September 29, 2011. http://washingtonindependent.com/99071/communities-opt-out-of-immigration-enforcement-program.

Ford, Jess T. 2002. *Border Security: Implications of Eliminating the Visa Waiver Program.* Washington, DC: Government Accountability Office. www.gao.gov/assets/240/236408.pdf.

_____. 2007. *Border Security: Security of New Passports and Visas Enhanced, But More Needs to Be Done to Prevent Their Fraudulent Use.* Washington, DC: Government Accountability Office. www.gao.gov/products/GAO-07-1006.

_____. 2008. *Visa Waiver Program: Actions Are Needed to Improve Management of the Expansion Process, and to Assess and Mitigate Program Risks.* Washington, DC: Government Accountability Office. www.gao.gov/new.items/d08967.pdf.

Freed Wessler, Seth. 2011. *Shattered Families: The Perilous Intersection of Immigration Enforcement and the Child Welfare System.* New York: Applied Research Center. http://arc.org/shatteredfamilies.

Gilbert, James. 2011. Yuma Sector Expands Operation Streamline. *Yuma Sun*, December 20, 2010. www.yumasun.com/news/sector-66298-operation-yuma.html.

Ginsburg, Susan and Kristen McCabe. 2011. Re-envisioning Security and the Movement of People. *Migration Information Source*, February 2011. www.migrationinformation.org/Feature/display.cfm?ID=829.

Goodwin, Jacob. 2011. CBP Aims to Boost Enrollment in its Trusted Traveler Programs. *Government Security News Magazine*, September 16, 2011. www.gsnmagazine.com/node/24541.

Greenhouse, Linda. 2011. Legacy of a Fence. *The New York Times*, January 23, 2011. opinionator.blogs.nytimes.com/2011/01/22/legacy-of-a-fence/.

Guttin, Andrea. 2010. *The Criminal Alien Program: Immigration Enforcement in Travis County, TX.* Washington, DC: Immigration Policy Center. www.immigrationpolicy.org/sites/default/files/docs/Criminal_Alien_Program_021710.pdf.

Haass, Aaron. 2006. Videoconferencing in Immigration Proceedings. *Pierce Law Review* 5 (1): 59-90. http://law.unh.edu/assets/images/uploads/publications/pierce-law-review-vol05-no1-haas.pdf.

Haddal, Chad C. 2010. *Border Security: The Role of the US Border Patrol.* Washington, DC: Congressional Research Service (CRS). www.fas.org/sgp/crs/homesec/RL32562.pdf.

Haddal, Chad C. and Alison Siskin. 2010. *Immigration Related Detention: Current Legislative Issues.* Washington, DC: CRS. http://digitalcommons.ilr.cornell.edu/key_workplace/707/.

Harty, Maura and Elaine Dezenski. 2005. DOS Special Briefing on Western Hemisphere Travel Initiative. Department of State briefing, April 5, 2005. http://2001-2009.state.gov/r/pa/prs/ps/2005/44286.htm.

Hing, Julianne. 2011. Counties Defy Feds, Vow Not to Detain Immigrants on ICE's Behalf. Colorlines, October 25, 2011. http://colorlines.com/archives/2011/10/counties_unable_to_opt_out_of_secure_communities_vow_not_to_detain_immigrants_on_ices_behalf.html.

Hite, Randolph and Richard M. Stana. 2007. Testimony of Director, Information Technology Architecture and Systems Issues, Government Accountability Office (GAO), and Director, Homeland Security and Justice Issues, GAO, before the House Committee on Appropriations, Subcommittee on Homeland Security. *US-VISIT Has Not Fully Met Expectations and Longstanding Program Management Challenges Need to Be Addressed*, 110th Cong., 1st sess., February 16, 2007. www.gao.gov/new.items/d07499t.pdf.

Hoefer, Michael, Nancy Rytina, and Bryan Baker. 2012. *Estimates of the Unauthorized Immigrant Population Residing in the United States.* Washington, DC: Department of Homeland Security, Office of Immigration Statistics. www.dhs.gov/xlibrary/assets/statistics/publications/ois_ill_pe_2011.pdf.

Home Office, UK Border Agency. 2010. *High value data sharing protocol - Five Country Conference, Privacy Impact Assessment.* London: UK Border Agency. www.ukba.homeoffice.gov.uk/sitecontent/documents/aboutus/workingwithus/high-value-data-sharing-protocol/.

Hong, J. Traci. 2002. *Objecting to Video Merits Hearings.* Washington, DC: American Immigration Law Foundation. www.ailf.org/lac/pa/lac_pa_080902.asp. http://digitalcommons.ilr.cornell.edu/cgi/viewcontent.cgi?article=1577&context=key_workplace&sei-redir=1#search=%22Nunez%20neto%20role%20US%20border%20patrol%22.

Lopez, Mark Hugo, Rich Morin, and Paul Taylor. 2010. *Illegal Immigration Backlash Worries, Divides Latinos*. Washington, DC: Pew Hispanic Center. www.pewhispanic.org/2010/10/28/illegal-immigration-backlash-worries-divides-latinos/.

Lopez, Mark Hugo, Ana Gonzalez-Barrera, and Seth Motel. 2011. *As Deportations Rise to Record Levels, Most Latinos Oppose Obama's Policy*. Washington, DC: Pew Hispanic Center. www.pewhispanic.org/2011/12/28/as-deportations-rise-to-record-levels-most-latinos-oppose-obamas-policy/.

Human Rights First. 2011. *Jails and Jumpsuits: Transforming the U.S. Immigration Detention System—A Two Year Review*. New York: Human Rights First. www.humanrightsfirst.org/wp-content/uploads/pdf/HRF-Jails-and-Jumpsuits-report.pdf.

Human Rights Watch. 2010. *Costly and Unfair: Flaws in US Immigration Detention Policy*. New York: Human Rights Watch. www.hrw.org/reports/2010/05/06/costly-and-unfair-0.

Human Rights Watch and American Civil Liberties Union (ACLU). 2010. *Deportation by Default: Mental Disability, Unfair Hearings, and Indefinite Detention in the US Immigration System*. New York: Human Rights Watch and ACLU. www.hrw.org/reports/2010/07/26/deportation-default-0.

Hutchinson, Asa. Remarks by Under Secretary for Border and Transportation Security on the Launch of US-VISIT. Speech, Center for Strategic and International Studies, May 19, 2003. http://csis.org/files/media/csis/events/030519_hutchinson.pdf.

ImmigrationWorksUSA. 2012. At a Glance: State E-Verify Laws. July 2012. www.immigrationworksusa.org/index.php?p=110.

Jimenez, Maria. 2009. *Humanitarian Crisis: Migrant Deaths at the U.S.-Mexico Border*. New York: ACLU of San Diego & Imperial Counties and Mexico's National Commission of Human Rights. www.aclu.org/immigrants-rights/humanitarian-crisis-migrant-deaths-us-mexico-border.

Jones, James L. and John O. Brennan. 2012. Letter from National Security Advisor and Assistant to the President for Homeland Security and Counterterrorism to The Honorable Carl Levin, Chairman, Committee on Armed Services, US Senate. May 25, 2010. www.whitehouse.gov/sites/default/files/Letter_to_Chairman_Levin.pdf.

Kahn, Carrie. 2011. Small Fishing Boats Smuggle People to California. NPR, November 16, 2011. www.npr.org/2011/11/16/142133395/small-fishing-boats-smuggle-people-to-california.

Kandel, Jason. 2011. Maritime Smuggling to California on the Rise. Reuters, July 30, 2011. www.reuters.com/article/2011/07/30/us-usa-mexico-boats-idUSTRE76T1J920110730.

Kelly, Erin. 2011. Arizona Border Security to Get an Upgrade. *Arizona Republic*, July 7, 2011. www.azcentral.com/arizonarepublic/news/articles/2011/07/07/20110707arizona-border-security-upgrade-0707.html.

Kennedy, Patrick F. 2010. Statement of Undersecretary of State for Management before the House Committee on the Judiciary. *Sharing and Analyzing Information to Prevent Terrorism*, 111th Cong., 2nd sess., February 10, 2010. http://travel.state.gov/law/legal/testimony/testimony_4830.html.

Kerwin, Donald. 1996. *Detention of Newcomers: Constitutional Standards and New Legislation: Part One*. Washington, DC: Federal Publications, Inc., 1996.

_____. 2001. *Chaos on the U.S.-Mexican Border*. Washington, DC: CLINIC. www.lexisnexis.com/practiceareas/immigration/pdfs/web305.pdf.

_____. 2005. *Revisiting the Need for Appointed Counsel*. Washington, DC: Migration Policy Institute. www.migrationpolicy.org/insight/Insight_Kerwin.pdf.

_____. 2011. *The Faltering US Refugee Protection Program: Legal and Policy Responses to Refugees, Asylum Seekers, and Others in Need of Protection*. Washington, DC: Migration Policy Institute. www.migrationpolicy.org/pubs/refugeeprotection-2011.pdf.

Kerwin, Donald M. and Serena Yi-Ying Lin. 2009. *Immigrant Detention: Can ICE Meet Its Legal Imperatives and Case Management Responsibilities?* Washington, DC: Migration Policy Institute. www.migrationpolicy.org/pubs/detentionreportSept1009.pdf.

Kerwin, Donald and Kristen McCabe. 2010. Arrested on Entry: Operation Streamline and the Prosecution of Immigration Crimes. *Migration Information Source*, April 2010. www.migrationinformation.org/Feature/display.cfm?ID=780.

Kerwin, Donald M. with Kristen McCabe. 2011. *Labor Standards Enforcement and Low-Wage Immigrants: Creating an Effective Enforcement System*. Washington, DC: Migration Policy Institute. www.migrationpolicy.org/pubs/laborstandards-2011.pdf.

Kerwin, Donald M., Doris Meissner, and Margie McHugh. 2011. *Executive Action on Immigration: Six Ways to Make the System Work Better*. Washington, DC: Migration Policy Institute. www.migrationpolicy.org/pubs/administrativefixes.pdf.

Kibble, Kumar. 2011. Statement of Deputy Director, Immigration and Customs Enforcement, before the House Committee on Homeland Security, Subcommittee on Border and Maritime Security. *Does Administrative Amnesty Harm Our Efforts to Gain and Maintain Operational Control of the Border?* 112th Cong., 1st sess., October 4, 2011. www.gpo.gov/fdsys/pkg/CHRG-112hhrg73358/pdf/CHRG-112hhrg73358.pdf.

Kim, Mallie Jane. 2011. Controversial Immigration Program Spurs Federal-State Spat. *US News and World Report*, June 27, 2011. www.usnews.com/news/articles/2011/06/27/controversial-immigration-program-spurs-federal-state-spat.

Krouse, William J. and Bart Elias. 2009. *Terrorist Watchlist Checks and Air Passenger Prescreening*. Washington, DC: CRS. www.fas.org/sgp/crs/homesec/RL33645.pdf.

Landy, Kevin. 2012. Testimony of Assistant Director, Office of Detention Policy and Planning, Immigration and Customs Enforcement (ICE), before the House Committee on the Judiciary, Subcommittee on Immigration Policy and Enforcement. *Holiday on ICE: The U.S. Department of Homeland Security's New Immigration Detention Standards*, 112th Cong., 2nd sess., March 28, 2012. www.judiciary.house.gov/hearings/Hearings%202012/Landy%2003282012.pdf.

Lee, Mike. 2011. Lee, Schumer Introduce Immigration Reform Bill. News release, October 20, 2011. http://lee.senate.gov/public/index.cfm/press-releases?ID=7d71bb4f-3752-4e86-af5f-85ec-c9c0c142.

Lee Koh, Jennifer, Jayashri Srikantiah, and Karen C. Tumlin. 2011. *Deportation Without Due Process*. Palo Alto, CA: Stanford Law School Mills Legal Clinic, Western State University College of Law, National Immigration Law Center. www.nilc.org/document.html?id=6.

Lemons, Stephen. 2010. Operation Streamline Costs Taxpayers Millions, Tramples on the Constitution, Treats Immigrants Like Cattle and Doesn't Work. So Why Are the Feds So Committed To It? *Dallas Observer*, October 21, 2010. www.dallasobserver.com/2010-10-21/news/operation-streamline-costs-taxpayers-millions-tramples-on-the-constitution-treats-immigrants-like-cattle-and-doesn-t-work-so-why-are-the-feds-so-committed-to-it/.

Lichtblau, Eric and John Markoff. 2004. U.S. Nearing Deal on Way to Track Foreign Visitors. *New York Times*, May 24, 2004. www.nytimes.com/2004/05/24/us/us-nearing-deal-on-way-to-track-foreign-visitors.html?pagewanted=all&src=pm.

Liptak, Adam. 2002. In the Name of Security: Privacy for Me, Not Thee. *The New York Times*, November 24, 2002. www.nytimes.com/2002/11/24/weekinreview/the-nation-citizen-watch-in-the-name-of-security-privacy-for-me-not-thee.html?pagewanted=all&src=pm.

Liptak, Adam and Julia Preston. 2009. Justices Limit Use of Identity Theft Law in Immigration Cases. *New York Times*, May 4, 2009. www.nytimes.com/2009/05/05/us/05immig.html?_r=1&scp=1&sq=aggravated%20identity%20theft&st=cse.

Lipton, Eric. 2006. Officials Seek Broader Access to Airline Data. *The New York Times*, August 22, 2006. www.nytimes.com/2006/08/22/washington/22data.html.

Lofstrom, Magnus, Sarah Bohn, and Steven Raphael. 2011. *Lessons from the 2007 Legal Arizona Workers Act*. San Francisco: Public Policy Institute of California. www.ppic.org/main/publication.asp?i=915.

Lutheran Immigration and Refugee Service (LIRS). 2012. *Unlocking Liberty: A Way Forward for U.S. Immigration and Detention Policy*. Baltimore, MD: LIRS. www.lirs.org/wp-content/uploads/2012/05/RPTUNLOCKINGLIBERTY.pdf.

Lydgate, Joanna Jacobbi. 2010. Assembly-Line Justice: A Review of Operation Streamline. *California Law Review* 98: 481-544. www.californialawreview.org/assets/pdfs/98-2/Lydgate_FINAL.pdf.

Massey, Douglas S. 2011. It's Time for Immigration Reform. CNN. July 7, 2011. globalpublicsquare.blogs.cnn.com/2011/07/07/its-time-for-immigration-reform/.

____. 2009. Testimony of Professor of Sociology and Public Affairs, Princeton University, before the US Senate Judiciary Committee. *Securing the Borders and America's Points of Entry, What Remains to Be Done?* 111th Cong., 1st sess., May 20, 2009. www.judiciary.senate.gov/hearings/hearing.cfm?id=e-655f9e2809e5476862f735da149ad69.

Meissner, Doris and Donald Kerwin. 2009. *DHS and Immigration: Taking Stock and Correcting Course.* Washington, DC: Migration Policy Institute. www.migrationpolicy.org/pubs/DHS_Feb09.pdf.

Mendelson, Margot, Shayna Strom, and Michael Wishnie. 2009. *Collateral Damage: An Examination of ICE's Fugitive Operations Program.* Washington, DC: Migration Policy Institute. www.migrationpolicy.org/pubs/NFOP_Feb09.pdf.

Meyers, Deborah Waller. 2005. *One Face at the Border: Behind the Slogan.* Washington, DC: Migration Policy Institute. www.migrationpolicy.org/pubs/Meyers_Report.pdf.

Miller, Candice. 2011. Letter from Representative to President Obama. April 1, 2011. http://candicemiller.house.gov/2011/04/miller-the-national-guards-mission-on-the-southwest-border-must-continue.shtml.

Morton, John. 2010. Testimony of Assistant Secretary, Immigration and Customs Enforcement, before the Senate Appropriations Committee. *ICE Fiscal Year 2011 Budget Request*, 111th Cong., 2nd sess., March 18, 2010. www.dhs.gov/ynews/testimony/testimony_1271443011074.shtm.

____. 2010. Memorandum for All ICE Employees: Civil Immigration Enforcement: Priorities for the Apprehension, Detention, and Removal of Aliens. ICE memorandum, June 2010. www.immilaw.com/FAQ/ICE%20prosecution%20priorities%202010.pdf.

____. 2011. Letter from Assistant Secretary, Immigration and Customs Enforcement, to the Honorable Jack Markell, Governor of Delaware. August 5, 2011. http://epic.org/privacy/secure_communities/SGN.pdf.

____. 2011. Testimony of Assistant Secretary, Immigration and Customs Enforcement, before the House Appropriations Committee, Subcommittee on Homeland Security. *The Budget for Immigration and Customs Enforcement*, 112th Cong., 1st sess., March 11, 2011. www.gpo.gov/fdsys/pkg/CHRG-112hhrg67979/pdf/CHRG-112hhrg67979.pdf.

____. 2012. Testimony of Assistant Secretary, Immigration and Customs Enforcement, before the House Appropriations Committee, Subcommittee on Homeland Security. *FY 2013 Appropriations for the Homeland Security Department's Immigration and Customs Enforcement*, 112th Cong., 2nd sess., March 8, 2012. www.micevhill.com/attachments/immigration_documents/hosted_documents/112th_congress/TranscriptOfHouseAppropriationsSubcommitteeHearingOnFY13ICEAppropriations.pdf.

Nakashima, Ellen. 2007. FBI Prepares Vast Database of Biometrics. *Washington Post*, December 22, 2007. www.washingtonpost.com/wp-dyn/content/article/2007/12/21/AR2007122102544.html.

Napolitano, Janet. 2009. Testimony of Secretary of Homeland Security before the Senate Committee on Homeland Security and Governmental Affairs. *Securing the Borders and America's Points of Entry: What Remains to be Done?* 111th Cong., 1st sess., May 20, 2009. www.gpo.gov/fdsys/pkg/CHRG-111shrg55033/pdf/CHRG-111shrg55033.pdf.

____. 2011. Remarks on Border Security at the University of Texas at El Paso. Speech, January 31, 2011. www.dhs.gov/ynews/speeches/sp_1296491064429.shtm.

____. 2011. Testimony of Secretary of Homeland Security before the Senate Homeland Security and Governmental Affairs Committee. *The Homeland Security Department's Budget Submission for Fiscal Year 2012*, 112th Cong., 1st sess., February 17, 2011. www.gpo.gov/fdsys/pkg/CHRG-112shrg66623/pdf/CHRG-112shrg66623.pdf.

____. 2011. Testimony of Secretary of Homeland Security before the US Senate Committee on Homeland Security and Governmental Affairs. *Securing the Border: Progress at the Federal Level*, 111th Cong., 2nd sess., May 3, 2011. www.dhs.gov/news/2011/05/03/secretary-janet-napolitano-senate-committee-homeland-security-and-governmental.

_____. 2011. Testimony of Secretary of Homeland Security before the US House Committee on the Judiciary. *Oversight of the Department of Homeland Security*, 112th Cong., 1st sess., October 26, 2011. www.dhs.gov/ynews/testimony/20111026-napolitano-house-judiciary.shtm.

_____. 2012. Testimony of Secretary of Homeland Security before the House Appropriations Committee, Homeland Security Subcommittee. *Budget Hearing - Department of Homeland Security – Secretary*, 112th Cong., 2nd sess., February 15, 2012. www.dhs.gov/news/2012/02/14/testimony-dhs-secretary-janet-napolitano-house-committee-appropriations-subcommittee.

_____. 2012. Testimony of Secretary of Homeland Security before the House Judiciary Committee. *Oversight of the Homeland Security Department*, 112th Cong., 2nd sess., July 19, 2012. www.micevhill.com/attachments/immigration_documents/hosted_documents/112th_congress/TranscriptOfHouseJudiciaryCommitteeHearingOnOversightOfTheHomelandSecurityDepartment.pdf .

_____. 2012. Exercising Prosecutorial Discretion with Respect to Individuals Who Came to the United States as Children. Memorandum, June 15, 2012. www.dhs.gov/xlibrary/assets/s1-exercising-prosecutorial-discretion-individuals-who-came-to-us-as-children.pdf.

National Commission on Terrorist Attacks Upon the United States. 2004. *Entry of the 9/11 Hijackers into the United States - Staff Statement No. 1*. Washington, DC: National Commission on Terrorist Attacks Upon the United States. http://govinfo.library.unt.edu/911/staff_statements/staff_statement_1.pdf.

_____. 2004. *The 9/11 Commission Report*. Washington, DC: National Commission on Terrorist Attacks Upon the United States. www.9-11commission.gov/report/index.htm.

National Immigrant Justice Center (NIJC), Detention Watch Network, and Midwest Coalition for Human Rights. 2010. *Year One Report Card: Human Rights & the Obama Administration's Immigration Detention Reforms*. Chicago: NIJC, Detention Watch Network, and Midwest Coalition for Human Rights. www.detentionwatchnetwork.org/sites/detentionwatchnetwork.org/files/ICE%20report%20card%20FULL%20FINAL%202010%2010%2006.pdf.

National Immigration Law Center (NILC). 2005. *Basic Information Brief: The Basic Pilot and SSNVS*. Washington, DC: NILC. v2011.nilc.org/immsemplymnt/IWR_Material/Attorney/Employment_Verification_Systems_4-05.pdf.

_____. 2011. DHS Proposes Fantasy Remedies to Cure Fundamental Flaws in the Secure Communities Program. Memorandum, July 2011. www.nilc.org/DHS-6-17-11-memos-QA-2011-07.html.

National Research Council of the National Academies. 2011. *Budgeting for Immigration Enforcement: A Path to Better Performance*. Washington, DC: The National Academies Press.

National Science and Technology Council. 2008. *Biometrics in Government Post-9/11*. Washington, DC: National Science and Technology Council. www.biometrics.gov/Documents/Biometrics%20in%20Government%20Post%209/11.pdf.

New York Times. 2011. Backward at the FBI: Overreaching New Rules for Surveillance Threaten Americans' Basic Rights. *New York Times*, June 19, 2011. www.nytimes.com/2011/06/19/opinion/19sun1.html.

New York University (NYU) School of Law Immigrant Rights Clinic, Immigrant Defense Project, and Families for Freedom. 2012. *Insecure Communities, Devastated Families: New Data on Immigrant Detention and Deportation Practices in New York City*. New York: NYU School of Law Immigrant Rights Clinic, Immigrant Defense Project, and Families for Freedom. http://familiesforfreedom.org/sites/default/files/resources/NYC%20FOIA%20Report%202012%20FINAL_1.pdf.

Nuñez-Neto, Blas. 2008. *Border Security: The Role of the US Border Patrol*. Washington, DC: Congressional Research Service. www.hsdl.org/?view&did=233395.

Nuñez-Neto, Blas and Stephen R. Vina. 2005. *Border Security: Fences Along the U.S. International Border*. Washington, DC: Congressional Research Service. http://fpc.state.gov/documents/organization/47819.pdf.

Passel, Jeffrey and D'Vera Cohn. 2010. *US Unauthorized Immigration Flows are Down Sharply Since Mid-Decade*. Washington, DC: Pew Hispanic Center. www.pewhispanic.org/2010/09/01/us-unauthorized-immigration-flows-are-down-sharply-since-mid-decade/.

_____. 2011. *Unauthorized Immigrant Population: National and State Trends, 2010*. Washington, DC: Pew Hispanic Center. http://pewhispanic.org/files/reports/133.pdf.

Passel, Jeffrey, D'Vera Cohn, and Ana Gonzalez-Barrera. 2012. *Net Migration from Mexico Falls to Zero—and Perhaps Less*. Washington, DC: Pew Hispanic Center. www.pewhispanic.org/2012/04/23/net-migration-from-mexico-falls-to-zero-and-perhaps-less/.

Pew Hispanic Center. 2006. Modes of Entry for the Unauthorized Migrant Population. Fact Sheet, May 22, 2006. Washington, DC: Pew Hispanic Center. www.pewhispanic.org/2006/05/22/modes-of-entry-for-the-unauthorized-migrant-population/.

Preston, Julia. 2011. Homeland Security Cancels 'Virtual Fence' after $1 Billion Is Spent. *New York Times*, January 14, 2011. www.nytimes.com/2011/01/15/us/politics/15fence.html?scp=1&sq=virtual%20fence&st=cse.

———. 2012. Young and Alone, Facing Court and Deportation. *New York Times*, August 25, 2012. www.nytimes.com/2012/08/26/us/more-young-illegal-immigrants-face-deportation.html?pagewanted=all.

Ragland, Susan. 2011. *Secure Border Initiative: Controls over Contractor Payments for the Technology Component Need Improvement*. Washington, DC: Government Accountability Office. www.gao.gov/new.items/d1168.pdf.

Ramji-Nogales, Jaya, Andrew I. Schoenholtz, and Phillip G. Schrag. 2009. *Refugee Roulette: Disparities in Asylum Adjudication and Proposals for Reform*. New York: New York University Press.

Richey, Warren. 2011. Iraqi Refugees in Kentucky Charged with Planning to Help Arm Al Qaeda. *Christian Science Monitor*, May 31, 2011. www.csmonitor.com/USA/Justice/2011/0531/Iraqi-refugees-in-Kentucky-charged-with-planning-to-help-arm-Al-Qaeda.

Robbins, Ted. 2010. Border Patrol Program Raises Due Process Concerns. National Public Radio, September 13, 2010. www.npr.org/templates/story/story.php?storyId=129780261.

Rodriguez, Cristina, Muzaffar Chishti, Randy Capps, and Laura St. John. 2010. *A Program in Flux: New Priorities and Implementation Challenges for 287(g)*. Washington, DC: Migration Policy Institute. www.migrationpolicy.org/pubs/287g-March2010.pdf.

Rosenblum, Marc R. 2011. *E-Verify: Strengths, Weaknesses, and Proposals for Reform*. Washington, DC: Migration Policy Institute. www.migrationpolicy.org/pubs/E-Verify-Insight.pdf.

———. 2012. *Border Security: Immigration Enforcement Between Ports of Entry*. Washington, DC: Congressional Research Service. http://fpc.state.gov/documents/organization/180681.pdf.

Rosenblum, Marc R. and Lang Hoyt. 2011. The Basics of E-Verify, the US Employer Verification System. *Migration Information Source*, July 2011. www.migrationinformation.org/Feature/display.cfm?ID=846.

Rosenblum, Marc R. and William A. Kandel. 2011. *Interior Immigration Enforcement: Programs Targeting Criminal Aliens*. Washington, DC: Congressional Research Service. http://digital.library.unt.edu/ark:/67531/metadc83991/m1/1/high_res_d/R42057_2011Oct21.pdf.

Rushing, Keith. 2012. Rights Groups Say New 287(g) Program in TN and SC to Lead to Bias. News release, Rights Working Group, March 21, 2012. www.rightsworkinggroup.org/content/rights-groups-say-new-287g-program-tn-and-sc-lead-bias.

Schriro, Dora. 2009. *Immigration Detention Overview and Recommendations*. Washington, DC: Immigration and Customs Enforcement. www.ice.gov/doclib/about/offices/odpp/pdf/ice-detention-rpt.pdf.

Simanski, John and Lesley M. Sapp. 2011. *Immigration Enforcement Actions 2011*. Washington, DC: Department of Homeland Security, Office of Immigration Statistics. www.dhs.gov/sites/default/files/publications/immigration-statistics/enforcement_ar_2011.pdf.

Siskin, Alison. 2005. *Monitoring Foreign Students in the United States: The Student and Exchange Visitor Information System*. Washington, DC: Congressional Research Service. www.ilw.com/immigrationdaily/news/2005,0421-crs.pdf.

———. 2011. *Visa Waiver Program*. Washington, DC: Congressional Research Service. www.fas.org/sgp/crs/homesec/RL32221.pdf.

Spagat, Elliot. 2012. AP Exclusive: Border Patrol to Toughen Policy. Associated Press, January 17, 2012. www.denverpost.com/immigration/ci_19757370.

———. 2012. US Stops Immigration Flights to Mexico. Associated Press, September 10, 2012. www.theledger.com/article/20120910/NEWS/120919988?p=1&tc=pg&tc=ar.

Srikantiah, Jayashri and Karen Tumlin. Stipulated Removal. Backgrounder, National Immigration Law Center and Stanford Immigrants' Rights Clinic, 2008. www.law.stanford.edu/program/clinics/immigrantsrights/pressrelease/Stipulated_removal_backgrounder.pdf.

Stana, Richard M. 1999. *Illegal Immigration: Status for Southwest Border Strategy Implementation*. Washington, DC: General Accounting Office. www.gao.gov/archive/1999/gg99044.pdf.

———. 2007. Letter from Director, Homeland Security and Justice Issues, Government Accountability Office (GAO) to the Honorable Mike Rogers. March 30, 2007. Washington, DC: GAO. www.gao.gov/new.items/d07540r.pdf.

———. 2007. Statement of Director, Homeland Security and Justice Issues, Government Accountability Office, before the House Committee on Homeland Security, Subcommittees on Border, Maritime, and Global Counterterrorism and Management, Investigations, and Oversight. *Secure Border Initiative: Observations on Selected Aspects of SBInet Program Implementation*, 110th Cong., 1st sess., October 24, 2007. www.gao.gov/new.items/d08131t.pdf.

———. 2008. Statement of Director, Homeland Security and Justice Issues, Government Accountability Office, before the House Committee on the Judiciary, Subcommittee on Immigration, Citizenship, Border Security, and International Law. *Employment Verification, Challenges Exist in Implementing a Mandatory Electronic Employment Verification System*, 110th Cong., 2nd sess., June 10, 2008. www.gao.gov/new.items/d08895t.pdf.

———. 2009. *Immigration Enforcement: Better Controls Needed Over Program Authorizing State and Local Enforcement of Federal Immigration Laws*. Washington, DC: Government Accountability Office. www.gao.gov/new.items/d09109.pdf.

———. 2009. *Secure Border Initiative Fence Construction Costs*. Washington, DC: Government Accountability Office. www.gao.gov/assets/100/95951.pdf.

———. 2010. *Employment Verification: Federal Agencies Have Taken Steps to Improve E-Verify, But Significant Challenges Remain*. Washington, DC: Government Accountability Office. www.gao.gov/new.items/d11146.pdf.

———. 2011. Statement of Director, Homeland Security and Justice Issues, Government Accountability Office, before the House Committee on Homeland Security, Subcommittee on Border and Maritime Security. *Border Security: Preliminary Observations on Border Control Measures for the Southwest Border*, 112th Cong., 1st sess., February 15, 2011. www.gao.gov/new.items/d11374t.pdf.

———. 2011. Statement of Director, Homeland Security and Justice Issues, Government Accountability Office, before the Senate Committee on Homeland Security and Governmental Affairs. *DHS Progress and Challenges in Securing the U.S. Southwest and Northern Borders*, 112th Cong., 1st sess., March 30, 2011. www.gao.gov/new.items/d11508t.pdf.

Stellin, Susan. 2011. A Long Wait Gets Longer. *The New York Times*, August 22, 2011. www.nytimes.com/2011/08/23/business/long-customs-lines-a-growing-concern.html?_r=1&scp=30&sq=fy%202011%20decrease%20in%20border%20patrol%20officers&st=cse.

Sternstein, Aliya. 2012. Feds Significantly Expand the Use of Iris-Recognition Technology. NextGov, July 13, 2012. www.nextgov.com/big-data/2012/07/feds-significantly-expand-use-iris-recognition-technology/56776/?oref=ng-HPriver.

Task Force on Secure Communities, *Findings and Recommendations*. 2011. Washington, DC: Homeland Security Advisory Council. www.dhs.gov/xlibrary/assets/hsac-task-force-on-secure-communities.pdf.

Taylor, Paul, Mark Hugo Lopez, Jeffrey Passel, and Seth Motel. 2011. *Unauthorized Immigrants: Length of Residency, Patterns of Parenthood*. Washington, DC: Pew Hispanic Center. www.pewhispanic.org/2011/12/01/unauthorized-immigrants-length-of-residency-patterns-of-parenthood/.

Terrazas, Aaron, Demetrios G. Papademetriou, and Marc R. Rosenblum. 2011. *Evolving Demographic and Human Capital Trends in Mexico and Central America and their Implications for Regional Migration*. Washington, DC: Migration Policy Institute and Woodrow Wilson International Center for Scholars. www.migrationpolicy.org/pubs/RMSG-human-capital.pdf.

Torres, John P. 2005. Statement of Deputy Assistant Director, Human Smuggling and Public Safety Division, Immigration and Customs Enforcement, before the House Committee on International Relations, Subcommittee on the Western Hemisphere, Gangs and Crime in Latin America. *Gangs and Crime in Latin America,* 109th Cong., 1st sess., April 20, 2005. www.ice.gov/doclib/news/library/speeches/042005Gang_testimony_torres.pdf.

Transactional Records Access Clearinghouse (TRAC). 2006. *Border Patrol Agents, 1975-2005*. Syracuse, NY: TRAC. http://trac.syr.edu/immigration/reports/143/.

____. 2007. *New Data on the Processing of Aggravated Felons*. Syracuse, NY: TRAC. http://trac.syr.edu/immigration/reports/175/.

____. 2010. *Federal Criminal Enforcement and Staffing: How Do the Obama and Bush Administrations Compare?* Syracuse, NY: TRAC. http://trac.syr.edu/tracreports/crim/245/.

____. 2011. Graphical Highlights Immigration: Lead Charges for Criminal Immigration Prosecutions FY 1986 – FY 2011. http://trac.syr.edu/immigration/reports/251/include/imm_charges.html.

____. 2011. *Immigration Prosecutions for 2011*. Syracuse, NY: TRAC. http://tracfed.syr.edu/results/9x754ec2fef8ab.html.

____. 2011. *New Judge Hiring Fails to Stem Rising Immigration Case Backlog*. Syracuse, NY: TRAC. http://trac.syr.edu/immigration/reports/246/.

____. 2012. *Historic Drop in Deportation Orders Continues as Immigration Court Backlog Increases*. Syracuse, NY: TRAC. http://trac.syr.edu/immigration/reports/279/.

____. 2012. Immigration Court Backlog Tool. http://trac.syr.edu/phptools/immigration/court_backlog/.

____. 2012. *Immigration Court Processing Time by Outcome*. Syracuse, NY: TRAC. http://trac.syr.edu/phptools/immigration/court_backlog/court_proctime_outcome.php.

____. Undated. Trac Fed tool. Accessed November 18, 2012. http://trac.syr.edu/cgi-bin/product/interpreter.pl?p_stat=fil&p_series=annual.

____. Undated. Going Deeper Tool. Accessed November 18, 2012. http://tracfed.syr.edu/trachelp/tools/help_tools_godeep.shtml.

United Nations Office on Drugs and Crimes. 2011. *Issue Paper—Smuggling of Migrants by Sea.* Vienna, Austria: United Nations Office on Drugs and Crime. www.unodc.org/documents/human-trafficking/Migrant-Smuggling/Issue-Papers/Issue_Paper_-_Smuggling_of_Migrants_by_Sea.pdf.

US Army. 2011. Army National Guard Operation Phalanx. *Stand-To!,* May 2011. www.army.mil/standto/archive/2011/05/20/.

US Border Patrol. 1994. *Border Patrol Strategic Plan: 1994 and Beyond.* Washington, DC: US Immigration and Naturalization Service.

____. 2004. *National Border Patrol Strategy*. Washington, DC: US Customs and Border Protection. www.au.af.mil/au/awc/awcgate/dhs/national_bp_strategy.pdf.

____. 2011. Border Patrol Agent Experience: FY 2004/FY 2006/FY 2011 YTD. Prepared for Migration Policy Institute. On file with authors.

____. 2011. Border Patrol Agent Staffing by Fiscal Year. Washington, DC: US Customs and Border Protection. www.cbp.gov/linkhandler/cgov/border_security/border_patrol/usbp_statistics/staffing_92_10.ctt/staffing_92_11.pdf.

____. 2011. Briefing by US Border Patrol, Representatives from the Office of Technology Innovation and Acquisition and Strategic Planning, Policy and Analysis Division for Migration Policy Institute. September 10, 2011. Notes on file with authors.

____. 2012. *2012-2016 Border Patrol Strategic Plan.* Washington, DC: US Customs and Border Protection. http://nemo.cbp.gov/obp/bp_strategic_plan.pdf.

____. Undated. Nationwide Illegal Alien Apprehensions Fiscal Years 1925-2011. Washington, DC: US Customs and Border Protection. Accessed November 15, 2012. www.cbp.gov/linkhandler/cgov/border_security/border_patrol/usbp_statistics/25_10_app_stats.ctt/25_11_app_stats.pdf.

———. Undated. Total Illegal Alien Apprehensions by Fiscal Year. Washington, DC: US Customs and Border Protection. Accessed November 19, 2012. www.cbp.gov/linkhandler/cgov/border_security/border_patrol/usbp_statistics/99_10_fy_stats.ctt/99_11_fy_stats.pdf.

US Census Bureau. Undated. Establishment. Accessed November 26, 2012. www.census.gov/econ/census02/text/sector31/31estab.htm.

———. Undated. Statistics of U.S. Businesses (SUSB) Main, U.S. & States, Total. Accessed November 21, 2012. www.census.gov/econ/susb/.

US Citizenship and Immigration Services (USCIS). 2004. *Report to Congress on the Basic Pilot Program*. Washington, DC: USCIS. www.aila.org/content/default.aspx?bc=1016%7C6715%7C16871%7C18523%7C11260.

———. 2009. Form I-9 Employment Eligibility Verification. Revised August 7, 2009. www.uscis.gov/files/form/i-9.pdf.

———. 2009. USCIS Adds Passport Data in E-Verify Process for Foreign-Born Citizens. News release, March 4, 2009. www.uscis.gov/portal/site/uscis/menuitem.5af9bb95919f35e66f614176543f-6d1a/?vgnextoid=b33c436d5f2df110VgnVCM1000004718190aRCRD&vgnextchannel=c94e6d26d17df110VgnVCM1000004718190aRCRD.

———. 2010. DHS Unveils Initiatives to Enhance E-Verify. Fact sheet, March 18, 2010. www.uscis.gov/portal/site/uscis/menuitem.5af9bb95919f35e66f614176543f6d1a/?vgnextoid=70beadd907c67210VgnVCM100000082ca60aRCRD&vgnextchannel=de779589cdb76210VgnVCM100000b92ca60aRCRD.

———. 2011. Penalties. Last updated November 23, 2011. www.uscis.gov/portal/site/uscis/menuitem.eb1d4c2a3e5b9ac89243c6a7543f6d1a/?vgnextoid=92082d73a2d38210VgnVCM100000082ca60aRCRD&vgnextchannel=92082d73a2d38210VgnVCM100000082ca60aRCRD.

———. 2011. Revised Guidance for the Referral of Cases and Issuance of Notices to Appear (NTAs) in Cases Involving Inadmissible and Removable Aliens. Memorandum, November 7, 2011. www.uscis.gov/USCIS/Laws/Memoranda/Static_Files_Memoranda/NTA%20PM%20(Approved%20as%20final%2011-7-11).pdf.

———. 2011. Transcript: Press Conference on E-Verify Self-Check. Press conference, Washington, DC: March 22, 2011. www.uscis.gov/USCIS/News/Transcript_SelfCheckSecrtry.pdf.

———. 2012. Deferred Action for Childhood Arrivals Process. http://www.uscis.gov/USCIS/Resources/Reports%20and%20Studies/Immigration%20Forms%20Data/All%20Form%20Types/DACA/DACA%20MonthlyDEC%20Report%20PDF.pdf.pdf.

———. 2012. E-Verify History and Milestones. www.uscis.gov/portal/site/uscis/menuitem.eb1d-4c2a3e5b9ac89243c6a7543f6d1a/?vgnextoid=84979589cdb76210VgnVCM100000b92ca60aRCRD&vgnextchannel=84979589cdb76210VgnVCM100000b92ca60aRCRD.

———. 2012. E-Verify Statistics and Reports. www.uscis.gov/portal/site/uscis/menuitem.eb1d4c2a3e-5b9ac89243c6a7543f6d1a/?vgnextoid=7c579589cdb76210VgnVCM100000b92ca60aRCRD&vgnextchannel=7c579589cdb76210VgnVCM100000b92ca60aRCRD.

———. 2012. Self-Check Background. www.uscis.gov/portal/site/uscis/menuitem.eb1d4c2a3e5b9ac-89243c6a7543f6d1a/?vgnextoid=bc417cd67450d210VgnVCM100000082ca60aRCRD&vgnextchannel=bc417cd67450d210VgnVCM100000082ca60aRCRD.

US Coast Guard. 2012. Alien Migrant Interdiction. Last updated May 23, 2012. www.uscg.mil/hq/cg5/cg531/AMIO/amio.asp.

US Customs and Border Protection (CBP). 2005. DHS Expands Expedited Removal Authority Along Southwest Border. News release, September 14, 2005. www.cbp.gov/xp/cgov/newsroom/news_releases/archives/2005_press_releases/092005/09142005.xml.

———. 2009. Border Patrol Search, Trauma, and Rescue (BORSTAR). Fact Sheet, June 3, 2009. www.cbp.gov/linkhandler/cgov/newsroom/fact_sheets/border/border_patrol/borstar.ctt/borstar.pdf.

———. 2009. Securing America's Borders: CBP Fiscal Year 2009 in Review. Fact Sheet, November 24, 2009. www.cbp.gov/xp/cgov/about/accomplish/previous_year/fy2009_stats/11242009_5.xml.

____. 2009. *Secure Borders, Safe Travel, Legal Trade: US Customs and Border Protection Fiscal Year 2009-2014 Strategic Plan*. Washington, DC: CBP. www.cbp.gov/linkhandler/cgov/about/mission/strategic_plan_09_14.ctt/strategic_plan_09_14.pdf.

____. 2011. CBP's 2011 Fiscal Year in Review. News release, December 12, 2011. www.cbp.gov/xp/cgov/newsroom/news_releases/national/2011_news_archive/12122011.xml.

____. 2011. Preclearance Locations. March 30, 2011. www.cbp.gov/xp/cgov/toolbox/contacts/preclear_locations.xml.

____. 2012. *Budget Request and Supporting Information*. Washington, DC: Department of Homeland Security. www.dhs.gov/xlibrary/assets/mgmt/dhs-congressional-budget-justification-fy2013.pdf.

____. Undated. Free and Secure Trade (FAST). Fact Sheet. Accessed November 19, 2012. www.cbp.gov/linkhandler/cgov/newsroom/fact_sheets/travel/fast/fast_fact.ctt/fast_fact.pdf.

____. Undated. Southwest Border Fence Construction Progress. Accessed November 19, 2012. www.cbp.gov/xp/cgov/border_security/ti/ti_news/sbi_fence/.

US Department of Homeland Security (DHS). 2003. *Budget in Brief FY 2004*. Washington, DC: DHS. www.dhs.gov/dhs-budget-brief-fiscal-year-2004.

____. 2003. Fact Sheet: US-VISIT Program. Fact Sheet, May 19, 2003. www.ice.gov/news/library/factsheets/us-visit.htm.

____. 2004. *Budget in Brief FY 2005*. Washington, DC: DHS. www.dhs.gov/xlibrary/assets/FY_2005_BIB_4.pdf.

____. 2005. *Budget in Brief FY 2006*. Washington, DC: DHS. www.dhs.gov/xlibrary/assets/Budget_BIB-FY2006.pdf.

____. 2005. *IDENT/IAFIS Interoperability Statistics*. Washington, DC: DHS. www.dhs.gov/xlibrary/assets/foia/US-VISIT_IDENT-IAFISReport.pdf.

____. 2005. Secure Border Initiative. News release, November 2, 2005. www.hsdl.org/?view&did=440470.

____. 2006. *Budget in Brief FY 2007*. Washington, DC: DHS. www.dhs.gov/xlibrary/assets/Budget_BIB-FY2007.pdf.

____. 2006. Secure Border Initiative Update. Fact sheet, August 23, 2006. www.hsdl.org/?view&did=476281.

____. 2007. *Budget in Brief FY 2008*. Washington, DC: DHS. www.dhs.gov/xlibrary/assets/budget_bib-fy2008.pdf.

____. 2007. *Privacy Impact Assessment for the Arrival and Departure Information System (ADIS)*. Washington, DC: DHS. www.dhs.gov/xlibrary/assets/privacy/privacy_pia_usvisit_adis_2007.pdf.

____. 2007. *Privacy Impact Assessment for the Central Index System*. Washington, DC: DHS. www.dhs.gov/xlibrary/assets/privacy/privacy_pia_uscis_cis.pdf.

____. 2008. *Budget in Brief FY 2009*. Washington, DC: DHS. www.dhs.gov/xlibrary/assets/budget_bib-fy2009.pdf.

____. 2008. *Privacy Impact Assessment for the Advance Passenger Information System (APIS)*. Washington, DC: DHS. http://foia.cbp.gov/streamingWord.asp?i=38.

____. 2009. *Budget in Brief FY 2010*. Washington, DC: DHS. www.dhs.gov/xlibrary/assets/budget_bib_fy2010.pdf.

____. 2009. *Privacy Impact Assessment for the US-VISIT Five Country Joint Enrollment and Information Sharing Project (FCC)*. Washington, DC: DHS, 2009. www.dhs.gov/xlibrary/assets/privacy/privacy_pia_usvisit_fcc.pdf.

____. 2009. Secretary Napolitano Issues Immigration and Border Security Action Directive. News release, January 30, 2009. www.dhs.gov/ynews/releases/pr_1233353528835.shtm.

_____. 2009. Secretary Napolitano Strengthens Employment Verification with Administration's Commitment to E-Verify. News release, July 8, 2009. www.dhs.gov/ynews/releases/pr_1247063976814.shtm.

_____. 2010. *Budget in Brief FY 2011*. Washington, DC: DHS. www.dhs.gov/xlibrary/assets/budget_bib_fy2011.pdf.

_____. 2010. *Congressional Budget Justification FY 2012, US Immigration and Customs Enforcement*. Washington, DC: DHS. www.dhs.gov/xlibrary/assets/dhs-congressional-budget-justification-fy2012.pdf.

_____. 2010. Press Conference with Secretary of Homeland Security Janet Napolitano; Immigration and Customs Enforcement Director John Morton; Los Angeles County, California, Sheriff Lee Baca; Harris County, Texas, Sheriff Adrian Garcia; Fairfax County, Virginia, Sheriff Stan Barry on New Immigration Enforcement Results. Briefing. Washington, DC: October 6, 2010. www.ice.gov/news/releases/1010/101006washingtondc2.htm.

_____. 2010. *Privacy Impact Assessment for the TECS System: CBP Primary and Secondary Processing*. Washington, DC: DHS. www.dhs.gov/xlibrary/assets/privacy/privacy_pia_cbp_tecs.pdf.

_____. 2010. *Privacy Impact Assessment for the Watchlist Service*. Washington, DC: DHS. www.dhs.gov/xlibrary/assets/privacy/privacy_pia_dhs_wls.pdf.

_____. 2011. DHS and DOD Announce Continued Partnership in Strengthening Southwest Border Security. Press release, December 20, 2011. www.dhs.gov/ynews/releases/20111220-dhs-dod-partnership-southwest-border-security.shtm.

_____. 2011. *FY 2012 Budget in Brief*. Washington, DC: DHS. www.dhs.gov/xlibrary/assets/budget-bib-fy2012.pdf.

_____. 2011. *Implementing the 9/11 Commission Recommendations Progress Report*. Washington, DC: DHS. www.dhs.gov/xlibrary/assets/implementing-9-11-commission-report-progress-2011.pdf.

_____. 2011. Statement by Secretary Napolitano on DOJ's Findings of Discriminatory Policing in Maricopa County. News release, December 15, 2011. www.dhs.gov/ynews/releases/20111215-napolitano-statement-doj-maricopa-county.shtm.

_____. 2011. *United States-Canada Beyond the Border: A Shared Vision for Perimeter Security and Economic Competitiveness, Action Plan*. Washington, DC: DHS. www.dhs.gov/xlibrary/assets/wh/us-canada-btb-action-plan.pdf.

_____. 2011. *US Department of Homeland Security Annual Performance Report Fiscal Years 2011-2013*. Washington, DC: DHS. www.dhs.gov/xlibrary/assets/mgmt/cfo_apr_fy2011.pdf.

_____. 2011. *Yearbook of Immigration Statistics: 2010*. Washington, DC: DHS. www.dhs.gov/xlibrary/assets/statistics/yearbook/2010/ois_yb_2010.pdf.

_____. 2012. *Budget in Brief FY 2013*. Washington, DC: DHS. www.dhs.gov/xlibrary/assets/mgmt/dhs-budget-in-brief-fy2013.pdf.

_____. 2012. *Congressional Budget Justification FY 2013*. Washington, DC: DHS. www.dhs.gov/xlibrary/assets/mgmt/dhs-congressional-budget-justification-fy2013.pdf.

_____. 2012. DHS Announces Taiwan's Designation into the Visa Waiver Program. News release, October 2, 2012. www.dhs.gov/news/2012/10/02/dhs-announces-taiwan%E2%80%99s-designation-visa-waiver-program.

_____. 2012. NEXUS. Fact Sheet, March 2012. www.cbp.gov/linkhandler/cgov/travel/trusted_traveler/nexus_prog/nexus_facts.ctt/nexus_facts.pdf.

_____. Undated. DHS' Progress in 2011: Southwest Border. Accessed November 16, 2012. www.dhs.gov/xabout/2011-dhs-accomplishments-southwest-border.shtm.

_____. Undated. Enforce and Administer Our Immigration Laws. Accessed November 18, 2012. www.dhs.gov/xabout/gc_1240610592951.shtm.

_____. Undated. Summary of Budget Authority by Appropriation. Accessed November 11, 2012. www.justice.gov/jmd/2013summary/pdf/budget-authority-appropriation.pdf.

____. Undated. US-VISIT at the US-Mexico Land Border. Accessed November 21, 2012. www.dhs.gov/xlibrary/assets/usvisit/usvisit_edu_us_mexico_land_border_info_card_english.pdf.

____. Undated. US-VISIT Biometric Identification Services. Accessed November 18, 2012. www.dhs.gov/files/programs/gc_1208531081211.shtm.

____. Undated. US-VISIT Enrollment Requirements. Accessed November 18, 2012. www.dhs.gov/files/programs/editorial_0527.shtm.

____. Undated. US-VISIT Resources and Materials. Accessed November 18, 2012. www.dhs.gov/files/programs/gc_1213298547634.shtm.

US Department of Homeland Security, Office of Immigration Statistics (OIS). 2009. *Immigration Enforcement Actions: 2008*. Washington, DC: DHS, OIS. http://www.dhs.gov/xlibrary/assets/statistics/publications/enforcement_ar_08.pdf.

____. 2010. *2009 Yearbook of Immigration Statistics*. Washington, DC: DHS, OIS. www.dhs.gov/xlibrary/assets/statistics/yearbook/2009/ois_yb_2009.pdf.

____. 2010. *Immigration Enforcement Actions: 2009*. Washington, DC: DHS, OIS. www.dhs.gov/xlibrary/assets/statistics/publications/enforcement_ar_2009.pdf.

____. 2011. *Immigration Enforcement Actions: 2010*. Washington, DC: DHS, OIS. https://www.dhs.gov/immigration-enforcement-actions-2010.

____. 2012. *Immigration Enforcement Actions: 2011*. Washington, DC: DHS, OIS. www.dhs.gov/sites/default/files/publications/immigration-statistics/enforcement_ar_2011.pdf.

US Department of Homeland Security, Office of the Inspector General (OIG). 2010. *The Performance of 287(g) Agreements: Report Update*. Washington, DC: DHS, OIG. www.oig.dhs.gov/assets/mgmt/oig_10-63_mar10.pdf.

____. 2011. *DHS Detainee Removals and Reliance on Assurances*. Washington, DC: DHS, OIG. www.oig.dhs.gov/assets/Mgmt/OIG_11-100_Nov11.pdf.

____. 2012. *Annual Review of the United States Coast Guard's Mission Performance*. Washington, DC: DHS, OIG. www.oig.dhs.gov/assets/Mgmt/2012/OIG_12-119_Sep12.pdf.

____. 2012. *US-VISIT Faces Challenges in Identifying and Reporting Multiple Biographic Identities*. Washington, DC: DHS, OIG. www.oig.dhs.gov/assets/Mgmt/2012/OIG_12-111_Aug12.pdf.

US Department of Justice (DOJ). 2002. Budget Trend Data for the Immigration and Naturalization Service (INS), 1975 Through the President's 2003 Request to Congress. Washington DC: DOJ Budget Staff, Justice Management Division. www.justice.gov/archive/jmd/1975_2002/btd02tocpg.htm.

____. 2009. *FY 2010 Budget Request*. Washington, DC: DOJ. www.justice.gov/jmd/2010summary/pdf/usa-bud-summary.pdf.

____. 2011. Assistant Attorney General Thomas E. Perez Speaks at the Maricopa County Sheriff's Office Investigative Findings Announcement. News release, December 15, 2011. www.justice.gov/crt/opa/pr/speeches/2011/crt-speech-111215.html.

US Department of Justice, Bureau of Justice Statistics. Undated. Federal Criminal Case Processing Statistics, Persons Entering Federal Prison. Accessed November 18, 2012. http://bjs.ojp.usdoj.gov/fjsrc/.

US Department of Justice, Executive Office of Immigration Review (EOIR). 2001. *Statistical Yearbook 2000*. Falls Church, VA: EOIR. www.justice.gov/eoir/statspub/SYB2000Final.pdf.

____. 2011. *FY 2010 Statistical Yearbook*. Falls Church, VA: EOIR. www.justice.gov/eoir/statspub/fy10syb.pdf.

____. 2012. Asylum Statistics by Nationality FY 2007. Falls Church, VA: EOIR. www.justice.gov/eoir/efoia/FY07AsyStats-Current.pdf.

____. 2012. Asylum Statistics by Nationality FY 2010. Falls Church, VA: EOIR. www.justice.gov/eoir/efoia/FY10AsyStats-Current.pdf.

_____. 2012. Asylum Statistics by Nationality FY 2011. Falls Church, VA: EOIR. www.justice.gov/eoir/efoia/FY11AsyStats-Current.pdf.

_____. 2012. *FY 2011 Statistical Yearbook.* Falls Church, VA: EOIR. www.justice.gov/eoir/statspub/fy11syb.pdf.

US Department of Justice, Office of the Inspector General, Audit Division. 2002. *Audit Report: Immigration and Naturalization Service Institutional Removal Program.* Washington, DC: DOJ, OIG. www.justice.gov/oig/reports/INS/a0241/final.pdf.

US Department of Labor (DOL). 1998. *Memorandum of Understanding Between the Immigration and Naturalization Service, Department of Justice, and the Employment Standards Administration, Department of Labor.* Washington, DC: DOL. www.docstoc.com/docs/42463920/Memorandum-of-Understanding-Between-the-Immigration-and-Naturalization.

_____. 2012. *FY 2013 Congressional Budget Justification: Wage and Hour Division.* Washington, DC: DOL. www.dol.gov/dol/budget/2013/PDF/CBJ-2013-V2-09.pdf.

US Department of Labor and DHS. 2011. *Revised Memorandum of Understanding Between the Departments of Homeland Security and Labor Concerning Enforcement Activities at Worksites.* Memorandum, DOL and DHS, December 7, 2011. www.dol.gov/asp/media/reports/DHS-DOL-MOU.pdf.

US Department of State (DOS). 2003. *Waiver of Personal Appearance Revision.* Cable to All Diplomatic and Consular Posts, May 3, 2003. http://travel.state.gov/visa/laws/telegrams/telegrams_1421.html.

_____. 2010. *Consular Consolidated Database Privacy Impact Assessment.* Washington, DC: DOS. www.state.gov/documents/organization/93772.pdf.

_____. 2011. US Passport Card Frequently Asked Questions. March 2011. http://travel.state.gov/passport/ppt_card/ppt_card_3921.html.

_____. Undated. *Foreign Affairs Manual.* Accessed November 19, 2012. www.state.gov/documents/organization/87421.pdf.

_____. Undated. Nonimmigrant Visa Statistics, FY 1997-2011 NIV Detail Table. Accessed November 18, 2012. http://travel.state.gov/visa/statistics/nivstats/nivstats_4582.html.

_____. Undated. Student Visas. Accessed November 18, 2012. http://travel.state.gov/visa/temp/types/types_1268.html.

_____. Undated. Visa Waiver Program. Accessed November 11, 2012. www.travel.state.gov/visa/temp/without/without_1990.html.

_____. Undated. Visa Waiver Program Frequently Asked Questions. Accessed November 18, 2012. http://travel.state.gov/visa/temp/without/without_1990.html.

US Embassy, Moscow. 2008. US Embassy Announces Waiver of Interview Requirement for Certain Visa Applicants. News release, October 17, 2008. http://moscow.usembassy.gov/intwaiver.html.

US Federal Bureau of Investigation (FBI). 2011. FBI Announces Initial Operating Capability for Next Generation Identification System. News release, March 8, 2011. www.fbi.gov/news/pressrel/press-releases/fbi-announces-initial-operating-capability-for-next-generation-identification-system.

_____. Undated. Next Generation Identification. Accessed November 18, 2012. www.fbi.gov/about-us/cjis/fingerprints_biometrics/ngi.

_____. Undated. Terrorist Screening Database, Frequently Asked Questions. Accessed November 18, 2012. www.fbi.gov/about-us/nsb/tsc/tsc_faqs.

_____. Undated. The Integrated Automated Fingerprint Identification System. Accessed November 18, 2012. www.fbi.gov/about-us/cjis/fingerprints_biometrics/iafis/iafis.

US Government Accountability Office (GAO). 2008. *Border Security: Summary of Covert Tests and Security Assessments for the Senate Committee on Finance, 2003 – 2007.* Washington, DC: GAO. www.gao.gov/new.items/d08757.pdf.

____. 2009. *Homeland Security: Key US-VISIT Components at Varying Stages of Completion, But Integrated and Reliable Schedule Needed*. Washington, DC: Government Accountability Office. www.gao.gov/new.items/d1013.pdf.

____. 2010. *Homeland Security: US-VISIT Pilot Options Offer Limited Understanding of Air Exit Options*. Washington, DC: Government Accountability Office. www.gao.gov/new.items/d10860.pdf.

____. 2012. *Secure Communities: Criminal Alien Removals Increased, But Technology Planning Improvements Needed.* Washington, DC: Government Accountability Office. www.gao.gov/assets/600/592415.pdf.

US Immigration and Customs Enforcement (ICE). 2008. Fact Sheet: Secure Communities. Fact sheet, March 28, 2008. www.aila.org/content/default.aspx?docid=25045.

____. 2008. *Second Congressional Status Report Covering the Fourth Quarter Fiscal Year 2008 for Secure Communities: A Comprehensive Plan to Identify and Remove Criminal Aliens*. Washington, DC: ICE. www.ice.gov/doclib/foia/secure_communities/congressionalstatusreportfy084thquarter.pdf.

____. 2009. ICE Announces Major Reforms to Immigration Detention System. News release, August 6, 2009. www.ice.gov/news/releases/0908/090806washington.htm.

____. 2009. ICE Fact Sheet: Alternatives to Detention for ICE Detainees. Fact sheet, November 6, 2009. www.kolkenandkolken.com/index.php?src=news&srctype=detail&category=Immigration%20Publications&refno=2488.

____. 2009. ICE Issues New Procedures for Asylum Seekers as Part of Ongoing Detention Reform Initiatives. News release, December 16, 2009. www.ice.gov/news/releases/0912/091216washington.htm.

____. 2009. Memo Re: National Fugitive Operations Program: Priorities, Goals, and Expectations. Memorandum, December 8, 2009. www.ice.gov/doclib/detention-reform/pdf/nfop_priorities_goals_expectations.pdf.

____. 2009. Secretary Napolitano Announces New Agreement for State and Local Immigration Enforcement Partnerships and Adds 11 New Agreements. News release, July 10, 2009. www.ice.gov/news/releases/0907/090710washington.htm.

____. 2009. *Secure Communities: Quarterly Report, Fiscal Year 2009 Report to Congress, Fourth Quarter*. Washington, DC: ICE. www.ice.gov/doclib/foia/secure_communities/congressionalstatusreportfy094thquarter.pdf.

____. 2010. Abercrombie and Fitch Fined after I-9 Audit. News release, September 28, 2010. www.ice.gov/news/releases/1009/100928detroit.htm.

____. 2010. ICE Announces Launch of Online Detainee Locator System. News release, July 23, 2010. www.ice.gov/news/releases/1007/100723washingtondc.htm.

____. 2010. ICE Arrests South Florida Residents for Transferring Obscene Material to a Juvenile. News release, November 24, 2010. www.ice.gov/news/releases/1011/101124fortpierce.htm.

____. 2010. ICE's Operation Community Shield Goes Global with a New Task Force in Honduras: Operation Double Impact from the Videographer's View. News release, August 11, 2010. www.ice.gov/news/releases/1008/100811washingtondc.htm.

____. 2010. *ICE Strategic Plan FY 2010-2014*. Washington, DC: ICE. www.ice.gov/doclib/news/library/reports/strategic-plan/strategic-plan-2010.pdf.

____. 2010. MS-13 Members Convicted of Federal Racketeering Charges. News release, December 8, 2010. www.ice.gov/news/releases/1012/101208washington.htm.

____. 2010. MS-13 Members Convicted of Federal Racketeering Charges. News release, December 8, 2010. www.ice.gov/news/releases/1012/101208washington.htm.

____. 2010. Secure Communities Presentation. www.ice.gov/doclib/foia/secure_communities/securecommunitiespresentations.pdf.

____. 2010. *Secure Communities Quarterly Report, Fiscal Year 2010 Report to Congress, First Quarter*. Washington, DC: ICE. www.ice.gov/doclib/foia/secure_communities/congressionalstatusreportfy101stquarter.pdf.

____. 2010. *Secure Communities Quarterly Report, Fiscal Year 2010 Report to Congress, Second Quarter.* Washington, DC: ICE. www.ice.gov/doclib/foia/secure_communities/congressionalstatusreport-fy102ndquarter.pdf.

____. 2010. *Secure Communities Quarterly Report, Fiscal Year 2010 Report to Congress, Third Quarter.* Washington, DC: ICE. www.ice.gov/doclib/foia/secure_communities/r_congressionalfy10rdquarter-report.pdf.

____. 2011. ERO Facts and Statistics. www.ice.gov/doclib/foia/reports/ero-facts-and-statistics.pdf.

____. 2011. Fact Sheet: Criminal Alien Program. Fact sheet, March 29, 2011. www.ice.gov/news/library/factsheets/cap.htm.

____. 2011. Fact Sheet: ICE Enforcement in Arizona. Fact sheet, November 14, 2011. www.ice.gov/news/library/factsheets/az-enforcement.htm.

____. 2011. ICE Establishes Hotline for Detained Individuals, Issues New Detainer Form. News release, December 29, 2011. www.ice.gov/news/releases/1112/111229washingtondc.htm.

____. 2011. *IDENT/IAFIS Interoperability Statistics.* Washington, DC: ICE. www.ice.gov/doclib/foia/sc-stats/nationwide_interoperability_stats-fy2011-feb28.pdf.

____. 2011. Memorandum Re. Exercising Prosecutorial Discretion Consistent with Civil Immigration Enforcement Priorities of the Agency for the Apprehension, Detention, and Removal of Aliens. Memorandum, June 17, 2011. www.ice.gov/doclib/secure-communities/pdf/prosecutorial-discre-tion-memo.pdf.

____. 2011. Next Steps in the Implementation of the Prosecutorial Discretion Memorandum and the August 18th Announcement on Immigration Enforcement Priorities. Memo, November 17, 2011. www.aila.org/content/default.aspx?docid=37684.

____. 2011. Organizational Chart. www.dhs.gov/xlibrary/assets/org-chart-ice.pdf.

____. 2011. *Secure Communities: Quarterly Report, Fiscal Year 2010 Report to Congress, Fourth Quarter.* Washington, DC: ICE. www.ice.gov/doclib/foia/secure_communities/congressionalstatusreport-fy104thquarter.pdf.

____. 2011. *Secure Communities: Quarterly Report FY 2011, Report to Congress, First Quarter.* Washington, DC: ICE. www.ice.gov/doclib/foia/secure_communities/congressionalstatusreportfy111stquar-ter.pdf.

____. 2011. *Secure Communities: Quarterly Report FY 2011, Report to Congress, Second Quarter.* Washington, DC: ICE. www.ice.gov/doclib/foia/secure_communities/congressionalstatusreportfy112nd-quarter.pdf.

____. 2011. Secure Communities: *Quarterly Report FY 2011, Report to Congress, Third Quarter.* Washington, DC: ICE. www.ice.gov/doclib/foia/secure_communities/r_congressionalfy10rdquarterreport.pdf.

____. 2011. *Student and Exchange Visitor Information System: General Summary Quarterly Review for Quarter Ending December 31, 2010.* Washington, DC: ICE. www.ice.gov/doclib/sevis/pdf/quarter-ly_report_ending_dec2010.pdf.

____. 2012. *Activated Jurisdictions.* Washington, DC: ICE. www.ice.gov/doclib/secure-communities/pdf/sc-activated.pdf.

____. 2012. *Deportation of Parents of U.S. Born Citizens: Fiscal Year 2011 Report to Congress.* Washington, DC: ICE. www.lirs.org/wp-content/uploads/2012/07/ICE-DEPORT-OF-PARENTS-OF-US-CIT-FY-2011.pdf.

____. 2012. Fact Sheet: Delegation of Immigration Authority Section 287(g) Immigration and Nationality Act. Fact sheet, October 16, 2012. www.ice.gov/news/library/factsheets/287g.htm.

____. 2012. ICE Opens its First-Ever Designed and Built Civil Detention Center. News release, March 13, 2012. www.ice.gov/news/releases/1203/120313karnescity.htm.

____. 2012. *Performance-Based National Detention Standards 2011.* Washington, DC: DHS. www.ice.gov/doclib/detention-standards/2011/pbnds2011.pdf.

_____. 2012. *Privacy Impact Assessment Update for the Enforcement Integrated Database (EID) Risk Classification Assessment (RCA 1.0), ENFORCE Alien Removal Module (EARM 5.0), and Crime Entry Screen (CES 2.0) DHS/ICE/PIA-015(d)*. Washington, DC: DHS. www.dhs.gov/xlibrary/assets/privacy/privacy_piaupdate_EID_april2012.pdf.

_____. 2012. *Secure Communities: Monthly Statistics through January 31, 2012*. Washington, DC: ICE. www.ice.gov/doclib/foia/sc-stats/nationwide_interoperability_stats-fy2012-to-date.pdf.

_____. Undated. Border Enforcement Security Task Force (BEST). Accessed November 18, 2012. www.ice.gov/best/.

_____. Undated. Rapid REPAT. Accessed November 18, 2012. www.ice.gov/rapid-repat/.

_____. Undated. Secure Communities Budget Numbers, FY 2008-FY 2011. Accessed November 21, 2012. www.ice.gov/doclib/foia/secure_communities/budgetnumbers.pdf.

US Immigration and Naturalization Services (INS). 1994. *1993 Statistical Yearbook of the Immigration and Naturalization Service*. Washington, DC: INS.

_____. 2001. *Yearbook of Immigration Statistics, FY 2000*. Washington, DC: INS. www.dhs.gov/xlibrary/assets/statistics/yearbook/2000/Yearbook2000.pdf.

_____. 2003. *Yearbook of Immigration Statistics, FY 2002*. Washington, DC: INS. www.dhs.gov/fiscal-year-2002-yearbook-immigration-statistics-0.

US Travel Association (USTA). 2011. *Ready for Takeoff: A Plan to Create 1.3 Million U.S. Jobs by Welcoming Millions of International Travelers*. Washington, DC: USTA. www.smartervisapolicy.org/site/documents/VisaReport.pdf.

US Transportation Security Administration (TSA). Undated. TSA Pre-Check. Accessed November 16, 2012. www.tsa.gov/what_we_do/escreening.shtm.

US-VISIT. 2011. 2011 Year in Review. Washington, DC: US-VISIT.

_____. 2012. 8th Anniversary Briefing, January 5, 2012. Notes on file with authors.

_____. Undated. US-VISIT Biometric Procedures: Applicability to Canadian Citizens. Accessed November 19, 2012. www.dhs.gov/files/programs/editorial_0695.shtm.

_____. Undated. US-VISIT Biometric Procedures: Applicability to Mexican Citizens. Accessed November 19, 2012. www.dhs.gov/files/programs/editorial_0696.shtm.

Venturella, David. Testimony of Executive Director of Secure Communities before the House Appropriations Committee, Subcommittee on Homeland Security. *Priorities Enforcing Immigration Law*, 111th Cong., 1st sess., April 2, 2009. www.aila.org/content/fileviewer.aspx?docid=28622&linkid=200232.

Vitello, Ronald D. and Martin E. Vaughn. 2012. Joint testimony of Deputy Chief, US Border Patrol, and Executive Director, Southwest Region, Office of Air and Marine, US Customs and Border Protection, before the House Committee on Homeland Security, Subcommittee on Border and Maritime Security. *Boots on the Ground or Eyes in the Sky: How Best to Utilize the National Guard to Achieve Operational Control*, 112th Cong., 2nd sess., April 17, 2012. www.dhs.gov/news/2012/04/17/written-testimony-us-customs-and-border-protection-house-homeland-security.

Wagner Dennis. 2010. Violence Is Not Up on Arizona Border Despite Mexican Drug War. *Arizona Republic*, May 2, 2010. www.azcentral.com/news/articles/2010/05/02/20100502arizona-border-violence-mexico.html.

Wasem, Ruth Ellen. 2011. *US Immigration Policy on Temporary Admissions*. Washington, DC: Congressional Research Service. www.fas.org/sgp/crs/homesec/RL31381.pdf.

_____. 2011. *Visa Security Policy: Roles of the Departments of State and Homeland Security*. Washington, DC: Congressional Research Service. www.fas.org/sgp/crs/homesec/R41093.pdf.

Westat. 2007. *Findings of the Web Basic Pilot Evaluation*. Rockville, MD: Westat. www.uscis.gov/files/article/WebBasicPilotRprtSept2007.pdf.

_____. 2009. *Findings of the E-Verify Program Evaluation*. Rockville, MD: Westat. www.uscis.gov/USCIS/E-Verify/E-Verify/Final%20E-Verify%20Report%2012-16-09_2.pdf.

White House Office of the Press Secretary. 2006. Basic Pilot: A Clear and Reliable Way to Verify Employment Eligibility. Fact sheet, July 5, 2006. www.swiftraid.org/media/articles/12-20-06BasicPilotFactSheet.pdf.

_____. 2011. Remarks by the President on Comprehensive Immigration Reform in El Paso, Texas. May 10, 2011. www.whitehouse.gov/the-press-office/2011/05/10/remarks-president-comprehensive-immigration-reform-el-paso-texas.

Witte, Griff. 2006. Boeing Wins Deal for Border Security. *The Washington Post*, September 20, 2006. www.washingtonpost.com/wp-dyn/content/article/2006/09/19/AR2006091901715.html.

Yale-Loehr, Stephen, Demetrios G. Papademetriou, and Betsy Cooper. 2005. *Secure Borders, Open Doors: Visa Procedures in the Post-September 11 Era.* Washington, DC: Migration Policy Institute. www.migrationpolicy.org/pubs/visa_report.pdf.

Zalud, Bill. 2002. Less Privacy Concern after Sept. 11. *SDM: Security Distributing & Marketing* 32 (4).

Zuniga, Bertha A. 2010. *Aggravated Felony Case Summary*. San Antonio, TX: Executive Office for Immigration Review. www.justice.gov/eoir/vll/benchbook/resources/Aggravated_Felony_Outline.pdf.

ACKNOWLEDGMENTS

The immigration enforcement policy landscape has been a central theme in the work of the Migration Policy Institute (MPI) since its founding in 2001. We are indebted to many individuals at MPI — past and present — who have collaborated in that work by contributing ideas, research, debate, and expertise that often draw on deep professional experience in various capacities in immigration enforcement and related fields. For this report, we want to acknowledge and thank a newer colleague, Faye Hipsman, our research assistant and a "graduate" of MPI's intern program, for providing essential, extensive support. Faye has worked tirelessly and creatively in making numerous contributions to the text and look and feel of the report.

We would also like to thank the very knowledgeable individuals who agreed to serve as outside reviewers for the report and gave us valuable feedback and suggestions for improving it. They are Randy Capps, MPI Senior Policy Analyst; Lucas Guttentag, Robina Foundation Distinguished Senior Research Scholar in Law and Lecturer in Law, Yale Law School; Marielena Hincapié, Executive Director of the National Immigration Law Center (NILC); David Martin, Warner-Booker Distinguished Professor of International Law, University of Virginia School of Law; and James Ziglar, MPI Senior Fellow and former Commissioner of the Immigration and Naturalization Service (INS).

We owe an exceptional measure of thanks to Michelle Mittelstadt, MPI's Director of Communications, whose skillful editing greatly improved the report. We deeply admire Michelle's ability to master enormous amounts of material and detail and render them more understandable and readable; she is a valued colleague and asset for MPI. We are also indebted to Demetrios Papademetriou, MPI's President, who continues to provide visionary leadership and enthusiasm for our work, amidst the broad-gauged contributions he makes to many aspects of migration policy thinking in the United States and around the world.

Finally, we are especially grateful for the generosity of our funders who have supported MPI and, in particular, MPI's Immigration Policy Program, with general operating support. The continuing encouragement and interest we receive from the Carnegie Corporation of New York, the Ford Foundation, the MacArthur Foundation, and the Open Society Foundations have been essential to this project and so many others at MPI.

ABOUT THE AUTHORS

Doris Meissner, former Commissioner of the US Immigration and Naturalization Service (INS), is a Senior Fellow at the Migration Policy Institute (MPI), where she directs the Institute's US immigration policy work.

Her responsibilities focus in particular on the role of immigration in America's future and on administering the nation's immigration laws, systems, and government agencies. Her work and expertise also include immigration and politics, immigration enforcement, border control, cooperation with other countries, and immigration and national security. She has authored and coauthored numerous reports, articles, and op-eds and is frequently quoted in the media. She served as Director of MPI's Independent Task Force on Immigration and America's Future, a bipartisan group of distinguished leaders. The group's report and recommendations address how to harness the advantages of immigration for a 21st century economy and society.

From 1993-2000, she served in the Clinton administration as Commissioner of the INS, then a bureau in the US Department of Justice. Her accomplishments included reforming the nation's asylum system; creating new strategies for managing US borders; improving naturalization and other services for immigrants; shaping new responses to migration and humanitarian emergencies; strengthening cooperation and joint initiatives with Mexico, Canada, and other countries; and managing growth that doubled the agency's personnel and tripled its budget.

She first joined the Justice Department in 1973 as a White House Fellow and Special Assistant to the Attorney General. She served in various senior policy posts until 1981, when she became Acting Commissioner of INS and then Executive Associate Commissioner, the third-ranking post in the agency. In 1986, she joined the Carnegie Endowment for International Peace as a Senior Associate. Ms. Meissner created the Endowment's Immigration Policy Project, which evolved into the Migration Policy Institute in 2001.

A graduate of the University of Wisconsin-Madison, where she earned bachelor of the arts and master of the arts degrees, she began her professional career there as Assistant Director of student financial aid. She was also the first Executive Director of the National Women's Political Caucus.

Donald Kerwin is Executive Director of the Center for Migration Studies, an educational institute of the Congregation of the Missionaries of St. Charles, Scalabrinians that studies migration policy issues and safeguards the dignity and rights of migrants, refugees, and newcomers. Mr. Kerwin is a Nonresident Senior Fellow at the Migration Policy Institute, where he served as Vice President for Programs.

During his MPI tenure, Mr. Kerwin coordinated MPI's national and international programs, and wrote and spoke extensively on legalization, refugee protection, labor standards enforcement, detention, the Department of Homeland Security (DHS), and executive action on immigration.

He previously worked for more than 16 years at the Catholic Legal Immigration Network, Inc. (CLINIC), serving as Executive Director for nearly 15 years. Upon his arrival at CLINIC in 1992, Mr. Kerwin directed CLINIC's political asylum project for Haitians. He became CLINIC's Executive Director in December 1993 and during his tenure, CLINIC coordinated the nation's largest political asylum, detainee services, immigration appeals, and naturalization programs.

Mr. Kerwin is a member of the American Bar Association's Commission on Immigration and a past member of the Council on Foreign Relations' Immigration Task Force. He serves on the Board of Directors of Jesuit Refugee Services-USA and the Border Network for Human Rights, and is an Associate Fellow at the Woodstock Theological Center.

He is a 1984 graduate of Georgetown University and a 1989 graduate of the University of Michigan Law School.

Muzaffar Chishti, a lawyer, is Director of MPI's office in New York, based at New York University School of Law. His work focuses on US immigration policy, the intersection of labor and immigration law, civil liberties, and immigrant integration.

Prior to joining MPI, Mr. Chishti was Director of the Immigration Project of the Union of Needletrades, Industrial & Textile Employees (UNITE).

Mr. Chishti serves on the Board of Directors of the National Immigration Law Center, the New York Immigration Coalition, and the Asian American Federation of New York. He has served as Chair of the Board of Directors of the National Immigration Forum, and as a member of the American Bar Association's Coordinating Committee on Immigration.

His publications include *Through the Prism of National Security: Major Immigration Policy and Program Changes in the Decade since 9/11* (co-author), *Delegation and Divergence: A Study of 287(g) State and Local Immigration Enforcement* (co-author), *A Program in Flux: New Priorities and Implementation Challenges for 287(g)* (co-author), *Testing the Limits: A Framework for Assessing the Legality of State and Local Immigration Measures* (co-author), and *America's Challenge: Domestic Security, Civil Liberties, and National Unity After September 11* (co-author).

Mr. Chishti was educated at St. Stephen's College, Delhi; the University of Delhi; Cornell Law School; and the Columbia School of International Affairs.

Claire Bergeron is a Research Assistant with the US Immigration Policy Program at MPI, where she works on immigration enforcement issues and co-authors the "Policy Beat" each month for the *Migration Information Source*.

In addition to her MPI duties, Ms. Bergeron is a third-year evening student at Georgetown University Law Center, where she is a member of the editorial board for the *Georgetown Immigration Law Journal*.

Prior to joining MPI, Ms. Bergeron worked as a paralegal and Board of Immigration Appeals (BIA) Accredited Representative at the National Immigrant Justice Center (NIJC) in Chicago.

She holds a BA in anthropology and legal studies from Northwestern University.